Disabled Veterans in History

Corporealities: Discourses of Disability

David T. Mitchell and Sharon L. Snyder, editors

Books available in the series:

"Defects": Engendering the Modern Body
  edited by Helen Deutsch and Felicity Nussbaum

Revels in Madness: Insanity in Medicine and Literature
  by Allen Thiher

Points of Contact: Disability, Art, and Culture
  edited by Susan Crutchfield and Marcy Epstein

A History of Disability
  by Henri-Jacques Stiker

Disabled Veterans in History
  edited by David A. Gerber

Disabled Veterans in History

DAVID A. GERBER, EDITOR

Ann Arbor

THE UNIVERSITY OF MICHIGAN PRESS

Published in the United States of America by
The University of Michigan Press
Manufactured in the United States of America
⊗ Printed on acid-free paper

2003   2002   2001   2000   4   3   2   1

*A CIP catalog record for this book is available
from the British Library.*

Library of Congress Cataloging-in-Publication Data

Disabled veterans in history / David A. Gerber, editor.
     p.   cm. — (Corporealities)
   Includes bibliographical references.
   ISBN 0-472-11033-0 (cloth : acid-free paper)
    1. Veterans, Disabled.   I. Gerber, David A., 1944–
II. Series.
   UB360 .D57   2000
   362.4'08697—dc21   00-008715

The editor gratefully acknowledges the assistance of
the Baldy Center for Law and Social Policy
at the State University of New York at Buffalo
with the preparation of the manuscript.

In memory of my brother,
Dr. Kenneth E. Gerber (1950–1997),
who for many years practiced clinical psychology
at the Department of Veterans Affairs
Long Beach, California Medical Center

Contents

David A. Gerber

Introduction: Finding Disabled
Veterans in History

Disabled veterans are neglected figures in the histories of war and peace, and
the historical scholarship about them at present is fragmentary. There is no
synthetic history of disabled veterans. This volume is the only historical collection on the subject. The volume exclusively reflects the histories of large
and relatively affluent Western societies, at times with particular emphasis
on the United States that reflects both imbalances in the literature and the
editor's own specialization. The volume also concentrates upon the experiences of regular armies as opposed, for example, to guerrilla forces. One
consequence is that the disabled veteran written about here is always "he,"
for women have been infrequent and statistically underrepresented participants in Western national armies, and have rarely served in active fighting
roles in such forces, though serving with distinction at times in irregular
combat forces, such as the World War II antifascist resistance movements.
To be sure, women have served in regular armies, mostly as uniformed
nurses, and have been injured in combat zones and become disabled while
doing so. If the American experience is representative, these disabled
women veterans have been seriously neglected by the governments they
have served. They have certainly been neglected by historians, whatever
their nationality, for there is even less written about their experiences than
those of men.[1]

   He, then, is a man injured or becoming chronically ill while in military
service, usually though not necessarily in combat. His military service is
often thus foreshortened. Technically, he becomes a veteran only when he
leaves the armed forces, but for our purposes we will begin to call him "veteran" from the moment it is clear that he cannot return to active duty, and
is headed for civilian life.* Whether physical or mental, injury or illness may
cause permanent impairment or disfigurement, and hence a changed

---

*For purposes of convenience, throughout this volume, the authors will continue to
contrast *veterans* with *civilians,* though the veteran, of course, eventually becomes a
civilian. We use *civilian* to mean those who have not served in armed forces.

appearance and a partial or complete loss of function and/or earning power and economic self-sufficiency. When especially severe, moreover, disabilities and disfigurements become a particularly significant marker for an individual's or group's social identity and self-understanding.[2] Especially traumatic, visible injuries have tended to become the primary way in which the general population of disabled veterans often seems to have been conceived in the minds of experts, artists, and the general citizenry. In much of the rehabilitation and medical literature about, and the cultural representations of, disabled veterans of the two world wars, we find amputees garnering attention vastly out of proportion to their relatively small numbers, and in effect, becoming representative of all disabled veterans.[3] The drama of their injury crowds out everything else about them, and about others, with different, less visible injuries or illnesses.

Awareness of the presence of disabled veterans in Western societies runs continuously, if mostly in muted forms, from ancient texts to the present. But that awareness has greatly grown, alongside the significant growth of their numbers, in the last two centuries, and particularly in the twentieth. The growth in numbers reflects the increasingly massive mobilizations of conscripted citizens by the nation-state to fight modern wars and the increasingly lethal potentialities of modern weaponry. It also reflects both a long, accelerating list of breakthroughs in such areas of general and military medicine as wound ballistics, vascular surgery, anesthesia, infection, and tropical disease, and the creation of systems for the delivery of medical services to frontline troops and for the evacuation of fighting forces to rear positions for intensive treatment.[4] One dramatic consequence of these developments may be seen in the stunning reversal of mortality rates for those men sustaining spinal cord injuries, and hence prone to deadly urinary tract infections, in twentieth-century conflicts. In World War I, only 20 percent of the Canadians and Americans with spinal cord injuries survived to be repatriated in North America; in World War II, largely because of the use of antibiotics, the figure was more than reversed, so that approximately 90 percent survived to return. Of *all* repatriated World War I injured survivors, 61 percent died in hospitals within two months of their return. In contrast, British, Canadian, and American data from World War II showed mortality rates of the repatriated cut to between 2.2 percent and 7.8 percent.[5] Sixty thousand Americans, Canadians and British, it is estimated, survived World War II hospitalization who would have died in World War I.[6]

Our growing awareness of the disabled veteran also results from the greater normalization of his existence. In the distant past, many disabled veterans were pauperized, roleless, and utterly dependent, and they were reduced to street begging, to residence in poorhouses and monasteries, or to thievery, while often also sentimentally lionized in the abstract as heroes. In the twentieth century, disabled veterans became a major project of the modern state, which endowed them with recognition as a group worthy of continuing assistance, and with entitlements in the form of advanced medical care and prosthetics, pension schemes, vocational rehabilitation, and job placement. Alongside this state assistance, activism by disabled veterans in behalf of enhancement of this special provision and of their right to a normalized existence contributed to the nearly complete social reintegration of even the most severely disabled men, such as bilateral limb amputees, the blinded, and those paralyzed by spinal cord injuries.[7]

If the visibility of the disabled generally, and for our purposes disabled veterans specifically, has increased in this century, so, too, has our ability to *see* them—to conceive of the meanings and consequences of disability and to understand the lived experiences of people with disabilities in the context of both war and peace. This conceptual breakthrough has advanced from a number of directions. In the twentieth century, war came to be associated with bureaucratized and technologized slaughter and large-scale environmental destruction that increasingly found its victims more or less indiscriminately among combatants and civilians alike. As Fussell demonstrated, in the hellish circumstances of trench warfare during World War I men fought desperately to survive, and war failed to retain the romantic haze of heroic values that was perhaps its principal ideological legacy from distant times to the imagination of modern cultures. Soldiers found their courage not in archetypes of good character, but in the desire to avoid displaying humiliating cowardice before their peers.[8] Much more common than the expectation of chivalric behavior has become the understanding of war one finds in the works of psychiatrists from Abram Kardiner to Jonathan Shay and of the neurologist William H. R. Rivers. Their reports on clinical practice document in excruciating detail the devastating psychoneurotic effects of war on the character of those who do the fighting. It is not difficult retrospectively to find these effects throughout history, but in the past they were mixed with the physical problems all soldiers faced from deprivation, disease, and exposure, so the balance of the mental and the physical was unclear. In the twentieth century, armies were healthier and better fed in the field than ever before; thus, the physical has been factored out increasingly, and we are left with war's destruction of the mind. Powerful antiwar implications are also found in the work of the philosopher Elaine Scarry, whose deconstruction of war and its official justifications and avowed purposes makes the case that war ultimately exists solely to create injury to

minds and bodies of individuals, and hence, to create victims.[9] Disability
and disfigurement are not incidental to war's purposes nor marginal to its
effects, but rather, alongside the murder of those killed, the point to begin
with. Only in making victims can war achieve its political ends. If we are to
understand war, we must come to intellectual, moral, and emotional terms
with the disabled veteran.

Changing conceptualizations of disability lead us in the same direction.
Beginning in the nineteenth century and accelerating in the early twentieth,
disability began to emerge from centuries of understandings based on
inchoate combinations of religion, humanitarianism, superstition, and psychic terror. It was increasingly being scientifically conceived according to a
medical model, founded on medico-scientific assumptions about pathology
and cure. Under the guidance of the medical model, students of disability
have come to possess large literatures about therapies and rehabilitation and
about the rise and development of public policies to subsidize research
about, and to provide varieties of social assistance for, the disabled. Many
fewer questions were asked about the identities and experiences of people
with disabilities or the ways in which they were culturally understood and
socially positioned in daily life by the able-bodied majority. If disability is
understood as a transient state pending cure, or alternatively, if permanent,
as evidence of the failures of our science, the reluctance to take on this second set of issues is understandable. But as the visibility and longevity of the
disabled have steadily grown and their voices have become more insistent,
disability has come increasingly to seem normal, if not necessarily in an
absolute statistical sense, certainly in terms of our ordinary expectations of
those whom we encounter in daily life and what may happen to any of us,
especially as we age. A new, social constructionist model of disability,
appropriate in light of this understanding of the normality of disability, has
emerged. It analyzes not only general shifts in cultural understandings and
social positioning of the disabled, but also the varieties of self-understand-
ings, social identities, and social groups they have formed.[10] This conception of disability lifts the disabled veteran out of the haze of ideology and
technical knowledge by which he has been obscured in the past and gives
him a voice in influencing how he is seen. At the least, we become aware
that we cannot take for granted that he is represented in what others have
said about him, or in the public policies and medical therapies developed in
his behalf.

In the context of these understandings, this introduction will proceed,
first, to review the current state of our knowledge of the history of disabled
veterans in Western societies, as we find it in a wide variety of scholarly,

medical, and policy literatures; and second, to introduce the essays themselves. The former discussion is organized along the lines of the categories—*representation, public policy, living with a disability*—by which the essays themselves are grouped in order to assist in effectively contextualizing them. In reality, we may separate these aspects of the disabled veteran's history only for analytical convenience. Meanings that culture and discourse have attached to the disabled veteran have much to do with how he has conceived his identity and how societies and political systems have defined his place. Public policy has shaped cohorts and identities by creating a separate and relatively generous system of benefits. The veterans' own agency in rehabilitation, reintegration, and public activism has influenced public perceptions and policy. Like other group histories, therefore, the disabled veteran's is a densely constructed, ramifying totality.

Representation

In Western cultures, we find the representation of disabled veterans at the juncture of the discourses of the warrior and of the disabled. Representation of disabled veterans is largely a product of the conflict and the negotiation of these discourses, which lie in a state of constant tension. These tensions begin to assert themselves in the earliest example of the archetype of the disabled veteran we possess: the narrative of Philoctetes, the subject of Martha Edwards's essay in this volume. The root of these tensions lies in gendered assumptions about manhood. On the one hand, the warrior may be valorized as a symbol of masculine honor; on the other, pity and fear, the common emotions associated with our response to disability, serve to subvert honor and infantilize and feminize the male.

The ideal traits of the warrior have been steeped in ideas of *masculine* honor, because war is the archetypal male experience, forming one of the borders of male and female. While the warrior's character traits of courage, toughness, endurance, and a capacity for action have been fairly stable throughout the centuries, the grounds have shifted for identifying sources of heroism. Chivalric values found heroism in the character inherent in a good man, who is fearless because he is noble. Postheroic assumptions associated with modern warfare find them in a peer group code of behavior that valorizes the individual's ability to respond effectively in war by doing a *job* in the face of fear, which is acknowledged to be inevitable. The measure of the individual lies in self-control, not in an honorable character.[11]

Injury and disability incurred in war have frequently been seen as, in Crane's ironically intended phrase, the "red badge of courage" of a warrior engaged in a cause worthy of his sacrifice. Though governments in wartime have sometimes been divided about allowing civilians to learn about the extent of death and traumatic injury experienced by fighting men in the belief that such knowledge was bad for morale,[12] the disabled veteran as warrior hero has served as a particularly potent symbol for inspiring war efforts. As Dunham notes, in Soviet World War II literature, he evokes gratitude, generosity, and guilt in civilians, and inspires the capacity for dedication and self-sacrifice. When war ends, however, and memories of it begin to fade in the general desire to return to a normal peacetime existence, the warrior hero gradually loses his luster and is reduced in stature to a beleaguered disabled man, whose needs may be perceived as an inconvenience.[13] Thus, the generosity his government and the public showed him in the way of preferential public employment, pensions, vocational rehabilitation, prostheses, and education begins to recede. As we shall see in the next section, this is what took place in a number of nations in the two decades after World War I, when governments found themselves needing to check the growth of the numbers of men receiving pensions and other assistance, or actually to retrench expenses because of massive war debts, the postwar recession, and the depression of the 1930s.[14]

As a disabled man, then, the veteran comes to be seen increasingly not as a warrior, but through the images by which people with disabilities have been conceived. As a number of writers have argued, impairments and illnesses have no meanings in and of themselves.[15] A disability incurred in adulthood takes a great deal of getting used to, but ultimately may well become a banal, if inconvenient, fact of life. But it is hardly a trivial fact of life, for culture has endowed disability with a broad range of symbolic meanings, so that, as Martin Norden has observed of movies featuring disabled characters, people with real disabilities cannot see themselves reflected in representations of disability that are ostensibly about their lives.[16]

In Western cultures, pity and fear are responses to disability and to the disabled veteran that are continuous over many centuries. They also overdetermine the use of disability as a dramatic device, for pity and fear have great representational value, as Aristotle observed in identifying them as the tragic emotions most likely to cause dramatic catharsis. They are evoked in the Philoctetes narrative, but they are a staple two millennia later of cinematic and novelistic treatments of disabled civilians and veterans.[17] They are protean responses, for they take a number of different forms and may be employed to suggest a variety of traits in a disabled character. Disabled characters may evoke fear because they are made to be demonic, or because prejudice leads them to be misunderstood, or because disability itself makes us insecure about our own body integrity. They may evoke pity for their dependence, or for their heroic efforts against great odds to be independent. But pity and fear are distinctive enough to contrast with responses to veterans' disabilities in at least some non-Western cultures. As the anthropologist Lindsay French discovered among the large population of Cambodian amputees who were members of guerrilla and resistance armies living in refugee camps in the 1980s and early 1990s, aversive meanings given to missing limbs were conceived within the framework of Theravada Buddhism. Amputations implied degradation, worthlessness, and weakness and presaged "a hopelessly degraded karmic destiny," throughout the cycle of the individual's continuous reincarnation.[18]

In contrast, fear, and the closely allied emotion, anxiety, are the products of several different perceptions rooted in abiding and overdetermined Western concerns. Physically and mentally impaired people have suggested both sinfulness and deformity of the soul and loss of moral and practical autonomy. One or the other account for the impaired individual as, alternately, revengeful, bitter, and self-absorbed; dependent, irresponsible, and parasitical; or monstrous, as in the long line of demented, demonic, and depraved fictional creations, such as Quasimodo and the Phantom of the Opera.[19] Neuropsychiatric disability also raises more immediate fears, for it is associated with a direct physical threat to the observer and to society. Though Americans associate the enraged, antisocial, unpredictable madman possessing advanced weapons training with Vietnam War veterans suffering from post-traumatic stress disorder,[20] in fact, societies have long been haunted by fears of the violent potential of veterans with unpredictable mental states. Two of the earliest domiciliary institutions established for the care of aged and disabled veterans, France's Hôtel des Invalides (1633) and Britain's Chelsea Hospital (1685), were founded in part to remove from the streets just such men, who, by the definitions of their time, were considered unstable. Impoverished as they mostly were, they turned to begging, picking pockets, and violent thievery.[21] Novels produced out of the experience of the two world wars, such as Eric Maria Remarque's *The Road Back* (1931) and Merle Miller's *That Winter* (1948), feature an unstable veteran with a potential for violence, who suffers lasting mental and emotional problems, sometimes alongside physical impairments, because of war and ends up taking his own life or someone else's.[22]

Pity (and self-pity, too) result from the perception that people with disabilities are innocent sufferers: in the case of veterans conscripted into armies, men injured through no fault of their own, and made thus to experience pain, a loss of autonomy, and exile from the community of the able-bodied, just as Philoctetes suffered physical exile on his lonely island.[23] While the impulse to feel kindly, if excessive, sympathy for the disabled veteran may be quite understandable, it frequently has been publicly manipulated for instrumental purposes, thus popularizing pity. Twentieth-century veterans' organizations, such as the American Legion and a broad array of World War I era German groups, learned the ease with which a democratic polity may be manipulated through the potent, guilt-inducing symbolism of badly wounded men, especially when backed by powerful veterans' lobbies and block voting. When confronted by legislative delay in approving entitlements for the general, able-bodied veterans' population, the American Legion brought greatly disabled men from nearby Walter Reed Army Hospital to lobby Congress in the 1920s.[24] During World War II, it used a well-orchestrated campaign of journalistic reports and biting newspaper cartoons highlighting the neglect of disabled veterans, to win congressional adherents to support passage of the G.I. Bill of Rights, which also dealt with the general veterans' population.[25] Governments, too, as in Britain, utilized the same symbolism in parades of disabled veterans during wartime to inspire enlistments, and in postwar commemorations, such as France's 1919 Festival of Victory, to orchestrate national celebration and to maintain wartime levels of political loyalty. Disabled warrior heroes could easily be transformed into "poster boys" for various political agendas.[26]

Pity, however, has not gone unchallenged. During World War I the idea of aggressive normalization through physical restoration and vocational training spread among all of the major belligerents. By the war's final year, it came to constitute a counterdiscourse to traditional ways of conceiving of disabled veterans' postwar prospects, for it insisted that every effort be made to return disabled veterans to the community and to the workforce. All that stood between the disabled veteran and self-sufficiency, it was said, was the pitying attitude that led his loved ones and well-meaning civilians to infantilize him and the self-pity that allowed him to accept a life as a recipient of charity.[27] While the practical achievements of this new program were quite uneven from one country to another, its message was conveyed in imaginative ways that extended the representation of disabled veterans. Advertising and published testimonials for prosthetics for disabled veterans were not new: lithographic images of active men with new prosthetic arms and legs burgeoned in the post–Civil War American press. Surveys of the rehabilitation of European disabled veterans from the World War I era now contained stunning photographs of handless men who had been fitted with efficient prosthetic metal hooks, which were much less masking of amputation than their Civil War era precursors, and were portrayed at work in factories, farmyards, and offices.[28] Out of these pictorial roots, in World War II the U.S. Army narrative training films, *Meet McGonegal* (1943) and *Diary of a Sergeant* (1945), both of which dealt with the rehabilitation of bilateral hand amputees and featured handless men telling their stories, developed their own visual style, which focused on the extent to which prosthetics geared to function rather than to aesthetics enabled a man to do just about anything. The effect is that of watching magicians perform tricks.[29] Post–World War II Hollywood movies, such as *The Best Years of Our Lives* (1946), about which I myself write in this volume, *The Men* (1950), and *Bright Victory* (1951), absorbed some of these conventions, and alongside the melodramatic narrative plot featured segments that were veritable advertisements for rehabilitation and demonstrated how assistive technologies and prostheses normalized the lives of blinded and paralyzed veterans and amputees.[30] That powerful shaper of Western consciousness, the American movie industry, would function throughout the twentieth century as a key purveyor of images of people with disabilities, including disabled veterans, about whom a narrative was created that seems, as we shall now see, particularly fitted for treatment as mass entertainment.

Pity, like fear, however, would never disappear, for it has been too deeply embedded in the reaction of the able-bodied to disability. Indeed, pity often is particularly prominent in the representation of the disabled veteran, and the public sentimentalizing of his losses, as in the controversial 1920 British film *Lest We Forget,* seems to mix effortlessly with patriotic and national feeling in the memory of war. Why should loss and pity be so prominent a feature of this representation, especially when the disabled veteran has also been conceived within the representational field of the warrior hero? The reason perhaps may be found in the crisis of gender that war and disability have created for men. As a number of feminist writers have explained, traditional war has upset the normal balance of gender expectations.[31] Men, who are supposed to behave courageously and show toughness in war, have been potentially feminized to the extent they may find themselves unable to live up to these expectations. Women have come to take over responsibilities at home, in the workplace, and in society that have been vacated by men serving in the armed forces. When injured or ill, and ultimately disabled, the male veteran moved further on the road toward compromised masculinity. He was not only unable to do his part in the war effort, but he became, at least for a time, dependent on a variety of institutions and individuals in the fulfillment of life's most elementary tasks.[32] In a telling example of the ways in which disabled men are instantly reduced in the terms of conventional masculinity under such circumstances, both

Koven and Bourke have demonstrated the potentially infantilizing effects on World War I British disabled veterans, who during the war shared treatment facilities, specialists, and assigned relationships with similarly disabled boys. Even the name of the principal organization, the Guild of the Brave Poor Things, that assisted these boys in peacetime was for a time retained, while it transformed its mission increasingly to the rehabilitation of adult disabled veterans. Only the strenuous objection of wounded men caused the guild to change its name to the Guild of the Handicapped.[33] The potential for infantilization of seriously injured men or women alike is implicit in hospitalization and rehabilitation, because they cannot care for themselves. If also smothered with pity and love, patronized and spoiled by family and caregivers, a man may in the gendered terms of culture be feminized if he exhibits indecision, weakness, passivity, and dependence.

That so many of those caring for him are women, whom he comes to depend on for the fulfillment of his basic needs and to whom he appears to lose authority, creates a psychological situation easily conceived as fraught with the Oedipal tensions that form one of the founding narratives of Western cultures, and that are the basis for the Freudian understanding of manhood. In examining the fragility of male identity and his own identity as a severely disabled man, the anthropologist Robert Murphy explained that in Freud's terms boys "are forced to lose the mother as both love object and model," in order to fulfill the cultural expectations for manhood, but that the male's "grasp of masculinity is threatened continually by the urge to fall back into her folds, to reverse our hard-won autonomy, and relapse into dependent passivity."[34] While the disabled veteran's goal in this situation is to reclaim his masculinity from the forces that feminize him, a woman's is more ambiguous, for she must help him succeed at his project, thus subverting her own claims to the newfound equality she has gained in wartime in his absence.[35]

Much twentieth-century representation of disabled veterans has been placed within narratives whose emplotment variously follows the outlines of such Oedipal drama. In novels such as Ernest Hemingway's *A Farewell to Arms* and Hollywood movies such as *Pride of the Marines* (1945), disabled veterans with compromised manhood because of injury or illness are rescued by a female savior, in the form of nurse, wife, or girlfriend, who functions simultaneously as both Mother and nurturer and mistress and sex object. In such dramas, the responsible woman's role is to coax and to manipulate the man into becoming "his old self" again, or in Jeffords's phrase, *remasculinized*. At the center of these dramas, however, are not such day-to-day aspects of living with a disability as mobility, accessibility, or work, but instead symbolic male dominance and heterosexual intimacy. Reclaiming manhood is thus conceived within the framework of a melodrama in which men and women ultimately sort themselves out by conventional gendered categories in their emotional and sexual relationship.[36] This project may also be tied symbolically, as it is in *The Best Years of Our Lives* and *Pride of the Marines,* to ensuring national vigor and power, which are made to seem dependent on the health of conventional masculinity and femininity.[37] Such dramas begin with realistic subject-matter—war, homecoming, heterosexual relationships, marriage, and disability—but in abstracting disability out of its larger social context and centering it exclusively in the melodrama of heterosexual romance, they lose their pretense to realism. It is certainly true, as the testimonies in Wolfe's collection of World War II disabled veterans' narratives suggest, that there were disabled veterans who found a source of strength in relationships with a generous, self-sacrificing woman. But there were many roads to rehabilitation and reintegration, and a consummated romance hardly resolved all of the challenges those fortunate enough to find it faced. Indeed, it created its own ongoing challenges for these couples. These narratives may be recognizable as cultural products reworking ancient themes, but they are not necessarily artifacts of daily life that can serve to help us understand disability. For this reason, it is well that, as Martin Norden observes here in his essay and elsewhere, the use of the Oedipal narrative has begun to play itself out in Hollywood movies featuring disabled veterans in favor, in films such as *Coming Home* (1978) and *Born on the Fourth of July* (1989), of more complex characters, more fluid gender roles, and a somewhat broader conceptualization of disability. The British novelist Pat Barker has achieved the same goals in her powerful trilogy featuring neuropsychiatric casualties of World War I. Stereotypes ultimately dependent on pity and fear remain, but under the influence of changing roles for both women and people with disabilities as well as feminist and disability criticism, the representational field has widened in the last quarter-century.[38]

Public Policy

Most Western societies historically have had at least two parallel tracks for providing assistance to those construed to be in need, one for veterans and another for the general civilian population. The former is not only older than the latter, but has been governed by different principles and rules and has been more generous in its provisions. The veterans' provision itself has not been a single entity. Though assistance for both groups has been governed by a common justification, disabled and able-bodied veterans have not been provided for equally. Disabled veterans consistently have been dealt with even more generously than able-bodied veterans and indeed than perhaps any other cohort in society, including the civilian disabled.[39]

The liberality of the veterans' provision results from the belief, widely articulated in seventeenth-century England and during the French Revolution and the American Civil War and universally accepted in the twentieth century, that assistance to veterans should not be charity or "welfare," in the sense that contemporary term is used to connote aid grudgingly provided those popularly considered the unworthy poor. It is instead a reward for, and implicitly an incentive to inspire, service. In the case of disabled veterans, it is also a repayment for especially significant personal sacrifice. It is *earned* assistance and a right of citizens. It has historically been provided mostly to disabled veterans. But increasingly in the twentieth century in modern, mass democracies, it has been given generously to all veterans, independent of the recipient's age and whether or not he is sufficiently self-supporting to pay for the medical care, prosthetics, vocational training, and general education that governments have continued to supply veterans long after their military service has ended. The provision for disabled civilians eventually grew, too, in the twentieth century, but the gap has never closed between disabled veterans and disabled civilians.[40]

In contrast to social provisioning for the poor, even when assistance to veterans is means-tested, it has come to be governed by understandings that the dignity of those to whom it is given must be preserved and that their provision is an entitlement.[41] Of course, to the extent that such public assistance to disabled veterans has been administered by impersonal bureaucratic processes and subject to the fiscal vagaries of the modern state, such understandings at times have been violated in practice. Nonetheless, the desire to treat disabled veterans as a favored class has had real and important consequences. One has only to contrast such historical institutional arrangements for assisting the poor as poorhouses, with domiciliary institutions, such as the Hôtel des Invalides, Chelsea Hospital, and the various branches of the National Home, which was created after the American Civil War, that have housed disabled and aged veterans who are homeless, indigent, or lack family support. (Poorhouses also took in the civilian disabled to the extent they were often also impoverished.) In order to discourage dependence, the poorhouse was a place intentionally bleak and uninviting, where work was compulsory and little more than drudgery, and the diet was monotonous and barely adequate. Though often characterized by the type of regimentation deemed necessary to control large numbers of single adult men, and sometimes, as at the Hôtel des Invalides under both the Bourbons and Napoleon, by differential levels of service to officers and regular troops, domiciliary institutions have offered clean, commodious accommodations and good food in a setting that aspired to be homelike and even aesthetic. They provided the opportunity for work, but did not always require it, and sometimes made education available. Men resident in them were usually given free medical care, pocket money, and the freedom to leave the grounds to shop, to seek entertainment, and to visit.[42]

The boundaries of civilian and veterans assistance have been well patrolled by governments both friendly to the veteran and eager to contain costs by limiting especially generous assistance only to them. They have also been patrolled by veterans themselves through their veterans advancement organizations, which have worked to ensure that the assistance given to their members was always construed as an entitlement, expanded or at least not cut, and mixed as little as possible with the civilian welfare system. Disabled veterans have belonged to and been represented in dealings with government by both general veterans organizations and organizations defined by a single disability, or uniting veterans across the lines of injury and illness. But whatever the exact composition of their organizations, veterans have been especially successful in achieving these goals in modern mass democracies, such as Australia and the United States, under three conditions: when they have been able to attain recognition as voting blocs and as lobbies; when they have found backing in influential sectors of civilian society, especially the mass media; and when their leaders and organizations have been brought into government or formed alliances with governments to consult on or actually to administer veterans programs. Veterans organizations of this type aspire to develop long-term client relations with the state, and define themselves less along the right-left ideological continuum than single-mindedly in terms of the economic interest of their members.[43]

Few groups in the twentieth century have succeeded in attracting expressions of gratitude and entitlement from political leaders and conserving as generous a social provision as disabled veterans. Governments of every type have appeared fearful of the bad impression made by retrenchments of programs to assist disabled veterans, though such retrenchments have been necessary during periods of fiscal difficulties, and they have been eager to appear to be a patron of the disabled veteran. Moreover, governments of all types, democratic and totalitarian, have been eager to exploit the symbolism of the disabled veteran to win legitimacy and public loyalty for the state. Attaining power in the midst of the Depression and soon dedicated to the expensive project of rearmament, the Nazi regime could do little more than its predecessor, the crisis-ridden Weimar Republic, to raise pension rates for the average disabled veteran. Indeed, the regime's pension rates were kept low enough to force men back into the labor market, and its administration of pensions was just as impersonal and cost-conscious as the Republic's. But the Nazis engaged in incessant propaganda extolling disabled veterans and in extravagant symbolic gestures, such as creating new military decorations for them.[44]

A comparison of the position in relation to the state of disabled veterans and disabled civilians, even those injured in industrial accidents doing war work, also establishes the privileged position of disabled veterans. The two groups have rarely been treated as representing one project in establishing provisions for assistance, whether in the liberal capitalist democracies or the former Soviet Union, where disabled veterans, especially of World War II, enjoyed an especially wide range of extraordinary privileges not enjoyed by others with or without disabilities. While they increasingly had the benefit of their own programs in the twentieth century, disabled civilians were usually shut out of opportunities to share in the better-funded and more broadly conceived programs created for the care, maintenance, rehabilitation, and retraining of disabled veterans. Indeed the benefits to the civilian disabled from programs to assist disabled veterans mostly have been indirect, through research, example, and the cumulative experience of medical or therapeutic practice, and they have only been gradually applied to civilians. Yet we should not underestimate these indirect gains, especially for the twentieth century, when the status of the civilian disabled greatly improved. War, as Steven A. Holmes has observed, is "the most efficient means for creating disabled people," and in ways we may only speculate on (to the extent they have never been systematically studied), the existence of a growing, if separate, disabled-veterans population, demanding rights, assistance, and group recognition, has no doubt influenced the position of all the disabled.[45]

Rare has been a process such as we may observe in Canada at the end of World War II, where the significant, federally subsidized strides made in the rehabilitation of spinal-cord-injured veterans were within a few years directly applied to the civilian population. Rarer still, this development may largely be attributed to the work of the veteran-founded Canadian Paraplegics Association, which not only opened its membership to spinal-cord-injured civilians, but broadened its agenda to include their needs and worked successfully to gain access for them to rehabilitation facilities created for paralyzed veterans.[46] In contrast, we find the more typical Paralyzed Veterans Association in the United States, which did not include civilians nor broaden its work to assist civilians with spinal cord injuries.[47] Disabled veterans' organizations defining themselves in the client mode, especially those defined by a single disability, have not typically made common cause with either civilian organizations or other veterans organizations.

Those not defined by a single disability, however, have a more complex political history, especially when moved by ideology as well as the quest for benefits. Both German and Austrian disabled-veterans organizations in the twentieth century did include civilian war victims, including not only injured civilians, but the wives and children of men killed in service.[48] This pattern is explained partly by the fact that activism within this framework, especially after World War I, stressed political solidarity as well as benefits, while in contrast the client-type organization limited itself to benefits and defined its political alliances expediently. The politics of the latter orientation was evident, for example, in France in the 1920s, when disabled-veterans organizations worked successfully for pension reform and usually eschewed ideological politics, while the general veterans organizations deeply divided along ideological lines. This self-interested style of politics is also clear in the behavior in 1944 of the Disabled Veterans of America, which usually cooperated in the quest for benefits with the organizations representing the general body of veterans, but opposed the G.I. Bill of Rights, which the latter sought, in fear that the more resources provided for the general veterans population, the less there would be for disabled veterans.[49]

Except perhaps when war touched the home front directly, exacting tremendous sacrifices from civilians, and incentives have been required to achieve solidarity and raise civilian morale, governments have rarely sought to dismantle any of these boundaries.[50] When they have done so outside these circumstances, even otherwise effective political leadership has failed. Consider these two contrasting examples. Because British industrial and farm workers during World War II were drafted into their jobs and subject to injury not only in war work but like other civilians in bombing raids, the extension of the same vocational rehabilitation programs to them as were created for disabled veterans seemed just to both planners and the general population, especially in the context of Britain's emerging postwar social democratic mood.[51] In contrast, in a context with a safe home front and a much more conservative political center of gravity, Franklin Roosevelt's support in 1943 for the creation of one common system of vocational rehabilitation for both civilians and veterans failed before an alliance of veterans organizations and pro-veteran, anti–New Deal majorities in Congress.[52]

In no area of the history of the disabled veteran has more been written than public policy. Only a brief sketch, focusing on the development of concepts and models accreted over time, may be accomplished here. What we are able to draw from such an exercise is an understanding of the extent to which during World War I a conceptual unity in the approach of most Western states to disabled veterans was achieved. Though subject to fine-tuning based on specific national circumstances, this approach has provided the framework for state disabled-veterans policy since that time. What we cannot analyze in depth here, because it is a vast subject in itself, is the extent to which states with veterans' provisions, as analysts such as Skocpol and Geyer have suggested and Robert Goler and Michael Rhode describe in this volume, have developed expertise in the exercise of some of their most significant modern state-building functions—record keeping; sorting, control, surveillance, and discipline of individual citizens; indexing needs of groups in the population; and maintenance of large, permanent bureaucratic agencies—through the creation and administration of veterans and particu-larly disabled-veterans policy. This development is understandable in light of the age, scope, and scale of programs for disabled veterans, relative to those for civilians, and of the extent to which governments confronting vet-erans' issues and evolving welfare states at the same points in time borrowed programmatic concepts and strategies from one another. We must keep in mind that disabled-veterans programs have provided policy and administra-tive contexts for the rise of the modern welfare state.[53]

The veterans' provision is an ancient and continuous feature of West-ern societies that has achieved its more developed forms where states are strong and have raised mass armies. Thus, we may assume that the ancient Greek state, which may have provided some form of assistance for indigent veterans disabled in battle, and Romans, who developed their finest medical care for treatment of soldiers and gave land to veterans, probably were more consistent and generous in the maintenance of their veterans than medieval Europe's feudal lords, who raised tenant-based armies in the context of weak states. The military lords provided mostly for their commanders, while the ordinary disabled veteran might at best end up a humble lay brother in a monastery to be looked after by monks.[54] It is in the early mod-ern era with the rise of the newly consolidated nation-states of Europe, headed by ambitious, state-building monarchs, that the roots of the modern disabled-veterans provision are to be found in such state-subsidized initia-tives as Chelsea Hospital and the Hôtel des Invalides and in the pensions schemes, such as the centralized system in France and the county-based sys-tem in Britain.[55] As long as armies remained small and episodically raised, these initiatives were not particularly systematic nor wide-ranging in their scope nor in the number of men to whom assistance was provided, and in France they were interlarded with royal patronage and aristocratic privilege. The rise of mass, at times conscripted, armies and increasingly democratic regimes, from the late eighteenth century on, necessitated more ambitious initiatives, especially in the United States, France, Prussia (and eventually Germany), and Britain and its neo-European, settler-based colonies. Nineteenth-century European pensions were small and preserved significant distinctions between officers and regular troops in rates of compensation. Britain and its colonies developed pension schemes depending on private subscriptions and administration.[56]

Though some elements of the program were prefigured in England in the seventeenth century and in France in the late eighteenth and early nineteenth centuries, as Geoffrey Hudson and Isser Woloch demonstrate in their contributions, only in the United States after the Civil War do we see the rise simultaneously, before World War I, of many of the features that would come to characterize the modern disabled-veterans provision. These were a network of publicly funded domiciliary institutions, free prosthetics for amputees, preference in state and federal government hiring, land grants, and a massive pension system, for men who had fought for the North. Suffering the role of a conquered people, Southerners were provided for not by the federal government they had rebelled against, but, much less ambitiously, by Southern state governments. The essays in this volume by Ethel Dunn, R. B. Rosenburg, and Gregory Weeks variously show that disabled veterans on the losing side in war often found even the most well-meaning governments under which they lived hindered in their effort to be of assistance by the economic, political, and moral consequences of defeat.[57]

Borrowing a feature from the much-studied French pension system, which was codified in 1831, the American federal system established rates on the basis of the nature and degree of physical injury. (It covered disability due to disease as well.) Along with Continental schemes, the American preserved a distinction between officers and regular troops in adjusting the size of pensions, but the rates attached by subsequent legislation to specific disabilities and the conditions arising out of them soon grew so variable and complex that the ordinary veteran, with the help of a doctor's testimony, easily might surpass the base rate. Such legislative tinkering is evidence of the extent to which the American system, in contrast to Continental ones at the time, was politicized. State-subsidized pension systems on the Continent in the nineteenth century were removed from popular politics, and largely in the control of central bureaucracies unresponsive to popular pressures. In consequence, rates were low, and many needy men were neglected. In the United States, popular political pressures in the late nineteenth century, resulting from a competitive electoral politics that thrust the veterans' vote into a position of importance in national and northern state elections and gave enormous political authority to the largest veterans organization, the Grand Army of the Republic, led to the enormous expansion of the population base of the American pension system. By 1893 over a million men were receiving pensions totaling $150,000,000 a year, fully 38 percent of the entire federal budget. Legislation in 1890 and 1906 extended the pension system further so that it became, in effect, an old-age pension available to any man age 62 or over who had served in the federal armed forces during the Civil War and made a representation that he was too infirm or feeble to work. By 1910, the American pension system, which thus had been transformed from a disability pension to a service pension scheme, was benefiting 28 percent of all Americans 65 or over. By World War I, the United States had spent $5,000,000,000 on military pensions since the founding of the Republic, the majority on Civil War pensions.[58]

This detail is significant because the fate of the American disability pension system would provide a negative reference point in the planning of World War I disabled veterans' benefits. It was notorious not only in the United States, but elsewhere as well. It came to epitomize what the Germans called *renten-hysterie* (pension psychosis), that is, the fixation of the disabled veteran and his organizations on compensation to the exclusion of all other issues and of thinking about rebuilding productive lives.[59]

The desire to produce schemes as generous in their multiple goals as the American system while avoiding the excesses that gave rise to pension psychosis in the masses of conscripted troops combined with fiscal conservatism, nationalism, the modern conservation and efficiency ethic, and a shortage of industrial labor during the war to produce a different programmatic emphasis among the belligerents on both sides of the fighting during World War I, even as they implemented other aspects of the American system. The scale of the problem, the most obvious challenge of the World War I experience, seemed to demand new ideas. Governments had never faced the task of human restoration in such dimensions. By April 1915, only eight months after the 50-month-long war had begun, Britain witnessed the return from the front of some 3,000 disabled men a month. In total, 752,000 British men were left permanently disabled, a severe challenge to the laissez-faire methods by which Britain in recent times had dealt with the disabled soldier. By war's end, over 4,000,000 Germans had been wounded and survived, and some 1,537,000 German veterans were categorized as disabled. In

France in that year, just over a million veterans were counted as sick or injured due to the war. In 1920, 70,000 Canadians and 200,000 Americans were disabled because of the conflict, significant numbers relative to the population size of Canada and the brief period the United States had been a combatant.[60] It was recognized during the war itself that human needs that might approach this magnitude required systematic, well-funded, and highly organized efforts. But careful planning and smoothly coordinated efforts were not possible amid such escalating numbers.

Though national variations in implementation and administration existed, the conceptual unity in the belligerents' approach began, as Jeffrey Reznick shows in the British case in his essay here, with a consensus around the goals of as complete a physical restoration of the individual as possible and aggressive socioeconomic normalization. These goals could profit the nation, and they were good for the individual. Assistance to them was conceived as a *right,* an entitlement that the veteran had earned through sacrifice, a belief shared among all the Continental belligerents of 1914–18. Another feature of this consensus was the view that normalization depended on the state's and cooperating private organizations' approaching the disabled man with practical programs that encouraged him to become self-supporting. The medical phase of treatment should be accompanied by occupational as well as physical therapy to accustom him to doing useful activities while gaining strength and agility. Even before completing medical treatment, injured men might be put to performing useful industrial work. The most complete physical restoration possible must have its complement in social and economic restoration, an argument recently advanced by civilian rehabilitation specialists, who had begun in the decades before the war to apply these ideas to disabled children and civilian victims of industrial accidents in Britain, Belgium, France, and Germany. The United States had just made a national commitment to do the same in legislation passed only months before it entered the war. Opportunities should be presented to the disabled veteran for vocational rehabilitation geared to what he might do in spite of the losses he had sustained. A man's work options should be fitted not only to his physical condition, but also to his prior occupation and class origins and to such aspects of the larger social and economic context as local job markets in the place from which he had come. Analogous arrangements were to be created to assist neuropsychiatric casualties and those suffering from chronic illnesses, the most common of which was tuberculosis. Pension systems, prosthetics that were free and emphasized function over aesthetics in the case of artificial limbs, preference in government employment, and subsidized medical care were promised, not as a substitute for, but as an aid to, normalization and as a reward.[61]

In working out the fine points of this program, states confronted a variety of questions, which they often resolved differently. Those questions touching upon pensions had been raised before, though the scale of need was, of course, never as great, but those touching upon state assistance in social reintegration were new. How were pension claims to be authenticated to make sure that injuries and illnesses were actually incurred in the line of duty, a matter that assumed considerable importance when men claimed service-connected medical conditions long after they left the armed forces? Should there be distinctions between officers and enlisted men in pension rates? Should pensions be geared to compensation for injury or to loss of earning potential? If the latter, would it serve as a disincentive for men to rehabilitate themselves in fear that they would lose their pensions as they improved their employment? Should disability or illness incurred in home service or far behind the lines be dealt with as generously in pension compensation as in cases in which they were incurred at the front? Should men be given a choice about whether to undertake vocational rehabilitation, and, if they chose, allowed to go home after leaving the hospital? Should men be kept under military discipline, and hence controlled, while being vocationally rehabilitated to make sure that they fully availed themselves of the opportunity? Should vocational training be combined with remedial or other education? Was the purpose of all of these restoration efforts to return a man to the exact same position he was in before the war, or to enable him to improve upon that position? What was to be the proper mix of public and private and local, regional, and national initiatives and obligations to ensure the efficient and cost-effective delivery of services? Should pension decisions be made at the local level, where boards were likely to be sympathetic of a neighbor, relative, or friend, or at the regional or national level, where officials might attain greater objectivity, if at the cost of cold and impersonal administration? What role would the veterans themselves have in administering these programs?[62]

The range of responses to these questions is impressive. Italy, Belgium, and Germany kept men under military discipline during rehabilitation, but the United States, Britain, and France did not. Italy, the United States, Canada, New Zealand, Belgium, and Australia opted for centralized administration of vocational rehabilitation. Britain established a combination of national, regional, and local administration that nonetheless attempted to leave as much as possible in the hands of private agencies and employers acting on a voluntary basis. Imperial Germany, which was able to build upon the world's most well developed, prewar infrastructure of services for the civilian disabled, did some of the most distinguished work of physical and social restoration. A bureaucratized, authoritarian, but cost-conscious regime, it depended on both existing and newly created private agencies for rehabilitation. Its democratic successor, the Weimar Republic, however, passed strong quota legislation providing for the opening of public and private employment to disabled veterans, just as did Italy—in contrast to Britain, where quota legislation that was poorly enforced had little impact on the employment of disabled veterans. The United States continued its tradition of informally maintaining similar pension rates for officers and enlisted men, but Germany, Britain, Australia, and Canada did not, though the inequalities varied greatly from one country to the other. Hoping to use the opportunity to improve the cultural standard of the southern peasantry and to further national integration as well as impart modern job skills, Italy combined vocational and literacy training. The Germans and French envisioned returning men to their former station in life. The United States allowed men to seek advanced academic education in the pursuit of improving theirs. In the belief it would do few of them any lasting benefit, Canada considered impractical the return to school for men who seemed to wish to advance themselves beyond their prewar social position.[63]

Intentions were good, but as Deborah Cohen establishes in her essay here on Britain and Germany, the results were often disappointing. To be sure, many individuals were helped, but many others were not assisted as much as they required or at all. From the start of the postwar era, varying combinations of war debt, badly damaged economic infrastructure, fiscal uncertainty, and recession set funding limits for pension schemes in Canada, Britain, and, of course, in defeated Germany, which also had to pay reparations to the victors. Private employers in France, Britain, and Canada proved reluctant to hire disabled workers, fearing that they would be unproductive and that they presented a serious liability problem. Efforts to assist neuropsychiatric casualties were marred by the belief that such men were shirkers or psychotic. Fraud, corruption, bad timing, and incompetence in administration haunted the elaborate American program, with its pension plan, life insurance scheme, hospital system, and rehabilitation programs. Vocational rehabilitation ended too soon to profit all of the men who could have made use of it in the United States, while in Europe men were often trained for old-fashioned village trades that had little future. And everywhere veterans complained of insensitive, indifferent, or hostile pension office bureaucrats, who rarely came from their own ranks. Civil servants sometimes treated them like beggars and frauds, created protracted procedural muddles, and arbitrarily reevaluated individual cases. Reevaluations could leave them with even less support, but, as in Canada and Germany, such decisions were difficult or impossible to appeal.[64] The 1930s depression led to cuts in pensions in Australia, Britain, France, and Germany. This did not occur in the United States. Roosevelt lost a battle to cut pension benefits that by 1934, in the American tradition, had again escalated dramatically beyond the original core of war-disabled men, because the definition of service-connection had been progressively widened by Congress. Nor did it take place in Canada, where much had already been done to clear the pension roles of marginal and illegitimate cases.[65]

During the balance of the century public policy sought to improve and to elaborate upon, rather than to find a substitute for, this program. Britain, France, and the United States discovered the hold of this model on the public mind in their efforts to reconstruct Germany after 1945. In order to combat militarism, at first they insisted that there be no separate benefit system for disabled veterans, whose needs the occupiers assimilated into the civilian disability system. This was, of course, the opposite approach from that developing in the Allied countries, in which imposing institutional structures, none more so than the massive Veterans Administration in the United States, had taken form between the wars to assist veterans, disabled and able-bodied alike. The policy was so unpopular among the Germans that it threatened to hinder efforts to win over the population in the emerging rivalry with the Soviet Union, and was gradually compromised. When Germans in the Western zone were allowed self-government in 1949, the first important task the new government accomplished was the reconstruction of much of the veteran benefits program of the Weimar Republic.[66]

The principal challenge that the improvement of the World War I program was seen to pose was finding ways to provide quality services, humanely administered to large numbers of needy and deserving men, while containing costs, especially *long-term* costs. It was accepted increasingly, as Neary has observed about Canada, that a heavy short-term investment was needed if long-term dependency was to be avoided. One innovation was bringing disabled veterans and their organizations into the process of administering and planning programs that affected the welfare of the military disabled in the belief they could get the job done both efficiently and compassionately. Canadian disabled veterans of World War I came during World War II to head the relevant principal agencies and to assist in planning for the provision of postwar services. Founded after World War I, Canadian organizations for the blinded, the hearing impaired veterans, and amputees during World War II were allowed to provide directly a number of government-funded services to their members. In the United States, where the American Legion played an informal role in the benefits process between the wars, the largest veterans organizations were given a permanent and formal role in representing disabled men in their efforts to obtain government benefits. Federal legislation was passed to subsidize the training of national service officers, most disabled veterans, who were to work for the major veterans organizations in local communities and were given the responsibility of applying for benefits for individuals.[67] Another development lay in applying lessons learned from dealing with the difficulty of precisely attributing disabilities and illnesses to service-connected circumstances. Pension officials found that medical and particularly psychological conditions often had existed prior to induction and were only exacerbated by military service, but as the result nonetheless, the basis for a national obligation to the individual was established. When and where circumstances allowed for systematic manpower planning, as in the United States, Australia, Canada, and Britain, much greater attention was paid in World War II to raising induction standards to exempt, or to create limited service opportunities in the armed forces for, already weak, sick, and emotionally unstable men. This policy was reinforced by the need to maintain significantly sized civilian workforces in industry and agriculture.[68] Together with the intensely analyzed World War I record of large numbers of neuropsychiatric casualties, the World War II experience of large numbers of draft exemptions and qualified classifications given for individual vulnerability to neuropsychiatric breakdown succeeded in spreading an awareness of psychological disability long before the war ended. In consequence, a widespread recognition of the inevitability and legitimacy of neuropsychiatric disability, which in the past was often seen as feigned and evidence of cowardice or psychosis, led to the proliferation of programs for dealing effectively with such disorders among veterans.[69] These efforts would continue throughout the century, particularly with the growing understanding of, and the rise of new psychopharmacological and psychotherapeutic treatments for, post-traumatic stress disorder that Americans and Australians developed out of the Vietnam War experience.[70] Moreover, old conditions no longer deemed hopeless, such as spinal cord injury, would be added to the list of disabilities and illnesses that became the responsibility of the state, and new ones, such as Agent Orange–related illnesses and Gulf War Syndrome that are related to the changing nature of warfare, have arisen for which veterans have demanded treatment and compensation.[71]

Improved subsidized, postservice medical care and vocational rehabilitation programs that placed a significant emphasis on training for modern industry rather than on anachronistic artisanal work came out of World War II and were further developed thereafter. Significant, too, were innovations in the development of prosthetics and assistive devices, such as folding wheelchairs, motorized wheelchairs, hand-controlled automobiles, and the long, white metal cane for facilitating the mobility of the blind, and adapted environments, such as homes fitted out for wheelchair users. Technological innovations for the disabled and free prosthetics have made disabled veterans among the most gadget-conscious consumers in the world.[72] The post-1945 experience of a quarter-century of unprecedented economic expansion in the West, which had its complement on a lesser scale in the Soviet Union and its Warsaw Pact allies, made possible these gains as well as generous pensions. The post-1970 economic contraction again made them problematic to the extent that American and Australian veterans of the Vietnam War and Russian veterans of the Afghanistan War returned home to find their governments were no longer able to deal with their needs in as unqualifiedly generous a way as they had dealt with their grandfathers' or fathers' needs after World War II.[73] In the wider span of historical time, however, growth in all facets of the disabled-veterans provision was the outstanding development in the relationship between these veterans and state and society in the twentieth century.

Living with Disability

The movements for rights and for the opportunity to live independently that formed among the civilian disabled in Western nations in the last quarter of the twentieth century were founded on the recognition of the lack of state support for ensuring the civic equality of people with disabilities. What made the development of these movements truly distinctive was not this recognition, however, but that the energies and leadership, and the very impulse toward organization and unity, came from the ranks of the disabled themselves.[74] While our historical understanding is hardly well developed at this point, there seems little evidence prior to the recent past of either group formation or activism by the civilian disabled in their own behalf, or of identities established among people with disabilities on the basis of their common ties, whether defined as sharing a particular disability or the general condition of being disabled. There are exceptions, to be sure, the outstanding one perhaps being the history of the deaf. The evolution among hearing-impaired people of sign languages and the rise in the eighteenth century of schools, at first church-supported but increasingly the project of states, created both cultural and institutional bases for deaf identity and group formation, and consequently a foundation for the activism of the hearing impaired in their own behalf. Such activism became evident, for example, in their campaigns in the United States in the late nineteenth and early twentieth centuries for sign language in its battles with oralism.[75] We may eventually find tracings of these processes among those with other disabilities, in other places, but a working hypothesis that seems warranted in light of current knowledge is that in the historical past the experience of civilian disability has been individual and family-based as well as local, and that the isolation of the experience of being disabled under such circumstances has hindered the development of identities, organizations, and politics based on disability.

In contrast, the disabled veteran's experience of disability has been collective. It has been rooted in cycles of a public experience of group formation and organization that repeat themselves on a significant scale with each war through which a nation and its people pass. There are three sources of this process: a historical event (participation and injury in a war, in specific temporal, cultural, and political contexts); an ongoing relationship to government (material benefits and symbolic recognitions); and a collectively experienced history of medical treatment, rehabilitation, and reintegration. These three sources of the disabled veterans' group history all have in common a relationship to the state, which has led Geyer to observe that the social identity of the disabled veteran is ultimately a product of his interaction with the state.[76] The point may be easily exaggerated. The ways in which disabled veterans have come to understand and organize themselves owe a great deal to social interactions with the able-bodied public and to cultural representation as well as to finding a place in the political order. Moreover, disabled veterans have organized to fill a number of needs, such as solidarity and sociability among men of the same generation, experience, and illness or injury, or to inspire self-help, beside ordering their relationship to governments. But it is clear that in comparison with the civilian disabled, disabled veterans have had a singular and broadly ramifying relationship to the state, which has endowed them with a special status and provided them with entitlements, subsidies, and recognitions. In addition, the state has been an advocate for disabled veterans in their relation to society, and it has often acted forcefully to facilitate their reintegration into the social order. In fulfilling these provider and advocacy roles, the state has contributed mightily to the rise of the disabled veterans' group consciousness, and provided them with a public context in which to be self-conscious and effective agents in advancing their interests.

Prior to the emergence in the late nineteenth and early twentieth cen-

turies of formal veterans organizations, which have given a concrete historical form to these relationships both among veterans and between veterans
and the state and society, it is difficult to identify the workings of the relevant processes. Domiciliary institutions, for example, may well have provided an institutional context for cohort formation and group self-
consciousness and activism, because they brought together a critical, if localized, mass of men who shared similar experiences, and the same relationship
to the state, on whom they depended to maintain them. In the midst of the
French Revolution and the international and internal conflicts that attended
it, movements among disabled and aged rank-and-file veteran residents,
who were infused with the spirit of the Revolution, developed in the Hôtel
des Invalides to equalize the conditions of life within the institution and to
democratize its governance. But the extraordinary democratic civic culture
of the Revolution soon faded, as did France's dependence on a massive citizen army. The absence of these inhibited the rise of such activism and its
transformation into lasting forms of identity and organization. In contrast to
the French experience, histories of state and national domiciliaries for
American Civil War veterans do not yield evidence among residents of
either group formation and politicization or the group understandings that
might give rise to them.[77]

But, unlike their French counterparts, American Civil War veterans in
the North had access to the first modern mass veterans organization in history, the Grand Army of the Republic, which proved an ideal context for
the development of these functions. What was *modern* about the Grand
Army of the Republic was not its size; it numbered only about 270,000 veterans at its height in 1885. The mass German veterans organizations, the first
national group of which was the conservative Kyffhauser Bund, were created after the Franco-Prussian War and had 3,000,000 members by 1914.
Instead, the Grand Army of the Republic was modern in the fusion of the
elaborate scale of its organization and the impressive scope of its activities.
The federal nature of its organization, on national, state, and local levels,
allowed it simultaneously to meet a number of different needs in the lives of
its members, from the socializing at the level of the local "post" between
men sharing common experiences and memories, to, on the local, state, and
national levels, consulting with government agencies, lobbying state legislatures and Congress on behalf of its members, and getting out "the old soldier" vote in behalf of candidates who would vote for enhancing pension
programs. While the Kyffhauser Bund was also, after 1900, a national organization, the narrower range of its political and advocacy activities reflected

both its own conservative, patriotic orientation and the centralized, bureau-cratized, and authoritarian state in Imperial Germany.[78]

The pattern of organizational types that characterize the formal groups to which disabled veterans have belonged emerged in the wake of World War I alongside both the dramatic rise in their numbers and the programs defining the state's commitment to the disabled veterans' social provision. There are three general types of organizations to which disabled veterans belonged in the twentieth century: mixed, comprised of both able-bodied and disabled veterans; composite, comprised of veterans with different dis-abilities; and single-population, comprised of those sharing the same injury or illness. For many men, membership has not been mutually exclusive; vet-erans might belong to organizations of each type simultaneously. As this tri-partite pattern of affiliation suggests, to understand the nature of each type is to understand a variety of the elements of the disabled veterans' history. But we shall spend the most time on the last of the three because, though these organizations have actually been small in total membership, they com-bine in one organization the most complete synthesis of disabled veterans' felt needs and articulated aspirations.

Mixed organizations with client aspirations, such as the American Legion, the Veterans of Foreign Wars in the United States, the Great War Veterans Association in Canada, the Canadian Legion, the British Legion, and the Returned Soldiers and Sailors Imperial League of Australia, often began dedicated primarily to aiding disabled veterans. But they resembled the Grand Army of the Republic in that they also sought to create one large organization of all veterans, both able-bodied and disabled, to preserve the solidarity of the military experience and to attain strength from numbers in dealing with the state. In maintaining this broad solidarity of all veterans, they do not necessarily lose sight of the former goals, but they had to take an interest in meeting the various needs of the majority, of able-bodied vet-erans, which created a tension over priorities in their membership. In turn, this contributed to the desire of disabled veterans to have their own organi-zations.[79] Nonetheless, there is evidence that disabled veterans have been attracted to the solidarity and the power of these large organizations. In his study of the membership of the French post–World War I mixed organiza-tions, Prost found that in both leadership and rank and file, disabled veter-ans were overrepresented. In the case of the leadership, it was the more seri-ously disabled men who were most likely to assume leadership roles. In the French case, these large organizations, in sharp contrast to the nonpartisan French organizations only for disabled veterans, were also likely to define themselves in ideological and political terms, which may well have made them attractive to men who were politicized along the conventional right-left continuum.[80]

Composite organizations arose in Canada, the United States, Great Britain, France, Germany, Austria, and Italy after the world wars and appear to have been motivated by largely material, but in the German case also ideological, considerations. Those for which we have membership data range in size from the relatively small Disabled Veterans of America, which had no more than 25,000 of the 350,000 American veterans receiving pensions in the interwar period, to the massive French and German organizations. The largest French organization, the Unione Federale, had 345,000 members in 1926, while the largest German organization, the Reichsbund, which was affiliated with the Social Democratic Party, had 640,000 members in 1921. In that year, all of the German war victims organizations together had over 1.4 million members.[81] The creation of these organizations was based on the perception that disabled veterans, across the lines of injury and illness, could not be adequately represented in mixed organizations or, at the least, would be more effective single-mindedly pursuing their own interests and must achieve solidarity and power based on their own numbers. This did not always mean complete independence, however: in Britain, the Disabled Society, though autonomous in advancing its own program, remained a part of the British Legion. In the case of the Italian Associazione Nazionale degli Invalide della Guerra, this impulse was furthered by the preexisting solidarity of the founders, all of whom were men of elite social background and officer status. Effectiveness was not only measured in material and political terms, for being agents in their own behalf was also conceived therapeutically, as an exercise in self-help and manly independence. As the general secretary of the Italian organization said at the founding meeting, activism would aid them to "regain the strength and will to be real men, useful to ourselves and our families."[82]

The desire for solidarity across the lines of injury and illness did not always lead to the emergence of one national organization such as the Disabled American Veterans. For example, France after World War I and both Canada and Germany after World War II had large and competing national organizations of disabled veterans that would not surrender their autonomy. The maintenance of autonomy in several of the largest of these French organizations was underscored by their growth out of local and regional associations during and just after the war. The Canadian organizations did agree to consult and to coordinate activities through a national council. In contrast to the more or less nonpartisan, client-oriented organizations that arose in most nations, the German war victims organizations founded after World War I were defined in partisan and ideological terms and were affiliated with parties and political groupings contending for power. Thus, they provided a means by which disabled veterans and, in the German and Austrian pattern, other war victims such as widows and orphans could pursue their own interests, while working for social and political transformation.[83]

Single-population organizations have never been large in size, but they were a routine feature of disabled veterans' history in the interwar years. Some had difficulty attaining enough stability to endure over a few decades and disappeared or, as in Canada in the interwar period, were absorbed by larger, more powerful organizations like the mixed Canadian Legion.[84] As a consequence of aggressive recruitment and in some cases changing their membership criteria, especially through acceptance as members of veterans disabled *after* leaving the service or of disabled civilians, a few were able to become permanent fixtures, though they might be transformed in character in the process. Organizations are known to have existed of blind, tubercular, hearing-impaired, facially disfigured, spinal-cord-injured, and brain-injured veterans as well as amputees in Canada, the United States, Austria, Great Britain, France, Germany, and Australia in the twentieth century, though no nation had organizations in all of these categories.[85] The sequence of creation of these organizations reflected the larger medical history of warfare. The two examples of spinal-cord-injured veterans organizations, the Paralyzed Veterans Association in the United States and the Canadian Paraplegics Association, were both founded after World War II because there were not enough survivors of spinal cord injuries, let alone healthy and functioning survivors, until after the introduction of antibiotics in the 1940s for there to be organizations of these men.[86] The small numbers of men involved also is a reflection of the seriousness of the initial injuries men sustained. Even among major belligerents, such as Germany in World War I and the United States in World War II, the blinded-veterans organizations contained no more than several thousand men. It was not that blinded veterans were less likely to be joiners. In fact, the opposite was the case—within a few years of its founding the Blinded Veterans Association (BVA) in the United States claimed the membership of 850 (60 percent) of the war's 1,400 blinded veterans. The German Bund Erblindeter Krieger actually claimed membership, in 1921, of 2,521 (98 percent) of the 2,547 men blinded in the war. (While we do not have membership data for the Canadian and British Sir Arthur Pearson Clubs, named for the founder of Britain's famed blind rehabilitation institution, St. Dunstan's, the stability they achieved in the first half of the twentieth century suggests they, too, had a relatively large percentage of the blinded.) It is instead that injuries causing blindness are head wounds and are that much more likely to lead quickly to death than to long-term impairment.[87]

One begins to understand the felt necessity for the existence of these organizations by noting the difficulties posed to individuals by the conditions and impairments they present. In contrast to a wound that continues to bring some pain episodically long after it has healed or produces, say, a permanent limp, each of the aforementioned conditions necessarily involves a major and to some extent continuous adjustment, especially when, like sudden blindness, it has been experienced in adulthood after a lifetime of able-bodied status and activity. In light of the depth and range of the adjustments the blinded face, which many of them believe that sighted people cannot really understand, it is not surprising blinded veterans have felt the need for their own organizations. As a member of the founding cohort of the BVA stated in explaining the need for a separate organization, "We were out there with our 'lights out,' and the other organizations just couldn't understand this."[88] In the case of tuberculosis, a major source of post–World War I disability because of a combination of the damp, cold weather and trench warfare on the Western Front, men faced a protracted period of hospitalization and continued removal from their homes and communities, and the possibility of further deterioration of their physical condition, while their comrades were being rapidly demobilized. A thousand (12 percent) of the 8,571 tubercular Canadian World War I veterans died in the two years after the war.[89] Circumstances such as these, creating many needs and demanding numerous types of adjustments, also seemed to require a separate organization.

Veterans with these serious conditions had an intensely communal experience from the beginning of their careers as disabled men. They had already shared the experience of a generation, living in its own historical time with a certain degree of usual generational self-consciousness already enhanced by military service and war, when an injury or illness placed them in a common situation of dependency and treatment. For the sake of efficiency in treatment and the psychological comfort of the patient, the practice of military medicine has been to separate seriously ill or injured men by their general or specific conditions as soon after field treatment as possible. From the time of that initial separation, a cohort began to take shape among men brought together in a common condition. In consequence, wards in both military hospitals and rehabilitation facilities, as James Jones observed in *Whistle,* an autobiographically inspired novel of World

War II injured soldiers, have been a locus classicus of the disabled veteran's identity. In them, cohorts begin a transformation into self-conscious groups, and men developed intense interpersonal relations, on the basis of which were created formal organizations to advance their various interests.[90]

Examples are to be found in the well-documented experiences of spinal-cord-injured Canadian and blinded American veterans of World War II. The central rehabilitation facility for all blinded American Army troops was maintained in a former prep school at Avon, Connecticut during 1944–47, and blinded veterans from two of the three military hospitals, at Menlo Park, California, and Phoenixville, Pennsylvania, were brought there for mobility, orientation, and vocational training after completing medical treatment. Nine hundred (64 percent) of the American World War II blinded veterans were trained there. The BVA was founded at Avon in March 1945 at a meeting attended by over 100 of the resident men.[91] Spinal-cord-injured Canadians were first gathered at a military hospital at Basingstoke in Britain, and then removed, beginning in 1944, to the Canadian armed forces Christie Street Hospital in Toronto, from which they were moved to rehabilitation facilities in Quebec, Manitoba, and British Columbia and, in Toronto, at Lyndhurst Lodge, which opened in January 1945. The Canadian Paraplegic Association (CPA) was founded by seven veterans resident at Lyndhurst Lodge in May 1945.[92] In their goals and ideologies, such organizations closely mirror the rapidly evolving consciousness of their disabled founders. From the intense, informal conversations among men sharing these facilities came collective understandings of the problems that must be faced and the opportunities that must be created by and for them, if they were to have the normalized existence to which the majority seem always to have aspired.[93] But they also had to decide just what it was to which they actually aspired when they thought of a normalized existence.

In these endeavors, it must be observed, most twentieth-century disabled veterans had few resources within their own experiences to serve as guides. The representation of the disabled has historically been heavily stereotyped with aversive images. The segregation of the civilian disabled in the historical past deprived able-bodied people of practical knowledge about living with disability. Thus, the blinded veterans' only initial reference point for thinking about their condition was the pathetic, dependent, helpless individual—the shut-in, the denizen of sheltered workshops, or the street beggar—they believed most blind people must inevitably be.[94]

Though much depended on the sensitivity of individual physicians, medicalized discourse in the period of the two world wars proved often to be impersonal and abstracted and had little to contribute to an understanding of what, from a social, economic, or interpersonal perspective, lay in the future for the severely disabled man. Of necessity, doctors dwelled on the body's trauma. Most did not feel themselves competent to address the mind, and in the end, they were left seeming to reduce the individual to a wound. Some blinded veterans recall that doctors ultimately did little more than inform them bluntly of the finality of their condition and ask them if they had any questions.[95] The section "Psychology" occupied but two of the more than 40-page Veterans Administration, 1948 state-of-the-art research report on spinal cord injury written for doctors.[96] The psychological counseling for the recently physically disabled adult that came to be taken for granted in the late twentieth century did not exist in most armed forces. During World War I, for example, the Germans were acknowledged to have gone the furthest in confronting the psychology of serious disability in promulgating five principles of normalization to guide their work. Suggestive of the approach used to influence the psyche of the individual disabled man was the hopeful: "When we muster the iron will to overcome it, the era of cripples will finally be behind us."[97]

Beyond such maxims, what came closest to formal, systematic psychological counseling for seriously disabled men in most armed forces was the occasional overworked professional psychologist, with an enormous caseload and competing obligations, and nonprofessionals, who were often assigned to individuals and trained to speak with them about their condition and give practical assistance with daily needs during the earliest postinjury phase. Typically, visiting disabled civilians and disabled veterans of past wars were employed as, in the World War I usage, "cheer-up" men. Initiated on the Western Front, this practice was intended to illustrate the possibility of normalization. The dependence on inspirational stories, whether in person, in print, or on film, was the principal method through which military, medical, and rehabilitation authorities sought to create a positive frame of mind in the injured through the two world wars.[98] The introduction of assistive devices, such as the braille watch for the blind, which "cheer-up" visitors from the American Foundation for the Blind distributed among blinded servicemen, who were instantly able to recover their time orientation, also was intended to serve the same purpose.[99]

Physical rehabilitation itself is a psychologically therapeutic exercise. A bilateral hand amputee like Harold Russell, whose hands were blown off in a training accident in 1944, and whose new prosthetic hooks allowed him to shave and to hold a cup of hot coffee for the first time since his injury, might take hope from regaining some of what seemed lost as the result of his injury.[100] But, as Russell himself was only too well aware, there is a vast territory between taking heart in the appearance of "cheer-up" men and in the small, incremental gains toward self-sufficiency and the return to civilian life, as a self-supporting and normally functioning adult. The peer group and the organizations that grow out of it played a large role in advancing many men toward this goal. Men recalling the liminal, rehabilitation period, between hospitalization and civilian life, have testified to their dependence on mutual counsel and instruction to deal with a wide variety of difficulties—establishing new relations with parents, wives, children, and girlfriends; handling staring and other types of unwanted attention by an insensitive able-bodied public in initial forays into the civilian world; confronting fears about sexual intimacy; learning to use prosthetics and assistive devices; defeating environmental obstacles; framing realistic employment aspirations; and above all perhaps, avoiding the roleless, self-pitying, and anger-filled life that led frequently, as James Marten's essay in this volume suggests, to abuse of alcohol, probably the most common maladjustment of disabled veterans throughout history.[101]

The ideology of organizations like the BVA and CPA grew out of a synthesis of informal, proactive responses to these challenges. As the previous quotation from one the founders of the Italian disabled-veterans association suggests, such ideologies of disability have frequently been expressed, whether explicitly or implicitly, in heavily gendered language in terms of the restoration of masculine identity. Simply put in those terms, the goal has been, in the words of a BVA publication, "to be men again."[102] Russell Williams, one of the founders of the BVA, who went on in 1948 to be the first director of the Veterans Administration Blind Rehabilitation Program, referred to this masculinized ethic as "respectability" in laying out those elements of the ideal blinded veteran's character that would reestablish him as, in Williams's phrase, a "man among men." For Williams, who established the world's first comprehensive program of blind mobility training based on white cane technique, "respectability" meant finding employment; refusing to surrender to self-pity or to accept pity from others; rejection of helplessness, especially in the form of overdependence on others for assistance with mobility; and solidarity with other blinded veterans.[103] The greatest source of ambivalence in such ideologies would lie in the response to the question of relations with the state. State assistance was conceived as an earned entitlement that was essential to the maintenance of individual dignity, but the dangers of the development of neurotic dependence on that assistance were only too well understood.

Adjusted for differences in impairments, most organizations of disabled veterans in the twentieth century came increasingly to have ideologies similar to Williams's formulation of respectability. But this did not necessarily predetermine the same political program. Because of the precariousness of national economies and of the constrained fiscal conditions of most capitalist states in the early 1920s and throughout the 1930s, pension issues exerted a powerful hold on disabled veterans' political activity at the time. In contrast, in the midst of the rapid economic expansion of world capitalist and state socialist economies after World War II, the focus shifted away from the struggle for adequate pensions, which were generally achieved, toward programs that furthered normalization.

The politics of disabled veterans organizations in their relations both to the state and to society grew directly out of the ideologies of disability conceived within these local and global contexts. In the case of the CPA, as Mary Tremblay shows in this volume and elsewhere, its creation followed several years of experimentation by John Counsell, a combat-injured paralyzed veteran who refused to accept the regime of invalidism that was the prescribed way of treating spinal-cord-injured men in Canada and everywhere else during the war years. Counsell ultimately brought together the self-propelling, folding Everest and Jennings wheelchair, a contrast to the conventional chair that was intended to be pushed from behind, with a hand-controlled automobile, and negotiated Toronto traffic on his own to do his visiting and shopping. Counsell, who enjoyed important social connections as a consequence of his own upper-class family background and the support of several influential doctors involved in veterans' spinal cord injury care in Toronto, lobbied the Canadian veterans affairs officials to make the Everest and Jennings chair available to all paralyzed veterans. He was at first turned down on the basis of cost, but officials relented in February 1945. Over 200 Canadian veterans were soon using the chairs as vehicles for independent living. As they came increasingly to do so, they began to understand that their rapid normalization depended not on the painful and frustrating effort to simulate walking, but rather on developing the strength and ability to use a wheelchair. Founded soon after Counsell had succeeded in changing official minds, the CPA reflected the possibilities for normalization that the change represented.[104]

Though these men certainly did not turn down pensions, their politics did not dwell on their pensions, which were generous anyway. The CPA struggled with Canadian officials to make sure that men did not have pension benefits cut as they were successfully rehabilitated and reintegrated into the civilian economy. But the CPA's most avidly pursued goals reflected a program of individual reentry into the community through both using tools of independent mobility and participating in active lifestyles.

The CPA sought government assistance for making hand-controlled auto-mobiles available to spinal-cord-injured veterans and for adapting their homes with such facilities as ramps to facilitate mobility. Eventually, as we have seen, the CPA called for the extension of government rehabilitation facilities and subsidized assistive technology to spinal-cord-injured civilians. In keeping with the masculine ethic that rejected dependence, it opposed subsidized sheltered workshops and developed a program of job counseling and placement in the mainstream economy. Moreover, its emphasis was on individual solutions: it did not call for legislation to create accessible environments or workplaces. Once assisted to travel independently, paralyzed veterans were invited to compete with able-bodied workers on the majority's terms. Though this no doubt made heavy demands on individuals, studies during the decade after the end of the war found that, in a variety of circumstances, from 60 percent to 90 percent of paralyzed veterans were employed.[105]

The BVA's political program also combined self-help, independent mobility, and public support, but it began with a pronounced emphasis on the need for solidarity of all blinded veterans, across the lines that normally divided Americans. The concentration of all blinded veterans, whatever their backgrounds, at Avon forced these men to negotiate racial, religious, and ethnic prejudices and partisan differences that characterized their society in their own ranks, while they were being rehabilitated, and these negotiations informed their new organization's politics. In contrast to the larger veterans organizations, including the Disabled American Veterans, which feared dividing their membership over social issues and sacrificing political effectiveness, the BVA took strong stands against racism and anti-Semitism from the beginning of its existence, integrated the leadership and rank and file of its national office and state and local chapters, and voiced strong support for civil rights legislation to further African-American equality.[106]

The BVA's formulation of aggressive normalization involved the effort to separate blinded veterans from the fate of the civilian blind, as the veterans understood it, and avoid the dependence on government that sapped individual initiative. The BVA also represented men in struggles with the Veterans Administration over pension ratings, which often had to be contested because of a failure to take into account the further deterioration of men's sight after leaving the service. But early in its history, its officials spoke strongly against members being tempted by generous pensions to join "the sitters' club" of unemployed pensioners content to stay at home and be cared for by their mothers or wives.[107] Indeed, one reason for the desire for a separate organization was the perception of the founding cohort that other veterans organizations had a "We'll take care of you" attitude toward them that promised little more than an active lobby for greater pension benefits. The BVA sought from government subsidies for the tools of independent living, and then it, too, invited blinded veterans to compete in the mainstream economy. Especially prominent here was support for a realistic program of rehabilitation. At Avon, rehabilitation had been based on a belief that the blind possessed "facial vision," a sensitivity in the nerves of the face that allowed them to anticipate environmental hazards. Moreover, army rehabilitation officials argued, the white cane was a stigmatizing marker of blindness. Without it, the blind could achieve normal street invisibility. Men who had been introduced to cane training at military hospitals were made to abandon their canes at Avon, and develop the ability, in effect, to listen to their faces. Though a few men seemed to possess this sixth sense, most did not. Just as the paralyzed Canadian veterans opted to use the potentially stigmatizing wheelchair because of its convenience, these blinded veterans opted for the white cane for the same reason. Their pressing the issue of cane technique was largely responsible for the decision of the Veterans Administration in 1948 to open a facility to teach use of the cane. Both the BVA and the CPA believed that by example and public education, they could break down the prejudices that led to stigmatizing canes and wheelchairs.[108]

Though the BVA went further than the CPA in seeking special accommodation for the blind, it, too, largely opted for a program of equal opportunity. Another set of BVA goals sought to oppose the segregation and cultural isolation they associated with blind civilians. The BVA rejected sheltered workshops, and armed with its motto, "Jobs not pity," aggressively engaged in job counseling and placement. It fought discrimination in housing and the barring of guide dogs from public places. It called for government subsidies for the publication of "talking books," because many men lacked the finger sensitivity to master braille, and because too little was published in braille for the blind to be exposed to a full range of the literatures of current events and cultural trends that would allow them to know deeply the world around them.[109]

All of these efforts achieved mixed results. The blinded American veterans of World War II and the Korean War led rich and active lives. Compared to the civilian blind, they were found in the 1960s to be less socially isolated, to have more sighted friends, to be more active in formal organizations, and to be more active in recreation and socializing. On the other hand, by 1958, still only half of the relatively youthful cohorts of World War II and Korean War blinded veterans were employed, and as they reached their middle years, many left the labor market. For all its efforts at opening up lines of communication to employers, the BVA found it difficult to break down employer assumptions about blinded workers' limitations.[110]

In these CPA and BVA programs of aggressive normalization, with their independent living and nascent disability rights orientations, we come closer to witnessing the emergence of the new disability politics of inclusion and equality that would emerge in the last quarter of the twentieth century. That politics would have to emerge along parallel tracks, however, for the gap in understandings, identities, and relations to the state that has separated the civilian and military disabled remains a feature of the lives of people with disabilities.

The Essays

All but three of the authors are historians by disciplinary training, but there is nonetheless a great variety to the interests within and the orientations toward the study of the past to be found in this volume. The authors are variously cultural and social and political historians, and their projects span the history of a number of European and neo-European societies from antiquity to the most recent past. None of them has a disability studies orientation. They have come by their interest in disability as a consequence of following the logic of various specialties, such as war and society or the formation of the state, in which they have been engaged. By and large then, in these essays disability is the dependent, rather than the independent, variable—it is the concept that helps to analyze and explain a larger phenomenon, rather than the thing to be explained. Thus, for example, the essays that illuminate how individual societies have crafted social provisions for disabled veterans are principally about how states behave under a variety of circumstances. But the lines between the two orientations are not hard and fast. How societies conceive of disability, and hence transform functional limitations into a basis for the social positioning and the identities of individuals, is a persistent thread running through many of the essays.

The first section has three essays on the representation of the disabled veteran. In the context of ancient Greek history and culture, Edwards analyzes the West's original myth of the disabled veteran, the Philoctetes narrative, which has been the subject of retelling and reinterpretation since the Homeric texts and Sophocles' play. She argues that without a stable, valorized place in the politics and public culture of the ancient Greeks, the disabled veteran was conceived in contradictory and polarized ways, through the lenses of pity and of fear. He inspired no consistent image, and his experience had no consistent meaning for his contemporaries. Edwards's essay stands in a state of tension with my own essay, which, with an explicit reference to the relevance of the Philoctetes narrative, finds pity and fear very much evident in the response of Americans to disabled veterans after World War II, by which time disabled veterans had a stable and much valorized place in official public culture and discourse in the United States. I analyze the character of the disabled veteran Homer, a bilateral hand amputee who is treated with great sympathy that evokes the audience's pity and respect, but who also inspires fear in the popular feature movie *The Best Years of Our Lives* (1946). The tension between these two essays invites us to speculate on the extent to which attitudes toward people with disabilities at some level may be quite consistent over historical time. Norden shifts the focus in the final essay in this section. He reviews a wide range of interpretations of the heavily gendered and metaphorized Hollywood products that have sought to comment on the Vietnam War, and how American society was transformed by that war, through narratives featuring disabled veterans, and he contrasts the disabled-veterans movies of World War II and the Vietnam War. Norden offers an alternative metaphor, the prodigal son, for interpreting these Vietnam era movies in order to explain both the singular burdens the disabled characters are made to bear as symbols of an unpopular and ultimately futile war, and the ways in which disability itself is represented. Norden's essay reflects on the growing, if inconsistent, trend toward greater diversity in the characters and narratives of Hollywood's disabled veterans.

The evolution of public policy toward disabled veterans is the subject of the essays in the next section, which develops examples from a number of different societies. In a pathbreaking essay, which is framed at once from the perspectives of the histories of social welfare, state-building, and medical theory and practice, Hudson analyzes the origins and development of Europe's first national pension system for disabled veterans. From 1593 to 1679, in a context of the transition to a more modern, centralized form of the state, England had a tax-based system of pensions, administered by county justices of the peace. This pension system prefigured the principal difficulties of such schemes that would evolve much later, in the nineteenth and twentieth centuries—for example, evolution into a general veterans' relief program based on need, especially among the disabled aged, rather than remaining centered around reward and recompense for honorable service, and administration that brought men's bodies and characters under invasive and impersonal state scrutiny. Woloch's essay examines the emergence of a number of the prominent elements of the modern disabled-veterans social provision under successive and radically different political regimes—monarchical, republican, revolutionary, and Napoleonic—in late-eighteenth- and early-nineteenth-century France. The state is, of course, not necessarily a stable entity; it has been configured and reconfigured frequently in history. Woloch, a pioneer in the history of social policy regarding disabled veterans, demonstrates the ways in which, under circumstances of frequent changes in regime, politics and ideology crafted and revised the understanding of the disabled veteran's place in society and position relative to the state. Goler and Rhode provide us with a case study of the disabled veteran's role in modern state-building through investigation of the Army Medical Museum, a unique institution established for the purpose of simultaneously recording, assessing, representing, and valorizing the injuries of Union veterans of the American Civil War. The museum, which displayed military and medical artifacts, including bones and skulls of war casualties, was an integral part of the federal pension assessment bureaucracy created to pass judgment on the claims to support of hundreds of thousands of Union veterans. Reznick's essay addresses the subject of the growth in rehabilitation consciousness and practice at the time of World War I. He writes of Britain's experiment in combining physical and mental rehabilitation through a program of work-therapy, which placed men in occupations useful to the war effort and prepared them for the post-war job market, while simultaneously repairing their bodies and minds. Acclaimed for its cost-effective qualities by public officials, the program was less enthusiastically embraced by war-injured men, who felt they had already done enough for the war effort, feared they were being prepared for low-wage drudgery after the war, and suspected that the more they proved able to work, the lower their pension support would sink.

Not all disabled veterans are injured in the war effort of the victors or of states that survive to carry through their commitments to assist them. As the next three essays demonstrate, a wide variety of circumstances define the context of defeat, and a considerable variety of responses to disabled veterans may be anticipated. Rosenburg's former Confederates and the people of the post–Civil War American South display little demoralization, and in terms suggestive of France's acceptance of a "sacred debt" to assist disabled veterans that Woloch evokes, through private and public means, they go about systematically aiding disabled Southern veterans. The impressive Southern state effort in behalf of assisting these veterans, and the prideful Southern consensus rejecting the possibility of aid to this relief effort by Northerners and by the federal government against which Southerners had unsuccessfully rebelled, are all the more impressive in light of the relative poverty of the post-1865 South. While the South dealt with its disabled veterans' needs on the basis of regional self-sufficiency and state government programs, this was not an option for defeated Austria following World War II. Weeks shows that Austria's complicated international history mixed with its historic culpability for World War II to influence the situation of Austrian disabled veterans. As a former ally of defeated Nazi Germany that was occupied by both Russian and Western armies, Austria was tracked into neutrality at the onset of the Cold War, and soon was being courted by both East and West. Its ties with Hitler were expediently forgiven by the various Allied occupiers, who thereby aided Austrians in avoiding the examination of their nation's participation in the war. Disabled veterans profited from the international competition of occupiers, but had to spend many years, during which they developed into an effective voice in their own behalf, convincing fellow Austrians, who showed little desire to reflect on their nation's role in the war, to take interest in assisting both military and civilian disabled war victims. In contrast to the Southern and Austrian examples, the various cohorts of World War II, Cold War (including those who served in the Afghanistan War), and post-Soviet disabled veterans found in Dunn's essay on contemporary Russia are severely demoralized and without any effective means of dependable state assistance. Amid the political paralysis and polarization and the economic chaos of contemporary Russia, the Russian state, heir to the defunct Soviet Union, seems largely to have abandoned them.

In the final section, three essays explore the disabled veteran's experience of life with disability and examine both positive and negative adjustments. Marten focuses on the prevalence of alcohol dysfunctions (both heavy drinking and addiction) among the disabled and elderly veterans residing in the opulent setting of the Milwaukee branch of the National Home, the post–Civil War network of residential, domiciliary institutions operated and generously supported by the federal government for Northern veterans. These men, to whom so much in the way of material support was given, appear to have had everything they needed but the public and private roles that make for a meaningful adult life. Their rolelessness, a common situation of many disabled people in modern societies, complemented their physical and mental disabilities in creating a basis for the problem many of them had with alcohol. In the only explicitly comparative essay in the volume, Cohen deals with a greatly different issue in the history of postwar adjustments—the contrasting political and psychological responses of British and German disabled veterans of World War I to the different systems of social provisioning that emerged in their homelands after the war. Foregrounding her discussion in the history of policy in both nations, Cohen shows how it was that the less assisted British veteran felt gratitude for the meager pension and unsystematized acts of private and local benevolence and assistance he experienced. Moreover, since he was not economically competitive let alone often even employed, able-bodied citizens did not resent him in the midst of the harsh economic situation of the postwar years. The German situation was the opposite. With the best of intentions, the state quashed the voluntary sector, provided ample pensions (even in the context of considerable fiscal constraints) and comprehensive rehabilitation programs, and placed the force of a strong, legally mandated quota system behind employment for disabled veterans. But the German disabled veteran resented the impersonal administration of these programs and the ingratitude of able-bodied citizens, who themselves resented the Weimar government's affirmative action programs in behalf of his employment. The German situation paradoxically bred the sort of bitterness and political alienation that helped to undermine the Weimar Republic. In the collection's final essay, Tremblay continues the analysis of the work of John Counsell and the Canadian Paraplegics Association, which she has recently examined in several articles. Tremblay shows the ways in which by example and influence, Counsell served as a pioneer in the work of normalizing the lives of spinal-cord-injured veterans and civilians. Counsell was aided in this important work by his own indomitable will, his allies among a number of like-minded medical practitioners, and his membership in the English-Canadian social elite, which provided him with authority and powerful political connections.

These essays leave much in the histories of disabled veterans unexamined. Many experiences, time periods, nations, and peoples are not touched. But the essays do provide a beginning to a project that—in light of the length of time societies have lived with those injured while fighting their wars—has been deferred much too long.

NOTES

1. Shelley Saywell, *Women in War* (New York: Viking, 1985); Jean Bethke Elshtain, *Women and War* (New York: Basic Books, 1989), 171–79. On the neglect of American women veterans; see Richard Severo and Lewis Milford, *The Wages of War: When America's Veterans Came Home—from Valley Forge to Vietnam* (New York: Simon and Schuster, 1989), 300–304, 424–25; June A. Willenz, *Women Veterans: America's Forgotten Heroines* (New York: Continuum, 1983); Elizabeth M. Norman, *We Band of*

Angels: The Untold Story of American Nurses Trapped on Bataan by the Japanese (New York: Random House, 1999).

2. On the problem of defining *disability*, see Simi Linton, *Claiming Disability* (New York: New York University Press, 1998), 8–33, 135, 138–39; Paul K. Longmore, "A Note on Language and the Social Identity of Disabled People," *American Behavioral Scientist* 28, no. 3 (1985): 419–23.

3. Douglas C. McMurtrie, *The Disabled Soldier* (New York: Macmillan, 1919), 113; Jafi Alyssa Lipson, "Celluloid Therapy: Rehabilitating Veteran Amputees and American Society through Film in the 1940s," B.A. thesis, Committee on History and Science, Harvard University, 1995, 32–36, 49, 60; Patrick J. Kelly, *Creating a National Home: Building the Veterans' Welfare State, 1860–1900* (Cambridge: Harvard University Press, 1997), 129–30.

4. Technical Information Division, Office of the Surgeon General of the Army, "The Physically Disabled," *Annals of the American Academy of Political and Social Science* 239 (May 1945): 10–19; Rose Entelman, *Two Hundred Years of Military Medicine* (Fort Detrick, Md.: U.S. Army Medical Unit, 1975); Peter Dorland and James Nanney, *Army Aeromedical Evacuation in Vietnam* (Washington, D.C.: United States Army Center for Military History, 1982).

5. Ernest Bors, M.D., "Urological Aspects of Rehabilitation in Spinal Cord Injuries," *Journal of the American Medical Association* 146 (May 1951): 225; Mary Tremblay, "Going Back to Main Street: The Development and Impact of Casualty Rehabilitation for Veterans with Disabilities, 1945–1948," in *The Veterans' Charter and Post–World War II Canada,* ed. Peter Neary and Jack L. Granatstein (Kingston, Ontario: McGill-Queen's University Press, 1997), 165–66; Ernest Bors, M.D., *Spinal Cord Injuries,* Technical Information Bulletin, TB10–503, December 15, 1948 (Washington, D.C.: Veterans Administration, 1948), 3–4.

6. Technical Information Division, "The Physically Disabled," 10.

7. On the increasing visibility of people with disabilities, including veterans, in the twentieth century throughout the world, see Richard K. Scotch, *From Good Will to Civil Rights: Transforming Federal Disability Policy* (Philadelphia: Temple University Press, 1984), 6–7, 31–40; James I. Charlton, *Nothing about Us without Us: Disability, Oppression, and Empowerment* (Berkeley and Los Angeles: University of California Press, 1998).

8. Paul Fussell, *The Great War and Modern Memory* (New York: Oxford University Press, 1975).

9. William H. R. Rivers, *Instinct and the Unconscious: A Contribution to a Biological Theory of the Psycho-Neurosis* (Cambridge: Cambridge University Press, 1920); Eric Dean, *Shook over Hell: Post-Traumatic Stress, Vietnam, and the Civil War* (Cambridge: Harvard University Press, 1997), 134; Terry Copp, "From Neurasthenia to Post-Traumatic Stress Disorder: Canadian Veterans and the Problem of Persistent Emotional Difficulties," in Neary and Granatstein, *Veterans' Charter,* 134; Abram Kardiner, *War Stress and Neurotic Illness,* 2d ed. (New York: Paul B. Hoeber, 1947); Jonathan Shay, *Achilles in Vietnam: Combat Trauma and the Undoing of Character* (New York: Simon and Schuster, 1994); Elaine Scarry, "Injury and the Structure of Modern War," *Representations* 10 (1985): 1–21.

10. Recent statements of the conceptual evolution of *disability* are Linton, *Claiming Disability,* and Charlton, *Nothing about Us.*

11. Fussell, *Great War;* Samuel Stouffer et al., *The American Soldier,* vol. 2, *Com-*

bat and Its Aftermath (Princeton: Princeton University Press, 1949), 84, 131–32, 150–51, 230, 264–71; S. L. A. Marshall, *Men against Fire* (New York: Morrow and Infantry Journal, 1947), 76, 150–52, 160–61; John Keegan, *The Face of Battle: A Study of Agincourt, Waterloo, and the Somme* (London: Jonathan Cape, 1976); Gwynne Dyer, *War* (New York: Crown, 1985), 104–22; James McPherson, *For Cause and Comrades: Why Men Fought the Civil War* (New York: Oxford University Press, 1997).

12. E.g., George H. Roeder Jr., *The Censored War: American Visual Experience during World War II* (New Haven: Yale University Press, 1993).

13. Vera Dunham, "Images of the Disabled, Especially the War Wounded, in Soviet Literature," in *The Disabled in the Soviet Union: Past and Present, Theory and Practice,* ed. William O. McCagy and Lewis Siegelbaum (Pittsburgh: University of Pittsburgh Press, 1989), 151–63; Sonya Michel, "Danger on the Home Front: Motherhood, Sexuality, and Disabled Veterans in American Postwar Films," in *Gendering War Talk,* ed. Marian Cooke and Angela Woollacott (Princeton: Princeton University Press, 1993), 260–61.

14. Desmond Morton and Glenn Wright, *Winning the Second Battle: Canadian Veterans and the Return to Civilian Life, 1915–1930* (Toronto: University of Toronto Press, 1987), 140–54, 63–167, 222–25; Robert Gerald Whalen, *Bitter Wounds: German Victims of the Great War, 1914–1939* (Ithaca: Cornell University Press, 1984), 141–70; Stephen R. Ward, "Land Fit for Heroes Lost," in *The War Generation: Veterans of the First World War,* ed. Stephen R. Ward (Port Washington, N.Y.: Kennikat, 1975), 31–35; Clem Lloyd and Jacqui Rees, *The Last Shilling: A History of Repatriation in Australia* (Melbourne: Melbourne University Press, 1994), 241–62; Davis R. B. Ross, *Preparing for Ulysses: Politics and Veterans during World War II* (New York: Columbia University Press, 1969), 25–29.

15. Sander L. Gilman, "Depicting Disease: A Theory of Representation," in *Disease and Representation: Images of Illness from Madness to AIDS* (Ithaca: Cornell University Press, 1988), 1–17; Leonard Kriegal, "Disability as a Metaphor in Literature," *Kaleidoscope* 17 (summer–fall 1988): 6–14; Susan Sontag, *Illness as Metaphor* (New York: Farrar, Straus and Giroux, 1977).

16. Martin F. Norden, *The Cinema of Isolation: A History of Physical Disability in the Movies* (New Brunswick, N.J.: Rutgers University Press, 1994), 1.

17. Oscar Mandel, ed., *Philoctetes and the Fall of Troy: Plays, Documents, Iconography, Interpretations* (Lincoln: University of Nebraska Press, 1981), 35–36; Dunham, "Images of the Disabled," 151–63; Paul Longmore, "Screening Stereotypes: Images of Disabled People," *Social Policy* 16 (summer 1985): 34–37; Albert Auster and Leonard Quart, *How The War Was Remembered: Hollywood and Vietnam* (New York: Praeger, 1988), 1–73.

18. Lindsay French, "The Political Economy of Injury and Compassion: Amputees on the Thai-Cambodian Border," in *The Existential Ground of Culture and Self,* ed. Thomas J. Csordas (Cambridge: Cambridge University Press, 1994), 69–99.

19. Douglas Bicklin and Robert Bogdan, "The Disabled: Media's Monsters," *Social Policy* 13 (fall 1982): 32–35; Shari Thurer, "Disability and Monstrosity: A Look at Literary Distortions of Handicapping Conditions," *Rehabilitation Literature* 41 (January–February 1980): 12–15.

20. See George Swiers, "'Demented Vets and Other Myths: The Moral Obligations of Veterans," in *Vietnam Reconsidered: Lessons from a War,* ed. Harrison Salisbury (New York: Harper and Row, 1984), 196–202, for an explanation of, and a protest against, this pervasive representation.

21. Marcel Prevost, "Aid for Disabled Soldiers in France before 1670," *American Journal of Care of Cripples* 8, no. 6 (1919): 405–18; McMurtrie, *The Disabled Soldier,* 20.

22. Eric Maria Remarque, *The Road Back* (Boston: Little, Brown, 1931); Merle Miller, *That Winter* (New York: William Sloane Associates, 1948).

23. Mandel, *Philoctetes and Troy,* 35–36, 40; McMurtrie, *The Disabled Soldier,* 47, 101–5, 120; William Waller, *The Veteran Comes Home* (New York: Dryden Press, 1944), 159–69, 289–91.

24. Jacob Armstrong Swisher, *The American Legion in Iowa* (Iowa City: Iowa State Historical Society, 1929), 65; Robert England, *Twenty Million War Veterans* (London: Oxford University Press, 1950), 216; Dorothy Culp, "The American Legion: A Study in Pressure Politics," Ph.D. diss., University of Chicago, 1939.

25. Ross, *Preparing for Ulysses,* 78–82; Michael J. Bennett, *When Dreams Come True: The G.I. Bill and the Making of Modern America* (Washington, D.C.: Brassey's, 1996), 94–95, 99–101; Albert Q. Maisal, *The Wounded Get Back* (New York: Harcourt, Brace, 1944).

26. M. Brady Brower, "Strategic Remembering: The Boundary Politics of Mourning in Post–Great War France," *Rethinking History* 1 (spring 1997): 25–28; Joanna Bourke, *Dismembering the Male: Men's Bodies, Britain, and the Great War* (Chicago: University of Chicago Press, 1996), 56, 58. For one among many other examples, an especially prominent one from the standpoint of frequency and self-consciousness of the disabled veteran's use as a public symbol in the post–Civil War American South, see Gaines Foster, *Ghosts of the Confederacy: Defeat, the Lost Cause, and the Emergence of the New South, 1865–1913* (New York: Oxford University Press, 1987), 194 and passim.

27. Douglas C. McMurtrie, *The Evolution of National Systems of Vocational Reeducation for Disabled Soldiers and Sailors* (Washington, D.C.: Federal Board for Vocational Education, 1918); McMurtrie, *The Disabled Soldier;* Edward T. Devine, *Disabled Soldiers and Sailors: Pensions and Training,* Preliminary Economic Studies of the War, no. 12 (New York: Oxford University Press, 1919).

28. Lisa Herschbach, "Prosthetic Reconstructions: Making the Industry, Re-Making the Body, Modeling the Nation," *History Workshop Journal* 44 (fall 1997): 28–33; Seth Koven, "Remembering and Dismemberment: Crippled Children, Wounded Soldiers, and the Great War in Great Britain," *American Historical Review* 99 (October 1994): 1193, 1196, 1198–99; McMurtrie, *Evolution of National Systems,* and *The Disabled Soldier;* R. Tait McKenzie, *Reclaiming the Maimed: A Handbook of Physical Therapy* (New York: Macmillan, 1918). The identical photographs (or very similar ones) tended to appear in these books, evidence of the perception of their representational value.

29. Lipson, "Celluloid Therapy."

30. *The Best Years of Our Lives* (1946), William Wyler, director, Robert Sherwood, screenplay, Samuel Goldwyn Productions; *The Men* (1950), Fred Zinnemann, director, Carl Foreman, screenplay, United Artists; *Bright Victory* (1951), Mark Robson, director, Robert Buckner, screenplay, Universal Pictures.

31. Bourke, *Dismembering the Male,* 56; Michel, "Danger on the Home Front," 260–79; Margaret Randolph Higonnet et al., eds., *Behind the Lines: Gender and the Two World Wars* (New Haven: Yale University Press, 1987), 1–10; Sandra M. Gilbert, "Soldiers' Hearts: Literary Men, Literary Women, and the Great War," in Higonnet et al., 200–226; Susan Gubar, "'This Is My Rifle, This Is My Gun': World War II and the Blitz on Women," in Higonnet et al., 228–55.

32. Waller, *The Veteran Comes Home,* 140; Willard Waller, *War and the Family* (New York: Dryden Press, 1940), 24–25, 47; Susan Hartman, *The Home Front and Beyond: American Women in the 1940s* (Boston: Twayne, 1982); McMurtrie, *The Disabled Soldier,* 96–105; Alexander Dumas and Grace Keen, *A Psychiatric Primer for the Veteran's Family and Friends* (Minneapolis: University of Minnesota Press, 1945), 41–74, 75–104, 105–57.

33. Koven, "Remembering and Dismemberment," 1177–85; Bourke, *Dismembering the Male,* 39, 41, 49–51.

34. Robert F. Murphy, *The Body Silent* (New York: H. Holt, 1987), 72–73.

35. Waller, *The Veteran Comes Home,* 289–91; Irvin L. Child et al., *Psychology for the Returning Serviceman* (Washington, D.C.: Infantry Journal, 1945), 85, 86, 154–80, 181–94, 218–19, 220–30, 289–90. This was a specific and dramatic instance of a more general problem that was well recognized in advice literature, addressed by experts to women, in the United States toward the end of World War II: how to reintegrate demobilized men into the life of the home. See Susan Hartman, "Prescriptions for Penelope: Literature on Women's Obligations to Returning World War II Veterans," *Women's Studies,* 5, no. 2 (1978): 233–39.

36. Susan Jeffords, *The Remasculinization of America: Gender and the Vietnam War* (Bloomington: Indiana University Press, 1989); Kaja Silverman, *Male Subjectivity at the Margins* (New York: Routledge, 1992), 65–90; Norden, *The Cinema of Isolation,* 314–23; Peter Roffman and Jim Purdy, *The Hollywood Social Problem Film: Madness, Despair, and Politics from the Depression to the Fifties* (Bloomington: Indiana University Press, 1981), 5–7, 227–28.

37. Michel, "Danger on the Home Front," 261; Koven, "Remembering and Dismemberment," 1188–89; Jeffords, *The Remasculinization of America.*

38. Don M. Wolfe, ed., *The Purple Testament* (New York: Doubleday, 1947); Ernest R. Mowrer and Harriet R. Mowrer, "The Disabled Veterans in the Family," *Annals of the American Academy of Political and Social Science* 239 (May 1945): 150–59; Martin F. Norden, "The Disabled Vietnam Veteran Revisited," in *In the Eye of the Beholder: Critical Perspectives in Popular Film and Television,* ed. G. Edgerton et al. (Bowling Green, Ohio: Bowling Green State University, 1997), 79–90, and "The Disabled Vietnam Veteran in Hollywood Films," *Journal of Popular Film and Television* 13 (spring 1985): 16–23; *Coming Home* (1978), Hal Ashby, director, Waldo Salt and Nancy Dowd, screenwriters, United Artists; *Born on the Fourth of July* (1989), Oliver Stone, director and screenplay, Universal; Pat Barker, *Regeneration* (New York: Dutton, 1992), *The Eye in the Door* (New York: Dutton, 1994), and *The Ghost Road* (London: Viking, 1995).

39. Sar Levitan and Karen A. Cleary, *Old Wars Remain Unfinished: The Veteran Benefits System* (Baltimore: Johns Hopkins University Press, 1973), ix and passim.

40. Deborah Stone, *The Disabled State* (Philadelphia: Temple University Press, 1984), 4–7, 24; Michael Geyer, "Ein Verbote des Wohlfahrtsstaates: Die Kriegsopferversorgung in Frankreich, Deutschland, und Grossbritannien nach dem Ersten Weltkrieg," *Geschichte und Gesellschaft* 9 (1983): 230–77; Theda Skocpol, *Protecting Soldiers and Mothers: The Political Origins of Social Policy in the United States* (Cambridge: Belknap Press of Harvard University Press, 1992), 148–51.

41. Skocpol, *Protecting Soldiers and Mothers,* 150; Edward D. Berkowitz, *Disabled Policy: America's Programs for the Handicapped* (Baltimore: Johns Hopkins University Press, 1987), 17, 169–70; Lloyd and Rees, *The Last Shilling,* 386–89; Devine, *Disabled Soldiers*

and Sailors, 101, 180, 386; Desmond Morton, "The Canadian Veterans' Heritage from the Great War," in Neary and Granatstein, *Veterans' Charter,* 22.

42. The prototypical expressions of this type of veterans organization come from the United States; see Mary Dearing, *Veterans in Politics: The Story of the GAR* (Baton Rouge: Louisiana State University, 1952); William Pencak, *For God and Country: The American Legion, 1919–1941* (Boston: Northeastern University Press, 1989). (This is not to overlook the American Legion *leadership's* outspoken patriotism and social conservatism, which, while deeply ingrained in the organization, are largely rhetorical and take a subordinate position to its single-minded pursuit of benefits.) Also see Lloyd and Rees, *The Last Shilling,* 416; Morton, "Canadian Veterans' Heritage," 22; James M. Diehl, "Germany: Veterans under Three Flags," in Ward, *The War Generation,* 175; Skocpol, *Protecting Soldiers and Mothers,* 116–17; Ross, *Preparing for Ulysses,* 78–82.

43. Robert England, *Twenty Million War Veterans* (London: Oxford University Press, 1950), 174; Bourke, *Dismembering the Male,* 43–44; Morton and Wright, *Winning the Second Battle,* 260 n. 35; Berkowitz, *Disabled Policy,* 203; Bernice Madison, "Programs for the Disabled in the Soviet Union," in McCagy and Siegelbaum, *Disabled in Soviet Union,* 172–88, Steven A. Holmes, "The Disabled Find a Voice and Make Sure It's Heard," *New York Times,* March 18, 1990.

44. James M. Diehl, "Change and Continuity in the Treatment of German *Kriegsopfer,*" *Central European History* 18 (June 1985): 173–76, and "Victors or Victims? Disabled Veterans in the Third Reich," *Journal of Modern History* 50 (December 1987): 705–36.

45. Mary Tremblay, "The Canadian Revolution in the Management of Spinal Cord Injury," *Canadian Bulletin of Medical History* 12 (1995): 142–45.

46. Mary Tremblay, "Going Back to Civvy Street: A Historical Account of the Impact of the Everest and Jennings Wheelchair for Canadian World War II Veterans with Spinal Cord Injury," *Disability and Society* 11 (1996): 165.

47. Ibid.

48. Whalen, *Bitter Wounds,* 162; James M. Diehl, *The Thanks of the Fatherland: German Veterans after World War II* (Chapel Hill: University of North Carolina Press, 1993), 89–93; Morton, "Canadian Veterans' Heritage," 27.

49. Ross, *Preparing for Ulysses,* 103–4; Antoine Prost, *In the Wake of War: Les Anciens Combattants and French Society, 1914–1939* (Oxford: Berg Publishers, 1992), 32–43.

50. William DeMaria, "Combat and Concern: The Welfare-Warfare Nexus," *War and Society* (Australia) 7 (May 1989): 71–85.

51. Ibid., 71–85; England, *Twenty Million War Veterans,* 5.

52. Ross, *Preparing for Ulysses,* 38–49.

53. Geoffrey Lewis Hudson, "Ex-Service Men, War Widows, and the English County Pension Scheme, 1593–1679," Ph.D. diss., Oxford University, 1996; Skocpol, *Protecting Soldiers and Mothers,* 3–23; Geyer, "Ein Verbote des Wohlfahrtsstaates," 230–77 (I want to thank Patricia Mazon for helping me with the translation of the Geyer essay). This point was missed by Michel Foucault in his influential *Discipline and Punish,* trans. Alan Sheridan-Smith (London: Allen Lane, 1977).

54. McMurtrie, *The Disabled Soldier,* 13; Devine, *Disabled Soldiers and Sailors,* 19–21; Prevost, "Disabled Soldiers in France," 405–18.

55. McMurtrie, *The Disabled Soldier,* 15–19, 21; Devine, *Disabled Soldiers and Sailors,* 20–23, 28–29; Hudson, "Ex-Servicemen, War Widows."

56. McMurtrie, *The Disabled Soldier*, 18–24; Devine, *Disabled Soldiers and Sailors*, 29–49; England, *Twenty Million Veterans*, 202–3; Alan Forest, *The Soldiers of the French Revolution* (Durham: Duke University Press, 1990), 144–54; Isser Woloch, *The French Veteran from the Revolution to the Restoration* (Chapel Hill: University of North Carolina Press, 1979); William G. Glasson, *Federal Military Pensions in the United States* (London: Oxford University Press, 1918), 9–98; Whalen, *Bitter Wounds*, 83–89; Lloyd and Rees, *The Last Shilling*, 7–16; Morton and Wright, *Winning the Second Battle*, 5–10.

57. R. B. Rosenburg, *Living Monuments: Confederate Soldiers' Homes in the New South* (Chapel Hill: University of North Carolina Press, 1993); Whalen, *Bitter Wounds;* Diehl, *Thanks of the Fatherland,* and "Treatment of German *Kriegsopfer,*" 170–87.

58. Skocpol, *Protecting Soldiers and Mothers*, 102–51; Glasson, *Federal Military Pensions*, 125–75; John William Oliver, *History of the Civil War Military Pensions, 1861–1885* (Madison: University of Wisconsin Press, 1917).

59. McMurtrie, *Evolution of National Systems*, 149; Devine, *Disabled Soldiers and Sailors*, 204, 290–91; Lloyd and Rees, *The Last Shilling*, 9; Morton and Wright, *Winning the Second Battle*, 12–13, 32.

60. Devine, *Disabled Soldiers and Sailors*, 131; Whalen, *Bitter Wounds*, 39–40, 55–56, 156; Prost, *In the Wake of War*, 3:13; Morton and Wright, *Winning the Second Battle*, ix; Severo and Milford, *The Wages of War*, 247–48; Antoine Prost, *Les Anciens Combattants et La Societé Françaises, 1914–1939* (Paris: Presses de La Fondation Nationale des Sciences Politique et Sociologie, 1977), 3:13.

61. Devine, *Disabled Soldiers and Sailors*, 385–446; McMurtrie, *The Disabled Soldier,* and *Evolution of National Systems;* Geyer, "Ein Vorbote des Wohlfahrtsstaates," 230–77. Prior to 1914–18, Russia and Great Britain provide the only examples of vocational rehabilitation for disabled veterans on a systematic basis. After the Russo-Japanese War disabled veterans were retrained at a St. Petersburg school for the nonveteran disabled; these arrangements seem to have been supported, in whole or in large part, privately. Disabled British veterans of the Boer War were aided by a private fund that facilitated retraining in special workshops and workrooms. In neither case do the numbers of veterans rehabilitated appear significant. See McMurtrie, *The Disabled Soldier*, 27.

62. Devine, *Disabled Soldiers and Sailors;* McMurtrie, *The Disabled Soldier,* and *Evolution of National Systems;* Whalen, *Bitter Wounds,* 131–40; Morton and Wright, *Winning the Second Battle,* 44–61; Lloyd and Rees, *The Last Shilling,* 20–34, 63–85, 133–52; Gustavus Weber and Laurence F. Schmeckebier, *The Veterans' Administration: Its History, Activities, and Organization,* Institute for Government Research Service Monographs of the United States Government, no. 66 (Washington, D.C.: Brookings Institution, 1934), 90–119.

63. Devine, *Disabled Soldiers and Sailors,* 180–88, 189–232, 240–65, 281–314, 319–73; McMurtrie, *The Disabled Soldier,* 160–208, 209–22, and *Evolution of National Systems,* 23–64, 65–76, 77–101, 109–31, 133–49, 205–33, 247–51. See Deborah Cohen, "Will to Work: Disabled Veterans in Britain and Germany after the First World War," in this volume.

64. Whalen, *Bitter Wounds,* 141–53; Prost, *In the Wake of War,* 29; Bourke, *Dismembering the Male,* 54, 60–67, 70–74; Ward, "Land Fit for Heroes," 16–30; Morton and Wright, *Winning the Second Battle,* 140–77; Lloyd and Rees, *The Last Shilling,* 187–208, 231–40; Weber and Schmeckebier, *The Veterans' Administration,* 106–85; Pencak, *For God and Country,* 176–97; Dixon Wecter, *When Johnny Comes Marching Home* (New York: Houghton Mifflin, 1944), 385–405.

65. See note 14 above. American pension costs increased 866 percent 1919–29; Wecter, *Johnny Comes Marching Home,* 403–4.

66. Diehl, *Thanks of the Fatherland,* and "Treatment of German *Kriegsopfer,*" 177–87.

67. Jeff Kashen, "Getting It Right the Second Time Around: The Reintegration of Canadian Veterans of World War II," in Neary and Granatstein, *Veterans' Charter,* 64–65; Peter Neary, introduction to Neary and Granatstein, *Veterans' Charter,* 11; Tremblay, "Back to Main Street," 166, 171; Theodore Newcomb and Amos H. Hawley, "Rehabilitation Services of Veterans Organizations," *Annals of the American Academy of Political and Social Science* 239 (May 1945): 160–64; American University, *Professional Curriculum: National Service Officers with Veterans Organizations,* Unit A-3/46.8, American University Archives.

68. William C. Menninger, "The Mentally or Emotionally Handicapped Veteran," *Annals of the American Academy of Political and Social Science* 239 (May 1945): 23; "N-P," *Time,* May 29, 1944, 44, 46; Wecter, *Johnny Comes Marching Home,* 391; England, *Twenty Million Veterans,* 164, 176; Lloyd and Rees, *The Last Shilling,* 266–77; Copp, "Neurasthenia," 151–52.

69. England, *Twenty Million Veterans,* 176–87; "Combat Detraining," *Newsweek,* July 9, 1945, 105–7; Menninger, "Mentally or Emotionally Handicapped," 28; Copp, "Neurasthenia," 153–54; Lloyd and Rees, *The Last Shilling,* 229.

70. Arthur S. Blank Jr., "Apocalypse Terminable and Interminable: Operation Outreach for Vietnam Veterans," *Hospital and Community Psychiatry* 33 (November 1982): 913–18; Robert Klein, *Wounded Men, Broken Promises* (New York: Macmillan, 1981), 355–74, 378; Lloyd and Rees, *The Last Shilling,* 375–76. The Canadian experience is somewhat ambiguous: the Canadian government has been generous in providing pensions for veterans with post-traumatic stress disorders, but not in developing treatment options; Copp, "Neurasthenia," 152–54.

71. Bors, *Spinal Cord Injuries;* Tremblay, "Canadian Revolution"; Klein, *Wounded Men, Broken Promises,* 154–81; Fred A. Wilcox, *Waiting for an Army to Die: The Tragedy of Agent Orange* (New York: Random House, 1983); Jock McCulloch, *The Politics of Agent Orange: The Australian Experience* (Richmond, Australia: Heineman, 1984); Seymour M. Hersh, *Against All Enemies—Gulf War Syndrome: The War between America's Ailing Veterans and Their Governments* (New York: Ballantine, 1998).

72. Madison, "Programs in Soviet Union," 187; England, *Twenty Million Veterans,* 117; Lloyd and Rees, *The Last Shilling,* 317–18; Tremblay, "Back to Civvy Street"; Richard Hoover, "The Cane as a Travel Aid," in *Blindness,* ed. Paul A. Zahl (Princeton: Princeton University Press, 1950), 353–65; Robert Brown and Hope Schutte, *Our Fight: A Battle against Darkness* (Washington, D.C.: Blinded Veterans Association, 1991), 15, 42–54; Roger Bates Boatwright, "The Social Adjustment of Eleven World War II Veterans to Paraplegia," M.A. thesis, Southern Methodist University, 1952.

73. Madison, "Programs in Soviet Union," 185–88; Paul D. Raymond, "Disability as Dissidence: The Action Group to Defend the Rights of the Disabled in the USSR," in McCagy and Siegelbaum, *Disabled in Soviet Union,* 245–46, 251 nn. 35, 47.

74. Scotch, *Good Will.*

75. John Vickery van Cleve and Barry A. Crouch, *A Place of Their Own: Creating the Deaf Community in America* (Washington, D.C.: Gallaudet University Press, 1989); Harlan Lane, *When the Mind Hears: A History of Deafness* (Random House, 1984).

76. Geyer, "Ein Verbote des Wohlfahrtsstaates," 230–34.

77. Woloch, *French Veteran;* Kelly, *Creating a National Home;* Rosenburg, *Living Monuments.*

78. Dearing, *Veterans in Politics;* Severo and Milford, *The Wages of War,* 167–68; Whalen, *Bitter Wounds,* 118–19; Diehl, "Germany," 137.

79. Pencak, *For God and Country,* 176–97; Lloyd and Rees, *The Last Shilling,* 187–208; Morton and Wright, *Winning the Second Battle,* 67–70; Morton, "Canadian Veterans' Heritage," 22, 27, 62–64; Prost, *In the Wake of War,* 35–37, 40, and *Les Anciens Combattants et La Société Française, 1919–1939,* 1:83.

80. Prost, *In the Wake of War,* 45.

81. Pencak, *For God and Country,* 50; Tremblay, "Back to Main Street," 171; Bourke, *Dismembering the Male,* 274 n. 218; Koven, "Remembering and Dismemberment," 1201–2; Prost, *In the Wake of War,* 29–33; McMurtrie, *Evolution of National Systems,* 132; Whalen, *Bitter Wounds,* 118–28.

82. McMurtrie, *Evolution of National Systems,* 132.

83. Whalen, *Bitter Wounds,* 118–28; Prost, *In the Wake of War,* 30–32; Mary Tremblay, "Lieutenant John Counsell and the Development of Medical Rehabilitation and Disability Policy in Canada," in this volume. Regionalism and developing rivalries among disabilities also divided British organizations, about which less is known; Bourke, *Dismembering the Male,* 71–72.

84. Morton, "Canadian Veterans Heritage," 27.

85. Brown and Schutte, *Our Fight,* 1–23; Tremblay, "Back to Main Street," 171; Lloyd and Rees, *The Last Shilling,* 277; Morton, "Canadian Veterans' Heritage," 27; Morton and Wright, *Winning the Second Battle,* 132, 135–36, 142, 169, 176, 185–86, 207–11; Koven, "Remembering and Dismemberment," 202; Whalen, *Bitter Wounds,* 55, 128, 173; Diehl, *Thanks of the Fatherland,* 93; Prost, *Les Anciens Combattants et La Société Française, 1919–1939,* 1:198, and *In the Wake of War,* 39–40.

86. Tremblay, "Back to Civvy Street," 165, *New York Times,* June 22, October 30, 1946.

87. Whalen, *Bitter Wounds,* 55, 128, 173; Lloyd Greenwood, "The Blinded Veteran," in Zahl, *Blindness,* 261, 269–70.

88. Brown and Schutte, *Our Fight,* 13.

89. Morton and Wright, *Winning the Second Battle,* 132.

90. James Jones, *Whistle* (New York: Delacorte, 1978), 36–38, 44, 134. Also see Laurence Stallings, "Vale of Tears," in *Men at War: The Best War Stories of All Time,* ed. Ernest Hemingway (New York: Crown, 1942), 377–407; Walter V. Bingham, " 'Start Climbing, Soldier!' The Army Program for Rehabilitating Casualties," *Annals of the American Academy of Political and Social Science* 239 (May 1945): 60–61; Harold Russell with Victor Rosen, *Victory in My Hands* (New York: Creative Age Press, 1949), 91–110; Brown and Schutte, *Our Fight,* 5–8, 11–17; Corrine Brown, *Body Shop: Recuperating from War* (New York: Stein and Day, 1973), 180.

91. Brown and Schutte, *Our Fight,* 5–8. The navy chose not to participate and developed its own program at the Philadelphia Naval Hospital; Francis Koestler, *The Unseen Minority: A Social History of Blindness in America* (New York: McKay, 1976), 266.

92. Tremblay, "Back to Civvy Street," 149–50, and "Canadian Revolution," 125–26, 135–40.

93. The desire for normalization accounts for the failure of all the schemes intro-

duced here and there in the twentieth century to create geographically separate communities, as distinct from sheltered workshops or domiciliary institutions, for disabled veterans; see McMurtrie, *The Disabled Soldier*, 93–95; Wecter, *Johnny Comes Marching Home*, 382–83.

94. Brown and Schutte, *Our Fights*, 2–3, 11; Howard Rusk, "Rehabilitation," *New York Times*, June 9, 1946.

95. Walt Stromer, "A Letter Too Late," *BVA Bulletin* 45 (July–August 1990): 8; Brown and Schutte, *Our Fight*, 4, 95; Greenwood, "The Blinded Veteran," 265; Blackburn, "The Army Blind in the United States," in Zahl, *Blindness*, 279.

96. Bors, *Spinal Cord Injury*, 32–33.

97. McMurtrie, *Evolution of National Systems*, 134. This rehabilitation dictum is attributed to Konrad Biesalski, an orthopedist who was the leading German theorist of rehabilitation during World War I, and appears in his *Kreigskrüppelfürsorge: Ein Aufklärungswort zum Trost und zur Mahnung* (Leipzig: Leopold Vess, 1915), 4.

98. Devine, *Disabled Soldiers and Sailors*, 319, 437; McMurtrie, *The Disabled Soldier*, 34–36; Lifson, "Celluloid Therapy"; Koestler, *The Unseen Minority*, 273–74; Greenwood, "The Blinded Veteran," 265; Blackburn, "Army Blind," 279–81; Bors, *Spinal Cord Injury*, 33; Waller, *The Veteran Comes Home*, 164.

99. Koestler, *The Unseen Minority*, 271–72.

100. Russell, *Victory in My Hands*, 103.

101. Brown and Schutte, *Our Fight*, 8; Russell, *Victory in My Hands*, 91–110; Greenwood, "The Blinded Veteran," 265; Child et al., *Psychology for Returning Veteran*, 148–49. There are so many testimonies, reprints, and comments about disabled veterans and the abuse of alcohol it is difficult to know how to begin to document them. What we lack are studies that synthesize this knowledge.

102. Brown and Schutte, *Our Fight*, 91.

103. Koestler, *The Unseen Minority*, 276–77; Ellen Papadimoulis, "Editorial," *VIS View* (winter 1989): 1–2; Russell Williams, "Some Historical Perspective on VIST and Blindness," *VIS View* (winter 1984): 5–8; Russell Williams, "Why Should I?" *VIS View* (winter 1989): 10–13; Russell Williams, "Believers," *VIS View* (winter 1989): 4–6.

104. Tremblay, "Back to Civvy Street," 149–57, and "Canadian Revolution," 125–40, and see Tremblay, "Lieutenant John Counsell and the Development of Medical Rehabilitation and Disability Policy in Canada," in this volume.

105. Tremblay, "Back to Civvy Street," 158–66, and "Canadian Revolution," 141–55.

106. Congress of Industrial Organizations Veterans Committee, *Veterans' Organizations* (Washington, D.C.: Congress of Industrial Organizations, 1946), 1–4; Koestler, *The Unseen Minority*, 278; *BVA Bulletin* 3 (April 1948): 1; 3 (May 1948): 1; 3 (July 1948): 1.

107. Brown and Schutte, *Our Fight*, iv, 16, 30–31, 80–81.

108. Koestler, *The Unseen Minority*, 264–65, 276–77, 303–4; Brown and Schutte, *Our Fight*, 7–10, 13–15, 42–53; *New York Times*, January 20, 1946.

109. Brown and Schutte, *Our Fight*, 22, 78–91; Koestler, *The Unseen Minority*, 282–83, *New York Times*, January 20, June 9, 1946, September 3, 6, October 20, 21, 22, 28, 1948, August 25, 1950; Greenwood, "The Blinded Veteran," 269–70.

110. Koestler, *The Unseen Minority*, 283–84, summarizing the results of two massive studies of the World War II and Korean War blinded-veteran cohorts: C. Warren Bledsoe, *War Veterans in a Post-War Setting* (Washington, D.C.: Veterans Administration, 1958), and Milton D. Graham, *851 Blinded Veterans: A Success Story* (New York: American Foundation for the Blind, 1968), using 1952 and 1962 data, respectively. Also see Hector Chevigny and Sydel Braverman, *The Adjustment of the Blind* (New Haven: Yale University Press, 1950), 287–88.

I. REPRESENTATION

Martha Edwards

Philoctetes in Historical Context

The tale of the wounded war-hero Philoctetes was spun over several centuries. Philoctetes' adventures were first recorded in the Homeric writings (*Iliad* 2.716ff.) around the eighth century B.C. They are best known through Sophocles' tragedy *Philoctetes,* produced at the end of the fifth century B.C., upon which this essay is based.[1] Many additional versions exist; for example, Ovid narrated the story at the end of the first century B.C., in his *Metamorphoses* (9.229, 13.45ff., 313ff.).[2]

The tale of the wounded war-hero is old, but it is not timeless. The Philoctetes myth must be viewed in its historical context. While the tale does not provide direct or specific historical information, it does illustrate several realities of the plight of the disabled veteran in the ancient world, particularly the lack of codified practice of matters such as medical care. While there may have been a small pension for injured war veterans, to be discussed below, there was no equivalent of the Veterans Administration hospital in the ancient Greek world, nor was there anything like the Department of Veterans' Affairs. Along with this lack of codified practice, there was little of the popular laudatory attitude toward the wounded and disabled soldier that is reflected in contemporary films such as *Forrest Gump* and *Born on the Fourth of July,* holidays such as Veterans Day, and celebratory events sponsored by the American Legion or by VFW posts. In other words, the category of the disabled veteran was not part of a package of patriotism as it is today. This is not a judgment that implies that the Greeks should have conformed to our standards; rather, it is an observation about the Greek world that helps put the tale of Philoctetes in context.

Summary of the Philoctetes Narrative

The story, which the Greeks set in the distant past of gods and heroes, begins when Philoctetes, taking with him the bow and arrows given to him by Heracles, joins the other Greek leaders and sets sail to make war on Troy.

During the voyage, he receives an injury to his foot by snakebite, according to most variations of the tale. The wound becomes infected, and Philoctetes is abandoned on the deserted island of Lemnos by his comrades, because they can bear neither the stench of the wound nor Philoctetes' screams of pain. Philoctetes remains on the island for nine years, in agony from this wound, which will not heal. Equipped with only his bow and arrows, he lives a miserable life foraging for food and searching for relief from his pain. Meanwhile, the Greeks learn that they will never be able to take Troy without the arrows of Heracles. Philoctetes and his weapons are fetched; the healers at Troy cure Philoctetes' wound. Troy falls, after which he returns to his native Thessaly.

Historical Interpretation

The narrative of the wounded soldier, then, is a very old one, and this particular narrative shows surprising resiliency. Of over 100 Sophoclean plays, *Philoctetes* is one of the seven that survive in their entirety. Furthermore, elements of the narrative have been adapted and interpreted over several centuries. In addition to the depiction of Philoctetes in art, the essence of the story survives through literary reworkings, most recently in Mark Merlis's *An Arrow's Flight,* a novel that weaves twentieth-century gay culture with the tale of Troy.[3]

From both an ancient and a modern perspective, the story of Philoctetes consists of elements that suggest attraction to and admiration for the wounded hero. The attraction is reflected in the artistic depictions of the sanitized and idealized agony of Philoctetes, such as is seen in figure 1. But there is also repulsion, reflected in the stench of Philoctetes' wound and his howls of pain, and rooted in the fear that nondisabled people have for disability. Pity, too, is expressed for Philoctetes by other characters in the play, such as Neoptolemus, who has come to lure Philoctetes and his weapons to Troy:

> I am filled with pity,
> Searing pity for this man,
> As I have been all along.

> (965–66)

The tale of Philoctetes is often discussed in mythological terms. Edmund Wilson, for example, in his essay "Philoctetes: The Wound and the Bow," compares Philoctetes' wound with Oedipus's transgressions.[4] Both Philoctetes and Oedipus are pariahs; Philoctetes is an outcast because of his disgusting wound, Oedipus because of his dreadful sins.[5]

FIG. 1 Pierre-Paul Prud'hon, *Philoctetes* (1807). (Reprinted by permission, The Museo de Arte de Ponce, The Louis A. Ferré Foundation, Inc., Ponce, Puerto Rico.)

While rich in timeless mythological symbolism, the story of Philoctetes is ahistorical in detail. The tale is also ahistorical in that it is heroic in proportion, rather than a depiction of ordinary people. Motifs such as Philoctetes' wound that seem obvious in their symbolism must be treated with caution. While it might be tempting for a modern audience to see Philoctetes' individual, physical suffering as symbolic of a larger, social suffering, R. A. Martin points out that Philoctetes' pain cannot be interpreted as social or political commentary—that it is only in modern realism that characters discover truth through their bodily experience. The Greeks discovered truth through divine interaction.[6]

It is also important to remember the context in which Sophocles told the story of Philoctetes. At Athens, tragedies were given only one performance, as part of a religious festival. Just as scholars must not impose a twentieth-century reading on a fifth-century narration, it is also important to realize that any Greek tragedy will have nuances that are not immediately apparent to a modern audience. Ismene Lada-Richards, for example, argues that Philoctetes' bow, the main stage prop in the _Philoctetes,_ activates a set of connotations associated with the Eleusinian Mysteries, in which a sacred object was also revealed as the culmination of the rite. The _thea,_ or mystical sight of a sacred object, is implicit when the bow is revealed and the audience is invited to gaze at it.[7]

While the dangers of reading too much or too little into the _Philoctetes_ must be taken into consideration, the Sophoclean version of the story is a cultural product of fifth-century Athens. Elements of the story provide a collage, if not a clear picture, of some historical realities.

While parallels between the modern and ancient disabled war veteran exist, historical context shapes many differences. The psychological trauma of battle is universal, as Jonathan Shay illustrates in _Achilles in Vietnam: Combat Trauma and the Undoing of Character._[8] In contrast, the Philoctetes myth illustrates some differences between the ancient and modern aftermath of combat, including war injury and its consequences. It also highlights the Athenians' apparent lack of a concept of the injured war veteran. There is no evidence that the wounded veteran was formally categorized in the Greek world. There is no trace of any memorial honoring a social category of the wounded veteran in speeches, public monuments, or special funerals. The only apparent recognition of the wounded veteran is in Plutarch's mention of state support for Athenian men who were maimed in war.

This state support does not necessarily indicate that there was an Athenian category of "the disabled veteran." First, its very existence is questionable. Although the biographer Plutarch attributed its genesis to the sixth-century statesman Solon (_Solon_ 31.2), Plutarch, who wrote in the first century A.D., is less interested in historical fact than in painting a portrait of his subject. The other reference to state support for injured veterans is the unreliable author Diogenes Laertius (1.55), in his third-century A.D. account of Solon.

The state support for wounded war veterans—if it existed as a separate category—was probably similar to the very small payment awarded by the Athenian state to those unable to fend for themselves (Aristotle, *Athenian Constitution* 49.4).[9] Matthew P. J. Dillon argues that the state pension was not merely altruistic, but rather was a mechanism that, by making it unnecessary for impoverished citizens to seek private financial help, prevented aristocratic patronage, which would have endangered the Athenian democratic system.[10] The state pension for injured war veterans, if it existed at all, was not a bureaucratic recognition of a social category. It was a mechanism of survival for those who, for whatever reason, could not survive on their own.

Wounded and disabled veterans did not constitute a bureaucratic category; rather, they were individuals who would survive or not, be cured or not, and be able to continue to participate in the military or not. As Herodotus has Solon, the wisest man in the world, say, no man should be counted lucky until he is dead, for the fortunate man is the one who ends his life "without disfigurement, sickness, or evil" (Herodotus 1.32).

Weaponry

Philoctetes had remarkable weaponry, "arrows that cannot miss—death-dealing always" (105). No ordinary Greek soldier owned the bow and arrows of Heracles, and while the bow was, for fifth-century Greeks, an archaic weapon, Philoctetes' ownership of Heracles' bow exemplifies the lack of uniformity of the citizen-army of any Greek community. Soldiers provided their own armor and weapons, and there was little standardization.[11] National uniforms, for example, were not common until the fourth century B.C.[12] That weapons were personal, individual possessions rather than standard, state-issued items is illustrated nicely by the seventh-century lyric poet Archilochus (frag. 2), who writes:

> By spear is kneaded the bread I eat, by spear my Ismaric
> wine is won, which I drink, leaning on my spear.[13]

Medical Care in Battle

Philoctetes' wound, like his Heraclean weaponry, had divine implications; his suffering, too, was larger than life. He suffers from excruciating pain—the sort of pain that one would not imagine tolerating more than a few moments—for nine years. As he relates to Neoptolemus:

Ah, it's going through me,
It's going through me!
Oh, what misery!
Yes, lost, my boy—this pain's devouring me.
For God's sake,
If you have a sword to hand, lad,
Strike my foot—here on the heel!
Mow it off, quickly!
Never mind my life!
Quick, quick, my boy!

(743–50)

This wound of heroic proportions reflects a more humble historical reality, that of the vulnerability of a citizen-soldier to incapacity for future battle from significant physical disability caused by a battle wound.

Neither during battle nor after was there an organized method of treating the wounded. Because of the intense, close range in classical Greek battle, which was fought shoulder-to-shoulder with one's comrades and face-to-face with one's enemies, there was no opportunity to gather one's own wounded during battle, and the enemy wounded were most likely killed or left to die.[14] These wounded were more pitiable than the dead. Thucydides (7.75) describes the wrenching scene at the disaster of Syracuse, which had occurred a few years prior to the production of the *Philoctetes:*

> The dead lay unburied, and each man as he recognized a friend among them shuddered with grief and horror; while the living whom they were leaving behind, wounded or sick, were to the living far more shocking than the dead, and more to be pitied than those who perished. These fell to entreating and bewailing until their friends knew not what to do, begging them to take them and loudly calling to each individual comrade or relative whom they could see, hanging upon the necks of their tent-fellow in the act of departure, and following as far as they could, and when their bodily strength failed them, calling again and again upon heaven and shrieking aloud as they were left behind.[15]

The stench of Philoctetes' wound suggests the stench of the dead and dying soldiers left on the battlefield, where, in the hot Greek summers, when battles were fought, corpses would be putrefying within a few hours.[16] The phenomenon of rotting corpses appears in ancient accounts of warfare often enough to suggest that it was perceived as a standard result of warfare.[17]

However, there is no suggestion that the wounded veteran was also perceived as a standard result of warfare.

There were no medical units attached to the army—indeed, rational medicine, as opposed to medicine dependent upon divine intervention, was in its infancy in classical Greece. Still, one soldier could attend another, as the famous vase painting of Achilles tending Patroclos suggests.

Medical Care after Battle

If a wounded man survived the battle, he returned home and hoped for the best. There were no hospitals, and certainly no equivalent of the rehabilitation unit. Permanent physical disability did not belong in the domain of rational medicine; in fact, a Hippocratic practitioner's recognition of an incurable case—a case in which he should not intervene—was part of his art.[18] The abandonment of Philoctetes by his comrades must have resonated with any soldier in the Greek world who had transported an injured comrade home, knowing that the wounded soldier might not join the next military engagement.

Men with severe wounds would have been left for dead on the battlefield,[19] but less-severely injured men who became permanently physically handicapped as a result of war wounds must have been numerous.[20] Even a simple injury by today's standards, such as a fall, could have irreversible consequences in the ancient world. Herodotus (3.129–30) tells us that the Persian king Darius, having dislocated his foot in the process of dismounting from his horse, lay in pain for several days. Finally a Greek physician was fetched, who was able to ease Darius's pain. Still, Darius gave up hope of ever using the foot again, and this despite having the best doctors. This passage is not a straightforward testimony, of course, but rather a showcase for the art of Greek medicine: only the Greek doctors could stop the pain.[21] Nevertheless, the underlying basis of the tale—that one risked permanent disability from a relatively minor accident—had to ring true with Greek audiences.

From the Homeric writings on, war injuries were noted as causes of permanent physical handicaps. In the *Iliad,* the god of war himself, Ares, reflects that he risked dying or living "strengthless by reason of the smitings of the spear" (*Iliad* 5.887), and an ancient Greek audience would know that Eurypylus, limping back from the battlefield with a wound in his thigh, was in serious danger (*Iliad* 11.809–11). An injury to the femur, the largest bone in the body, leads to complications such as torn muscles and long-lasting infections.[22] The author of the Hippocratic treatise on dislocations and other injuries to bones and joints, *On Fractures* (19), observes that the fractured thigh bone will lead to a shortened thigh (19), and that the thigh bone distorts easily (20).[23]

There is, of course, a wide range of additional war injuries that would have led to permanent physical handicaps if the injured person survived. Injuries of any sort, whether as a result of improper healing, or as the result of infection, were much more likely to lead to a permanent physical disability in the ancient world, where even the most minor injury could have permanent consequences, than in the modern, developed world.[24] In the developed world, for example, we take for granted that, with medical attention, even the most severe fracture will be undetectably repaired. Without medical attention, fractures sometimes spontaneously and completely heal, but not always.[25]

While it is assumed in the developed world that medical attention to a broken bone will result in its healing, a visit from a doctor in classical Greece had many possible results. A Hippocratic writer (*On Fractures* 1) warns that some doctors, through their showy bandagings—for example by bandaging fractured arms in exotic rather than natural positions—do the patient more harm than good. We read spine-tingling instructions for setting bones, which, in most cases, could only have caused further damage. For a dislocated foot, for example, the physician is instructed as follows:

> As a rule two men suffice, one pulling one way and one the other, but if they cannot do it, it is easy to make the extension more powerful. Thus, one should fix a wheel-nave or something similar in the ground, put a soft wrapping round the foot, and then binding broad straps of ox-hide about it attach the ends of the straps to a pestle or some other rod. Put the end of the rod into the wheel-nave and pull back, while assistants hold the patient on the upper side both at the shoulders and hollow of the knee. The upper part of the body can also be fixed by an apparatus. (*On Fractures* 13)

A broken thigh bone that results in a shortened thigh because of faulty medical treatment, we are told (*On Fractures* 19), is evidence of poor medical judgment. It is not clear if the Hippocratic writer is giving literal advice or simply making a point when he advises the physician that it is better to break both legs and at least have them in equilibrium.[26]

Even if a bone is tended to and set properly, one must remain immobilized to effect complete healing. While animals with broken bones do this by instinct, the need to tend a shop or a field probably overrode any instinct to remain idle.[27] A Hippocratic writer (*On Fractures* 9) notes that while a patient with a broken foot should remain immobile for 20 days,[28] "patients, despising the injury, do not bring themselves to do this, but go about before they are well."

A Greek would be lucky if the bone simply healed crookedly, as every bone injury was susceptible to infection.[29] Untreated by antibiotics, an infection can spread throughout the surrounding tissues, then the bone itself, attacking even the bone marrow.

Although in the Sophoclean tragedy, Philoctetes' wound is a religious pollution that keeps his comrades from sacrificing to the gods, thus forcing his comrades to abandon him (1–10), it is also a literal wound, graphically portrayed from the beginning of the play. Neoptolemus identifies Philoctetes' lair by various clues, including his bandages:

> Aha! Here's something else! Yes, some rags drying in the sun. They're reeking with matter from some terrible sore. (38–39)

The stench of the wound could have easily been drawn from real experience. Colin Hodgkinson, in *Best Foot Forward,* a 1957 account of his amputation, relates that his injured foot never healed, but stank for months. The stench, more than anything, led him to decide to have his foot amputated.[30] If the injured person survives severe infection, the necrotic bones become extremely deformed, not just at the injury, but around the whole area.[31]

Philoctetes, having spent nine years in agony from an open wound, reflects:

> And so I pine for the tenth year,
> Miserable, starving, sick,
> Working to feed my insatiable disease.
>
> (312–14)

While a decade of an unhealed wound is an exaggeration, it may have highlighted anxiety over the fact that some limbs did not heal at all, but were lost. Ischemia (localized anemia) and gangrene (decay of tissue resulting from this lack of blood supply) are common results of injury.[32]

Today, minor amputation can forestall or prevent major limb amputation, and, in an age of antibiotics, no amputation need necessarily mean infection, as various antibiotics are now prescribed for the healing process of any limb amputation.[33] Preventative amputation seems not to have been practiced during the classical period. In the Hippocratic Corpus, amputation is always a passive matter; that is, the limb falls off on its own, or is pulled off only when it is ready to come away anyway.[34]

Philoctetes spent 10 years on an island fending for himself, deep in his agony of pain and solitude. The chorus laments the pitiful situation:

> He has no friend to nurse him, not a man.
> He sees no other face,
> He must be wretched, always alone, sick and in pain.
> He must go nearly mad,
> Wondering how to cater for his daily needs.
> How does a man endure such hardships?
>
> (171–76)

An ordinary wounded Greek soldier would be with his family, for physical care for an ordinary handicapped person was a family matter.[35] Still, Philoctetes' bare survival on the island of Lemnos provides symbolic parallels to the ordinary injured veteran's life. The economics of chronic disability suggest that all but the wealthiest of families would have been burdened; thus the quality of life for a significantly disabled veteran could not have been optimal.[36] As mentioned above, the disabled soldier, along with anyone who was unable to support himself, may have been eligible to receive a very small payment from the state, but only if he were destitute.[37] We can only guess at the range of conditions that must have existed for physically handicapped people who required care, for we do not have any direct information. The surviving literature shows us examples only of the extremes of children's solicitousness and neglect for their incapacitated parents.[38]

The Philoctetes myth highlights the lack of standardization in several areas of ancient Greek military life, including weaponry, medical care in battle, care for the wounded soldier after battle, and provision for the disabled veteran thereafter. In addition, because there was no category of "disabled veteran" and no custom of valorizing men wounded in battle, the myth highlights the dual reaction of admiration and disgust for the disabled soldier. In the twentieth-century Western worldview, there is an emotional and institutional category for the disabled veteran of war that did not exist in the ancient Greek world. This lack of standardization in the Greek world is a central consideration in an investigation of the ancient disabled veteran of war.

Absence of the Category of Disabled Veteran

When it became clear that his arrows were needed to win the Trojan War, Philoctetes' former comrades were apparently able to bear Philoctetes' cries and stench after all. He was retrieved from Lemnos and taken forcibly to Troy, asking his captor,

> How is it, cursed wretch, I am not *now* lame, evil-smelling?
>
> (1031)

We see the flexibility of the category "able" in our own century: during World War II, people who had been considered incapable by nature, such as women and people with mental retardation, suddenly were deemed quite capable. Intelligence tests that would have labeled a potential soldier mentally retarded, thus unfit for service, were discarded in favor of simple screening processes. Steven Gelb reports that "many previously institutionalized soldiers compiled war records that caused the attitude of institution superintendents to shift from one of disapproval and skepticism to pride in the accomplishments of 'their boys.'"[39]

This phenomenon is documented in the ancient Greek world as well. The same people who were deemed useless by nature of their physical configuration (whether by age, gender, or ability) were, in emergency situations, employed to defend the city walls.[40] There was not so rigid a distinction as there is today between those who were fit to serve and those who were not. One did not have to be in near-perfect bodily condition to serve. In classical Greek hoplite battle, one needed to be able to hold one's ground in order to keep the line intact, not to run or move quickly.[41]

At the end of the Sophoclean play (1438–39) Philoctetes is promised a cure by the healing god Asclepius after nine years of intense suffering. While this cure is on one level the play's final divine intervention,[42] the symbolism reflects reality. Philoctetes' cure is not the only tale of complete recovery. While rational Hippocratic physicians recognized incurable cases, the Asclepiadic dedications at Epidaurus include many testimonies of miraculous cures of blindness, deafness, lameness, and so on.[43] Given the perceived possibility for spontaneous, miraculous cure, the concept of disability's permanence in the ancient Greek world was much less rigid than today in the developed world. The Greeks could certainly hope for, if not expect, an imminent cure for any ailment, including ailments we in the modern world would call incurable. An example similar to Philoctetes' miraculous cure is seen in the case of a certain Cephesias, recorded on a fourth-century B.C. stele at Epidaurus. Cephesias, who had been thrown from his horse, injured his foot so badly that he had to be carried into the temple. He received this injury as divine punishment because he had laughed at the Asclepiadic cures for lameness, and was cured only after he recanted.[44]

Conclusion

In modern warfare, medical units quickly distinguish between the dead and the living, and the wounded are gathered, treated, and, if need be, rehabilitated. If the wounded become permanently disabled, they join a bureaucratic and social category, the disabled veteran. In ancient warfare, the line between wounded, dying, and dead was less clear. Philoctetes' persistent wound is an emblem of this ambiguity.

Because there was no military, social, or economic category of the wounded veteran, the plight of the individual wounded and disabled veteran could produce mixed feelings of pride and pity, admiration and repulsion. The scars of the disabled veteran were tangible reminders to the citizens of any given community of past wars as much as were the weapons on display in public buildings.[45] Without the social positioning of the disabled veteran that we have in the twentieth century, the ancient disabled soldier starkly represents the very real horrors of war.

NOTES

I thank William Ashcraft, Janet Davis, Julia DeLancey, Christine Harker, Sara Orel, and Steven Reschly for their generous help with this essay. I also thank David Gerber for his helpful suggestions.

1. All translations of Sophocles' *Philoctetes* are by Kathleen Freeman, in *Ten Greek Plays in Contemporary Translation,* ed. L. R. Lind (Boston: Houghton Mifflin, 1957), 160–210.

2. A full account of the textual history of the tale of Philoctetes is found in Oscar Mandel, ed., *Philoctetes and the Fall of Troy: Plays, Documents, Iconography, Interpretations* (Lincoln: University of Nebraska Press, 1981).

3. Mark Merlis, *An Arrow's Flight* (New York: St. Martin's Press, 1998). Mandel catalogs the various interpretations of the play.

4. Edmund Wilson, *The Wound and the Bow: Seven Studies in Literature* (New York: Oxford University Press, 1965), 232–33.

5. Ibid., 233.

6. R. A. Martin, "Metaphysical Realism in *Philoctetes,*" *Classical and Modern Literature* 13, no. 2 (1993): 127–38.

7. Ismene Lada-Richards, "Neoptolemus and the Bow: Ritual *Thea* and Theatrical Vision in Sophocles' *Philoctetes,*" *Journal of Hellenic Studies* 117 (1997): 179–83.

8. Jonathan Shay, *Achilles in Vietnam: Combat Trauma and the Undoing of Character* (New York: Simon and Schuster, 1995).

9. As I argue in "Constructions of Physical Disability in the Ancient Greek World: The Community Concept," in *Discourses of Disability: The Body and Physical Difference in the Humanities,* ed. David Mitchell and Sharon Snyder (Ann Arbor: University of Michigan Press, 1997), 37–38, the speech that is about this pension, Lysias 24, illustrates that the pension is for any Athenian unable to fend for himself, not for disabled people in particular. Matthew P. J. Dillon, "Payments to the Disabled at Athens: Social Justice or Fear of Aristocratic Patronage?" *Ancient Society* 26 (1995): 27–57, catalogs the source material for the existence of a pension.

10. Dillon, "Payments to Disabled," 57. Dillon assumes (31, 37, 40) that physical disability meant economic dependence; otherwise, the essay is very useful.

11. Equipment of the hoplite soldier is discussed by Victor Davis Hanson, *The Western Way of War: Infantry Battle in Classical Greece* (New York: Alfred A. Knopf, 1989), 55–88, and by J. K. Anderson, "Hoplite Weapons and Offensive Arms," in *Hoplites: The Classical Greek Battle Experience,* ed. Victor Davis Hanson (London: Routledge, 1991), 15–37.

12. Everett L. Wheeler, "The General as Hoplite," in Hanson, *Hoplites,* 140.

13. Translated by Richmond Lattimore, *Greek Lyrics,* 2d ed. (Chicago: University of Chicago Press, 1960), 1.

14. John Lazenby, "The Killing Zone," in Hanson, *Hoplites,* 103.

15. Translated by Richard Crawley, in Robert Strassler, ed., *The Landmark Thucydides* (New York: Free Press, 1996), 471.

16. Pamela Vaughn, in "Identification and Retrieval of Hoplite Battle-Dead," in Hanson, *Hoplites,* 51.

17. The phenomenon is discussed by Vaughn, ibid., 51–53.

18. Heinrich von Staden, "Incurability and Hopelessness: The *Hippocratic Corpus,*" in *La Maladie et les maladies dans la Collection hippocratique,* ed. P. Potter, G. Maloney, and J. Desautels (Quebec: Les Éditions du Sphinx, 1990), 110–11, concludes that "going on record in a more or less public way with an accurate prognostication of incurability enhances the ancient healer's standing, paradoxically at the very moment when the pronouncement itself unveils the limits of his powers."

19. E.g., Lazenby, "The Killing Zone," 102–3; Hanson, *Western Way of War,* 210–11.

20. Robert Garland, *The Eye of the Beholder: Deformity and Disability in the Graeco-Roman World* (Ithaca: Cornell University Press, 1995), 22, points out that war must have produced many disabling injuries.

21. Warren Dawson, "Herodotus as a Medical Writer," *Bulletin of the Institute of Classical Studies* 33 (1986): 88–89, summarizes Herodotus's narrative of Darius and Democedes.

22. René Bridler, "Das Trauma in der Kunst der griechischen Antike," Ph.D. diss., Universität Zürich, 1990, 50–86, catalogs the artistic representations from the seventh through fifth centuries B.C. of injuries inflicted during war. Guido Majno, *The Healing Hand* (Cambridge: Harvard University Press, 1975), 142–47, discusses wounded soldiers, as does Hanson, *Western Way of War,* 210–18.

23. The Hippocratic Corpus is a compilation of material that spans the fifth through the second centuries B.C. It includes writings by Hippocrates himself, although

nothing is identified securely. The corpus also includes writings by the students of Hippocrates and other medical writers.

24. Srboljub Živanović, *Ancient Diseases: The Elements of Paleopathology,* trans. L. Edwards (New York: Pica Press, 1982), 171–72, writes that "the morphological deformities that arose are really beyond imagination at the present time." Maciej Henneberg and Renata Henneberg, "Biological Characteristics of the Population Based on Analysis of Skeletal Remains," in *The Chora of Metaponto: The Necropoleis,* ed. Joseph Coleman Carter, vol. 2 (Austin, Tex.: Institute of Classical Archaeology, 1998), 527, report that "despite the often fragmentary state of preservation which precludes observation of all possible sites of pathological processes on many skeletons, over 40% of the individuals showed some bone pathologies."

25. Paul Janssens, *Paleopathology: Diseases and Injuries of Prehistoric Man,* trans. I. Dequeecker (London: John Baker, 1970), 32–33; Donald Ortner and Walter Putschar, *Identification of Pathological Conditions in Human Skeletal Remains,* Smithsonian Contributions to Anthropology 28 (Washington, D.C.: Smithsonian Institution Press, 1985), 64. Lawrence Angel, "Ancient Skeletons from Asine," in S. Dietz, *General Stratigraphical Analysis and Architectural Remains,* Asine II: Results of Excavations East of the Acropolis, 1970–1974 (Stockholm: Paul Åströms Förlag, 1982), 109 notes, for example, the evidence in a male from the Middle Bronze Age of a right humerus fracture with 15 degrees angulation and shortening of the bone; in another male from the Protogeometric period, a fracture of the left tibia shaft with 5 degrees angulation and shortening; and, in a male from the Hellenistic period, a fracture of the left femur angled 20 degrees and thickened.

26. Majno, *The Healing Hand,* 188–89, discusses dangerous ancient medical practices in general; see also Lawrence Bliquez, "Greek and Roman Medicine," *Archaeology* 34 (1981): 10–17.

27. Ortner and Putschar, *Identification of Pathological Conditions,* 65, explain that in both small and large fractures, the sensory nerve may be lost, in which case the lack of pain allows continued use of the broken bone, which of course prevents healing.

28. Actually, Ortner and Putschar, ibid., 63, estimate six weeks, in ideal conditions, for the primary callus to develop, which suggests that the Hippocratic doctors' underestimation of the time needed for healing would result in permanent injury.

29. Živanović, *Ancient Diseases,* 176.

30. Colin Hodgkinson, *Best Foot Forward: The Autobiography of Colin Hodgkinson* (London: Odhams Press, 1957), 80–85.

31. Živanović, *Ancient Diseases,* 177–78.

32. Živanović, ibid., 128, discusses gangrene in the ancient world.

33. John Bergan and James Yao, "Performance of Debridement and Minor Amputation in Patients With Ischemia," in *Gangrene and Severe Ischemia of the Lower Extremities,* ed. J. Bergan and J. Yao (New York: Grune and Stratton, 1978), 403.

34. We learn the details of when and how the necrotic bones might fall off from Hippocratic writers: for example, we learn in *On Fractures* 33 that "the more porous bones come away more quickly, the more solid more slowly." Similarly, *Prognostic* 9: if the fingers and feet are blackened, the patient will lose the blackened parts. It is difficult to determine exactly when amputation became a medical practice; it could have existed all along as a sort of barbershop service.

35. Garland, *Eye of the Beholder,* 30.

36. Garland, ibid., points out that while the very rich might employ a staff of slaves, this would be the exception.

37. Arthur Hands, *Charity and Social Aid in Greece and Rome* (London: Thames and Hudson, 1968), 17–18, discusses the difference between charities as institutions that exist in their own right and the charity of the classical city-state, which had no legal personality and which was a matter of individual arrangements.

38. For literary examples, see Edwards, "Constructions of Physical Disability," 41.

39. Steven Gelb, "'Mental Deficients' Fighting Fascism: The Unplanned Normalization of World War II," paper presented at Cheiron Conference, June 1989, Kingston, Ontario, Canada, 4. See also Gelb, "The Problem of Typological Thinking in Mental Retardation," *Mental Retardation* 35, no. 6 (1997): 448–57.

40. Barry Baldwin, "Medical Grounds for Exemption from Military Service at Athens," *Classical Philology* 62 (1967): 42–43.

41. Hanson, *Western Way of War,* 95; also see Edwards, "Constructions of Physical Disability," 39–41.

42. Martin, "Metaphysical Realism in *Philoctetes,*" 137.

43. These testimonies are collected and translated by Emma Edelstein and Ludwig Edelstein, *Asclepius: A Collection and Interpretation of the Testimony,* 2 vols. (Baltimore: Johns Hopkins University Press, 1945).

44. Ibid., 1:236.

45. A. H. Jackson, "Hoplites and the Gods: The Dedication of Captured Arms and Armor," in Hanson, *Hoplites,* 235.

David A. Gerber

Heroes and Misfits: The Troubled Social Reintegration of Disabled Veterans in *The Best Years of Our Lives*

With a sharply divided consciousness that both honored the veteran and feared his potential to disrupt society, Americans in 1945 prepared to receive and reintegrate millions of demobilized men. The return of the disabled veteran gave rise to particularly acute anxieties, for his difficulties in adjusting to civilian life would be compounded by his injuries. During the war, experts in social work, the military, and the social sciences had begun to prepare the public for the likelihood of a major social crisis prompted by the sudden demobilization of millions of men, able-bodied and disabled alike. These experts also attempted to mobilize American women on behalf of an effort, at the level of the individual family and household, to take responsibility for assisting veterans in their readjustment struggles.

There was nothing new, let alone unique to America, in this divided consciousness about veterans. We find it in classical narratives of Western antiquity. In the movies, however, American society now possessed a powerful agent for representing its anxieties and for instantly and cathartically resolving the anticipated problems that prompted so much expert and lay concern. One of Hollywood's best-loved and most commercially successful movies, *The Best Years of Our Lives* (1946), served this function for its postwar audience. The narrative elements of the movie closely follow the expert discourse of "the veterans problem," both in its depiction of the able-bodied and disabled veterans' readjustment difficulties and in its dependence on gendered prescriptions to resolve them. The movie's most brilliant and, for its audience, most unanticipated representations involve the struggle of Homer Parrish, a navy veteran and bilateral hand amputee who uses two metal prosthetic hooks in place of the hands he lost in battle. Homer, portrayed by Harold Russell (a bilateral hand amputee), faces a tremendous reintegration struggle, which results as much from his attitude toward his disability as from the attitudes of others. He moves painfully and slowly toward spiritual rehabilitation as he sets his life with his family and his girl-friend, Wilma, on a positive course. His struggle culminates in a conventional happy ending, their marriage, which sends a powerful message of hope and reconciliation.

After briefly reviewing the conflicting representations of veterans—particularly disabled veterans—and analyzing the expert discourse about World War II veterans, this essay examines Homer's reintegration struggle. I view *The Best Years of Our Lives* as a cultural event, deeply rooted in its time and in the conventions of the Hollywood system, through which we may locate the consensus of beliefs and attitudes surrounding the figure of the disabled veteran. The movie broke new ground in its use of a severely disabled actor and in its realistic visualization of severe disability. Because of the imaginative limitations imposed by the conventionalized, romantic narrative that envelopes Homer and Wilma, however, the movie did little to challenge the long-prevailing stereotypes of people with disabilities that prompt pity and fear.[1]

The divided consciousness of Americans contemplating the return of World War II servicemen reflects an abiding tension in the response of Western societies to the recently demobilized veteran. On the one hand, the veteran's heroism and sacrifices are celebrated and memorialized, and debts of gratitude, both symbolic and material, are paid to him. On the other hand, the veteran also inspires anxiety and fear and is seen as a threat to social order and political stability. This second, much less officially acknowledged response is based on a plausible, though greatly exaggerated projection: remove young men from the restraining influences of educational institutions, employment, and family; provide them with advanced weapons training and send them off on a violent adventure; expose their minds and bodies to horrific injuries; and then attempt to return them speedily to the life they had previously known, and you have a prescription for individual and social chaos.

Aspects of this tension in Western perceptions of the return of the veteran may be traced back at least as far as the Homeric narrative of Odysseus. This tension emerges especially strongly in twentieth-century American representations of veterans.[2] Contemporary Americans are most acquainted with it in connection with the return of Vietnam veterans. Few are aware that the same divided consciousness accompanied the prospect of the return of World War II servicemen. In contrast to the Vietnam War, "the Good

War" has always evoked national pride. It is assumed that the men who fought in it were, unlike Vietnam veterans, greeted universally as heroes when they left the armed forces.[3]

Few remember today that the prospect of the World War II veterans' demobilization and reintegration was a cause for widespread concern, indeed alarm, that began long before V-J Day. Social workers, psychologists, psychiatrists, sociologists, physicians, clergymen, and military officials all predicted a demobilization crisis. They were haunted by memories of the social and political chaos that followed World War I and by a fear of the return of the Great Depression after the war ended. Moreover, they claimed, by 1941 the Depression had already blighted the hopes of the generation of men now in uniform by leaving them without skills and work experience. What would happen to these men when they returned from war to find themselves without the opportunities they felt they were owed for the loss of years of their lives, the risks they had taken, and the wounds to their minds and bodies? Would not outrage follow the realization that profiteers, black-market operators, men with draft exemptions, and millions of others—including women and African Americans—normally barred from effective competition had made good money at home?[4]

The former soldiers—low in rank, poorly educated, and accustomed to obeying orders—some argued, had lost the capacity to think for themselves. These bitter, unreflective men, like the World War I German veterans who formed a significant portion of the early Nazi cohort, would be easily influenced by demagogues. The Bonus March of 1932 had demonstrated the potential power of American veterans' mobilizations. Willard Waller, a Columbia University social work professor who was a thoughtful analyst of veterans, stated confidently that "the political history of the next 25 years" in the United States would be determined when recently demobilized men concluded precisely whom to "hate" among such potential targets as racial and ethnic minorities, capitalists, and those with draft exemptions. "Will the vets of World War II turn into the Storm Troopers who will destroy democracy?" he asked.[5]

To these chilling projections, Waller appended an even more disturbing qualification. He was certain that disabled veterans would be the most bitter and dangerous of all demobilized men. They had given up so much that they had nothing to lose in following a violent, antisocial path as civilians.[6] Few went as far as Waller in this particular prediction, but the belief that the disabled veteran constituted a particularly difficult problem was widespread. This belief, too, was hardly new. Speculation on the character of the disabled veteran is also rooted in classic antiquity.

Sophocles' Philoctetes, a warrior who fights alongside Odysseus, may be taken as the model that forms the boundaries within which the disabled veterans continually would be imagined. If Odysseus's well-known story is one of romantic wandering, exotic adventure, sexual intrigue, and violent revenge on the men who court his wife in his absence, Philoctetes' more obscure narrative, as Martha Edwards informs us in this volume, is characterized by repulsion, stigmatization, humiliation, bitterness, and loss of self-regard. Neither narrative provides much reassurance to anxious civilians. But Philoctetes' story evokes the intense emotions with which we most commonly respond to severe disability: fear for the terrible vulnerabilities of the flesh, which are also our own vulnerabilities, and pity (sorrow, regret, and compassion) for innocent suffering that cannot be eliminated.[7] The man who must be helped—yet, all too frequently, cannot be restored to the manly figure he was before his injury (unlike Philoctetes, whom the gods cure so that he may fight again)—the disabled veteran has cast a troublesome shadow over the already difficult problem posed by the demobilized man.[8] To the extent the able-bodied respond to him with pity and fear, they know neither what they have in common with him nor what his potential is for a normal existence. Thus, his presence is rendered even more problematic.

For Americans, World War II casualty statistics could only feed these anxieties and give credibility to Waller's warnings. By the war's end, approximately 671,000 Americans had been wounded, 300,000 seriously enough to require long-term hospitalization and often systematic rehabilitation. No less pressing were the neuropsychiatric casualties, whose numbers mounted steadily in the last two years of the war, as large numbers of men from every condition of life were called up to fill draft quotas. As many as 500,000 men were said to have been hospitalized for neuropsychiatric causes in 1945 alone. Contemplating such data, the Veterans Administration director of social work predicted that the release of men from the military would occasion "a psychiatric problem of a dimension never before experienced in any country." Many of these hospitalizations, it is true, were for minor "nervous disorders," depression, and anxiety, and the patients responded well to rest and short-term hospitalization. But to the extent that they suggested—to the experts and lay public alike—the possibility of millions of men exhibiting lasting, unpredictable, irrational behavior that might take antisocial forms, this class of disabilities inspired dread. Moreover, the discourse of the veterans problem served to cast doubt on the mental stability of every demobilized man, able-bodied or physically disabled. Every veteran was a potential "mental case," even if he showed no symptoms. As it turns out, these fears were vastly exaggerated, just as they would be in the case of the Vietnam veterans. But they were popularly aired so often in 1945 and 1946 that veterans, themselves, began to speak out against the stereotypes of criminality, violence, and psychopathology that branded them misfits.[9]

The search for solutions to these anticipated problems began during the war. By V-J Day, there were two distinct sets of solutions to the reintegration question. One, concretized in the G.I. Bill of Rights, involved a significant extension of the New Deal corporatist welfare state and depended for its execution on the cooperation of the Congress, the Veterans Administration, and the major veterans organizations. This massive mobilization of public resources was controversial from the beginning. Its great costs, inefficient and impersonal administration, and uneven effects impressed thoughtful people with the advantages of the second set of solutions, which involved individuals acting within the private sphere of family, kinship, friendship, and community.[10]

By the war's end, there existed a body of advice literature, authored by experts in the veterans problem, that was intended to give conscientious individuals confidence and instruction in appropriate private initiatives. Much of the literature was aimed at women because the writers, male and female, shared the traditional assumption that women bore singular responsibility in the family and in caring for men. These experts, like the majority of politicians and bureaucrats with authority in postwar social policy, shared the view that the restoration of peace must lead to the restoration of the status quo antebellum in gender relations. They acknowledged that many women had grown self-sufficient through wartime employment and maintaining their households. But the experts told women to use their new self-confidence not to break down gender barriers, but to reestablish them by deliberately assisting men to reclaim the dominant roles of breadwinners and heads of their families. Women were told to give up their employment and their independence and to devote themselves to the domestication of the returning men.[11]

Susan M. Hartmann has analyzed this large literature, so we need only summarize its central prescriptions.[12] As we shall see, the character of Wilma in *The Best Years of Our Lives* is largely constructed around the outstanding womanly features of these prescriptions. Women were told to use the full repertory of traditional female strategies (mothering, crying, sexual playfulness, etc.) for manipulating men to make the veteran feel at home and to want to reclaim his dominance. Women were alerted to expect competition from the strong emotional claims of male bonds forged in the armed forces. In efforts to preserve the excitement of irresponsible action-seeking with their buddies, veterans would carouse, drink, fight, refuse to keep regular hours, and resist going back to work. Women would have to act determinedly, if diplomatically, to break those bonds. While the advice writers also sought the rapid normalization of disabled veterans, they recognized that these men constituted a special reintegration problem. Acknowledging that there would be a natural tendency not to make demands on such men, the literature argued that neurotic invalidism and lifelong alienation would result if protective feelings governed relationships with disabled veterans. While they might require more time to reenter civilian life, these men, too, must be brought to reclaim the obligations and prerogatives of manhood.[13]

Though the domestic order these experts projected closely approximated the white, American, middle-class family ideal of the 1950s, this literature hardly determined the course of gender relations in the postwar years. Most women were too busy with the practical demands of life to consult it, or they were too sure of how to organize their own lives to feel the need to consult it. While it probably bolstered the confidence of those who did read it, this literature's principal value to this inquiry lies in setting out some of the parameters of the cultural consensus that developed around the reintegration problem. Although other factors also defined the cultural consensus, the literature's matter-of-fact systematization of the terms of that consensus makes it a convenient place from which to begin an analysis of what was understood about the veterans problem. Other forms of cultural expression, the movies prominent among them, attempted to describe the same dilemmas and prescribe the same remedies.

Much of what is now popularly understood about World War II, the return of servicemen from the war, and the renegotiation of postwar gender roles has been learned by watching Hollywood movies.[14] Several reintegration dramas, foremost among them *The Best Years of Our Lives,* provide us with images of veterans that often have been perceived as upbeat and positive, largely because they establish formulaic happy endings for the interpersonal and social confusions that seemed to attend demobilization.[15] In light of the pervasive anxieties about these men, however, it was probably inevitable that the subtext of this movie, which served as an emotional reference point for its audience of millions of Americans living out their own demobilization dramas,[16] contained suggestions that are sharply at variance with its positive symbolic moments. Beneath the surface lurk the ominous messages about veterans' anger, bitterness, violence, alcoholism, and personality disorganization that were part of the discourse of the veterans problem.

Nowhere are these messages more disturbing than in the character of Homer Parrish, who simultaneously reflects the tensions in the representation of the veteran's character and the limited, stereotypical representations of the disabled. Homer's story is the vehicle for a great deal of uplifting emotion. In the service of uplift, director William Wyler played on the most conventionalized theme in the representation of the disabled in mass culture: courageous effort can overcome even the most limiting personal circumstances. Emphasizing Homer's positive attitude, Wyler's camera focuses frequently on the great range of tasks he can perform with his hooks. In doing so, the movie greatly expands the possibilities for realistic visual representation of a severe disability. In such moments, we feel pity for Homer, who, though greatly impaired, tries so hard to overcome practical difficulties. Yet, at other times, Homer personifies all the anxious projections about veterans. In developing the underside of Homer's character, Wyler was willing to exploit both the able-bodied audience's body anxieties and the well-established cultural archetypes of the physically disabled as freakish and menacing.

The dualism in Homer's character is never resolved—unless one considers as a resolution the emotional ceremony in which Homer and Wilma are married in the movie's final sequence. It is in that ending, and more precisely in the narrative devices that work to make it plausible, that *The Best Years of Our Lives* served as a powerful ally to the advice literature. Like the advice literature, the movie promised its audience that if women played their prescribed role in the demobilization drama, all would work out well for the nation, their loved ones, and themselves. Moreover, if there could be a positive denouement to the story of the severely disabled Homer, with all his practical and emotional needs, a normal civilian existence would be within the grasp of all veterans.

The project that eventuated in *The Best Years of Our Lives* began with producer Samuel Goldwyn's insight in the summer of 1944 that a timely postwar movie about the difficulties of reintegration would have considerable box-office potential because so many Americans would simultaneously be living through similar homecomings.[17] Goldwyn commissioned screenwriter and combat journalist MacKinlay Kantor to write a screenplay dealing with readjustment difficulties. Within six months, Kantor produced a 268-page novel, published as *Glory for Me* (1945), which Goldwyn found unsuitable. Overwhelmed by the classical provenance of his theme, Kantor wrote in Homeric blank verse that could not establish an authentic voice for his mid-twentieth-century, American characters. Furthermore, the characters themselves hardly seemed good material to attract a mass audience. Kantor's story revolves around three, variously disabled and disaffected men, each somewhat less than likable. The most traumatically injured is the sailor Homer Wermels, whose brain injury has left him paralyzed on one side of his body and, hence, severely spastic and unable to speak clearly.[18] Goldwyn felt that Homer's disability, bitterness, alcoholism, and suicidal rages produced a character so thoroughly repellent that no actor could play him without permanent risk to his career and no audience could watch him without extreme discomfort. Goldwyn also disliked the political edge to Kantor's novel. All his characters' readjustment problems result not only from personal difficulties but also from bigotry, social inequities, and prejudices against the disabled and the poor. As their own readjustment problems become manageable, they dedicate themselves, as a matter of principle, to struggling to overcome American society's many weaknesses. This social criticism offended Goldwyn's patriotism and prompted his fears of attacks from the Right that might limit box-office receipts. Like most studio executives, he preferred uncontroversial formula entertainments.[19]

Goldwyn turned to planning an epic based on the life of General Eisenhower, but he could not interest William Wyler, who owed him a movie under contract, in the project. Wyler's recent personal experience, however, led him to want to make a realistic movie about the readjustment difficulties of returning servicemen. While in the air force, Wyler made documentaries, notably *Memphis Belle* (1944), which was about the crew of a B-17 that flew combat missions over Germany. He knew many young crewmen of such B-17s who had died fiery deaths in the skies, and he lost a cameraman during one such mission. While shooting *Memphis Belle,* Wyler was exposed to such engine noise that he lost the hearing in one ear; he returned to Hollywood fearing his hearing loss would imperil his career. His sense of solidarity with the troops, living and dead, and his own personal reintegration struggle led him to feel disgust over the superficiality of his prewar artistic goals. The war, he later wrote, had provided him with an "escape into reality" that had led to a new artistic goal—the desire to explore the potential of film to illuminate the daily lives of ordinary people.[20] Goldwyn hired Pulitzer Prize–winning playwright and former Roosevelt advisor Robert Sherwood, who was a World War I veteran, to work with Wyler in developing concepts for a movie about postwar life. A staunch New Dealer and champion of the ordinary citizen, Sherwood also wanted to do a realistic film and was concerned especially with exploring uncomfortable social issues—such as joblessness, the housing shortage, and prejudice against the disabled—that were raised by the ongoing process of the reintegration of veterans.[21]

Both Wyler and Sherwood were attracted to Kantor's novel because of its critical realism and timeliness. They understood that it would have to be greatly revised to be the basis for a screenplay. Both men were sufficiently schooled in the Hollywood system to know the limits within which they would need to work in order to avoid serious controversy with censors and reviewers. Hesitant to jeopardize box-office receipts, they accepted the need to meet the audience's expectations for glamour and romance. As Wyler explained at the time in interviews and in an article he wrote, he continued to believe that audiences required a Hollywood-style, emotion-gripping drama to make realism more palatable.[22] In final form, therefore, *The Best Years of Our Lives* certainly has the gritty look of real life, but it is a testament to ordinary people and daily life of a distinctly Hollywood type. It contains iconoclastic, and occasionally bitter, messages about the pretensions of the wealthy and powerful and the insensitivity of institutions, such as the military, the banks, the press, and big business. But it does so, like other movies of the social problems genre, within the boundaries of a formula entertainment that focuses not on the workings of public social processes and institutions but on individuals who are embedded in private dramas of blocked ambition, failed marriage, sexual disloyalty, frustrated romance, and family misunderstanding.[23] The movie handles these themes with an admirable candor that lifts them above ordinary, soap opera melodrama. But, in the process, the balance is struck in the direction of interpersonal relationships and personal problems, the answers to which are to be found only in individual solutions.[24] This is evident in the different endings of the novel and of the movie. In contrast to Kantor's brooding, critical conclusion, in which the characters determinedly face the "savage . . . weather of a peace" characterized by intense prejudices and abiding inequities, Sherwood creates closure by pairing the protagonists in stable relationships. Thus, *The Best Years of Our Lives* accomplishes what Thomas Schatz has noted Hollywood social problem films often do: it simultaneously criticizes and profoundly reinforces existing cultural ideals and aspirations.[25]

The movie preserves the structure and general plot outlines of Kantor's novel. The lives of three recently demobilized men, each from a distinct level of society, become intertwined initially when they accept a ride home to Boone City on a military airplane. The flight sequence introduces us to

each man and suggests the difficulties he is likely to face as a civilian. Each
has the problem of putting the traumas and dislocations of war behind him,
of finding his way back into his family, and of reestablishing a relationship
to a wife or girlfriend. The focus consistently is on the men's readjustment.
In contrast, the parallel problems the women face as they interpret and react
to the men's needs are mostly implied. Explicit instead is the gendered
stance we find in the advice literature: women are responsible for the welfare of men and, by caring for men, contribute greatly to social harmony.

The movie's core is formed, as was Kantor's book, by the increasingly
complex connections between two of the veterans: Al Stephenson (Fredric
March), a middle-aged banker who is drafted late in the war and attains the
rank of sergeant, and Fred Derry (Dana Andrews), a much younger air force
lieutenant who is the product of a disorganized working-class home. Fred,
whose hastily arranged wartime marriage to Marie (Virginia Mayo) begins
to unravel shortly after his return, meets Al's daughter Peggy (Theresa
Wright). They soon fall in love. Apprehensive about the prospect of his
return to the cold, self-interested world of banking and troubled that his
daughter and son have grown up in his absence, Al—though Wyler handles
the issue comically—begins to drink heavily. Because Fred is married, Al at
first rejects Fred's liaison with Peggy and insists on breaking up the relationship. But, by the end of the movie, Marie and Fred have split up; this
clears the way for the declaration of love that he and Peggy share, which
constitutes the movie's final frames. Wyler and Sherwood dropped many of
the complexities and much of the depth Kantor developed for these two
characters. Al's wounds disappeared, he stays at the bank rather than leave it
for landscape gardening, and he does not experience an ideological conver-
sion from Republican conservatism to New Deal liberalism. The post-
traumatic stress disorder and neurological problems Fred suffers in the book
are muted in the movie, which frames him as torn between two women and
lacking the self-confidence to find work consistent with an emerging and
enlarged sense of self, which he has gained through travel, war experiences,
and responsibilities as an officer.

Wyler and Sherwood did wish to have a severely disabled veteran as
the third of this group, but they agreed with Goldwyn that Kantor's Homer
Wermels was a cinematic impossibility. Visiting military and Veterans
Administration hospitals, they searched for alternative ideas. The inspiration
they sought eluded them until, in mid-1945, they saw an Army training
film, *Diary of a Sergeant,* which had been recently made to offer encouragement to the 15,000 men who had lost hands or arms. The short film cast a
bilateral hand amputee, Harold Russell, in the main role and followed some

of the general outlines of Russell's own rehabilitation story. While working as a demolitions instructor at a North Carolina base in June 1944, he was the victim of a training accident. After some months of agonizing about his helplessness and disfigurement, Russell accepted his situation; rejected the useless, glove-covered cosmetic hands he was at first tempted to wear; and learned quickly to manipulate the functional prosthetic hooks with which he was fitted. A butcher before the war, he had no acting experience, but his rapid spiritual and physical rehabilitation recommended him to the staff of Walter Reed Army Hospital, which had been asked to select a young amputee to act in the training film. Impressed by his positive attitude, winning smile, and screen presence, Wyler and Sherwood wanted Russell for the part. Goldwyn was unsure and worried about the same fears of audience rejection that Kantor's character had prompted. But a poll Goldwyn commissioned on a broad range of postwar issues convinced him that Americans possessed a great deal of humanitarian concern for disabled veterans. This moved him to uncharacteristic boldness, and he cast Russell alongside March and Andrews.[26]

Homer (now with the more euphonious surname "Parrish") was the movie's most complexly conceived character. Sherwood's Homer was an amalgam of aspects of Kantor's character, whom he closely resembles in the severity of his disability and the emotional turmoil into which it impels him and those around him, of Russell's own postinjury experiences, of the stories of men whom Russell had known in the hospital, and even of Franklin Roosevelt's experiences. (Sherwood had had many discussions with Roosevelt about his paralysis.)[27] From the earliest publicity, however, the studio did nothing to contradict the inevitable tendency to assume that the actor and his character were somehow the same. The press and reviewers almost universally accepted the idea that the congruence was much greater than the difference, though, as we shall see, this was hardly the case.[28] Russell's convincing acting enabled him to come across on the screen as simply himself, and this intensified the emotions his character evoked.

The dramatic impact of Russell's portrayal of Homer was also intensified because, of the three veterans, his story was the most disturbing for the audience—not only from the standpoint of the narrative plot and the manner in which Wyler and his cinematographer Gregg Toland realized the character, but also in the context of the veterans problem Americans anticipated. Al and Fred have problems, but these were familiar to the audience and amenable to familiar solutions: find a job and make peace with its indignities; cut back on your drinking; accept estrangement from your maturing children; terminate a failed marriage, and so forth.

Harold Russell/Homer Parrish can never get his hands back and will always bear the disfiguring, disabling condition resulting from his accident. This was terra incognita for the audience. Most people knew that fighting men had been maimed, but their chances of knowing an amputee, let alone a bilateral hand amputee (of whom there were only 63 among World War II veterans), were small. Newsreels and news magazines, most significantly *Life,* had a policy against publishing images of dead, dying, or severely wounded American combat forces. Over the years, a few feature-length movies—such as *The Big Parade* (1926), *Since You Went Away* (1943), and *Till the End of Time* (1945)—had alluded briefly to veterans with traumatic amputations, but none of them had developed narratives of physical or spiritual rehabilitation, as did Wyler's film.[29] Nor had the camera in these movies focused on the body of the amputee in the protracted, delving, and—some would feel—intrusive manner of Wyler and Toland. To watch the sequences featuring Russell is inevitably to feel a degree of anxiety about the vulnerability of one's body.[30] Homer also creates anxiety in another way: his anger, which emerges repeatedly, yet unpredictably, throughout the movie. Such injuries, we are being told, make men angry and desperate and perhaps menaces to society, just as some experts were predicting. Homer creates considerable dramatic tension for the able-bodied audience, which feels pity for him and wants to sympathize with him but is nonetheless frightened by his anger. That Homer closely parallels Philoctetes—in his emotions and in the emotions he evokes in others—may well have been deliberate on Kantor's part. We cannot know for certain, though we do know that Kantor was well aware of the cultural history of the materials with which he was dealing. We need to take note, however, of the continuity of the limitations within which we conceive of the disabled veteran and, more generally, of people with disabilities.

What are the problems Homer must resolve? His hands were burned beyond saving in a naval battle that claimed the lives of hundreds of his shipmates. He explains to Al and Fred that the navy provided him with excellent training in the use of the hooks but that he still dreads returning home. His parents know what has happened to him but have never seen the hooks. Worse still, there is the problem of Wilma (Cathy O'Donnell), his next-door neighbor's daughter, whom he promised to marry when he returned. Like Al's daughter Peggy, and in sharp contrast to the selfish, insensitive Marie Derry, Wilma is a conventionally good woman—loyal, chaste, and principled in relations with both men and women. But neither Wilma nor Peggy is weak. Though Homer fondly dismisses Wilma as "just a kid," we find that she has matured and become self-confident during the war as she waited for the homecoming of a loved one she knew might not survive. Wilma has definite plans to begin their life together as soon as Homer returns, and she pursues this goal openly, though tactfully and patiently.[31]

Homer is evasive and uncommunicative. He fears she mistakes pity and duty for love. Moreover, as is finally and delicately established in the scenes, providing the emotional breakthrough that resolves their impasse over the future, he is troubled by the prospect that he will not be able to play the dominant role in their sexual relations after marriage. When he retires for the night, he must take off his hooks, and this leaves him, he tells her, "as dependent as a baby."

For some time after his return, he awkwardly fends off her efforts to obtain a commitment from him, and he does little to plan for the future. She forces the issue by presenting him with a choice: either he commits himself, or she will go away, as her parents wish, to live with an aunt. At this late point in the movie—for reasons that may be given to sharply conflicting interpretations—Homer finally finds his own voice. While the circumstances will be described in greater depth later, it is enough for now to know that he speaks of his fears, to the extent the Production Code made this possible, and removes his hooks in front of her. For the first time, he exposes her and the audience at length to both of his handless forearms. Finding Wilma neither disgusted nor horrified, but confident and supportive, Homer now accepts her love, and they achieve instantaneously a resolution to the impasse that has characterized their relationship. The movie ends with their wedding, at which Fred and Peggy are reunited.

Most reviewers at the time and movie analysts in later years have explained Homer's evolution through the conventions of a scenario of embattled manhood common to American social problem movies about men, veterans and others, with severe disabilities.[32] In this view, which evokes our pity, Homer struggles to salvage his self-respect and to create a new masculine identity to fill the void created by the trauma of his amputations. This narrative establishes Homer as alternately a highly resilient and highly vulnerable—and, in some crucial matters, quite helpless—character.

The themes Wyler presents here are the disabled veterans' positive embrace of physical rehabilitation and self-help and the solidarity of all veterans in the face of countless personal difficulties and social prejudices that bedevil their return to civilian life. There is the strong suggestion of a desire to awaken the conscience and to quicken the guilt of the vast percentage of the audience that did not serve in the armed forces. The public has a responsibility to men such as these. It must offer not only sympathy and material assistance but also support in creating a world that will never again have to call on anyone to make the sort of sacrifices Al, Fred, and especially Homer have made. These points are all underscored in the movie's only sequence that is explicitly politically charged. While skillfully eating a sundae at the drugstore fountain counter where Fred works unhappily as a lowly soda jerk, Homer falls into a conversation with a right-wing ideologue, who prominently wears an American flag pin in his lapel. The stranger tells Homer that he lost his hands, and hundreds of his shipmates their lives, for nothing, because the United States was on the wrong side. A fight ensues; at the end of it, symbolically salvaging the nation's honor, Homer picks the lapel pin off the floor and puts it in his pocket.

In this narrative, Homer has embraced physical rehabilitation and even expresses gratitude for the training the navy gave him in the use of the hooks. ("I had it easy," he says of his postsurgery rehabilitation; Al and Fred are stunned by the courage Homer here reveals.) His repertory of physical skills is constantly before the camera: target shooting; opening a pack of cigarettes; endorsing a check; taking piano lessons and playing a rendition of "Chop Sticks" with his tavern-owner uncle Butch (Hoagy Carmichael); and, finally, effortlessly placing a wedding ring on Wilma's finger.

But eager and proficient in small acts, for much of the movie he lacks competence and self-confidence in the larger matters that would determine a successful reintegration from the perspective of the authors of the advice literature. He refuses to plan for the future, whether regarding a job or his life with Wilma. The crucial bedroom scene, built around the nighttime ritual of removing the hooks (usually performed with his father's help) provides the climax to this conception of Homer. It is here that the relationship with Wilma—including not only the issue of their marriage but also, by obvious suggestion, the problem of sexual relations—is finally resolved. Once Homer and Wilma are married, one may imagine the necessity, too, that Homer will find a job, perhaps, as Wilma's father suggests, selling insurance out of the office where he works.

This conception of Homer inspires sympathy. He is portrayed as a well-intentioned, brave man caught in a pitiable dilemma that is fraught with unbearable psychological tension. He does not want to hurt Wilma, but he lacks the courage to break out of the personal impasse that his way of dealing with his disability has created. The viewer is provided with a way to explain Homer that allows us easily to maintain sympathy for someone whose misfortunes are no fault of his own, whose problems result from service in our behalf, and whose dominant tendency is to want to do what is right.

But this is not all there is to Homer's character, though it has proven reassuring and emotionally satisfying over the decades to understand him only in this way. The other side of Homer's character subverts pity and replaces it with fear. This puts a considerable psychological burden on many American viewers, whose democratic inclinations predispose them to believe that the *proper* public response to people with disfiguring disabilities is to deny the usual immediate response of fear, pity, and hence aversion, and to act as if we perceive no difference between them and us.[33] Perhaps this is the reason why the underside of Homer's character has proven elusive for movie reviewers and analysts. Homer emerges here as the menacing, embittered veteran that haunted advice writers and much of the lay public; his metal hooks make him more menacing still. We cannot avoid acknowledging that he is greatly disfigured because he is so angry about what has happened to him. As we shall see, however, while these contrasting ways in which Homer may be understood prove disturbingly different in their immediate narrative implications, the movie was plotted so that it can, ultimately, be optimistic about the future it projects for Homer.

We turn now to the underside of Homer's character. Homer may be sexually passive for most of the movie, but, in other respects, he is often assertive, even disruptive. He drinks with gusto and takes pride in participating in the male drinking culture, as is evident when he says enthusiastically of his prowess with his hooks, "You ought to see me open a bottle of beer!" On his first night home, after Wilma's father suggests he should consider going to work selling insurance, and do so soon, he becomes tense and upset, spills a glass of lemonade, and retreats from the living room domestic circle to Butch's tavern. Thereafter, he spends more time drinking at Butch's—to the extent that, at one point, his uncle tells him "to stay away for awhile." But this behavior is not simply an escape from the normalizing pressures of domestic culture. He enjoys drinking, carousing, and the masculine company of the tavern. Adding to his enjoyment, Butch gives him piano lessons in an effort to provide him with something to do other than drinking when he is allowed to return to the tavern.

That he is at Butch's during the day rather than planning for the future and looking for work, a prospect to which he seems not to give a second thought after the abortive conversation with Wilma's father, demonstrates another troublesome feature of Homer's character. He seems fully content to live off his generous federal pension and do nothing else. When he stops at the bank where Al works to cash his government disability check, he shows Al the fat wad of cash he receives and exclaims with obvious pleasure, "Look at it, Al—two hundred leaves of cabbage. That's what I get every month from old Mr. Whiskers [Uncle Sam]. Pretty soft, eh?" Few Americans would have begrudged a lifelong subsidy to a veteran who had made sacrifices such as Homer's. But it is doubtful they would have been completely satisfied with the pleasure he takes in his freedom from responsibility and with his willingness to spend his days, at their expense, visiting taverns and playing the piano.

Though it challenges the official hope that men like Homer would settle down quickly, none of this constitutes a threat to the social order. More disturbing, however, is the undercurrent of violence in Homer. In Kantor's novel, Homer's violence is turned on himself; he attempts to shoot himself but cannot hold the gun steady enough to succeed. In the movie there is a strong suggestion that Homer is capable of aggression against others. Avoiding both Wilma and his family, he retreats with his rifle to the garage, where he practices target shooting; this provokes confusion and concern in his father, who tells Wilma that he would have thought his son had had enough exposure to weaponry in the war to exhaust his interest. Homer is evidently annoyed to be interrupted while shooting when Wilma one day comes to the garage to talk with him about their future. Discomforted by the noise and the very presence of a weapon, she voices concern about whether he knows how to handle a gun safely. The father's remark and Wilma's anxious question implant the idea that there is danger in the situation. The threat shortly becomes quite real. While Homer and Wilma talk, Luella, his younger sister, has been at the window with some playmates, looking in, pointing, and whispering with gestures about the hooks and Homer and Wilma's relationship. Seeing the children, Homer is diverted from the tense meeting with Wilma and angrily shouts, "You want to see how these hooks work? You want to see the freak? All right, I'll show you. Take a good look!" He thrusts the hooks through the window and sends glass flying near the children, who run away in terror and, in Luella's case, in tears. He is ashamed of himself but bitterly refuses Wilma's overture of comfort. She, too, retreats in tears. The menace in the scene is enhanced musically by an eerie, tense rendition of a traditional children's song.

In this conception of Homer, the resolution of his story ultimately grows out of his capacity for a violent assertion of manhood. The drugstore scene, in which Homer argues with the opinionated stranger, proves crucial to understanding this resolution. It is sometimes interpreted as an example of Homer's faltering masculine identity and his vulnerability as a disabled man[34]—this view, however, is based on an understandable misreading of anyone that seems intentionally to have been made to be confusing in order to heighten its dramatic tension and to move Fred's story, too, toward resolution. But this interpretation is also based on our reluctance to perceive a disabled man as an aggressor. We are more comfortable thinking of him as a victim, perhaps because that is the way we prefer to see the disabled. The alternative is to imagine, as Waller did in his wartime writings on the veterans problem, that such men as Homer really do have nothing left to lose; if so, the rage they feel is too terrible to contemplate.

In the scene, Homer perceives in the stranger's remarks the implication that his 800 dead shipmates and he, the disabled survivor, were "suckers." Out of feelings of patriotic duty, personal grievance, and outrage at the stain on the memory of his dead buddies, he reaches to tear the American flag pin from the man's lapel. As he does so, he says with frustration, "If only I had my hands . . ." But there is no doubt that he is the aggressor. The stranger correctly sees his action as an assault. Moreover, the script informs us, Russell was directed to use the hooks as instruments in intimidation and to hold them menacingly before the man's face. The stranger is terrified and in a trembling voice says "You put those down" as the hooks move toward his eyes.[35]

Fred, who sees the situation unfolding from the middle distance, interprets what is going on differently. When the man grabs Homer by the arms in self-defense, Fred assumes that it is his disabled friend who is being assaulted and steals the scene by punching the hapless superpatriot and sending him through a display case. All this happens very quickly, and, before we can reflect upon the scene, attention has shifted from Homer to Fred. Fred has captured the action, and the pressing personal dimensions of his own narrative now come into play once more. We already know that he has had trouble finding a job and that the drugstore position, though degrading to his mind, has been his only opportunity to work. We know, too, that his high-living wife, Marie, looks at his low wage with contempt and that her estimation of him has fallen greatly. Will Fred be fired? Will his troubled marriage finally collapse, just as his promising relationship with Peggy already has? The drama of these tense relationships, thus, refocuses the viewer's attention, and we find that we have lost track of who started the drugstore altercation and why.

Yet the drugstore sequence is significant for understanding Homer. It provides the only logical basis, in narrative terms, for making sense of the subsequent scenes, in which the impasse in the relationship between Homer and Wilma is finally resolved. This resolution has often eluded the movie's analysts. It has remained unclear how Homer gains the courage to explain to Wilma what troubles him when he considers the future of their relationship. Just after the drugstore sequence, Fred does tell him to marry Wilma, and Wilma herself does force the issue by coming to Homer and telling him that unless there is a resolution, she will leave Boone City to live with her aunt. But these pressures in themselves hardly account for the extraordinarily articulate revelation that Homer makes. Beneath the surface of the narrative text there is another, more psychologically realistic explanation, which ties the violent temper Homer displays at the drugstore to the masculine assertiveness that allows him suddenly to assume a dominant role in directing the process of his meeting with Wilma. Since Homer's revelation comes on the heels of the drugstore brawl, we cannot help but wonder what the relationship is between these sequences. Wyler and Sherwood do not explicitly define the connection. But I suggest Homer's voice has been liberated by his violent, angry self-assertion, about which he does not have to feel shame, as he does when he terrifies Luella, because the target of his anger is another—and an able-bodied—man.

Wyler plays upon audience fears as he sets the stage for the fateful conversation with Wilma, which begins in the kitchen of Homer's house and ends in the bedroom. Homer's request that Wilma accompany him to his bedroom was probably unsettling for the audience, but not simply because of its suggestiveness. The film has been candid about sexuality. Al and Milly (Myrna Loy) share a passionate embrace in their bedroom. Fred and Peggy kiss, though he is married to Marie. We are led to believe, too, that both Al and Fred had sexual adventures outside their marriages while overseas and that Marie was no more loyal to Fred than he was to her.[36] Marie is a hard, worldly woman, however, and Wilma, who may have a strong character, is still girlishly innocent and wears teenage clothes and light makeup. But more than anything else, the metal hooks, which are unlikely to be perceived as sensual objects, stir sexual anxieties. Enhancing the sexual tension is Toland's acclaimed deep-focus camera work, which here highlights spaciousness, shadows, and deep background tones as Homer and Wilma ascend the stairs. She is wide-eyed and appears frightened when asked to accompany him to the bedroom. As they climb the stairs, he is in front, and his back, which is to the camera, is massive and muscular. She looks all the more isolated, vulnerable, and childlike. She does not have to follow, but seems incapable of resisting. The music, tense and expectant, repeats refrains already linked to Homer's story. But now, the refrains are keyed to suggest menace. As they enter his room, the camera shot is centered in such a way that it highlights the rifle and bayonet that are on the wall. They are decorations, of course, but they may send a message of danger, especially in light of Homer's angry target shooting.[37]

Clearly Wyler and Sherwood had no intention of having Homer hurt Wilma. But Wyler is playing on audience fear. There is the fear that had been implanted by current discourse about the harm a troubled, angry veteran could cause, and there is the sadistic expectancy (common to the horror film genre, which often features disabled villains) that a monster or freak will violate a vulnerable, virginal female. Thus, though the scene has the look and to some extent the feel of film noir, with its deep shadows and its suggestion of male passion gone haywire, it ultimately depends on exploiting the fear of Homer as a disabled man.[38] There had been foreshadowing of these fears throughout the movie—in Homer's drinking, target shooting, and menacing the stranger and breaking windows with his hooks.

The brilliance of the scene is that the outcome—compassion, mutual understanding, and loving commitment—are the opposite of those we were, very shortly before, led to expect. Indeed, the sequence ends with Wilma again seizing the initiative she had gained originally in coming to Homer's house. After Homer's admission of his sense of helplessness and loss of manhood, she tells him his condition has never made a difference in her feelings for him. They embrace, as they have not done since his return because he has been too embarrassed to hold her in his arms, and she initiates an enthusiastic kiss; then, with maternal gentleness, she tucks him into bed and turns off the lights. The scene ends with a close-up, shot in a faint light, of a smiling Homer, who is framed against his pillow, and who has tears in his eyes. This is the last of the three parallel scenes in which first Al and then Fred are tucked into bed by women we know are capable of devoting themselves to healing the wounds of war. Like Milly and Peggy, Wilma has established herself as mother, girlfriend, and lover, and we may imagine that soon she will be a successful wife. Under the most difficult circumstances, she has proved that she possesses the full repertory of emotions and beliefs that the experts deemed necessary to the reestablishment of the domesticity and the dominance of the recently demobilized men.

For many Americans living out the drama of the veteran's return, life would imitate the ultimate course of Wyler and Sherwood's drama. In spite of the fears about the veteran, most of these men wanted simply to leave the war behind them, get on with their lives, and embrace the security of a job, family, and home. Though specific elements of the emerging gender order would certainly be contested terrain, most women had a similar, domestic vision of the future.[39] As Wyler himself explained, and some reviewers agreed, the message for contemporaries seemed to be that, in their postwar adjustments, individuals might well be in for a hard time for awhile. But their futures would be resolved for the better, if, without dependence on government for special favors, like Homer and Wilma, they all worked hard to attain the life of domesticated security held out to them with such powerful emotional evocation, at the end of the movie.[40]

At another level of inquiry, however, one has to wonder just what the

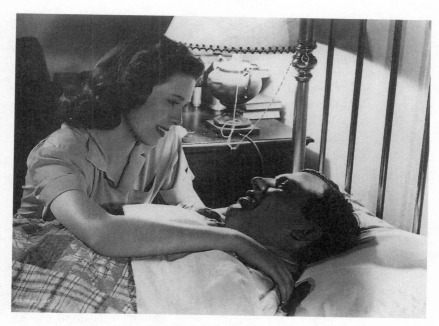

FIG. 2. *The Best Years of Our Lives* (1946). The emotional resolution of the impasse in the relationship of Homer and Wilma comes late one night in Homer's bedroom, when Homer for the first time reveals sexual anxieties prompted by his disability. The scene ends with Wilma (Cathy O'Donnell) passionately kissing Homer (Harold Russell) and maternally tucking him into bed. (Courtesy Film Stills Archive, Museum of Modern Art, New York City.)

movie accomplished for people with disabilities. While Wyler employed a disabled actor to bring Homer to life—and this was surely a breakthrough in the realistic depiction of disability—Homer's dualistic character actually failed to take us much beyond Philoctetes, and thus it improved little on existing stereotypes of the disabled that evoke fear and pity. In either case, fear or pity, his handlessness frames his character; his character does not frame his handlessness.

At the close of the movie, he has not been able, beyond his commitment to Wilma, to reintegrate himself into a normal social existence. What he will do for a living, whether he will seek more education, whether he will grow critical of American society, whether he will change his political preferences—that is, the whole range of practical issues that, along with their problematic relations with the women they loved, concern Fred and

Al—all seem irrelevant to Homer. His disability overwhelms all aspects of his life and abstracts him from the workaday social world. People with disabilities increasingly have come to recognize this constricted conception of the disabled as a fundamental source of their oppression.[41]

Of course if one finds Homer's response to his handlessness plausible, this criticism seems a case of substituting a contemporary, ideologically driven viewpoint for the complexity of the "real life" of the mid-1940s Wyler had hoped to capture. How then are we to understand disabled veterans? Must Philoctetes' bitter, self-pitying, suffering alienation be our only working model?

In responding to these questions, we may benefit from comparing Harold Russell's postinjury experiences to Homer's story. In his two memoirs, Russell writes that while recovering in the hospital and then during his months of rehabilitation, he was hardly immune from depression, hopelessness, and self-pity. Yet he also took practical steps to remake his life and, in doing so, vastly boosted his self-confidence. Within months of his accident, he resumed a love affair with one woman and then became engaged to another he had been too shy to pursue before the war. He applied successfully to Boston University's School of Business, where he wanted to get training in public relations. The choice of career was premised on Russell's realization, based on countless public encounters, that if he could make strangers comfortable with his hooks, he could convince them of anything. Even the crucial bedroom scene—one we want so much to believe because it creates such a powerful, cleansing emotional catharsis—was premised on a falsehood, one just as misleading as the assumption that disabled men like Russell were sexually passive. One of the first things Russell learned in rehabilitation was to put on and remove his hooks by himself, precisely so that he would never be "as dependent as a baby."[42]

To a large extent therefore, Homer became Homer in spite of, rather than because of, the emotional profile of the man employed to play him. Russell accepted the logic of the script he was given, dredged up appropriate emotions based on memory but also imagination, and was carried along as he discovered that he enjoyed acting. An interviewer who assumes that he and Homer were the same person will find that Russell carefully differentiates between the character he played and the man he was in 1945. Wyler came to understand this. During production, he grew so impatient with Russell's problems portraying anger, confusion, and passivity that he actually threatened to require that Russell spend two weeks at a military hospital, where it was assumed that soon he would become bitter and miserable.[43] Of course, the audience knew none of this. Having no opportunity to distinguish between Homer Parrish and Harold Russell, the audience could not be effectively challenged in its limited imaginative response, pity and fear, toward disability.

NOTES

This essay is a revised version of "Heroes and Misfits: The Troubled Social Reintegration of Disabled Veterans in *The Best Years of Our Lives,*" *American Quarterly* 46 (December 1994): 545–74. © 1994 The American Studies Association. Reprinted by permission of the Johns Hopkins University Press.

1. In spite of its commercial success and technical achievements, *The Best Years of Our Lives* has been the subject of little in the way of substantial and systematic analysis, whether from an aesthetic or contextual point of view. There is a useful, synoptic treatment of the project and the reception of the movie in its historical context by Martin A. Jackson, "The Uncertain Peace: *The Best Years of Our Lives,*" *American History/American Film: Interpreting the Hollywood Image,* ed. John E. O'Connor and Martin A. Jackson (New York: Routledge, 1992), 65–90. Proceeding on the basis of the Freudian formulation of castration, Kaja Silverman, *Male Subjectivity at the Margins* (New York: Routledge, 1992), understands the veterans' injuries, mental and physical, transhistorically in the context of traumatic demasculinization. Silverman's analysis assists us brilliantly in decoding certain especially powerful cinematic elements of the film, but it cannot provide a historical framework for understanding the film. The veterans in the movie can best be appreciated in their historical context by placing them in such frames as the expert discourse of the 1940s veterans problem, the cultural history of images of the veteran, and the genre conventions of Hollywood movies, all of which formed the bases on which the characters were conceived and consciously understood.

2. See, for example, for the two worlds wars, John Dos Passos, *Three Soldiers* (New York: George Doran, 1921); Laurence Stallings, *Plumes* (New York: Charles Scribner's Sons, 1924); Ernest Hemingway, *The Sun Also Rises* (New York: Charles Scribner's Sons, 1926); James Jones, *Whistle* (New York: Delacorte Press, 1978). For movies, in addition to *The Best Years of Our Lives,* see n. 14 and n. 19.

3. Richard Severo and Lewis Milford, *The Wages of War: When America's Soldiers Came Home—from Valley Forge to Vietnam* (New York: Touchstone, 1990), 283–314, 419–26; Albert Auster and Leonard Quarter, *How the War Was Remembered: Hollywood and Vietnam* (New York: Praeger, 1988), 23–130.

4. Willard Waller, *War and the Family* (New York: Dryden Press, 1940), 19–36, and *The Veteran Comes Home* (New York: Dryden Press, 1944), 30, 121, 130–40, 175–78, 234–41; Charles Bolte, *The New Veteran* (New York: Regnal and Hitchcock, 1945), 145–46, 150–59, 191–94; Sonya Michel, "American Women and the Discourse of the Democratic Family in World War II," in *Behind the Lines: Gender and the Two World Wars,* ed. Margaret Randolph Higonnet et al. (New Haven: Yale University Press, 1987), 154–67.

5. Robert Nisbet, "The Coming Problem of Assimilation," *American Journal of Sociology* 50 (January 1945): 267; Waller, *The Veteran Comes Home,* 159–69, 183–91, 248; Bolte, *The New Veteran,* 81–82.

6. Waller, *The Veteran Comes Home*, 159–62.

7. Sophocles, *Philoctetes*, in *Four Plays by Sophocles*, trans. Thomas Howard Banks (New York: Oxford University Press, 1966), 119–59; Oscar Mandel, ed., *Philoctetes and the Fall of Troy: Plays, Documents, Iconography, Interpretations* (Lincoln: University of Nebraska Press, 1981), 3–45 (and, esp., 35–36 on "pity and fear").

8. Robert Klein, *Wounded Men, Broken Promises* (New York: Macmillan, 1981); Leonard Quart and Albert Auster, "The Wounded Vet in Postwar Film," *Social Policy* 13 (fall 1982): 24–31; Martin Norden, "The Disabled Vet in Hollywood Films," *Journal of Popular Film and Television* 13 (September 1985): 16–24; Waller, *The Veteran Comes Home*, 159–69, 289–90.

9. *Time*, May 29, 1944, 44, 46; Waller, *The Veteran Comes Home*, 165–69; "Combat Detraining," *Newsweek*, July 11, 1945, 105–7; Benjamin Bowker, *Out of Uniform* (New York: Norton, 1946), 34, 74–80; Bill Mauldin, *Back Home* (New York: William Sloan Associates, 1947), 53–55; Joseph Goulden, *The Best Years, 1945–1950* (New York: Atheneum, 1976), 37–39.

10. Davis R. B. Ross, *Preparing for Ulysses: Politics and Veterans during World War II* (New York: Columbia University Press, 1969); Klein, *Wounded Men, Broken Promises*, 30, 46–49, and passim; Robert S. Havighurst et al., *The American Veteran Back Home* (New York: Norton, 1951), 99–129, 130–78.

11. Susan M. Hartmann, *The Home Front and Beyond: American Women in the 1940s* (Boston: Twayne, 1982), 69–70, 209–16; Elaine Tyler May, *Homeward Bound: American Families in the Cold War Era* (New York: Basic Books, 1988), 58–91. Representative titles include Waller, *The Veteran Comes Home;* Irvin L. Child et al., *Psychology for the Returning Serviceman* (Washington, D.C.: Infantry Journal, 1945); Howard Kitching, *Sex Problems of the Returned Veteran* (Verplanck, N.Y.: Emerson, 1946); John Mariano, *The Veteran and His Marriage* (New York: Council on Marriage Relations, 1945); Alanson Edgerton, *Readjustment or Revolution: A Guide to Economic, Educational, and Social Readjustment of Our War Veterans, Ex-War Workers, and Oncoming Youth* (New York: McGraw-Hill, 1946); George K. Pratt, *Soldier to Civilian: Problems of Readjustment* (New York: McGraw-Hill, 1944).

12. Susan M. Hartmann, "Prescriptions for Penelope: Literature on Women's Obligations to Returning World War II Veterans," *Women's Studies* 5, no. 2 (1978): 223–39.

13. On the disabled veteran as a special problem, see, e.g., Waller, *The Veteran Comes Home*, 289–91; Child et al., *Psychology for Returning Serviceman*, 85, 86, 154–80, 181–94, 218–19, 220–30, 289–90.

14. Peter Roffman and Jim Purdy, *The Hollywood Social Problem Film: Madness, Despair, and Politics from the Depression to the Fifties* (Bloomington: Indiana University Press, 1981), 227–34, analyzes reintegration dramas focusing on disabled veterans. In addition to *The Best Years of Our Lives*, the authors discuss *Pride of the Marines* (1945; dir. Delmer Daves); *Till the End of Time* (1946; dir. Edward Dmytryk); *Home of the Brave* (1949; dir. Stanley Kramer); *The Men* (1950; dir. Fred Zinnemann); and *Bright Victory* (1951; dir. Mark Robson).

15. The enormous, instant popularity of the movie suggests its cultural and emotional functions at the historical moment. It grossed $10 million in the year after its release and became the second largest moneymaker in the history of talking motion pic-

tures, surpassed only by *Gone with the Wind* (1939). See A. Scott Berg, *Goldwyn: A Biography* (New York: Knopf, 1989), 419–20, 428.

16. Shari Turer, "Disability and Monstrosity: A Look at Literary Distortions of Handicapping Conditions," *Rehabilitation Literature* 41 (January–February 1980): 12–15; Douglas Bicklen and Robert Bogdan, "The Disabled: Media's Monster," *Social Policy* 13 (fall 1982): 32–35.

17. Berg, *Goldwyn*, 392–93; Arthur Marx, *Goldwyn: A Biography of the Man behind the Myth* (New York: Norton, 1976), 305; Jackson, "The Uncertain Peace," 147–65.

18. MacKinlay Kantor, *Glory for Me* (New York: Coward-McCann, 1945).

19. Clayton R. Coppes and Gregory D. Black, *Hollywood Goes to War: How Politics, Profits, and Propaganda Shaped World War II Movies* (New York: Free Press, 1987), 162; Marx, *Goldwyn*, 305–7.

20. Axel Madsen, *William Wyler: The Authorized Biography* (New York: Thomas Crowell, 1973), 257–59, 266–68; Marx, *Goldwyn*, 307 (quote); Berg, *Goldwyn*, 405–6; *The Best Years of Our Lives*, Press Kit, Film Library, Museum of Modern Art, New York City.

21. John Mason Brown, *The Worlds of Robert E. Sherwood: Mirror to His Times, 1896–1930* (New York: Harper and Row, 1965); Coppes and Black, *Hollywood Goes to War*, 22–23, 33, 54–55, 192, 198; Marx, *Goldwyn*, 308.

22. Thomas Pryor, "William Wyler and His Screen Philosophy," *New York Times*, November 17, 1946; Hermine Rich Isaacs, "William Wyler: Director with a Passion and a Craft," *Theater Arts* 31 (February 1947): 22–23; William Wyler, "No Magic Wand," in *Hollywood Directors, 1941–1976*, ed. Richard Koszarski (New York: Oxford University Press, 1977), 102–16.

23. Thomas Schatz, *Hollywood Genres: Formulas, Filmmaking, and the Studio System* (Philadelphia: Temple University Press, 1981), 14–41; Roffman and Purdy, *Hollywood Social Problem Film*, 5–7.

24. Schatz, *Hollywood Genres*, 222; Roffman and Purdy, *Hollywood Social Problem Film*, 227–28; Andrea Walsh, *Women's Film and Female Experience, 1940–1950* (New York: Praeger, 1974), 43; Molly Haskell, *From Reverence to Rape: The Treatment of Women in Movies* (New York: Holt, Reinhardt, and Winston, 1974), 124; Franklin Fearing, "Warrior's Return: Normal or Neurotic?" *Hollywood Quarterly*, October 1945, 91–109.

25. Kantor, *Glory for Me*, 268; Schatz, *Hollywood Genres*, 35.

26. Marx, *Goldwyn*, 309–11; Madsen, *William Wyler*, 262–63; Harold Russell, with Victor Rosen, *Victory in My Hands* (New York: Creative Age Press, 1949), 1–85, 153–60; Harold Russell, with Dan Ferullo, *The Best Years of My Life* (Middlebury, Vt.: Paul S. Erikson, 1981), 23–30.

27. Russell, *Victory in My Hands*, 187–88, 197; Harold Russell, taped interview with author, June 27, 1990, tapes in author's possession.

28. Rusk, "Rehabilitation—New Film on Broadway Called 'Significant Portrayal of the Emotional and Physical Problems Facing Veterans,'" *New York Times*, November 24, 1946; "New Picture—*The Best Years of Our Lives*," *Time*, November 25, 1946, 103–4; "Film of the Week—*Best Years of Our Lives*," *Life*, December 16, 1946, 71; Richard Griffith, review, *National Board of Reviewers*, January 1947, 4–5; "Harold Russell's 'Oscar,'" editorial, *New York Times*, March 15, 1947.

29. George H. Roeder Jr., *The Censored War: American Visual Experience during*

World War II (New Haven: Yale University Press, 1993); Vicki Goldberg, "Setting the Standards of War Pictures," *New York Times,* June 5, 1994. In King Vidor's *The Big Parade* Jim (John Gilbert) appears briefly as a veteran with an amputated leg. David O. Selznick and John Cromwell's *Since You Went Away* has a very short sequence on a train that features a sailor whose arm has been amputated. Edward Dmytryk's *Till The End of Time* features Perry (Bill Williams) as a bilateral leg amputee, who is one of a trio of veterans experiencing readjustment problems.

30. John McCarten, "Goldwyn's Longest," *New Yorker,* November 23, 1946, 70–71; Andrew Sarris, *"The Best Years of Our Lives," Village Voice,* July 15, 1965, 11. On media depictions of disability and audience body anxieties, see Shari Thurer, "Disability and Monstrosity: A Look at Literary Distortions of Handicapping Conditions," *Rehabilitation Literature* 41 (January–February 1980): 14.

31. Wilma and Peggy are representative variations of the respectable, strong, and deliberate but patient women who routinely appear in "the women's films" (domestic and romantic melodramas). See Molly Haskell, *From Reverence to Rape,* 189; Marjorie Rosen, *Popcorn Venus: Women, Movies, and the American Dream* (New York: Coward, McGann, Geoghegan, 1973), 193–94, 204–5; Walsh, *Women's Film and Female Experience,* 89–165.

32. Roffman and Purdy, *Hollywood Social Problem Film,* 227–34; Quart and Auster, "Wounded Vet," 24–31; Silverman, *Male Subjectivity,* 65–90; Dana Polan, *Power and Paranoia: History, Narrative, and American Cinema, 1940–1950* (New York: Columbia University Press, 1986), 87–96.

33. I analyze this matter in "Anger and Affability: The Rise and Representation of a Repertory of Self-Presentation Skills in a Disabled Veteran of World War II," *Journal of Social History* 27 (fall 1993): 1–21.

34. Quart and Auster, "The Wounded Vet in Postwar Film," 26–27; Michael Anderegg, *William Wyler* (Boston: Twayne, 1979), 143–44.

35. *The Best Years of Our Lives,* script dated April, 9, 1946 (Hollywood: Script City, reprint), 186.

36. Leonard Leff and Jerold L. Simons, *The Dame in the Kimono: Hollywood, Censorship, and the Production Code from the 1920s to the 1960s* (New York: Grove Weidenfeld, 1990), 136; National Legion of Decency, *Class B Pictures Reviewed This Week and Reasons for Their Classification: December 12, 1946,* Film Library, Museum of Modern Art.

37. Madsen, *William Wyler,* 268–272.

38. David Hogan, *Dark Romance: Sexuality in the Horror Film* (Jefferson, N.C.: McFarland, 1986), 90–121; Frank Krutnik, *In Lonely Street: "Film Noir," Genre, and Masculinity* (London: Routledge, 1991), 75–91; Thurer, "Disability and Monstrosity," 13–134; Bicklen and Bogdan, "The Disabled," 32–35; Linda Williams, "Film Bodies: Gender, Genre, and Excess," *Film Quarterly* 44 (summer 1991): 3–4.

39. Hartmann, *Home Front and Beyond,* 23–27, and "Prescriptions for Penelope," 235; May, *Homeward Bound,* 58–91; Michel, "American Women and Discourse," 154–55, 160–61, 166–67.

40. Madsen, *William Wyler,* 264; Abraham Polonsky, *"The Best Years of Our Lives: A Review,"* *Hollywood Quarterly,* April 1947, 257–60.

41. Robert F. Murphy, *The Body Silent* (New York: Henry Holt, 1987), 85–194; Adrienne Asch and Michelle Fine, "Introduction: Beyond Pedestals," *Women with Disabilities: Essays in Psychology, Culture, and Politics,* ed. Asch and Fine (Philadelphia: Tem-

ple University Press, 1988), 12–26; Irving Kenneth Zola, *Missing Pieces: A Chronicle of Living with a Disability* (Philadelphia: Temple University Press, 1982), 198–211.

42. Russell, *Victory in My Hands,* 91–167, and *Best Years of My Life,* 11–30. On the theme of sexual passivity in the relationship of Homer and Wilma, see Siegfried Kracauer, "Those Movies with a Message," *Harper's,* June 1948, 571; Robert Warshow, *The Immediate Experience: Movies, Comics, Theater, and Other Aspects of Popular Culture* (Garden City, N.Y.: Doubleday, 1962), 161.

43. Russell, interview. I investigate Russell's motivations in making the movie and realizing the character of Homer in "Anger and Affability."

Martin F. Norden

Bitterness, Rage, and Redemption: Hollywood Constructs the Disabled Vietnam Veteran

The American movie industry has represented disabled people in its products since the 1890s, but, as I have argued elsewhere, its images have only occasionally resembled the people on whom they are supposedly based. From a political perspective, we might say that such images are designed primarily to serve the needs of—indeed, perpetuate—a mainstream society that has long subjected its disabled minority to alternating rounds of paternalism, bigotry, and indifference.[1]

The movie representation of disabled Vietnam veterans is very much a part of this tradition. Of all disabled movie figures, severely injured veterans have generally received the most sympathetic and favorable treatment from Hollywood filmmakers,[2] but such constructions, particularly ones related to Vietnam, remain problematic. Guided by the belief that people often turn to the popular culture that surrounds them for information about disability, the Vietnam War, and the intersecting concerns of the two,[3] this essay examines the Hollywood construction of disabled Vietnam veterans within the contexts of the war and American society during and after the war. As I hope to show, Hollywood's images have gone well beyond simply "standing in" for actual disabled Vietnam veterans and serve as integral parts of a metaphoric framework that embraces larger aspects of America and the war, such as national identity and gender roles. If we agree with the argument that Hollywood helps maintain a patriarchal society by perpetuating conventionalized gender roles, its Vietnam-related disabled characters are something of a conundrum; as we shall see, Hollywood typically endowed such figures with the privileged status of white heterosexual masculinity but simultaneously coded them as highly disruptive "Others," in part because of their participation in a morally ambiguous war, in part because of what may be read as their symbolic castration and its potential for weakening patriarchal values.[4] Faced with this representational dilemma, Hollywood typically attempted to neutralize the vets' disruptiveness in a manner consistent with the cautionary biblical tale of the prodigal son: lay blame on them, redeem them if they demonstrate a new worthiness, and then reabsorb them. This study, which also incorporates alternative interpretations of the films offered by other commentators and a comparison of the disabled Vietnam vet images with their World War II counterparts, should provide a better understanding of the sociopolitical forces that have shaped these particular movie images and the ways audiences may have received them.

Basic Narrative Patterns

The surface narratives of the films that present disabled Vietnam vets in major roles—*Coming Home* (1978), *Cutter's Way* (1981), *Born on the Fourth of July* (1989), and *Scent of a Woman* (1992)—are well known and need not be recounted here in detail,[5] but it is worth noting that they differ with regard to their points of attack; in other words, their narrative trajectories begin at different stages in the main characters' lives. *Born on the Fourth of July* commences with Ron Kovic's youth in Massapequa, New York, well before his service in Vietnam, while *Coming Home* introduces Luke Martin after he has returned from Vietnam and is undergoing rehabilitation in a VA hospital. *Cutter's Way* and *Scent of a Woman* follow a third option: they start after the lead characters (Alex Cutter and Frank Slade, respectively) have completed the rehabilitative process and returned to civilian life. If we treat the main characters' evolution as the defining narrative, however, we find that the productions follow a distinctly similar pattern: each film constructs its vet, postinjury, as a lonely, embittered substance-abuser who, after an epiphany (and often with the assistance of a politically naive character), redirects his pent-up rage toward some larger purpose.

   This observation merits closer scrutiny. *Coming Home* first presents the symbolically disempowered Luke Martin as rage-filled (in a memorable scene in a VA hospital, he splatters his urine bag while thrashing about on a gurney) but then shows him becoming partially "remasculinized" through his affair with the politically ingenuous Sally Hyde. Saddled with saintly monikers, Luke becomes something of a saint himself—and completes his remasculinization process—after learning that a friend at the VA has committed suicide; he shackles himself to the gates of a Marine Corps recruitment facility in a symbolic attempt to stop others from going to Vietnam and later gives an emotional speech to high-school students about the needlessness of the war. *Cutter's Way* shows the highly abrasive Alex Cutter to

be utterly without purpose until he learns about a murder in his home town
of Santa Barbara. He convinces himself that a corporate executive named J.
J. Cord is guilty of the crime and relentlessly pursues him with the help of
his self-centered and noncommittal friend Rich Bone, even though Cord's
guilt may be entirely the product of Alex's imagination. In *Born on the Fourth
of July,* Ron Kovic evolves from a war supporter to an impassioned antiwar
activist who leads a protest at the 1972 Republican National Convention.
Scent of a Woman initially portrays Frank Slade as a suicidal misanthrope, but
at the end of the film he comes to the aid of Charlie Simms, a fresh-faced
young man who had been hired as Frank's caretaker and now risks losing a
Harvard scholarship if he does not inform on a prep school peer.

Disabled vets who occupy relatively minor roles follow a different pattern; they are often quietly reintegrated into their society with little if any
acknowledgment about Vietnam. *Alice's Restaurant* (1969) shows Jacob, an
African American who lost a hand in Vietnam, as one of several people who
have been unobtrusively accepted into a commune in Stockbridge, Massachusetts. In *The Deer Hunter* (1978), the severely injured Stevie is initially
shown to have readjustment problems—he refuses to leave the VA hospital—but by the end of the film he has rather anonymously blended back
into his circle of friends with no recognition of any moral issues surrounding Vietnam. A subnarrative of *Modern Problems* (1981) involves Brian Stills,
an extremely well adjusted disabled vet who runs his own publishing company. Among the former 1960s radicals who gather for a friend's funeral in
The Big Chill (1983) is Nick, a veteran who appears able-bodied but nevertheless alludes several times to an emasculating injury suffered in Vietnam.[6]
The title character of *Suspect* (1987), a deafened vet named Carl Wayne
Anderson, is accused of committing a murder and is eventually "rescued"
by a public defender and a jurist illegally collaborating on his behalf. Like
most of the films cited above, however, *Suspect* avoids confronting any
moral issues arising from the intersection of Vietnam and disability.

Forrest Gump (1994), the most recent of the films discussed in this essay,
presents a disabled vet who occupies a kind of middle ground; Dan Taylor,
Forrest Gump's commanding officer in Vietnam, is not the film's main
character, but he does appear in many scenes. Dan loses both legs above the
knee during an attack and, like the major characters of the other films noted
above, is constructed postinjury as extremely bitter, alcoholic, and suicidal.
Unlike them, however, he does not engage in any "rescue mission." He is
instead helped out of his deep depression by the childlike Gump and eventually reabsorbed into the mainstream.

What are we to make of these images? What did *Forrest Gump* director

Robert Zemeckis mean, for instance, when he said, "I saw characters [in the film] as metaphors for different aspects of the American character"?[7] If we accept the view that movies are politically charged commodities that contain perspectives on issues that filmmakers are asking audiences to "buy," we are forced to ask questions about the movies described above: What are the films attempting to "sell," and for what purpose? In particular, what are the filmmakers trying to encourage spectators into believing about disabled veterans, the Vietnam War, and American society? In a sense, the images described above are mythic icons produced by a major cultural industry ostensibly to help general audiences understand the war and its aftermath. Susan Mackey-Kallis provided a start toward understanding these figures with her general suggestion that "the image of the [disabled] Vietnam vet reconstructing his life stateside, such as Stevie in *The Deer Hunter,* Luke in *Coming Home,* Alex Cutter in *Cutter's Way,* and Ron Kovic in *Born on the Fourth of July,* also became metaphoric for the American public's attempt to do likewise."[8] As I argue below, however, the situation is considerably more complex.

A Historical Overview of the Film Imagery

Albert Auster and Leonard Quart suggested in *How the War Was Remembered: Hollywood and Vietnam* that Hollywood initially tried to make the Vietnam War accessible to the general public—to mythologize it, in effect—through the creation of two archetypal figures: the wounded vet and the superman. The wounded-vet image took on two forms: the psychologically injured veteran frequently given to mindless rampages as a result of post-traumatic stress disorder (PTSD), and, to a lesser extent, the physically injured vet whose wounds symbolized the guilt of the nation. The superman, on the other hand, "lived beyond conventional values [and projected] an aura of almost superhuman courage and power and personal invulnerability," in Quart's words.[9] Auster and Quart suggested that the madman/victim and superman metaphors ultimately failed because audiences wanted more resonant figures to have the war explained to them. "The cautiously evolved Vietnam symbols and protagonists of the 1970s (the wounded vet and the superman) had only partially filled the need for acceptable and accessible Vietnam metaphors," they wrote. "As a matter of fact, instead of supplying a satisfying basis for any kind of Vietnam genre, [the moviemakers'] attempts succeeded in only confusing the audience— sometimes even inspiring remorse, guilt, and anxiety—and in stifling further cinematic consideration of the war."[10]

Though this latter point is certainly moot, Auster and Quart's comments on the failure of these images are apt. The wounded-vet and superman archetypes, the first of which lent itself too readily to sensationalistic or pitiable representations, while the second was too closely associated with the John Wayne–Audie Murphy type of figure found in World War II era films, were eventually replaced by a round of less exaggerated images, ones that stressed the veterans' roles as "survivors" and their ability to persevere.[11]

Coming Home serves as an important transitional film from the first wave of Vietnam vet depictions to the second. It constructs Luke Martin at first as a person mindlessly raging about (though, importantly, he does not harm anyone during such outbursts), but by the end of the film he is portrayed as a survivor: a thoughtful, impassioned antiwar activist who raises people's awareness of the war through various strategies. It helped pave the way for "survivor" films of the 1980s and 1990s such as *Cutter's Way, Born on the Fourth of July, Scent of a Woman,* and *Forrest Gump.*

As Auster and Quart have observed, *Cutter's Way* works particularly well as a survivor film (even though Alex is ironically the only disabled Vietnam veteran among the ones discussed in this essay to die as a result of his beliefs). "*Cutter's Way* succeeds in managing to touch upon the tortured Vietnam and the ambiguous counterculture legacies without indulging in sentimental cliches or egregious stereotypes," they wrote. "The film takes the Vietnam metaphors developed in the films of the 1970s and deepens them by creating a more complex synthesis of them. Consequently, as evoked by the character of Alex Cutter, the wounded vet no longer resembles the passive victim of earlier Vietnam films, to be either pitied or feared, nor in his moments of grandiosity is he touched by the superman romanticism that surrounds Michael Vronsky in *The Deer Hunter* or the metahistorical Kurtz in *Apocalypse Now.*"[12] Though the film's murder mystery is only tangentially related to Vietnam, it serves as a powerful metaphor for the Vietnam experience as seen from Alex's perspective. As I argued in a previous essay, Alex's "way" of making sense of the world around him includes seeing himself as a war protestor, the businessman Cord as a Vietnam policy-setter who demands unquestioning loyalty, the murdered teenager as a "grunt" who died as a result of power politics, and his bland, self-absorbed friend Rich Bone as an initially uncommitted citizen who eventually turns against the war. On a more abstract level, *Cutter's Way* suggests all people are disabled (or incomplete) in some way and that they need each other to achieve the wholeness necessary to accomplish moral and political goals.[13]

Coming Home, Cutter's Way, and the others not only represent their lead characters as survivors but, as noted above, also show them pursuing larger goals: protesting the war on either a micro level *(Coming Home)* or a macro one *(Born on the Fourth of July)*, snaring an alleged murderer *(Cutter's Way)*, helping a friend in danger of losing a college scholarship *(Scent of a Woman)*. Denied the heroic status bestowed on veterans of other wars, particularly World War II, they seek to become what we might call "alternative heroes." In other words, the above films construct their main characters as survivors and then as heroes of a different sort who struggle with a society that treats with them with hostility or indifference, or both.

The Disabled Vietnam Vet Images in Their Societal Context

The relationship between the survivors-cum-alternative-heroes and their society needs to be explored more closely. The films suggest that society had conditioned the vets to want to be heroes, rejected them as the war turned increasingly unpopular at home, and then treated them as modern-day equivalents of the biblical prodigal son by accepting them back into the fold if they had redeemed themselves by performing heroic deeds (or, in the case of the minor-character films, if they were redeemed by others) by the films' conclusion.[14] The society depicted in these films is as much a part of the metaphoric design as the vets themselves, as a closer examination reveals.

Born on the Fourth of July is perhaps the most self-conscious of the films in its attempt to metaphorize different aspects of the war and American society. The trope at the heart of both the film and the autobiography is simple yet powerful: America *is* the disabled Vietnam veteran, and vice versa. In other words, Ron Kovic and his country, coincidentally "born" on the same day, undergo a similar maturation; his evolution from a war supporter crippled by his beliefs to an antiwar activist parallels the country's own development from the 1950s to the 1970s.

The filmmakers were quite conscious of the America/Kovic metaphor and emphasized it frequently in interviews. Tom Cruise, the actor who played Kovic, stressed the point that *Born on the Fourth of July* is more than a simple coming-to-terms kind of story: "The film isn't about a man in a wheelchair. [It's about] the country, what it went through, was, became. You know, an invalid . . . It was a crippling time for this country, and you had to get beyond this man and a chair." The film's director, Oliver Stone, expressed similar sentiments. "We wanted to show America, and Tom, and through Tom, Ron, being put in a wheelchair, losing their potency," he said. "We wanted to show America being forced to redefine its concept of heroism."[15]

For some reviewers, this trope proved too heavy-handed and discouraged audiences from regarding the Kovic character as a fully fleshed-out
human being. Writing in *Commonweal,* Christian Appy suggested that many
of the film's individual moments "may seem on the mark—'the way it really
was'—but Stone is constantly basting them with a mythic sauce. And so
what comes out this time is not a searching examination of Ron Kovic's life,
but a symbolic life, the effort to make Kovic's experience represent the history of an entire nation." His perspective echoes that of *Newsweek* reviewer
David Ansen, who suggested that the film is "trying so hard to be archetypal
it ends up feeling unreal. You can't connect to the characters because
they've been deprived of personality: they're simply white-bread symbols of
deluded American patriotism."[16]

In my view, the America/Kovic metaphor fails for another reason; in
both the book and the movie, Kovic spends considerable time separating
himself (or finding himself separated) from the very society that the
filmmakers insist he "is." For example, the free-verse poem that begins the
autobiography, and which was later adapted into a bit of Kovic's dialogue
for the film's demonstration scene at the 1972 Republican National Convention, features an "I-You" strategy that serves mainly to differentiate
Kovic from his country:

> I am the living death
> the memorial day on wheels
> I am your yankee doodle dandy
> your john wayne come home
> your fourth of july firecracker
> exploding in the grave[17]

In *Film Nation: Hollywood Looks at U.S. History,* Robert Burgoyne has
read into *Born on the Fourth of July* an alternative (and richer) metaphor, one
that hinges on gender roles, national identity, and Freud's notion of "rescue": America is a woman that needs to be saved. "Linking the symbolism
of nationalism to the iconography of gender in an overt way, the film anat-
omizes the failure of masculinist national ideals in the Vietnam period,
offering in its closing scenes an alternative image of nation based on the
metaphor of a maternal, social body America," he wrote. On the other
hand, the film "restores the privileged place of the male hero by appealing
to another cultural paradigm, what Freud called 'the rescue fantasy' in
which the male hero gains authority by 'rescuing' the nation, figured as a
woman, from its own weakness. In its portrait of the Vietnam veteran as

FIG. 3. *Born on the Fourth of July* (1989). Ron Kovic (Tom Cruise) reclaims his manhood by protesting his government's policies in Vietnam.

victim of patriarchy on the one hand and as savior of the nation on the other, *Born on the Fourth of July* solicits a more complex reading of masculine agency in the Vietnam film than has been given to date."[18]

Whether or not we agree fully with Burgoyne's Freudian interpretation, it should be clear that gender issues have played a pivotal role in the construction of national identity in *Born on the Fourth of July* and, by extension, the other films discussed in this essay. As Susan Jeffords has argued convincingly in her book, *The Remasculinization of America: Gender and the Vietnam War,* "gender is the matrix through which Vietnam is read, interpreted and reframed in dominant American culture."[19] Issues of sexual difference also loomed large in World War II era films that presented the stateside reintegration of disabled veterans, and a comparison of the movie constructions of disabled Vietnam vets, their World War II counterparts, and their respective societies will help bring these issues into sharper focus. Though Auster and Quart have insisted that the permanent injuries of Hollywood's World War II disabled veterans "were mainly symbols of anxiety and fear over the adjustment to postwar American society," while "the Vietnam-produced wounds were marks of equivocation, disillusion, and rage with war itself,"[20] I maintain that the intersection of disability, war, gender, and American identity makes for a more intricate reading.

The Evolving Image of Disabled Veterans
since the 1940s

The manifest narratives of the World War II era films that represented disabled veterans had among their chief concerns the vets' rehabilitation and successful reentry into civilian life. In film after film—*Since You Went Away* (1944), *Thirty Seconds over Tokyo* (1944), *The Enchanted Cottage* (1945), *Pride of the Marines* (1945), *Till the End of Time* (1946), *The Best Years of Our Lives* (1946), *Home of the Brave* (1949), *The Men* (1951), *Bright Victory* (1951), and doubtless others—the disabled vets' psychological conflicts, readjustment problems, and ultimate rehabilitation took up significant screen time. In the exemplary and justly famous film *The Best Years of Our Lives,* a sailor who lost both hands in a shipboard accident is one of three ex-servicemen who find the road to readjustment rough, if, with the support of friends and family, eventually maneuverable.

As a number of historians have observed, post–World War II American society was deeply divided about the returning vets; it wanted to welcome them but at the same time was concerned about the disruptive effects that these millions of demobilized men, able-bodied and disabled alike, might have on it.[21] The films that depicted disabled veterans reflected these anxieties on a subtextual level, but their surface stories revealed a very different perspective, one redolent of "spin control": they suggested that the vets were returning to a mostly unified and welcoming society that shared in their triumph when they inevitably overcame physical and psychological obstacles.

The films' preoccupation with the successful reabsorption of disabled veterans into society is traceable in part to concerns both political and economic. During the early years of American involvement in World War II, Hollywood combined patriotic sentiments with a desire to protect profitable overseas markets and began turning out numerous products that promoted the war effort. By the latter years of the conflict and throughout the postwar period, a time when disabled veterans were on the minds of many,[22] it often included disabled-vet characters in its productions. Since the industry's general philosophy dictated that almost every American veteran it depicted would automatically wear the mantle of heroism, Hollywood found itself in the peculiar position of having to resolve a paradox largely of its own making; it somehow had to inscribe the heavily masculinized notion of heroism upon symbolically castrated, feminized males to demonstrate that patriarchal values had not been permanently vitiated. In previous decades, Hollywood frequently resorted to the repaternalizing "miracle cure" scenario to reward disabled characters coded as "good" (for example, almost half of the approximately 200 disability-related feature films produced during the 1920s showed the disabled characters undergoing a cure),[23] but, by World War II, most filmmakers realized that audiences were no longer buying that facile idea, if they ever did.[24] A partial solution was to cast virile actors such as Van Johnson ("the rhapsodized dream boy of virtually every romantic female fan," according to New York Times critic Bosley Crowther)[25] and Marlon Brando in several of the roles (in Thirty Seconds over Tokyo and The Men, respectively) while concomitantly having the women in the vets' lives remasculinize them by serving as both wives and mothers to them. These films insisted that the veterans needed to be heroized, remasculinized, and reassimilated into society at all costs, and that the women on the home front were the primary agents for these tasks.[26]

This cycle of disabled-vet films continued into the 1950s, but the onset of the Korean War and fears of a global Communist menace led filmmakers to reconsider their position. They were no doubt influenced by the box-office failure of The Men, a study of wheelchair-using World War II veterans whose title left little doubt about the way its makers wanted the vets to be perceived. Though it received widespread critical acclaim, The Men had the misfortune of opening two weeks after the outbreak of the Korean War. "Designed as a post-war picture it was suddenly facing a pre-war mentality," wrote its director, Fred Zinnemann. "No wonder that people whose sons, husbands and fathers were going to fight could not bear to watch a movie such as ours. It folded in two weeks."[27] Filmmakers were still interested in exploring the lives of disabled World War II veterans but, in the wake of the new war, began altering their strategies for representing them. The severely injured veteran at the center of Bad Day at Black Rock (1954) amply demonstrates his karate and judo expertise in his one-person battle against townspeople who had murdered a Japanese-American during World War II, for example, while The Eternal Sea (1955) and The Wings of Eagles (1957) show their disabled vets fighting for, and receiving, the chance to return to wartime duty after their rehabilitation. We may surmise that filmmakers in the 1950s found it insufficient to show the vets merely blending into mainstream society; with the Cold War as their backdrop, they began showing postrehabilitative disabled vets in more traditionally heroic situations with women playing little if any role in their remasculinization.[28]

The major films discussed in this essay went a step beyond this latter set of World War II disabled-vet films by showing the veterans as maladjusted and alienated from women from the start. Several early Vietnam vet films—Coming Home, Modern Problems, The Big Chill—do eventually show women acting as remasculinizing agents but in ways more problematic than in the World War II films: *Coming Home,* which was widely criticized for its conflation of political and romantic issues,[29] presents Luke committing adultery with the woman who had been an early target of his rage; *Modern Problems* shows Brian (an avatar of the "modern problem" of Vietnam, perhaps) developing a loving relationship with a woman but well after his success as a businessman; and *The Big Chill* has Nick spending the night with the quirky, enigmatic girlfriend of the man whom he and his friends had just buried.[30] The other films treat female figures in a very different way; the women are either ineffective or, worse, carry blame for the vets' misfortune. This scenario is most powerfully realized in *Born on the Fourth of July,* which splits the mother-spouse construction so prevalent in the World War II era films into separate characters with disastrous results for its lead character: Kovic's mother is demonized for having pushed him into the war and his war-protestor girlfriend Donna, despite her platitudes about wanting to help him, plays no role in his remasculinization. He turns to a Mexican prostitute in desperation, and she seems sympathetic at first, but he soon realizes that her interest in him is related solely to her role as a sex-for-hire mercenary.

Similar sentiments guided other films in this tradition. Until their concluding moments, *Scent of a Woman* and *Forrest Gump* show prostitutes to be the only possible female partners for Frank Slade and Dan Taylor, while Alex Cutter's adulterous and heavily depressed wife Mo communicates mainly by hurling verbal barbs at her disabled husband or lapsing into silence. Unless we accept Robert Burgoyne's reading of America in *Born on the Fourth of July* as a woman in need of rescue and extend it to the other films, we find that the female imagery in the disabled Vietnam vet films consists largely of demons, whores, and do-nothings.

Concluding Thoughts

To "help" audiences understand the Vietnam War, these films suggested that the vets had sought their manhood in Vietnam and with high irony lost it there, and that, as participants in an unpopular war, they did not deserve the traditional remasculinization process afforded the World War II vets. The seemingly automatic reabsorption of disabled veterans into American society (and, typically, into the waiting arms of adoring women) so commonly represented in the World War II films found little expression in the Vietnam films a generation later; instead, the major-character vets had to "prove" their heroism and manhood (to paraphrase Don Kunz, they had to fight to reclaim their masculinity in this country, having lost it in another) before a reintegration could possibly occur. On this point, Christian Appy's commentary on *Born on the Fourth of July* applies equally well to the other main movies discussed in this essay: "The film's nagging implication is that the real motive behind Kovic's antiwar activities is the desire to recover his manhood; that he found in this crusade an outlet for the heroic self-expression he had been looking for his whole life." In some cases, that reintegration is epitomized by mainstream romance or, at least, the promise of it. Near the end of *Scent of a Woman,* for example, Frank offers a spirited, heroic defense of Charlie at the youth's disciplinary hearing and then, heady with his success, flirts with a female teacher shortly thereafter. She is not unreceptive to his forwardness, raising the distinct possibility that women other than prostitutes might now take an interest in this newly remasculinized figure. The film concludes with the sense that Frank has taken the first steps toward a successful reentry into his society.[31]

Forrest Gump, with its secondary character of Dan, merits special attention for its unusual strategy of heroizing a relatively passive if undeniably rage-filled veteran. As revealed in the film's closing moments, the "vet reclamation" process is already under way on a number of fronts. Firstly, the film shows Dan as newly reconstituted; when he appears at Forrest and Jenny's wedding, he wears prostheses under his formal attire and looks "whole" for the first time since his accident. Forrest greets him with "You've got new legs—new legs," to which Dan replies, "Yeah, I got new legs." Secondly, the film associates him with an exceptionally high-ranking group of heroic icons: astronauts. Earlier in the film, when Forrest mentions that he plans to harvest shrimp for a living, Dan taunts him by cackling drunkenly, "If you're ever a shrimp boat captain, that's the day I'm an astronaut." Forrest does eventually become a shrimp boat captain, a highly successful one at that, and hires Dan as his first mate. Now, at Forrest and Jenny's wedding, Dan notes that his prostheses are made of a titanium alloy, pointedly adding that "it's what they use on the space shuttle." The *Forrest Gump* filmmakers thus manage to heroize Dan, if in an oblique way, by linking him with astronaut imagery. The film leaves no doubt about the thoroughness of his remasculinization when he introduces Forrest and Jenny to his fiancée, Susan. Though Susan is a marginal figure (she is on screen for less than a minute and speaks but one line—"Hi, Forrest"), her presence speaks volumes.

The films as a whole carry other perspectives that can charitably be labeled as questionable, some relating to the rather bland and politically naive helper/rescuers who serve as foils to the often overheated veterans, others to the vets themselves. For example, the filmmakers would have their audiences believe that characters such as Forrest Gump, Charlie Simms, Rich Bone, and Sally Hyde are stand-ins for America as it wanted to see itself. As an advertising tagline for *Forrest Gump* puts it, "Forrest is the embodiment of an era, an innocent at large in an America that is losing its innocence." More disturbingly, the makers of the three most recent films— *Born on the Fourth of July, Scent of a Woman,* and *Forrest Gump*—imply that the veterans themselves were responsible for their injuries. As Eben Muse has noted of *Born on the Fourth of July,* "Kovic seems to believe that his crippling wounds are divine justice for his accidentally shooting a young soldier in his squad,"[32] while *Scent of a Woman*'s Frank Slade had inadvertently blinded himself in a stunt with a hand grenade after being passed over for a promotion. In the case of *Forrest Gump,* its makers hold Dan Taylor up to ridicule for wanting to die on the battlefield in the tradition of his forebears. As he snarls to Forrest, his erstwhile rescuer, "I was supposed to die in the field, with honor. That was my destiny, and you cheated me out of it!" In addition, a brief montage of images shows Dan's Revolutionary War, Civil War, World War I, and World War II ancestors—all played by Gary Sinise, the same actor who portrayed Dan—comically collapsing and expiring in battle while Forrest intones offscreen: "I guess you could say he had a lot to live up to."

The filmmakers, in their rewriting of U.S. history from the 1960s onward, chose to minimize or negate the long-standing place of war within American national identity. By absolving the general populace of blame and concomitantly pinning the Vietnam War on a few self-destructive and "Otherized" soldiers—to make them bear, in Quart and Auster's words, "the stigma of guilt for the whole society"[33]—the filmmakers turned their historical revisionism into a denial of massive proportions. Their basic attitudes toward the veterans, which can be summarized as "blame and then save the wayward victims," are unsettling, to say the least, and undermine whatever good intentions they had in attempting to present the lifestyles of newly disabled military men.

In this regard, the vets bear more than a passing resemblance to a well-known biblical figure alluded to several times in this essay: the prodigal son. As noted in Luke 15:11–32 (King James Version), the son "gathered all together, and took his journey into a far country, and there wasted his substance with riotous living." The passage suggests that he had spent huge sums on whores—he "hath devoured thy [bequest] with harlots," his elder brother tells their father—and it is certainly worth pointing out that prostitutes figure prominently in *Born on the Fourth of July, Scent of a Woman,* and *Forrest Gump.* Later, the young man sees the error of his ways and returns to his father, saying "I have sinned against heaven, and in thy sight, and am no more worthy to be called thy son," whereupon the father welcomes him with a feast. "For this my son was dead, and is alive again; he was lost, and is found," he proclaims. Though the prodigal son does not engage in any alternative heroics on the level of Luke Martin, Alex Cutter, Ron Kovic, or Frank Slade, we might argue that his simple acts of returning to the father— or, perhaps more appropriately, to the Law of the Father—and admitting guilt take courage, just as the veterans' deeds do. The vets for their part typically do not admit guilt or ask for forgiveness (if they do, it is with high reticence),[34] but the films seem to argue that their heroic acts are tantamount to admissions of culpability: that is, that the vets embark on these acts in part to assuage their guilt. And, as the Bible, one of American society's defining texts, makes clear, the proper action for a society encountering Others defined as repentant sinners is to rejoice and embrace them.

With few exceptions, films that depict disabled Vietnam veterans are ultimately concerned with the reintegration of these highly Otherized figures. In the case of the major-character productions, the filmmakers, realizing that audiences no longer accept the idea of "miracle cures," give the vets the opportunity to redeem themselves; in other words, they are "cured" in a different way. In a sense, they cure themselves with help from able-bodied people before their reentry into society. As for the films that offer disabled Vietnam veterans as minor characters, they show the preferred outcome that the other films struggle toward: the vets' relatively unobtrusive integration.

Though not commenting specifically on these films, the philosopher Roland Barthes offered some insights into mainstream society that may help explain the decisions of the filmmakers responsible for this imagery. In his seminal book *Mythologies,* Barthes suggested that a mainstream society typically acts on its fear of Others and their potentially disruptive power by either transforming them into parts of itself or condemning them. "Any otherness is reduced to sameness," he wrote, "because the Other is a scandal which threatens [mainstream] existence." It is essentially a "cure or kill" philosophy, as Robin Wood has suggested in his extension of Barthes's views. The majority society deals with Otherness, Wood argued, "either by rejecting and if possible annihilating it, or by rendering it safe and assimilating it, converting it as far as possible into a replica of itself."[35]

By bestowing a double stigma on disabled Vietnam veterans (i.e., disabled status and involvement in an unpopular war), society thus coded them to be among its most Otherized and potentially troublesome people. In response, filmmakers working on behalf of mainstream society have mostly advocated the "cure" option; with the exception of Alex Cutter, whose Otherness is so extreme that it leads to his death, these highly marginalized figures are eventually reabsorbed into mainstream society. They have "come home," in effect—a point underscored by Ron Kovic's final words in *Born on the Fourth of July*: "Just lately I've felt like [pause] I'm home. You know, like, uh, maybe we're home." Indeed, the later Vietnam films are typified, in Michael Clark's words, by "a vision of historical continuity that represents the veteran's presence in Vietnam as a memory of home; our collective relation to the past as a family reunion; and the restoration of the prodigal son as our national identity."[36] Though we can perhaps take heart in knowing that Hollywood has not routinely advocated the rejection or annihilation of disabled Vietnam veterans, its use of them to further a political agenda concerned with the perpetuation of patriarchal values remains highly problematic and troubling.

NOTES

1. Martin F. Norden, *The Cinema of Isolation: A History of Physical Disability in the Movies* (New Brunswick, N.J.: Rutgers University Press, 1994), 314.

2. Ibid., 318–20.

3. This point is vividly illustrated by an anecdote concerning Holly Koester, a former army captain whose vertebra was crushed at the T7 level in a 1990 vehicular accident near Huntsville, Alabama. "When my doctor told me I was going to a V.A. hospital, I cried," she said. "I had just seen *Born on the Fourth of July* and was convinced I would live the same nightmare as Tom Cruise did in the movie if I went to one of these medical centers." Quoted in Cynthia Bizal, "The 'Real' G.I. Jane," *Paraplegia News*, November 1997, 47.

4. Susan Jeffords suggests that the term *masculinity* refers to "the set of images, values, interests, and activities held important to a successful achievement of male adulthood in American cultures" and is "*the* category of privilege in patriarchy." We might argue that a patriarchal society regards disabled Vietnam vets as one of several groups described by Jeffords as "oppressed via defined categories of difference [and] treated as women—'feminized'—and made subject to domination." Their "remasculinization," simply put, is the reclamation of their manhood and the reestablishment, on a micro level, of patriarchal values. See Susan Jeffords, *The Remasculinization of America: Gender and the Vietnam War* (Bloomington: Indiana University Press, 1989), xii.

5. For more information on these narratives, see the corresponding entries in *Vietnam War Films,* ed. Jean-Jacques Malo and Tony Williams (Jefferson, N.C.: McFarland, 1994). See also Martin F. Norden, "The Disabled Vietnam Veteran in Hollywood Films," *Journal of Popular Film and Television* 13 (spring 1985): 16–23, and "Hollywood's Disabled Vietnam Vet Revisited," in *In the Eye of the Beholder: Critical Perspectives in Popular Film and Television,* ed. Gary Edgerton, Michael Marsden, and Jack Nachbar (Bowl-

ing Green, Ohio: Bowling Green State University Popular Press, 1997), 179–90. Major cast and crew credits may be found in the filmography at the end of this essay.

6. For example, Nick extinguishes an amorous woman's passion by asking, "Did I ever tell you what happened to me in Vietnam?" and later informs a male friend that "the equipment doesn't work at all." We can only surmise that Nick's impotence is the result of a physical injury, however; the film never explicitly indicates whether it is physically or psychologically based, or some combination of the two. There is also a remote possibility that he is simply lying about his impotence to avoid relationship commitments.

7. Quoted in Jerry Adler, "'Tis a Gift to Be Simple," *Newsweek,* August 1, 1994, 59.

8. Susan Mackey-Kallis, *Oliver Stone's America* (Boulder, Colo.: Westview Press, 1996), 73.

9. Leonard Quart, "*The Deer Hunter:* The Superman in Vietnam," in *From Hanoi to Hollywood: The Vietnam War in American Film,* ed. Linda Dittmar and Gene Michaud (New Brunswick, N.J.: Rutgers University Press, 1990), 159. Auster and Quart discuss the superman throughout their book, arguing that this larger-than-life figure is best epitomized by Michael Vronsky of *The Deer Hunter,* Kurtz of *Apocalypse Now* (1979), and John Rambo of *Rambo: First Blood Part II* (1985). See Albert Auster and Leonard Quart, *How the War Was Remembered: Hollywood and Vietnam* (New York: Praeger, 1988).

10. Auster and Quart, *How War Was Remembered,* 85.

11. Ibid., 130.

12. Ibid., 88.

13. Martin F. Norden, "Portrait of a Disabled Vietnam Veteran: Alex Cutter of *Cutter's Way,*" in Dittmar and Michaud, *From Hanoi to Hollywood,* 217–25.

14. On this latter point, *Cutter's Way* is a notable exception.

15. Tom Cruise, interview, *The Today Show,* NBC-TV, December 19, 1989; Stone quoted in Paul Chutkow, "Cruise Declares Independence," *Providence Sunday Journal,* January 7, 1990, as reprinted in Don Kunz, "Oliver Stone's Film Adaptation of *Born on the Fourth of July:* Redefining Masculine Heroism," in *The Films of Oliver Stone,* ed. Don Kunz (Lanham, Md.: Scarecrow Press, 1997), 160.

16. Christian Appy, "Vietnam according to Oliver Stone," *Commonweal,* March 23, 1990, 187; David Ansen, "Bringing It All Back Home," *Newsweek,* December 25, 1989, 74.

17. Ron Kovic, *Born on the Fourth of July* (New York: Pocket Books, 1977), 11.

18. Robert Burgoyne, *Film Nation: Hollywood Looks at U.S. History* (Minneapolis: University of Minnesota Press, 1997), 13–14.

19. Jeffords, *The Remasculinization of America,* 53.

20. Auster and Quart, *How War Was Remembered,* 42.

21. For example, see David A. Gerber's essay in this volume.

22. See Norden, *The Cinema of Isolation,* 167–68.

23. Ibid., 58–59.

24. *Pride of the Marines,* which presents the story of blinded veteran Al Schmid, is one of the very few World War II era films to raise the possibility of a miracle cure. It concludes with the suggestion that Schmid's vision is starting to return—a situation that did not happen to the actual veteran on whose life the film was based. See David A. Ger-

ber, "In Search of Al Schmid: War Hero, Blinded Veteran, Everyman," *Journal of American Studies* 29 (April 1995): 1–32.

25. Bosley Crowther, "Hollywood's New Fair-Haired Boys," *New York Times,* July 15, 1945, sec. 6, p. 14.

26. For a case study, see Martin F. Norden, "Resexualization of the Disabled War Hero in *Thirty Seconds over Tokyo,*" *Journal of Popular Film and Television* 23 (summer 1995): 50–55.

27. Fred Zinnemann, *A Life in the Movies: An Autobiography* (New York: Charles Scribner's Sons, 1992), 85. History almost repeated itself 40 years later when CBS-TV was preparing for the network-television premiere of *Born on the Fourth of July.* The film was scheduled for broadcast in early 1991, but network executives decided to shelve it indefinitely because of the Gulf War. As Oliver Stone noted, "They basically said that if there's no war, we'll air it, and if there is a war, we'll pull it." The movie eventually had its network premiere on January 21, 1992. Stone quoted in Monica Collins, "Bringing *Born on the Fourth of July* to TV," *TV Guide,* December 28, 1991–January 3, 1992, 27.

28. Further discussions of these films may be found in Norden, *The Cinema of Isolation,* 196–201.

29. See, for example, Michael Anderegg, "Hollywood and Vietnam: John Wayne and Jane Fonda as Discourse," in *Inventing Vietnam: The War in Film and Television,* ed. Michael Anderegg (Philadelphia: Temple University Press, 1991), 21–22; and Tony Williams, "Narrative Patterns and Mythic Trajectories in Mid-1980s Vietnam Movies," in Anderegg, *Inventing Vietnam,* 122.

30. Though technically outside the scope of this essay, the 1977 made-for-TV production *Just a Little Inconvenience,* about a disabled Vietnam veteran ultimately rehabilitated by the love of a good woman, is perhaps the closest in spirit to the World War II disabled-vet films; in fact, Jill Beerman expressly links it to such films as *Pride of the Marines, The Best Years of Our Lives,* and *The Men.* See Jill Beerman, *"Just a Little Inconvenience,"* in Malo and Williams, *Vietnam War Films,* 226–27. See also Eben J. Muse, *The Land of Nam: The Vietnam War in American Film* (Lanham, Md.: Scarecrow Press, 1995), 93–94.

31. Kunz, "Oliver Stone's Film Adaptation," 161; Appy, "Vietnam according to Stone," 188–89.

32. Muse, *The Land of Nam,* 148.

33. Leonard Quart and Albert Auster, "The Wounded Vet in Postwar Film," *Social Policy* 13 (fall 1982): 31.

34. An example is Ron Kovic's confession to the Wilsons, the family of the young man whom he believes he accidentally shot in Vietnam. Though he does not ask for forgiveness, he does say (with his voice trailing off), "I think I was the one that killed your son that night. I was the one. I was the one." Luke Martin is more indirect about any feelings of culpability; he tells a group of high-school students that he does not "feel good about" having killed for his country and that certain unstated things he did are now "hard to live with." His contrition is foreshadowed in the film's very first sequence; the camera slowly zooms in on him as he lies on a hospital gurney, deep in thought, while another veteran speaks offscreen: "I have to justify being paralyzed, I have to justify killing people, so I say [fighting in Vietnam] was OK. But how many guys you know can make the reality and say 'What I did was wrong, and what all this other shit was

wrong, man?' And still be able to live with themselves 'cause they're crippled for the rest of their fuckin' life?"

35. Roland Barthes, *Mythologies,* trans. Annette Lavers (New York: Hill and Wang, 1972), 151; Robin Wood, *Hollywood from Vietnam to Reagan* (New York: Columbia University Press, 1986), 73.

36. Michael Clark, "Remembering Vietnam," in *The Vietnam War and American Culture,* ed. John Carlos Rowe and Rick Berg (New York: Columbia University Press, 1991), 204.

FILMOGRAPHY

Alice's Restaurant (1969). United Artists. Produced by Hillard Elkins and Joe Manduke. Directed by Arthur Penn. Screenplay by Venable Herndon and Arthur Penn, based on the song "The Alice's Restaurant Massacre" by Arlo Guthrie. Photographed by Mike Nebbia. Edited by Dede Allen. Music by Arlo Guthrie, Woody Guthrie, Joni Mitchell, and Gerry Sherman. With Arlo Guthrie (Arlo), Pat Quinn (Alice), James Broderick (Ray), Simm Landres (Jacob).

The Big Chill (1983). Columbia. Produced by Michael Shamberg. Directed by Lawrence Kasdan. Written by Lawrence Kasdan and Barbara Benedek. Photographed by John Bailey. Edited by Carol Littleton. Original music by Meg Kasdan. With Tom Berenger (Sam), Glenn Close (Sarah), Jeff Goldblum (Michael), William Hurt (Nick), Kevin Kline (Harold), Mary Kay Place (Meg), Meg Tilly (Chloe), JoBeth Williams (Karen).

Born on the Fourth of July (1989). Universal. Produced by A. Kitman Ho and Oliver Stone. Directed by Oliver Stone. Written by Oliver Stone and Ron Kovic, based on Kovic's 1976 autobiography. Photographed by Robert Richardson. Edited by David Brenner. Music by John Williams. With Tom Cruise (Ron Kovic), Kyra Sedgwick (Donna), Raymond J. Barry (Mr. Kovic), Caroline Kava (Mrs. Kovic), Willem Dafoe (Charlie), Cordelia Gonzalez (Maria Elena).

Coming Home (1978). United Artists. Produced by Jerome Hellman. Directed by Hal Ashby. Screenplay by Waldo Salt and Robert C. Jones, based on a story by Nancy Dowd. Photographed by Haskell Wexler. Edited by Don Zimmerman. Music edited by George Brand. With Jane Fonda (Sally Hyde), Jon Voight (Luke Martin), Bruce Dern (Bob Hyde), Robert Carradine (Billy Munson).

Cutter's Way, a.k.a. *Cutter and Bone* (1981). United Artists. Produced by Paul R. Gurian. Directed by Ivan Passer. Screenplay by Jeffrey Fiskin, based on the novel by Newton Thornburg. Photographed by Jordan Cronenweth. Edited by Carol Ferriol. Music by Jack Nitzsche. With John Heard (Alex Cutter III), Jeff Bridges (Rich Bone), Lisa Eichhorn (Mo Cutter), Ann Dusenberry (Valerie Duran), Stephen Elliott (J. J. Cord).

The Deer Hunter (1978). Universal. Produced by Barry Spikings, Michael Deeley, Michael Cimino, and John Peverall. Directed by Michael Cimino. Screenplay by Derek Washburn. Photographed by Vilmos Zsigmond. Edited by Peter Zinner. Music by Stanley Myers. With Robert De Niro (Michael Vronsky), Christopher Walken (Nick), Meryl Streep (Linda), John Savage (Stevie), John Cazale (Stanley).

Forrest Gump (1994). Paramount. Produced by Wendy Fineman, Steve Tisch, and Steve Starkey. Directed by Robert Zemeckis. Screenplay by Eric Roth, based on the novel by Winston Groom. Photographed by Don Burgess. Edited by Arthur Schmidt. Music by Alan Silvestri. With Tom Hanks (Forrest Gump), Robin Wright (Jenny Curran), Mykelti Williamson (Bubba Blue), Gary Sinise (Dan Taylor), Sally Field (Mrs. Gump).

Modern Problems (1981). 20th Century–Fox. Produced by Alan Greisman and Michael Shamberg. Directed by Ken Shapiro. Screenplay by Ken Shapiro, Tom Sherohman, and Arthur Sellers. Photographed by Edmond Koons. Edited by Michael Jablow. Music by Dominic Frontiere. With Chevy Chase (Max), Patti D'Arbanville (Darcy), Mary Kay Place (Lorraine), Dabney Coleman (Mark), Nell Carter (Dorita), Brian Doyle-Murray (Brian).

Scent of a Woman (1992). Universal. Produced and directed by Martin Brest. Screenplay by Bo Goldman, based on the 1974 film *Profumo di Donna*. Photographed by Donald Thorin. Edited by Harvey Rosenstock and William Steinkamp. Music by Thomas Newman. With Al Pacino (Frank Slade), Chris O'Donnell (Charlie Simms), James Rebhorn (Mr. Trask), Gabrielle Anwar (Donna).

Suspect (1987). Tri-Star Pictures. Produced by Daniel A. Sherkow. Directed by Peter Yates. Screenplay by Eric Roth. Photographed by Billy Williams. Edited by Ray Lovejoy. Music by Michael Kamen. With Cher (Kathleen Riley), Dennis Quaid (Eddie Sanger), Liam Neeson (Carl Wayne Anderson), John Mahoney (Judge Helms).

Other productions have included disabled Vietnam veterans, but, in my view, they lack the significance of the films I discussed in this essay. (Some disappeared from theaters very quickly and are difficult to access today; others were originally created for television or went straight to video, and still others are non-U.S. productions that received limited distribution in this country.) I provide a simple listing of them below. Information on all may be found in *Vietnam War Films,* ed. Jean-Jacques Malo and Tony Williams (Jefferson, N.C.: McFarland, 1994). These films are: *Article 99* (1991), *Beg, Borrow . . . or Steal* (1973), *Blind Fury* (1989), *Cage* (1989), *Coach of the Year* (1980), *The Desperate Miles* (1975), *Enemy Territory* (1987), *Just a Little Inconvenience* (1977), *The P.O.W.* (1973), *Riders of the Storm* (1988), *Savage Dawn* (1985), *To Kill a Clown* (1972), *Vietnam War Story* ("Home" episode) (1989–90).

II. PUBLIC POLICY

Geoffrey L. Hudson

Disabled Veterans and the State in Early Modern England

The ships were "much dyed with blood, their masts and tackle being moiled with brains, hair, [and] pieces of skulls."[1] This description of warships entering Dover harbor in 1653 illustrates the havoc war wrought on the bodies of servicemen in this period. The bodies of those who survived were a political problem; for the early modern state, the move from tenant-based armies to nationally raised forces necessitated consideration of relief measures for the demobilized. In the late sixteenth century the English Parliament responded to this problem by creating Europe's first state system of benefits for rank-and-file disabled veterans. This important development has been virtually ignored by scholars.

In this essay I examine the reasons for the creation in 1593 of a nationwide pension scheme for ex-servicemen, administered in the counties by local justices of the peace until its effective end nationally in 1679. I will provide also an overview of the legislation that governed the operation of the scheme, the numbers and social status of those pensioned, and the administration of the system. As well as discussing law and practice, I will examine the history of the state's treatment of chronically disabled ex-servicemen from the perspective of how it regulated their bodies. From this perspective progress was indeed made, but toward increased state control and discipline of its former warriors, within the county system and, later, within military hospitals. I consider also the effects of war on the body—quantifying the physical damage—and contemporary attitudes to disability. The attitudes explored include both life-cycle poverty and its import for notions of pensionable disability, and how the men's bodies were experienced by themselves in the light of humoral medical theory.

I

In some respects the introduction of the pension scheme fits into well-known patterns. There was a move in sixteenth-century Europe to secular poor relief, influenced by the ideas of Christian humanism, and an increase in the social and political problem of poverty concomitant with demographic change and urbanization. In England the manner in which those in authority responded changed fundamentally—from individual and church relief of the poor via traditional hospitality and alms, to increasingly sophisticated public regulation and relief of the poor. One historian, commenting on this political response to the problem of poverty, has observed that "the rule throughout was to relieve the disabled, at first by voluntary means, but later by means of a statutory tax."[2] The English Privy Council, the administrative organ of central government, acted in a manner consistent with this observation in response to the problem of maimed ex-servicemen.

Prior to 1593 the Privy Council, in responding to disabled veterans, revealed its conservative view of the social order. The council was forced to change policies, and ultimately to sponsor parliamentary legislation, by events and demands for assistance. After the start of war with Spain in 1585 the council at first reacted only when difficulties with veterans arose, requesting that local authorities assess the problem and relieve the soldiers through voluntary charitable donations. This traditional approach, however, could no longer meet the needs of the new situation, and other methods of relieving disabled veterans were tried. The council tried to use the royal prerogative to grant almsrooms to ex-servicemen in cathedral and collegiate almshouses, institutions that provided lodging for paupers. This failed miserably. Why? One reason was the shortage of almsrooms. From the council's perspective, this shortage existed because lands bequeathed for charitable lands were misused and inappropriately alienated. Those who ran the almshouses, however, harbored an understandable intransigence against the council's insistence that the almshouses pay to keep men who had been foisted on them. There was also the fact that many maimed veterans had been pressed vagrants and convicted felons—not exactly the types almshouse administrators welcomed with open arms.

The royal prerogative was also used by the council in mid-1591 when it reinitiated attempts to have towns and parishes support disabled veterans. These methods of relief failed because local authorities, both civil and ecclesiastical, resisted privy conciliar initiatives on behalf of ex-servicemen, sometimes questioning the legality of the council's orders.[3] In 1589 the relief of disabled veterans had been listed by councillors as a potential subject for parliamentary legislation.[4] By 1593 it was evidently a necessary subject for a statute, and the council sponsored successfully the act for relief of soldiers.[5] This act created a system of compulsory parochial taxation to be administered on a countywide basis by special county treasurers and the justices in court (quarter sessions). These statutory measures had a basis of entitlement that was unique among the poor laws. Poverty was not the criterion for relief. Physical disability suffered in the service of the state entitled ex-servicemen to pensions.

The shift from traditional patrons in the localities to the law of the realm was a consequence of the change in composition and control of the armed forces.[6] The state no longer relied on local magnates to raise, lead, and subsequently oversee the well-being of tenant-based military forces. Instead it created and tried to sustain its own armies and consequently had to take responsibility for those mutilated while fighting in its service. Furthermore, as a stable and relatively centralized state, with low numbers of maimed ex-servicemen (compared to its European neighbors) England was able to enact these legislative measures without undue political difficulties.[7]

Those historians who have examined (albeit cursorily) the reasons for the creation of this law have tended to emphasize its distinctiveness. Joan Kent and C. G. Cruickshank highlighted the fact that disabled soldiers were accorded a separate act because they were different from the rest of the suffering poor.[8] Special measures for the soldiers' relief were necessary because of the martial nature of the problem. The pension scheme was adopted in order to encourage Englishmen to fight and fight well, and reward their services rather than grant them charity. It was viewed as a practical preventative measure against desertion, evasion of impressment, and the unfortunate and all too public spectacle of former servicemen, destitute, maimed, and begging in the streets. In addition, it was established to relieve the tensions created by demobilized soldiers around London in the late 1580s and early 1590s. These tensions prompted the council to appoint provost marshals to capture and punish vagrant soldiers, and force the demobbed to return to their home counties.[9] That the pension scheme complemented the government's repressive measures is clear from the council's swift action after the Parliament of 1593 in sending home poor maimed soldiers who had been begging around London.[10] The council sought to restore peace and order in that city. Thus the reasons for relief measures for disabled soldiers were distinctive from the other poor laws in several ways.

These arguments are sound, as far as they go. In its attempts to relieve disabled soldiers from 1589 to 1593 the council demonstrated that it agreed with comments made by Lord Admiral Charles, Lord Howard, to the then secretary of state, Sir Francis Walsingham, in 1588—England's soldiers needed to be treated decently so that others would be willing to serve.[11] Parliament in the preamble to the 1593 act and Secretary of State Sir Robert

Cecil in the Parliament of 1601 also stated clearly that they believed that maimed soldiers, as distinct from the impotent poor, *merited* relief for good service.[12]

The argument based on military distinctiveness stops short, however, of a full explanation of why the act to relieve soldiers was introduced. There is a more fundamental motivation for the government's action: the need to sustain the complex *social* order and the government's place in it. It is not possible to understand why those in authority acted in the way they did if we do not comprehend how they thought society should operate. In responding to the soldiers' difficulties, the council and Parliament were acting in a manner typical of the contemporary social dynamic. Keith Wrightson and others argue that the social order was maintained both because England's governors acknowledged a responsibility to protect their inferiors from economic and social insecurity *and* because the lower orders expected that their betters would act accordingly. The council's 1587 *Book of Orders* for the relief of dearth was an example of this process.[13] It provided strict regulation of grain supplies and prices so that the poor would be able to sustain themselves. Middlemen sellers of grain were vilified in the *Orders*. The government wanted local authorities to discipline them harshly if necessary in deference to the needs of the poor. Since government and commoners agreed on how the economy should be ordered in the event of dearth, the poor did not react initially by rioting but instead appealed to local authorities to stop the export of grain, which they often did.[14]

In the case of soldiers and mariners there are striking parallels. Mutinies and riots normally followed petition and were organized, ritualistic affairs designed to achieve a limited objective—usually back pay.[15] Two important examples of independent action by English servicemen were the London riots of 1589 and 1592. In these soldiers and mariners sought redress from their betters and used the military skills of discipline and order that they had learned in service to petition for their back pay.[16]

Although it put down the servicemen's protests in 1589 and 1592, the council acted quickly to address the concerns of the soldiers, establishing a commission to investigate the problems with back pay in 1589, and announcing the creation of a new pay system in March 1593. In stating why this change was necessary the council blamed the captains—the middlemen. They were declared responsible for the soldiers not having received proper pay, food, and clothing.[17]

There is considerable evidence that maimed veterans themselves sought redress from members of Parliament. The council commented after the conclusion of the 1593 parliament that disabled soldiers had "assembled"

themselves in London for the "occacion of the late Parlyament." Members of
both houses were also affected by the sight of many maimed soldiers near Parliament.[18] The MP Sir Michael Hickes, in a speech prepared for the Commons, argued that "the poore soldiars you hear cry uppon us daylie in the
stret for releif assure your self they will cry out uppon us, yea curse us if we
do nothing for them and, upbryd us that we have charity in our mouths, but
none in our hands."[19] Hickes—who was the lord treasurer's servant—
directed his appeal to Parliament's perception that the disabled ex-servicemen
expected a statutory solution to the ongoing problem of relief. This perception would not have been unreasonable given the actions of servicemen in
London as recently as three months previous in the mariners' riot of December 1592. They had demanded assistance from their betters and demonstrated
this expectation. Thus Hickes affirmed the ex-servicemen's right to press
their governors for benefits through their appeal to the elite's perceptions of
their obligations to the lower orders. Further evidence that maimed soldiers
could and did seek legislative remedies from Parliament is provided by a petition submitted to the 1597–98 House of Commons by a number of disabled
ex-servicemen. In their petition the disabled ex-servicemen gave reasons why
they believed the statute was not being enforced correctly and suggested ways
of solving the problems.[20]

In his speech Hickes also implied strongly that to refuse to relieve the
disabled soldier would be shameful. Hickes, in using such arguments, was
playing on the contemporary association between aristocracy, honor, and
hospitality in which good hospitality assured a reputation for good lord-
ship.[21] Hickes was not alone in employing this traditional ideology in connection with this cause—in March 1593 the council maintained that England's inadequate treatment of its ex-servicemen brought "dishonoure to
the Realme, in comparison to other Countries."[22] The use of such ideas in
connection with the relief of ex-servicemen—who earlier in the century
would have gone to war as the tenants of substantial lords—goes some way
in explaining why the 1593 act for the relief of soldiers does not include
poverty as a criterion for relief. Soldiers and sailors, wounded in the service
of the realm, were to be treated as members of the community of honor,
with hospitality extended to them in a way reminiscent of traditional noble
hospitality. Even though the veterans were economically and socially infe-
rior they were nevertheless to be treated as part of the social world of the
host. To inquire too closely into their financial resources would have been
dishonorable. Governed (veterans) and governors (council and Parliament)
in Elizabethan England thus agreed that disabled ex-servicemen were entitled to statutory relief. This strong conception of entitlement was not, it

should be noted, rooted in modern notions of equality or citizenship but in premodern ideals of hierarchical social obligation based on status.

II

The 1593 act was amended in 1598, and then, in 1601, a new act was passed that incorporated the earlier acts and introduced some changes, including rate increases.[23] In 1647 the Long Parliament passed three ordinances that supplemented the 1601 act. These ordinances denied pensions to Royalists and increased the maimed-soldier rates. They also required disabled ex-servicemen to show that they were "disabled in body for work."[24] This change reflected transformations in practice since the mid-1610s, discussed later in this essay, with justices introducing selection criteria related to contemporary norms about which disabilities impoverish. In 1662 an act was passed that supplemented the 1601 act in ways similar to that of the 1647 ordinances. The differences: taxation was raised yet again, and Parliamentarians were denied relief instead of Royalists.[25]

In 1679 the 1662 act lapsed and so too did the trebling of the 1601 tax burden provided for in the 1662 act.[26] As a result the county pension scheme established in 1593 became a dead letter in practice over the ensuing decades. With rate caps that were now far too low, it was superseded by the provisions of the national military hospitals of Chelsea (army) and Greenwich (navy), effectively in operation from 1685 and 1705 respectively. Some jurisdictions stopped implementing the county pension scheme altogether in 1679–80, thereby ending its active application throughout the entire kingdom.

In addition to the county pension scheme disabled veterans had access to other forms of relief. A pension scheme of similar antiquity to the county pension scheme was that of the Chatham Chest, funded from deductions of 6d. per month from navy seamen, and its governance was sanctioned by the prerogative of the Crown. The Chest became significant only after the three Dutch wars of 1652–54, 1665–67, and 1672–74. The numbers of pensioners grew as follows: 41 in 1617, 55 (1637–83), 54 (1643–44), 442 (1656), 253 (1665), and 885 (1676).[27]

As well as the Chatham Chest a central government fund was created by the parliamentary regimes in October 1643, overseen by a committee of the House of Commons for sick and maimed soldiers and widows. It provided pensions to veterans and war widows and orphans and funded the national military hospitals at the Savoy and Ely House, established in 1644 and 1648 respectively. These two hospitals had space for about 350 men, with war widows given preference as nurses. By the late 1650s this fund was providing pensions for over 6,500 men and women.[28] The central fund and the two military hospitals were discontinued in late 1660.[29]

Nine county and corporation treasurers' accounts survive circa 1671, enough to permit a fairly reliable estimate of the numbers of county pensioners throughout England at this time. Numbers would have been down from a peak in the years 1663–65, when Royalist ex-servicemen rushed forward by the thousands to take advantage of the supplementary act of 1662. Scholars who have considered the state's relief of ex-servicemen in the early modern period have concentrated on the national military hospitals and given little attention to the county scheme. John Keevil in *Medicine and the Navy,* for example, dismissed the county system as "no more than thinly disguised and inefficiently administered charity."[30] This is simply not true. Given 123 pensioners per 100,000, and a population of 4,982,000 (5,331,000 with Wales), an estimate of the number of county pensioners in England, circa 1671, is 6,128 (6,557 in England and Wales). Chelsea and Greenwich hospitals would not relieve this many veterans until well into the eighteenth century.[31]

Over the century there was an increase in numbers and a decline in the pension levels. This is apparent in the comparison of figures for Cheshire in 1598 (10 pensioners at £5.2.8 per year on average) and 1671–72 (178 at £1.8s.); Devon in 1602 (51 at £3.12.10) and 1673 (200 at £2.1.6); Hampshire in 1608 (31 at £3.8s.) and 1662 (60 at £2.3.8).[32] Although the level of the county pension decreased over time, it did so as the parochial pension scheme became firmly established all over England and parish pension levels increased.

III

After passage of the 1593 act the government continued to encourage private philanthropy—almshouse building for example—but very much as a supplement to, rather than a substitute for, public taxes. Indeed, the council placed a priority on the strict and uniform enforcement of the new statutory pension scheme. In so doing, it responded to the petitions of aggrieved veterans seeking conciliar intervention with local authorities, required detailed reports from the counties about their implementation of the act, and sought tax increases and other amendments to the legislation in order to address enforcement problems.[33]

The council failed in its attempt at a rigorous, consistent implementation of the act. But the history of the council's efforts to enforce the pen-

sion scheme is not about failure—the local authorities *did* implement the
legislation after all. Instead it is better characterized as a struggle between the
national and local levels of government over who should control enforcement.

One area of conflict was over interpretation of the act. Fiscal difficulties, partly from problems of local collection and administration, resulted in
justices of the peace sending ex-servicemen to other counties for relief on
legally spurious grounds. The Privy Council believed that pensioners who
took up employment, served again in the army, or were granted almsrooms
should not have their pensions withdrawn or reduced. The county authorities, with limited resources, disagreed.

The lack of funds led to discrepancies between law and practice. Justices of the peace were quick to implement the 1593 legislation. But when
the numbers of eligible men increased, the justices failed—despite council
pressure—to use the statutory powers given to them in 1598 and 1601 to
raise the rates. The political pressures are apparent: it was one thing to set a
rate, another to collect it, and yet another to attempt to increase it.[34] Instead
of raising taxes the justices resorted to traditional practices that had been
used by cathedral almshouses and guilds. They restricted the number of
pensions available, granted pensions in reversion, and awarded onetime
composition payments in lieu of future payments.[35]

Some local authorities made use of payments in lieu of pensions and,
indeed, withdrew pensions from certified ex-servicemen, in cases where
they did not approve of their character and/or behavior. In these instances
the discretionary basis upon which the English system of justice operated
serves to explain the justices' actions. Relief, after all, was administered in
court—the same court in which decisions in criminal cases were often
influenced crucially by the defendant's social status, testimony as to his character by neighbors, his demeanor in the courtroom, and any personal
knowledge of the defendant on the part of the justices.

In several counties justices exercised discretion as a tool with which to
attempt the control—the regulation—of drunkards and other misbehaving
local ex-servicemen. These men's pensions were revoked and reissued frequently. Others fared worse—masterless men and convicted criminals,
pressed in large numbers, were precisely the kind of men justices wanted to
discipline not pension, disabled or not, entitled or not.[36]

Although the council sought a strict and uniform execution of the act,
it was not and could not have been successful because it was trying to
achieve certain objectives with which the county magistrates fundamentally
did not agree. The consent of the governed was crucial, illustrating com-

ments made by Fletcher, Wrightson, and others about the inevitable failure of any conciliar enforcement of social welfare measures if it lacked the support of county authorities.[37] There was perhaps a significant difference between the Privy Council and the local authorities prior to 1642 in their understanding of the way the relief measures were supposed to operate and, indeed, about the objective of the act to relieve ex-servicemen. The council, over and over again, emphasized that pensions were to be granted for life. In the counties, grants were almost invariably given "until further order." The 1597 and 1601 acts to relieve the poor, which were framed to avoid central interference, had run counter to traditional ideas of hospitality and charity. The act to relieve ex-servicemen went even further. Traditional charity was a privilege extended to the lower orders who were in need. The 1601 act to relieve disabled soldiers, however, made relief for maimed ex-servicemen a right for which the payment of taxes was required by law. And need—that is, poverty—was not a requirement. For justices and other local authorities there was an understandably difficult adjustment to make, especially since it involved a loss of power. It is not surprising that they exercised traditional discretion in their implementation of the act. The pensions were, after all, paid out of local rate monies. The provisions enacted by Parliament for disabled ex-servicemen also ran counter to assumptions about the purpose of the new poor relief measures. Some magistrates believed that as the poor were getting poorer and potentially more disorderly it was their Christian duty to relieve their wants and make them respectable. While understanding the actions of the local justices and rate payers the results of these actions must not be overlooked. Maimed ex-servicemen were being denied their pensions.

After 1647 many of the discrepancies between law and practice of the pre-1642 period were incorporated into the legislation. The legislation reflected the concerns of local county and corporation benches in two important respects: it was now legal to discriminate on the basis of need and to require certificates from local justices of the peace as to the suitability of the ex-serviceman for relief. Discrepancies between law and practice continued because of the continuing problem of a lack of funds to pension adequately all those entitled to a county stipend.

Concern with pensioners' moral probity as a manifestation of social disorder virtually disappears after 1642. There are a very few cases of this concern but no systematic attempt to regulate the behavior of county pensioners.[38] Instead the pre-1642 regard for the social disorder caused by immorality was replaced by a concern with security and allegiance. This is a shift that has been delineated by other historians.[39] Bastardy, drunkenness, and vagrancy were to some extent supplanted, in the late 1640s and 1650s, by Royalism and Quakerism, and, after 1660, by nonconformity and Catholicism.[40] For maimed soldiers the shift was explicit in the legislation of 1647 and 1662 that discriminated against first Royalist, and then, parliamentary, veterans. In the latter 1670s in Middlesex Roman Catholic pensioners, and those Protestant veterans not conforming to the Church of England, were also targeted.[41]

IV

One important difference between law and practice resulted in increased regulation of the bodies of ex-servicemen. In this section I will combine an analysis of that development with a discussion of contemporary notions of disability, including the ways in which veterans experienced their own bodies and struggled to deal with their postwar circumstances.

After the collapse of the county pension scheme disabled veterans would be confined in the new purpose-built Chelsea and Greenwich hospitals. These institutions would enable the state to exercise greater bureaucratic control and discipline of veterans. In the hospitals the men were issued uniforms, ranked, and punished, often quite severely, for a wide variety of infractions of the hospitals' rules. The veterans were not so much inhabitants as captives, imprisoned by poverty, with only the officers, civilian staff, and medics given free movement over the institutions. To some extent Michel Foucault's theory of bio-power informs an understanding of this process. For Foucault, this new regime of power was increasingly exercised by early modern states, the body becoming an object to be controlled by various disciplinary technologies with the goal of improving it for the good of the state. These technologies developed to include the use of enclosure and control of space, standardization of actions over time, and were "always meticulous, often minute," creating a "new microphysics of power." Indeed, for Foucault, "discipline is a political anatomy of detail," in that discipline, examination, and its documentation function as a procedure of objectification and subjection.[42] The move to increased regulation of the body that was concomitant with the creation of the national military hospitals of Chelsea and Greenwich was foreshadowed in the law and practice of the county pension scheme, especially with regards to the use of examination and the documentation thereof.

The Elizabethan legislation provided for pensions as a right based on disability experienced in military service. Poverty did not have to be proved. Instead a given ex-serviceman had to acquire first a certificate from his captain, listing the soldier's injuries and service record. This certificate had to be countersigned by the muster master general in London to prevent counterfeiting. Thus the state relied on the maimed ex-serviceman and his military superiors to create the application; local justices of the peace were to use this documentation rather than create their own. The law, therefore, placed the onus for documentation of the ex-serviceman's disabilities on the soldier and authorities who were not responsible for administering the county pension scheme. And from 1601, once a pension was granted, justices were not permitted arbitrarily to revoke, diminish, or alter the pension without just cause (i.e., contrary to the statutory provisions). Thus these statutory measures for the disabled men meant that they could claim pensions as a right without submitting to physical examination or a means test.

Examining the qualitatively richest quarter sessions files (Cheshire, Kent, and Wiltshire), I found that the statutory system for determining eligibility was followed for the first two decades of the pension scheme's operation. Petitioners and their supporters based their arguments for relief on the terms of the statute. Applications were made on the basis that the individual had served in the military, had been physically maimed in service, and had been pressed or born in the county. Thus, for example, George Jodrell applied to the Cheshire bench in 1602 with a letter of recommendation from William Waad, the general muster master. The letter stated that the soldier, pressed in the county, had been "so hurt and maymed in the Warrs as he is not able to serve anie longer."[43]

Toward the middle and end of the first decade of the century, however, ex-servicemen *and* their champions began to introduce arguments based on other criteria. Poverty was cited. These citations included mention of the inability of the ex-serviceman to labor or otherwise maintain himself, age, that he had a wife and a number of children to support, that his wife was disabled to work by age or sickness. Some also argued that the man had done all in his power to avoid dependence on public funds.

Many of these new criteria are found in the parish certificate forwarded to the Kent bench in January 1617/8 in support of an application by a maimed soldier for a county pension. In the certificate the parish declared that the man, a carpenter, had been maimed in the hand in France in the service of Queen Elizabeth. On his return "by his painfull labour in his calling" he "kept & mainteyned himself his wife & manye Children so long as he was able to frome his worke." But now, unable to work because of his war wound, he had fallen into "great want & povertie." On the reverse of the parish certificate was a certificate from the daughter-in-law of the man's commander in France as to his service in which he was "hurt . . . which now in his age is a great trouble unto him." She also stated that he "hath ever lived an honest laboringe man."[44]

These changes in the application procedure and the basis for application are reflected in two long-term developments between 1593 and 1641. Increasingly, applicants cited their inability to work rather than to serve again in the military, and the latter disappeared as a stated reason why a pension should be granted. Indeed, by the middle and late 1620s, when England was at war, ex-servicemen claimed that they were too disabled to work rather than to fight again for king and country—reflecting the change to nonstatutory criteria being used to determine eligibility for pensions.

There is also evidence that justices in sessions increasingly expected that maimed soldiers be able to reveal their wounds upon application for pension benefits.[45] In addition, men were increasingly denied pensions and had pensions withdrawn, because they had other means of subsistence.[46]

The statutory basis for entitlement was turned on its head. Need, associated with life-cycle poverty, became the basis for the application and award of relief and pension level increases, rather than mutilation in recent military conflict. The meaning of disability within the context of the ex-serviceman pension scheme became, in time, almost identical to what Tim Wales and Margaret Pelling have shown was its meaning in the parish poor relief system. Relief was granted to those who were disabled by age or casualty in order to maintain themselves and their families. The only difference was that retired and elderly ex-servicemen, unlike the parish poor, had to cite their loss of blood, bruises, and wounds, suffered often decades earlier in war. Younger disabled ex-servicemen encountered accepted categories of pensionable disability into which they did not fall; adult males, especially those in their twenties and thirties, were not granted parish pensions, as were single mothers with young children, the elderly, and very large, poor families. Such men were the hole in the middle of the pensionable poor.[47] As a result, younger disabled men had very much to demonstrate that they were physically disabled to work.

Despite discrepancies between law and practice, disabled ex-servicemen managed to play the system quite effectively. Ex-servicemen used and manipulated powerful friends to intercede with the local justices, combined (petitioned in groups), skillfully told the justices what they wanted to hear, and exploited institutional weaknesses (e.g., magisterial amnesia). Disabled veterans also demonstrated a keen notion of entitlement. By the latter years of James's reign veterans referred to the granting of pensions as not only lawful—the constant refrain in earlier years—but also customary. They also called the pension "recompence," "satisfaction," and "justice." Local poor ex-servicemen used their advantage over those entitled to pension who lived elsewhere. In a society like early-seventeenth-century England living in the county gave a soldier the necessary knowledge of how the pension scheme in his county operated and the contacts vital in order to secure relief for himself. Others did manage to operate at the national level—using the central authorities in order to secure relief in more than one jurisdiction, making use of statutory loopholes and administrative deficiencies in the quest for benefits. Example of a loophole: men were entitled to apply for relief to counties in which they had been born, had lived three years prior to service, or where they had been impressed. Through record linkage I have discovered that several became multiusers, collecting a number of stipends simultaneously.[48]

Changes in law and practice from the 1640s on made it more difficult for maimed ex-servicemen to use the system on a national level. The body came under more scrutiny. Under ordinances passed in 1647 and the 1662 act disabled ex-servicemen had to show that they were "disabled in body for work" and do so in the place in which they were last settled before taking up arms. In that location the applicant had to produce a certificate from his military superiors as to his record of military service and disabilities and give it to the two nearest justices who would examine the truth of the certificates.

Disabled ex-servicemen were thus henceforth *legally* obliged to conform to contemporary notions of what kind of disabilities impoverish. The stipulation that they had to return to the place in which they had resided before service meant they could no longer as easily operate on a national level and use or abuse the Elizabethan loopholes. This situation was compounded by the fact that the republican regimes, and the Privy Council after the Restoration, did not play as active a role as had the early-seventeenth-century Privy Council in intervening on behalf of ex-servicemen in their counties and towns. A number of counties made the norm of disability more systematic by requiring periodic reviews of pensioners to ensure that they were, indeed, disabled to work. And in the case of the populous county of Devon, surgeons were hired regularly after the Restoration to examine the men's bodies to determine eligibility.[49]

Given contemporary notions of disability it was particularly difficult for adult men—the group in the demographic hole in the pensionable poor— to argue that they were disabled to work. In doing so many argued that they were physically disabled to practice their specific trade. The inability to continue a trade was cited more often than the inability to labor. This was the case because men with a trade could more easily link a specific physical problem to an inability to do a specific trade than an inability to do any form of labor. As the test for disability was incapacity to work, a tradesman met the test with less difficulty than a laborer, who could be expected to perform a much wider variation of activities to earn his subsistence.[50] William Leak of Cheshire could thus argue that his incurable hand injuries prevented his continuing as a gunsmith and expect (and receive) a pension.[51] Ex-servicemen who cited their trade were also playing on contemporary notions of status; a tradesman who could no longer practice was in a different category of the impoverished from a laborer. Like an impoverished junior officer, a pension was expected and granted partially in recognition of a man having fallen from a certain station in life. In this respect the county pension scheme still adhered to its Elizabethan origins—recognizing to some extent the importance of status honor by providing for the shame-faced poor.[52]

Lists of new pensioners in 1647 in Somerset and Cheshire reveal the types of disabilities that ex-servicemen claimed and the justices were prepared to recognize immediately after war by the granting of a county stipend. Hands, arms, and legs were the most affected (see table 1). As well as pensioning civil war ex-servicemen justices of the peace in both counties reinstated pre–Civil War pensioners, many of whom were quite old.

Evidence from quarter sessions petitions for the entire period 1593–1679 reveals that most petitioners mentioned that they had been maimed (see table 2). Some did cite colds and disease, violent fevers and fluxes, that they had contracted in service. These continued to plague them after the wars, so as to make labor difficult.[53] Several of the citations of cold and disease correspond to contemporary understandings of the humoral theory of the body.

Within humoralism the body was believed to be a semipermeable, irrigated vessel in which moved the four humors (blood, phlegm, yellow bile, and black bile). Health was maintained by the preservation of internal stability, through evacuation of bodily fluids, and the avoidance, if possible, of environments and conditions of life that upset one's internal stability. The humors moved with differing degrees of fluidity. And they left with varying degrees of efficiency. Heat was believed to promote solubility, cold to hamper it.[54] Several petitioners demonstrated a keen awareness of the permanent effect of heat and, especially, cold in military service upon their physical state. A John Rigby in 1656 maintained that service at Worcester "hath brought him to much weaknesse by the length of the march & heats and colds therein so [he is] not able to labour." So too one William Hoult declared that he had "gott into his bodie An extreame Could by Lying in the open feild in the extreametie of weather that caused great Aches and paine in his Lymbes and Joynts that hee is theire by sore troubled at Change of weather to follow his dayly Labour." William Wimpennye cited a "cold in his lims" that he had received in service. The result: he had become a "cripple" who could not "stirre forth but uppon his Crutches and is alto-geather unable to worke." All the above were granted some form of relief, as was Margaret Massey, who petitioned in 1650 for permission to build a cottage upon the waste. The justices, perhaps demonstrating a shared under-standing of the nature of illness and disability based on humoralism, noted

TABLE 1.   New Pensioners in Somerset and Cheshire and Their Disabilities in 1647

Disability	Somerset	Cheshire
One limb inoperative	8	16
One limb lost	4	1
More than one limb inoperative	2	2
Head wound	2	2
Sickness	0	1

Source: Somerset Record Office, Q/SO5, fols. 34r–35v; CRO, QJB, 1/6, fols. 35r–36v.

TABLE 2.   Disabilities of Applicants for Pensions, Cheshire, 1593–1680, and Devon, 1660–1692

Disability	Cheshire			Devon
	1593–1642	1646–60	1660–80	1660–92
Service related				
General description: "maims in service"	25	44	71	216
One limb inoperative	9	35	16	33
More than one limb inoperative	3	9	8	10
One limb lost	1	5	4	11
More than one limb lost	1	1	0	1
Visual	2	2	4	11
Hearing	1	0	0	0
Mental	0	0	0	2
Cold/disease	7	4	5	11
Not service related				
Age	6	3	15	9

Source: Cheshire Record Office, QJB 2/6–2/7, 3/1–3/3; QJF 1593–1680; Devon Record Office, Q/S, 1/9–1/13; Q/S 128.

that her husband had died "by reason of the Coold which hee gott in his limbes in that [military] service."[55]

Many petitioners did not mention the effects of the heat and cold experienced on long marches and during lengthy sieges in open country (so vividly described by C. Carlton).[56] This is probably because of potential skepticism about the legitimacy of the facts of their claims. This skepticism is revealed in a petition by the officers of a county bench. They sought to be relieved of the burden of an ex-serviceman's court-ordered parish pension. In the petition they maintained that he "pretends hee got his colds" but that in reality he was capable of working and, in addition was unworthy, having not served well: "wee are credibly informed hee overrunne his Coulors."[57] The officers were not disputing that cold could disable, but that this individual had experienced such cold.

In their general descriptions of injuries in service, men sometimes mentioned their loss of blood and bruises (the extravasation of blood) suffered on the battlefield. This was often combined with citing old age. Thus Thomas Oulton in 1651 declared that he was growing old, had received many dangerous wounds, and was in a weak state because of "the very much blood that hee hath lost in the late warres."[58] It is clear that people believed that a significant loss of blood, or its being forced from its proper vessel in the case of serious bruising, could have permanent effects on the human body. The blood was believed to be the vehicle of the humors, and as such, an inordinate loss of it could irreparably upset one's internal balance. As one got older, the loss of a great deal of blood on one or more occasions would have a greater effect on one's health and strength. This was because it was believed that the bodies of the aged contained less blood than the bodies of younger adults. Aging was a process of gradually drying out. Thus although in 1628 Harvey revealed that blood circulated, and that more of it flowed through the heart than could be created as a result of digestion, people continued to believe for some time that the body's production of blood was related to consumption and other factors such as age.[59]

Age was important in contemporary notions of pensionable disability, but one had to be quite old to be considered: men and women were expected to work as long as possible. The pre–Civil War Privy Council had a notion that men who retired from the military should be given pensions, but this did not sit well with contemporary ideas of pensionable disability in which there was no real idea of retirement, except for the very old and decrepit. The significance of age as a factor in pensionable disability is demonstrated in Devon. Between 1660 and 1692, 83 of 240 (34.6 percent) mention age as well as other causes of disability to work.[60] Those who cite a specific age confirm conclusions reached by Margaret Pelling—that only the very elderly were considered unable to work.[61] Thirty-three of the Devon applicants cited their age, the mean average of which was 74 years.[62] Throughout the operation of the county pension scheme old age was an acceptable reason for a pension increase as well as an initial stipend award.

In addition to the effects of cold, disease, blood, and age, specific causes of wounds were cited for a number of ex-servicemen. In pre–Civil War Cheshire the cause of the disability was given for 10 cases. Of these nine had been shot (the other had been cut by a sword). From 1646 to 1660, 32 of the 39 for whom mention of the cause of disability was given had been shot, with five receiving sword wounds; one was mutilated by a dart. Another ex-serviceman had received both sword and musket wounds. A wound by gunshot was frequently cited without any further specification about the nature of the disability. In total, thus 15 of the 44 Cheshire ex-servicemen in the "general description: 'maims in service' " (table 2) had been shot.[63] The cause of wounds in Cheshire for the period between 1660 and 1680 is found in table 3. Two others not listed in table 3 received musket-related injuries: one suffered from a vicious recoil of a musket, and the other received a harsh blow from a musket.[64]

In Devon the overwhelming preponderance of gunshot wounds was also in evidence (see table 4). Two other wounds were described: one man had a cannon fall and crush his foot; the other suffered from a musket butt to the head.

TABLE 3.   Cause of Wounds of Applicants for Pensions in Cheshire, 1660–1680

Shot	22
Sword	4
Sword and shot	5
Scalded by powder	1

Source: Cheshire Record Office, QJB, 3/1–3/3; QJF, 1593–1680.

TABLE 4.   Cause of Wounds of Applicants for Pensions in Devon, 1660–1692

Shot	36
Sword	1
Sword and shot	16
Splinters from ship	4
Scalded by powder	3

Source: Devon Record Office, Q/S, 1/9–1/13; Q/S, 128.
Note: Whereas Cheshire ended the county scheme in 1680, Devon continued it.

Gunshot wounds were notoriously dangerous. The widow of Richard Buckly in her petition for a pension described her husband's wound. He had been "shott throw the sholder with a bullet which proued a verie dangerous wound, had seuen bones taken out of his sholder, and had extreame great paine of it and after wards proued to bee the occasion of his death as Mr gates the surgeon can make it appeare." His wounds had made it impossible to practice his trade as a shoemaker. As well as drawing a pension he had run errands "to gett a poore Liuelihood till he dyed by reason of the great swellinge of his sholder." Having had a "holt pultis layd to it the swellinge remoued into his side and soe ascended upward to his harte whereupon hee dyed."[65]

Contemporary links between illness and divine providence, as discussed by Andrew Wear for example, did not arise within the context of the county pension scheme—in petitions, letters of support, or pension award orders. Injuries experienced in good service were the work of *other* men, and not God (no matter which side he fought on).[66]

Pauper survival strategies and the nature of their by-employments were described by some veterans in their petitions for relief. In Cheshire from 1647 to 1680, for example, 35 ex-servicemen gave 40 explanations of how they had managed to subsist prior to applying for benefits (see table 5). Ex-servicemen had to rely on the assistance of siblings, parents, neighbors, and patrons. Thomas Hall mentioned that for the previous six to seven years his brother had provided him with food, drink, and clothing. Another man declared that "his poore sister" had "kepte him for the Space of about three yeares last past & is not able to keepe him any longer beinge soe great a charge both for his dyet & tendinge." The support of a patron was crucial for a Royalist maimed ex-serviceman, John Wright, during the Interregnum, when he was not entitled to a county pension. Wright, petitioning in 1662, mentioned that he had nothing "but what hee houldeth of the Right Worshipful Wilougbly Aston Barronet uppon the Racke who is verrie respective unto him by reason of his fidelty and true loyalty." Others relied on neighbors, as in the case of Thomas King, who received their help whenever his wife and children were sick. As well as mentioning the assistance of others, men also included information about their work. Richard Harrison lived as a servant in a Mr. Bennet's house. He commented that his wages were so low that he received most of his maintenance from his father, who was now old, blind, and no longer able to help his disabled son. Thomas Hall declared the he had been

very laborious & Industrious in a way by tradeinge in boyinge & sell-
inge of smale wares whoe upon his Creditt gott a stocke to sett up with
the helpe of his brother . . . since which time . . . had his shopp broken
& goods taken from him in the night to the value of Tenn Pounds.

Two ex-servicemen had been kept on by the military, despite their disabilities: one was in the trained band until it was disbanded: another was "constrained to continue a Souldier at this present in the Garrison at Chester."[67]

Other ex-servicemen petitioned for permission to erect a dwelling
upon the waste or common and later became pensioners. Permission to
build a cottage not only helped an ex-serviceman to survive, but there is
evidence that it was considered necessary to have a dwelling in order to
apply for a county pension. James Richardson commented in his cottage
application that as he was "destitute of a place wherein to putt his head" he
had "lost the opportunity for present of puttinge in for a pention from his
Majesty."[68]

In some counties pensioners were given jobs to increase their income.
In Devon County pensioners were employed as county postmen and house
of correction governors. The Devon bench also paid eight county pensioners 10 shillings extra on their pensions in 1664 for traveling extensively in
the county to assist the justices in the suppression of conventicles.[69] On
occasion disabled veterans faced difficulties in the course of carrying out
official responsibilities. Dennis Brayne, county pensioner, was put on watch
by the town of Nantwich in 1650 because of the plague. Subsequently he
petitioned the bench for the prosecution of a man who attacked him while
he was on watch. Brayne complained that "your petitionr having but the
use of one hand, the said Sheene gott him downe [and] gave him many

TABLE 5.   Tales of Subsistence, Ex-servicemen in
Cheshire, 1647–1680

Supported by family, friends, or neighbors	19
Worked	14
Sold belongings/consumed estate	2
Parish relief	2
Forced to beg	3

Source: Cheshire Record Office, QJF, 1647–1680.

Note: Four applicants stated that they had previously relied on
work and the support of family, friends, and neighbors. A fifth stated
that he had relied on parish relief and work.

blowes [and] swore extremely hee wold bit your petitoners nose off."
Neighbors intervened to assist Brayne in his struggle.[70] Worries about such
physical difficulties did not prevent sick and maimed soldiers about London
in 1651 volunteering to guard Parliament gratis. The council of state
thanked the ex-servicemen but declined, declaring that "through the good-
ness of God, the state of affairs is such that they have no need of any other
guards than what are already appointed."[71]

The administration of the county pension scheme tells us much about the
effect of war on the body, including the harmful effects of shot wounds and
the role of humoral ideas. It also informs about disabled veterans' survival
strategies and contemporary notions of disability. The only recognized disability was the disability to work. Men were expected, if at all possible, to
work however affected in body by their wartime experiences. In addition it
was expected that they would utilize their personal and family resources
before applying for county benefit. And aging was a process of very gradual
withdrawal from economic productivity and self-support.

V

The Elizabethan Privy Council sponsored and enforced the county pension
scheme to national military problems. Soldiers, disabled in service, needed
to be properly provided for if men were to be encouraged to serve. For
councillors like Sir Robert Cecil maimed soldiers were a special category.
Unlike the impotent poor who needed relief and idle vagabonds who had
to be punished, disabled ex-servicemen *merited* lifelong pensions, regardless
of their financial circumstances. Ex-servicemen, wounded in the service of
the realm, were to be treated as members of the community of honor. In
their administration of the disabled soldier act, county justices did not
demonstrate an appreciation of this national and aristocratic perspective and
its significance for the status of ex-servicemen. As the number of eligible
disabled grew, county justices, with limited resources (due to the unpopu-
larity of the rates), preferred to pension deserving county men *who were disabled to work*. Therein rose the discrepancies between law and practice that
developed in the early seventeenth century and were eventually incorporated into law in midcentury. These changes brought with them increased
examination of men's bodies at the local level and disentitled ex-servicemen
who had some means or ability to work.

By 1679 the attitudes and concerns of the Privy Council had changed.

There was a marked decline in its enforcement of the county scheme after the Restoration. And, indeed, when the 1662 act lapsed in 1679, the council initially met local questions about the status of the act with assurances that it was still in force.[72] This was not true; only the 1601 act still survived, with its inadequate rate base. Instead of devoting attention to the county scheme the king and advisors became increasingly interested in the creation of a national hospital for ex-servicemen. And from 1670 this was especially the case, given the example of Louis XIV's Hôtel des Invalides in France.[73] Such institutions promised greater and more visible central, royal control of ex-servicemen. Such institutions would clearly be the product of monarchs in charge of their armed forces. And in the late seventeenth century most county authorities seem to have been happy to transfer onto central funds (in time, a system of deficit financing ultimately borne by customs and excise duties) a burden previously borne on local rates (politically unpopular taxes on land). In this context the hospitals of Chelsea and Greenwich would come to stand as monuments to a new fiscal arrangement within the realm. They were part of what Joanna Innes has called the domestic face of the fiscal–military state.[74]

Chelsea and Greenwich also continued the process, already begun under the county scheme, of even greater regulation of veterans' bodies. Indeed, an examination of discipline within the hospitals reveals that these institutions do not seem an improvement when compared to the county out-pension system, as asserted previously by scholars. In addition to having to experience harsh discipline within the hospitals, disabled veterans were separated from their families, who were left to beg at the gates for food and struggle with reluctant local parochial officials for parish relief. Another significant change with the move to the hospitals of Greenwich and Chelsea was that whereas previously men had received pensions funded by county rates as per statute, the hospitals were royal charities paid for principally by deductions from pay. The hospital system was a form of insurance, not insurance that provided statutory tax-based relief to the men as their entitlement but, rather, insurance as charitable bounty from the Crown, paid from servicemen's own wages.

In answer to critics of the cost of the construction of Greenwich hospital Nicholas Hawksmore, in 1728, commented that "in effect" it "cost us nothing but the Labour and Industry of our own Poor; and [its] Production [is a] Memorial of the Care and Industry, as well as [an] evident mark of a Polite Government."[75] As monuments Greenwich and Chelsea were successful, prominent places on the Thames, places to impress the foreigner and subject with the strength, commitment, and foresight of the Crown, Great Britain, and its armed forces; the disabled veterans colorful ornaments in their uniforms.

NOTES

I wish to thank the Wellcome Trust for financial support that partially assisted the research for this paper.

1. S. R. Gardiner and C. T. Atkinson, eds., *Letters and Papers relating to the First Dutch War, 1652–4,* vol. 4 (London, 1899–1930), 111, cited in B. Capp, *Cromwell's Navy* (Oxford, 1989), 81.

2. A. L. Beier, *The Problem of the Poor in Tudor and Early Stuart England* (New York, 1983), 13. The following discussion of the council and disabled soldiers prior to 1593 is a shortened and altered version of chapter 2 in G. L. Hudson "The English Privy Council and Relief of Disabled Soldiers, c. 1558–1625," M.A. thesis, McMaster University, 1988.

3. *Acts of the Privy Council,* ed. J. R. Dasent, 32 vols. (London, 1890–1907), (hereafter cited as *APC*), vols. 14–24, passim; C. Read, ed., *William Lambarde and Local Government* (Ithaca, 1962), 183–84; British Library (hereafter BL), Lansdowne MSS, 65, fol. 21; Public Record Office (hereafter PRO), State Papers Domestic (hereafter SP Dom.), 12/244/68; the dean and chapter of Durham, for example, declared that the almshouse grant was not legally binding. *APC,* 21:79.

4. PRO, SP Dom., 12/218/55.

5. The council's sponsorship of the 1593 act is well documented; see Hudson, "English Privy Council," chap. 3; and J. R. Kent, "Social Attitudes of Members of Parliament with Special Reference to the Problem of Poverty, circa 1590–1624," Ph.D. diss., University of London, 1971, chap. 1, sec. 1.

6. See J. Goring, "Social Change and Military Decline in Mid-Tudor England," *History* 60 (1975): 185–97. See also the chapter "Force and Arms" in P. Williams, *The Tudor Regime* (Oxford, 1979).

7. For the relative centralization of the English state and its importance for the development of social legislation see P. Slack, *Poverty and Policy in Tudor and Stuart England* (London, 1988), 12–14. For the significant difference between the numbers of troops on active service for England and countries like France and Spain at this time see J. R. Hale, *War and Society in Renaissance Europe, 1450–1620* (London, 1985), 62–63.

8. C. G. Cruickshank, *Elizabeth's Army,* 2d ed. (Oxford, 1966), 183–86; Kent, "Social Attitudes of Members," chap. 1, sec. 2. J. J. N. McGurk reiterates Kent's arguments in "Casualties and Welfare Measures for the Sick and Wounded of the Nine Year War in Ireland, 1593–1602," *Journal of the Society for Army Historical Research* 68 (autumn 1990): 189–90.

9. L. Boynton, "The Tudor Provost Marshall," *English Historical Review* 87 (1962): 437–55; A. L. Beier, *Masterless Men: The Vagrancy Problem in England, 1560–1640* (London, 1985), 152–53; J. Pound, *Poverty and Vagrancy in Tudor England,* 2d ed. (London, 1986), 2–3; J. Calnan, "County Society and Local Government in the Country of Hertford, c. 1580–c. 1630, with Special Reference to the Commission of the Peace," Ph.D. diss., Cambridge University, 1978, 235–40.

10. *APC,* 24:170–71, 178–80, 191–96.

11. Letter from Charles, Lord Howard to Sir Francis Walsingham, PRO, SP Dom., 12/215/66. Lord Howard observed that as "we are to like to have more of theire servyes . . . the men should be carred for better then to . . . starve and die."

12. BL, Cotton MSS, Titus, F.ii, fol. 58r; BL, Harleian MSS, 1888, fol. 154.

13. *Orders devised for the reliefe of the present dearth of Graine* (London, 1586), *A Short Title Catalogue of Books Printed in England, Scotland, and Ireland and of English Books Printed Abroad, 1475–1640,* ed. W. A. Jackson, F. S. Ferguson, and K. F. Pantzer, 2d ed. (London, 1986), vol. 1, vol. 2, 9194.

14. J. Walter and K. Wrightson, "Dearth and the Social Order in Early Modern England," *Past and Present* 71 (1976): 22–42, especially at 38–42; K. Wrightson, "Social Order of Early Modern England: Three Approaches," in *World We Have Gained: Histories of Population and Social Structure,* ed. L. Bonfield et al. (Oxford, 1986), 177–202; D. Levine and K. Wrightson, *Making of an Industrial Society: Wickham, 1560–1765* (Oxford, 1991), especially chap. 4. See also P. Clark, "Popular Protest and Disturbance in Kent, 1558–1640," *Economic History Review,* 2d series, 29, no. 3 (1976): 380–81; J. Walter, "A Rising of the People? The Oxfordshire Rising of 1596," *Past and Present* 107 (1985): 90–143; J. Walter, "Social Economy of Dearth in Early Modern England," in *Famine, Disease, and the Social Order in Early Modern Society,* ed. J. Walter and R. Schofield (Cambridge, 1989), chap. 2; M. Braddick, "State Formation and Social Change in Early Modern England: A Problem Stated and Approaches Suggested," *Social History* 16, no. 1 (1991): 1–17, especially at 7, 10, 14, 17.

15. G. Parker in *The Army of Flanders and the Spanish Road, 1567–1659* (Cambridge, 1972) comments that "once resolved on disobedience, the mutineers organized themselves with considerable sophistication in order to achieve their objectives. They elected leaders to govern them, followed a rational and orderly plan, and concentrated their efforts on limited and attainable goals" (187).

16. *APC,* 18:54–56, 320; *Calendar of Letters and State Papers relating to English Affairs preserved in, or originally belonging to, the Archives of Simancas,* ed. Martin A. S. Hume IV, Elizabeth 1587–1603 (London, 1899), 558–59.

17. *APC,* 17:46–48; *Tudor Royal Proclamations,* ed. P. L. Hughes and J. F. Larkin, 3 vols. (London, 1964–69), 3:715: soldiers were ordered to return to the county where they had been impressed and approach their local justices concerning their back pay. The latter were to then approach the lord lieutenants, who would in turn ask the Privy Council to forward the necessary sums. Parker, *Army of Flanders,* 205; PRO, SP Dom., 12/244/71.

18. *APC,* 24:178–80, 193–96; Sir Simonds, *The Journals of all the Parliaments during the Reign of Queen Elizabeth* (London, 1682), 463; PRO, SP Dom., 3/244/118; BL, MSS Lansdowne 104, fol. 39.

19. BL Lansdowne 73 (38).

20. Salisbury MSS 169/21 (BL, M 485/45); *Historic Manuscripts Commission,* vol. 4 (London, 1892), 457, lists 1593 as a possible date for this petition. This date is incorrect—the petition refers to problems connected with the implementation of the pension scheme only just created in 1593. As the petitioners cite the establishment of the pension scheme by "the Last Sessyon of Parliament" and mention difficulties connected with provisions unique to the 1593 act (which were altered in 1598), it is probable that it was submitted to the 1597–98 meeting of the Commons.

21. For a discussion of aristocratic honor and hospitality, see F. Heal, *Hospitality in Early Modern England* (Oxford, 1990), 393, 11–12. Not surprisingly the misuse of hospital lands and revenues that was deemed to have caused this deficiency was also believed to have resulted in a decay of hospitality in general, to the detriment of the poor. PRO, SP Dom., 12/244/68. For a discussion of attempts by the English government of the 1590s to revive hospitality and catholicity in giving see Heal, 127–30.

22. PRO, SP Dom., 12/244/68. Spain had the most elaborate system of hospitals for disabled servicemen in Europe (Parker, *Army of Flanders,* 167, 169; Parker, *The Military Revolution: Military Innovation and the Rise of the West, 1500–1800* [Cambridge, 1988], 53–55). Parliament could eliminate the dishonor through legislation.

23. *Statutes of the Realm* (hereafter cited as *SR*), 35 Eliz. c. 4, 39 Eliz. c. 21, 43 Eliz. c. 3. A detailed outline of this legislation is provided in G. L. Hudson, "Ex-servicemen, War Widows, and the English County Pension Scheme, 1593–1679," (D.Phil. diss., Oxford University, 1995), 21–28. Although it was not renewed in 1610—when James I's first parliament ended—the 1601 act did not lapse in practice, as is made clear by the fact that in 1624 an act (*SR*, 21 Jac. I c. 28) continued the 1601 act and adjudged it to have been in force ever since the end of the 1610 session. The 1601 act was continued also by 3 Car. I c. 5 and 16 Car. I c. 4. The latter act provided for the indefinite continuation of the 1601 act until another act was passed affecting it.

24. An order of Parliament of November 1645 required that "the ancient Rates and Leavies usually paid of Goals and maimed Souldiers in the said severall counties, be from time to time assessed and collected as formerly, and be duly paid and imployed for the said uses." The order did not make it clear, however, whether the county benches or committees were to administer these monies, and there is little evidence of either body having successfully revived the Elizabethan scheme. BL, E 309 (30). County committees did award funds sequestered from Royalists to disabled ex-servicemen. PRO, SP, 28, 224 and 225 (Cheshire), 227 (Devon and Essex), 230 (Hampshire), 235 (Kent), 237 (London and Middlesex). In addition to the 1647 ordinances in September 1651 an act was passed that required county justices of the peace to relieve the sick and maimed ex-servicemen, war widows, and orphans of the Scottish and Irish campaigns. *Acts and Ordinances,* 1:938–40 (May 28, 1647), 997–98 (August 10, 1647), 1055 (December 24, 1647); 2:556–59 (September 30, 1651).

25. *SR*, 14 Car. II. c. 9. For passage of the bill through Parliament see *Journals of the House of Lords* (hereafter *LJ*) 2:153, 398, 400, 405, 471; *Journals of the House of Commons* (hereafter *CJ*), 8:321, 329, 345, 350, 352, 358, 368, 376. For more on this legislation see P. Seaward, *Cavalier Parliament and the Reconstruction of the Old Regime, 1661–1667* (Cambridge, 1989), 208–11.

26. *CJ*, 9:582. The committee appointed to inspect the temporary laws that would expire in this session of Parliament considered the 1662 county pension act. No decision about renewing the act can be found in the parliamentary journals.

27. PRO, SP Dom., 352/81 cited in I. G. Powell, "The Chatham Chest under the Early Stuarts," *Mariner's Mirror* 8 (1922), 181; National Maritime Museum, Soc. 15 (Chest accounts, 1637–43); PRO, Admiralty (hereafter ADM), 82/2 (1656); Bodl. Rawl. MSS C199 (1665); Bodl. Rawl. MSS A229 (1676).

28. PRO, *Calendar of State Papers, Domestic Series* (hereafter *CSPD*), 1657–58, 363. This central fund was maintained for most of the period by central government excise duties and monies received from naval prizes, and in an ordinance of May 1654 its income was guaranteed at a rate of £26,260 per annum. This was increased to £38,270

per annum by letters patent dated November 18, 1654. *Acts and Ordinances,* 1:102–3, 328–30, 466–68, 484, 989–90, 1004–7, 2:9–13, 213–33, 889–90. House of Lords Record Office, Main Papers, *LJ,* 10:231 and 232 (April 5 and 14, 1648), draft parliamentary orders for maimed soldiers to have use of Ely House. BL, Add. MSS 9305, fol. 117r and v.

29. C. H. Firth, *Cromwell's Army* (London, 1902), 262, 267, 268–69. For the final efforts at supporting, and eventual decision to wind down, this central fund, see *CJ,* 5:16 (May 7, 1660), 46 (May 26, 1660), 66 (June 18, 1660), 122 (August 15, 1660), 147 (September 3, 1660), 158 (September 7, 1660), 170–71, 204 (December 11, 1660), 212–13 (December 17, 1660).

30. J J. Keevil, *Medicine and the Navy, 1200–1900,* vol. 1 (London, 1957), 52, 54.

31. Treasurers accounts: Gloucestershire (1673–74), Wiltshire (1669–70), Somerset (1668), Devon (1673), Middlesex and Westminster (1669), City of London (1671), Shropshire (1671), West Riding of Yorkshire (1668), and Cheshire (1671–72). For pensioner numbers, references and population calculations see Hudson, "Ex-servicemen, War Widows," 55.

32. Cheshire Record Office (hereafter CRO), Quarter Sessions Files (hereafter QJF), 28/2, QJF, 100/2, fol. 32; Devon Record Office (hereafter DRO), Q/S, 1/2, n. fol.; Q/S, 1/11, n.f.; Hampshire Record Office (hereafter HRO), Q1/1; Q1/4, fols. 109–12 (Trinity 1662).

33. For enforcement of the pension scheme prior to the civil wars see Hudson, "English Privy Council," chaps. 4 and 5 and "Ex-Servicemen, War Widows," chap. 2. See also Slack, *Poverty and Policy,* 127. McGurk is mistaken in adopting Kent's view that the government of James I was not active in enforcing this legislation. McGurk, "Casualties and Welfare," 198; Kent, "Social attitudes," 57–60.

34. Conclusions based on detailed study of sessions materials from City of Oxford, Kent, Cheshire, and Devon. Oxford City Library, O.5.9; N.4.2; Kent Archive Office, Q/FM 1–11; Q/SO WI; CRO, Quarter Sessions Books (hereafter QJB) 1/4, fols. 89v, 90r; QJF, 28/4, fol. 8 (Hilary 1598–99); QJF, 35/2, fol. 30 (Trinity 1606); DRO Q/S, 1/1, fol. 298 (Hilary 1599–1600); 1/2, n. fol. (Hilary 1603–4), n. fol. (Easter 1607).

35. The legal principle behind these practices was made explicit by two Staffordshire JPs. In a 1640 decision concerning a poor law matter they concluded that practices that ran counter to an act of Parliament, even an act passed as recently as 1601, are legal if these practices are begun and continued by the consent and agreement of the interested parties. Staffordshire Record Office, QS files (Easter 1640), cited in S. C. Newton, "Staffordshire Quarter Sessions: Archives and Procedures in the Earlier Seventeenth-Century," in *Essays in Staffordshire History,* ed. M. W. Greenslade, Collections for a History of Staffordshire, 4th ser., 6 (1970), 80.

36. For a detailed discussion see Hudson, "Ex-Servicemen, War Widows," chap. 2.

37. Hudson, "English Privy Council," chaps. 4 and 5; A Fletcher, *A Country Community in Peace and War: Sussex, 1600–1660* (London, 1975), part 3; Fletcher, *Reform in the Provinces* (London, 1986), 43–44, 60–61, 354–55, 373; Wrightson, *English Society, 1580–1680* (London, 1982), 151–55, 172.

38. DRO, Q/S 1/8–1/13; Q/S 128.

39. Example: Fletcher, *Reform in the Provinces,* 352–53.

40. Two recorded orders for watch and ward in the 1650s Devon reveal the concern for political security. Beggars are associated with the benches' ideological opponents

in July 1651. DRO, Q/S, 1/8, n. fol (Trinity 1651). See also DRO, Q/S, 1/9, n. fol. (Trinity 1565).

41. Greater London Record Office, MJ/SBB/356, fol. 39 (Michaelmas 1678); MJ/SBB/357, fol. 37 (December 1678). The pre-1670 shift has been characterized as civil war (or the continuation thereof) by other means by Andrew Coleby in an unpublished paper entitled "Local Sufferers and the State: The Case of Maimed Soldiers in England, 1645–1670" (1988). Coleby argued that "there was a growth of partisanship in the attitude of central rulers to the localities and by extension within these localities. This process is well illustrated by the treatment meted out to a particularly vulnerable group within local society: those wounded on active service in the royalist and parliamentary armies in the 1640s."

42. Discussion of Greenwich and Chelsea hospitals in this essay based on research in progress. G. L. Hudson, "Secular Glory Incarnate? English Military Hospitals in the Seventeenth and Eighteenth Centuries," paper delivered at Wellcome Institute for the History of Medicine, London, February 1998, "Body and the State in Early Modern England," paper delivered at All Souls College, Oxford, May 1998. M. Foucault, *Discipline and Punish: The Birth of the Prison*, trans. A. Sheridan-Smith (New York, 1979), 139, 184–85. See also M. Foucault, *Madness and Civilization*, trans. R. Howard (New York, 1965); M. Foucault, *The Order of Things: An Archaeology of the Human Sciences*, trans. A. Sheridan-Smith (London, 1970); M. Foucault, *Power/Knowledge: Selected Interviews and Other Writings*, ed. C. Gordon (New York, 1980), esp. "The Politics of Health"; M. Foucault, *The History of Sexuality*, vol. 1 (London, 1979). In my ongoing examination of the English military hospitals I am attentive to social agency and relations in ways that are critical of Foucault's tendency to see power as omnipresent.

43. CRO, QJF, 31/2, fol. 1 (Trinity 1602). Other examples: Arthur Bulkley, CRO, QJF 24/4, fol. 33 (Hilary 1594–95); William Brown, CRO, QJF, 31/2, fols. 2 and 3 (Trinity 1602); John Goodridge, Kent Archives Office (hereafter KAO), QM/SB, 63 and 86 (June 1595); Thomas Bean, KAO, QM/SB, 589 (September 1605); Andrew Simes, Wiltshire Record Office (hereafter WRO), A1 110 (Michaelmas 1606), fol. 149 (Trinity 1609), fol. 101; Thomas Pooer, WRO, A1 110 (Easter 1608), fols. 141–43; Henry Baker, WRO (Trinity 1609), fol. 105; Thomas Tattom, WRO (Easter 1611), fol. 131; Thomas Jones, WRO (Hilary 1612–13), fols. 137–40.

44. KAO, QM/SB, 1316.

45. CRO, QJB and QJF, 1593–1641.

46. Examples: WRO, A1/150/7 (Trinity 1631); DRO, Q/S 1/3, fol. 77v (Hilary 1609–10); Q/S, 1/4, n. fol. (Easter 1616). The evidence from the Privy Council registers confirms the timing of the shift in how eligibility was determined. There is a clear change in the nature of the disabilities by which soldiers applied, and were recommended, for pensions. *APC*, 22–39, passim; PRO, SP Dom., 11/174/83, 11/180/94.

47. T. Wales, "Poverty, Poor Relief, and the Life-Cycle: Some Evidence from Seventeenth Century Norfolk," in *Land, Kinship and Life-Cycle*, ed. R. M. Smith (Cambridge, 1984), 351–404; M. Pelling, "Healing the Sick Poor: Social Policy and Disability in Norwich, 1550–1640," *Medical History* 29 (1985): 115–37; M. Pelling, "Illness among the Poor in an Early Modern English Town: The Norwich Census of 1570," *Continuity and Change* 3, no. 2 (1988): 273–90; M. Pelling, "Old Age, Poverty, and Disability in Early Modern Norwich," in *Life, Death, and the Elderly*, ed. M. Pelling and R. M. Smith (London, 1991), 74–101, 77. See also W. Newman Brown, "Receipt of Poor Relief and Family Situation: Aldenham, Hertfordshire, 1630–90," in *Land, Kinship, and Life-Cycle*, 405–21, 411.

48. For a detailed discussion of social agency and the disabled veteran see Hudson, "Ex-servicemen, War Widows," chap. 3. At the national level Parliament was treated to numerous demonstrations and petitions from ex-servicemen at key moments, bringing pressure to bear on their betters to relieve them, enact and/or improve legislation. The key dates: the early and mid-1590s, 1647, later 1650s, and early 1660s.

49. DRO, Q/S, 1/9, n. fol. (Michaelmas 1661); 1/10, n. fol. (Trinity 1663).

50. For a discussion of early modern disability to work see J. C. Riley, "Sickness in an Early Modern Workplace," *Continuity and Change* 2, no. 3 (1987): 363–85, 383.

51. CRO, QJF, 83/4, fol. 120 (Trinity 1655–56).

52. As Stuart Woolf has asked rhetorically: "who was better known or better recommended than the respected noble, merchant or artisan, whose misfortune threatened his ability to uphold his status . . . ?" *The Poor in Western Europe* (London, 1986), 20.

53. Example: Richard Greene, CRO, QJF, 99/2, fols. 40, 131 (Trinity 1671).

54. V. Hutton, "Humoralism," in *Companion Encyclopedia of the History of Medicine,* ed. W. F. Bynum and R. Porter, vol. 1 (London, 1993), 281–91; A. Wear, "Making Sense of Health and the Environment in Early Modern England," in *Medicine in Society,* ed. A. Wear (Cambridge, 1992), 119–47; G. K. Paster, *The Body Embarrassed* (Ithaca, 1993), introduction.

55. Rigby, CRO, QJF, 84/1, fol. 103 (Easter 1656); Hoult, QJF, 90/3, fol. 204 (Hilary 1662–63); Wimpennye, QJF, 99/1, fol. 166 (Easter 1671); Massey, QJB, 1/6, fol. 268v (Michaelmas 1650).

56. C. Carlton, *Going to the Wars: The Experience of the British Civil Wars, 1638–1651* (London, 1992), 102–5.

57. CRO, QJF, 85/1, fol. 100 (Easter 1657).

58. CRO, QJF, 79/2, fol. 117 (Trinity 1651).

59. Paster, *Body Embarrassed,* 21, 65–66, 69–71, 74, 96.

60. DRO, Q/S, 1/9–1/13; Q/S, 128.

61. M. Pelling, "Old Age, Poverty and Disability in Early Modern Norwich: Work, Remarriage and Other Expedients," in *Life, Death and the Elderly: Historical Perspectives* (London, 1991), 78–82.

62. DRO, Q/S, 1/9–1/13; Q/S, 128.

63. CRO, QJB, 1/6; QJF.

64. In terms of the total numbers mentioning that they were wounded for 1646 to 1660, 33 of 100 mentioned that they had been shot. From 1660 to 1680, 27 of 107 (25 percent) did likewise.

65. CRO, QJF, 85/2, fol. 171 (Trinity 1657) and 88/4, fol. 32 (Hilary 1660–61). Another example: a surgeon's certificate for a Humphrey Briscoe mentioned that Briscoe had been "shot with a Brace of Bullets verie Danroulsy into the shoulder out of which came many Bones and he a longe time in Cure." In his petition Briscoe maintained that he was "disabled to follow his vocation as formerly." CRO, 88/4, fol. 62 (Hilary 1660–61). Gunshot wounds in the head were particularly dangerous. An Anthony Taylor in Devon, shot in the head, went insane. He had to be pensioned and cared for, off and on, from 1657 to at least 1684 in the St. Thomas Apostle House of Correction (which, among others, housed the county distracted). DRO, Q/S, 1/9, (Hilary 1657–58, Hilary 1658–59); Q/S 1/10 (Michaelmas 1661); 1/11 (Hilary 1672–73, Trinity 1674, Hilary 1669–70); 1/12 (Easter 1680); Q/S, 128/146/10–13.

66. L. M. Beier, *Sufferers and Healers: The Experience of Illness in Seventeenth-Century England* (London, 1987), 122–23; A. Wear, "Puritan Perceptions of Illness in Seven-

teenth Century England," in *Patients and Practitioners: Lay Perceptions of Medicine in Pre-industrial Society*, ed. R. Porter (Cambridge, 1985), 71, 75–77; H. J. Cook, "Good Advice nad Little Medicine: The Professional Authority of Early Modern English Physicians," *Journal of British Studies* 22 (January 1994): 1–31; R. Porter, "The Patient in England, c. 1660–1800," in Wear, *Medicine in Society, 95.*

67. Hall, CRO, QJF 79/1, fol. 99 (Easter 1651); Man and sister, QJF, 90/3, fol. 99; Wright, QJF 90/3, fols. 202–3 (Michaelmas 1662); King, QJF 79/4, fol. 90 (Hilary 1651–52); Harrison, QJF 84/4, fol. 106 (Hilary 1656–57); men in military, QJB, 1/6, fol. 145r (Easter 1647) and QJF 79/2, fol. 117 (Trinity 1651).

68. CRO, QJF, 89/2, fol. 207 (Trinity 1661). For further discussion of cottage petitions in Cheshire and by-employments see: J. S. Morrill, *Cheshire, 1630–1660* (Oxford, 1974), 247–49; A. Everitt, "Farm Labourers," in *The Agrarian History of England and Wales, 1500–1750*, vol. 4, ed. J. Thirsk (rpt. Cambridge, 1990), 190–95.

69. Postmen, DRO, Q/S, 128/1/5 (1676); Q/S, 1/10, n. fol. (Easter 1665, Easter 1666). House of Correction governors, Q/S, 1/9, n. fol. (Hilary 160–61); Q/S, 1/10, n. fol. (Trinity 1664, Michaelmas 1665, Easter 1666). S. Roberts, *Recovery and Restoration in an English County: Devon Local Administration, 1646–1670* (Exeter, 1985), 195–96. DRO, Q/S, 1/9, n. fol. (Easter 1656); Q/S, 1/10 (Trinity 1667, Michaelmas 1667). Justices also gave county contracts on the basis of military service. In 1686 the bench cited one John Spry's "loyalty in the actuall service of his late Matie" and granted him the job of glass-ing the county workhouse. DRO, Q/S, 1/13, n. fol. (Trinity 1686). BL, Additional MSS, 34012 (glassier). Conventicle suppressers, DRO, Q/S, 1/10, n. fol., Hilary 1663–64; Q/S, 146/7, 146/14. The first conventicles act (*SR,* 16 Charles II, c. 4) made it illegal for any person aged 16 or older to attend a meeting of five for worship without using the Anglican prayer book and liturgy.

70. CRO, QJF, 78/2, fol. 29 (Trinity 1650).

71. PRO, *CSPD, 1651,* 402.

72. PRO, PC2/68, fol. 325 (December 17, 1679).

73. Although some historians have argued that Chelsea and Greenwich were cre-ated as a result of the example of the Savoy and Ely House hospitals there is evidence to suggest that this is not true; those in authority were much more mindful of continental, and especially French, hospitals rather than those of the rebels who ruled England in the mid-century. William Blathwayt, Secretary at War from August 1683, chose consciously to follow the administrative methods of the French army including modeling the regu-lations which were employed at the Chelsea on those of l'Hôtel des Invalides. J. Childs, *The Army of Charles II* (1976), 103; J. Childs, *The Army, James II, and the Glorious Revolu-tion* (Manchester, 1980), 84; J. H. Plumb, *Growth of Political Stability in England 1675–1725* (London, 1967), 24–25; G. A. Jacobsen, *William Blathwayt* (New Haven, 1932), 223–24. For the French experience see C. Jones, "The Welfare of the French Foot-Soldier from Richelieu to Napoleon," in *Charitable Imperative: Hospitals and Nursing in Ancien Régime and Revolutionary France* (London, 1989).

74. J. Innes, "Domestic Face of the Military-Fiscal State: Government and Society in Eighteenth-Century Britain," in *An Imperial State at War: Britain from 1689–1815,* ed. L. Stone (London, 1994), 96–127.

75. N. Hawksmore, *Remarks on the Founding and Carrying on of the Buildings of the Royal Hospital at Greenwich* (London, 1728), 23.

Isser Woloch

"A Sacred Debt": Veterans and the State in Revolutionary and Napoleonic France

War veterans as a group straddle civil and military society. True, they can be studied strictly within the context of the military profession, as André Corvisier did in his book on the eighteenth-century French soldier and the career of soldiering. But most elderly or disabled veterans at that time, and certainly during the revolutionary-Napoleonic era, found themselves upon demobilization in the lower reaches of civil society.[1] Since needy veterans formed a particular stratum of the poor, veterans policy (while also an element of the state's military structure) was likely to be a frontier of social welfare, dependent in turn on the nature of the regime and its ideology. Between 1789 and 1815, France experienced a dizzying succession of such regimes—constitutional monarchy until 1792; Jacobin republic between 1792 and 1794; moderate republic during the Thermidorian reaction and the Directory, 1794–99; Bonaparte's Consulate between 1800 and 1804, followed by the Napoleonic empire after that date—while embroiled in an almost continuous and ever-expanding war between 1792 and 1815. During the French Revolution, as we shall see, veterans policy briefly entered a totally uncharted territory of egalitarian liberality. Ultimately, however, the revolutionary and Napoleonic state failed to sustain this remarkable policy, as provisions for war veterans receded in disarray and slipped back to more traditional and inadequate levels. In this paper I will sketch the unprecedented mutations in France's provision for veterans; the implementation of these new policies that paralleled oscillations in the Revolution's character; and the subsequent derogations, retreats, and failures.

I

A century before the French Revolution, the precociously centralized and militarized state of Louis XIV adopted at least some aged and disabled ex-soldiers and officers as favored wards. Whereas poor relief generally remained a local matter, religious or municipal in nature, Louis XIV created an impressive state institution, the Hôtel Royal des Invalides, to serve this needy constituency. The National Assembly of 1789 inherited that venerable establishment, along with other provisions for veterans, striking both for their unusual scope compared to the rest of Europe and for their blatant deficiencies. While providing some form of assistance to as many as 35,000 former officers and soldiers, these benefits were riddled with inequities and the spoils of aristocratic privilege. War ministry reformers had long advocated uniform and standardized retirement pensions that would encourage and reward longevity, and in the 1760s Choiseul's government had created the rudiments for such a system when it offered annual pensions to privates and NCOs who could not be accommodated at the Hôtel des Invalides after the heavy casualties and demobilizations of the Seven Years War: 54 livres *(solde)* for a private after 24 years of service, for example, or 27 livres *(demi-solde)* annually after at least 16 years. Choiseul likewise sought to create a standardized scale of retirement pensions for officers with at least 30 years of service, starting at 360 livres for lieutenants, and 500 to 700 for captains, with increments for further longevity.

Most money paid out in royal pensions, however, was not being allocated under any such rationalized criteria, and when the National Assembly managed to secure the royal pension list for 1789, the contours of an abusive spoils system unfolded. Of approximately 24,000 individuals receiving royal pensions (about half being military officers), over half drew amounts less than 600 livres, but these individuals accounted for only 14 percent of the money. At the other end of the spectrum a mere 90 individuals accounted for 9 percent of the money. As Baron de Wimpffen, an influential member of the National Assembly and himself the recipient of an 8,000-livre pension, noted in 1789, "under the same title of *Pension* are confounded the feeble compensation for a long career of privations, dangers, and suffering and the recompense that pride accords to baseness."[2]

The net balance of the pension list's two functions—providing benefits for retired or disabled officers, and dispensing royal largesse to favorites—was drawn by Wimpffen's military committee. Military pension obligations totaled 6,162,000 livres for around 10,000 officers, and 9,772,000 livres for 857 generals (many of them high aristocrats still on active duty). And this disproportion was merely the most striking part of a system that limited the resources available to the neediest veterans of the rank and file. The 25,000 to 28,000 veterans retired as *soldes* and *demi-soldes;* the residents of the Hôtel des Invalides; and the old professionals who lingered on in the "detached

companies of *invalides*" on sedentary duty were supported on a budget totaling only 6,346,000 livres, about one-third of which went to the Hôtel. As
the revolutionary legislator Dubois-Crancé observed: "Enormous pensions
demonstrate the munificence of the royal government toward the superior
officers who have held commands, while even the physical means of subsistence have been denied to their needy comrades in arms."[3] With the triumph of the Revolution in the summer of 1789, the National Assembly
could entirely eliminate the royal prerogative in this area and rationalize the
treatment of veterans from top to bottom. Henceforth under the pension
law of August 3, 1790, all retiring professional officers and soldiers of the
same rank would receive uniform compensation based on their rank and
length of service.

What about the future of the Hôtel des Invalides—that suspect monument to Louis XIV's grandeur? Despite its European-wide renown, the
institution was seething with discontent over harsh regimentation, inadequate rations, and inequities. Old-regime authoritarianism and paternalism
had papered over this discontent, but in July 1789 it exploded for all to hear.
Royal army veterans in and out of the Invalides seized the revolutionary
upheaval around them as an occasion to articulate their grievances and
demands. But the problems at the Invalides seemed so serious that the first
report of the National Assembly's military committee called not for reforms
but for closing down the institution altogether. Besides invoking fiscal arguments about the cost-effectiveness of maintaining the establishment, the
abolitionists questioned its very function and maintained that it stood in the
way of a modernized and equitable veterans policy. On the level of symbolic politics, they attacked it as an embodiment of the "despotism" and
"aristocracy" that all good patriots now opposed.[4] But Dubois-Crancé's
report calling for abolition and the pensioning-off of the present *invalides*
provoked determined opposition, which argued that both the material and
moral welfare of certain veterans was best served by this large institution.
After an acrimonious debate the Assembly rejected the report. Instead, the
law of March 24, 1791 initiated a historic policy of free choice for qualified
veterans between residence in the Hôtel and generous pensions based on
the August 1790 law—a choice that prompted about half the present complement of 3,000 *invalides* to vacate the institution almost immediately. This
principle of choice remained one cornerstone of French veterans policy
throughout the revolutionary and Napoleonic eras.

Given this new lease on life, the Hôtel des Invalides became the object
of a sweeping reorganization by the Legislative Assembly, which succeeded
the National Assembly in the fall of 1791. As finally codified in the law of

May 1792, the Hôtel des Invalides would be responsible for 4,000 veterans, at least half of whom were not expected to reside in the institution but to live outside on special pensions at the new rates, while the lower ranks of resident *invalides* would receive higher monthly pocket-money allowances. The law pointedly brought self-government to the Invalides, whose administrative council would now be elected by the residents, while surveillance of the institution was shifted from the War Ministry to the Interior Ministry and the Seine department. Further, to combat the old image of despotic control, the law introduced the new French system of justice to the precincts of the Hôtel in the form of an elected "tribunal of conciliation" to deal with disciplinary infractions. It also restructured the institution's fiscal administration, previously a classic example of arcane old-regime practices. In its architects' eyes, this comprehensive blueprint for reform would create in the Hôtel des Invalides a model commonwealth exemplifying the Revolution's liberal values.[5]

Meanwhile the prospects improved for other old-regime veterans. Those collecting minuscule pensions lobbied successfully for an across-the-board rise in their stipends, while the old regime's "detached companies of *invalides*" (the third alternative for long-serving soldiers reaching retirement age) were redeployed from isolated garrisons to the more hospitable capital of each new department. All in all by May 1792 the Assembly had completed a sweeping project of reform for the veterans of the old royal army, in which it balanced fiscal limitations with a sense of humanitarian obligation. The Assembly sifted the status quo carefully, listened to the vocal demands of different categories of veterans, maintained what seemed soundest, and modified what seemed most deficient.

War and "revolution in the Revolution," however, rendered these plans obsolete almost immediately. Designed for a relatively small-scale, peacetime, and professional military establishment, they now had to be adapted to a massive wartime mobilization of citizen-soldiers who were grafted onto the army's professional core. While never ignoring professional considerations such as the career aspirations of NCO and officer cadres, the National Convention (September 1792–October 1795) understood the democratic implications of this mobilization.[6] Preoccupied though it was with waging a life-and-death struggle on its frontiers, the Convention concerned itself with veterans and military dependents as well as draftees and soldiers at the front. Its initiatives included provision of home relief for the needy families and dependents of soldiers, and pensions for war widows whose husbands died from wounds or illness in service.[7] Above all the Convention broke new ground with its law of June 6, 1793, a response to two novel ideas: that seriously wounded soldiers deserved especially high compensation for their painful and debilitating sacrifice for the republic, and that the gap between benefits going to superior officers and to the rank and file should be narrowed. Accordingly, the new law brought an unprecedented weakening of the claims of rank in determining veterans benefits.

Under the law of June 6, 1793, seriously wounded privates and NCOs (those who lost a limb, or the use of a limb, or who suffered other incapacitating wounds) were mustered out as honorary sublieutenants and either pensioned at 600 livres annually (raised a few months later to 800 to compensate for inflation), or else admitted to the Invalides as lieutenants. Double amputees and the blind were made honorary captains and granted pensions in amounts heretofore reserved for generals.[8] Compared to the reforms of 1790 to 1792—which in many respects implemented plans conceived but obstructed under the old regime—this was a veritable revolution in status and in the allocation of the state's resources. Like the sans-culottes from the ranks of master artisans and shopkeepers who dominated some of the clubs and revolutionary committees of 1793, the wounded honorary lieutenant was a new man of the Revolution.

And unlike some of the Revolution's most utopian plans, this law was applied integrally. Pension lists, surviving copies of certificates of "national recompense," and admissions registers of the renamed Maison Nationale des Militaires Invalides all testify to the varied military origins of France's disabled revolutionary veterans: regulars of the line army, volunteers of 1792, and draftees of 1793–94. In their detail these sources not only document the generous levels of compensation pledged by a grateful republic, but they evoke the severity of the trauma for the wounded men lucky enough to survive combat.[9] Amputees were the most common type of disabled revolutionary veteran simply because the standard medical technique of that era called for amputating wounded hands, arms, or legs as the only feasible means of saving lives from lethal infection and gangrene.

The war dragged on, however, and new applicants for veterans benefits eventually overwhelmed the War Ministry. By February 1797, while the extensive paperwork for over 10,000 pensions had been completed, about 25,000 applications were still pending, these veterans collecting in the meanwhile a minimal daily subsistence allowance (solde provisoire). More important, veterans suffered disastrously from the hyperinflation and monetary collapse that beset the republic between 1795 and 1797. Agonizing concern by both the Directory and the legislature would be unavailing until the collapsing paper currency could be stabilized and converted back to hard money. There was scarcely any point in paying veterans with worthless *assignats* or *mandats* (the successive paper currencies of the revolutionary regime). As the municipality of Cambrai in northern France wrote in March 1797: "The disabled soldiers have received no payment whatsoever for six months. We watch with anguish as these men who have sacrificed everything for the defense of the fatherland are reduced to the most dreadful indigence."[10]

The War Ministry shared this frustration. Frantic over its inability to assure "a comforting security and honorable subsistence" to the veterans, to acquit the republic's "sacred debt," the ministry considered trying a system in which the responsibility would be assumed directly by each veteran's community as long as the state's "circumstantial insufficiency" lasted. Under this abortive plan, every needy veteran who wished to do so could temporarily turn over his title to a veterans pension or *solde provisoire* to the local authorities where he had settled. In exchange the commune would provide him with a daily ration of one-and-a-half livres of bread and a half livre of meat. This would be financed by assessing "the wealthy individuals of the commune."[11]

This desperate situation was obviously temporary, and once the national currency was stabilized veterans benefits could be salvaged from the wreckage. A long debate in the directorial legislature ensued, however, in which a retreat from egalitarian values occurred parallel to a renewed emphasis on professional considerations within the armed forces. In the resultant comprehensive veterans law of September 1799 wounded veterans lost ground in two ways compared to their generous treatment under the law of June 1793. First, the basic scales for most categories of pensions were lowered, beyond readjustments for previous inflation; second, the determination of pensions would henceforth depend not only on the seriousness of wounds, but on rank and length of service. Rank again became the prime determinant of recompense and—outside of the Hôtel des Invalides—there would be no more disabled honorary lieutenants.[12]

The Hôtel des Invalides weathered the same cycle of changes. Obviously all-out war mobilization would transform the size and profile of its population completely. While the institution continued to serve as a refuge for the aged and destitute soldiers who had retired earlier from the royal army, it was soon flooded with young common soldiers wounded in the revolutionary wars, most of whom held the new rank of (honorary) lieutenant.[13]

The figures in table 6 reflect the two types of veterans who sought sanctuary in the Invalides, with 75 to 80 percent of the lieutenants in the cohort of 1798 being young disabled privates or NCOs of the revolutionary armies[14]—men like Martin Herzoque of Rhinefeld in Alsace. Twenty-six years old at the time of his admission to the Invalides as an honorary lieutenant, Herzoque had been a chasseur in the first battalion of the Hautes-Alpes when he was seriously wounded at the siege of Toulon in 1793 by a bullet that traversed his jaws, partially severing his tongue and leaving him deaf and dumb. Or Alexandre Moulin, a 26-year-old volunteer in the first battalion of the Nord who was wounded in November 1792 after only a few months of service, "his left hand destroyed by artillery fire at Varneton."[15]

The "second revolution" had other dramatic consequences at the Invalides. To begin with, frenetic politicization in Paris destroyed the fragile experiment in self-government inaugurated by the Legislative Assembly in 1792. Accused, paradoxically, of not republicanizing the institution rapidly enough, the council of elected *invalides* was badgered by a handful of critics inside, attacked by Jacobins and Cordeliers on the outside, and ultimately replaced in 1794 by a revolutionary agency appointed by the Committee of Public Safety for the duration of the emergency.[16] This typical scenario of the Year II (1793–94) was in fact only half the story, however. The other, positive half arose in the same context and from the same source: the intervention of radical Jacobins and Montagnard deputies in the Convention. For at the same time that it suppressed the elected council of *invalides,* the Committee of Public Safety also ordered equal food service for all *invalides (égalité des tables),* thereby obliterating the most significant distinction of rank, apart from pocket-money allowance, lodging assignments, and fuel allotments.[17]

Then, in perhaps the most far-reaching of all measures, the committee established a school for veterans at the Invalides. Under the guidance of its dedicated director, Nicholas Brard, this school took on several functions: to

TABLE 6.   Composition of the Hôtel des Invalides by Rank before and after the Revolutionary Influx

	February 1793	January 1798
Officier supérieur	18 (1%)	133 (3%)
Capitain	89 (6%)	600 (12%)
Lieutenant	139 (9%)	1,642 (33%)
Maréchal des logis	70 (5%)	283 (6%)
Sous–officier	186 (12%)	342 (7%)
Soldat	993 (66%)	2,014 (39%)
Total	1,495	5,014

teach illiterate veterans to read and write; to improve the skills of veterans in order to qualify them for preferential employment as government clerks or teachers; to offer the "consolation" of study to aged veterans who had no ulterior use for education; and to teach right-handed amputees to write with their left hands. Brard's school—the only form of rehabilitation offered to veterans apart from simple prosthetic devices—flourished for several years until it was suppressed by the Consulate in favor of a school for war orphans.[18]

The ebb and flow of the Revolution registered in still other ways at the Hôtel des Invalides. The devastating inflation that destroyed the purchasing power of veterans pensions increased the demand for admission to the Invalides. But once there, veterans found that *égalité des tables* had turned into a temporary equality of privation, while their once-generous pocket-money allowances were virtually worthless by 1796. Still, the institution offered a buffer of security lacking on the outside. At a time when other hospitals and institutions experienced sharply rising mortality amid a severe subsistence crises, the Invalides had no appreciable rise in its death rate.[19]

Moreover, only at the Hôtel des Invalides were veterans politically active as a group during the Revolution. This did not occur in the Year II (1793–94), when there were as yet relatively few revolutionary veterans on the scene, for the buildup was just beginning at the time of Robespierre's fall in July 1794. But by 1798—when the Directory had restored an element of self-government to the Invalides—a veterans movement did develop. It emanated from a nucleus of veterans who had links with civilian Neo-Jacobins and were popular among their comrades, several being elected by the residents to the newly reconstituted administrative council. The Directory, intensely hostile to any stirring of Jacobinism, plausibly linked agitation within the institution against commander Berruyer and other officials with Neo-Jacobin dissidence in the capital. It all came to a head when the government—for legitimate reasons, perhaps, but in a blatantly arbitrary and discriminatory manner—prepared to transfer many of the revolutionary veterans out of Paris to an inadequate and extremely unappealing annex at Versailles.

Taking their stand on the law of June 6, 1793, the dissidents attacked this policy as a grievous derogation from the republic's pledges. The veterans succeeded in having one of their number—an amputee of the legendary battle of Jemappes, honorary lieutenant Jean Gomegéon—chosen for the Parisian legislative deputation in the elections of 1798. But the Directory shortly annulled the entire slate of Parisian deputies (along with those of about 30 other departments) in one of its periodic resorts to arbitrary measures against political opponents. As far as veterans were concerned, the clock had run out on the republic's toleration for political activism. The next year the Directory even tried to prevent the participation of the *invalides* in the annual elections altogether through various pretexts. Likewise it purged and reorganized the Invalides council to assure that its top administrators would henceforth control that body completely. Perhaps it was no coincidence that these callously repressive measures by the Directory came at about the same time that the legislature formally scrapped the law of June 6, 1793, and adopted the new veterans pension law that restored traditional hierarchies of compensation according to rank.[20]

II

Napoleon's ascendancy had surprisingly mixed results in the area of veterans policy. To his credit First Consul Bonaparte personally ordered a crash program to process the enormous backlog of applicants for pensions.[21] He followed this by asking counselor of state J.-G. Lacueé (author of the first reform plan of 1792) to inspect the Hôtel des Invalides and also to provide a comprehensive report on the entire population of pensioned veterans as of 1801, which he referred to, rather curiously, as the *armée morte* (literally, the dead army). Lacueé concluded that they numbered about 45,000 post-1792 veterans plus 6,500 *invalides;* that the *armée morte* was too costly, its benefits allocated too liberally. Another revision of the pension laws followed in which the rates of compensation were again ratcheted down, proportionately more so at the lower ranks. In addition, a narrower and more skeptical approach in assessing the seriousness of disabilities was introduced with a resultant diminution in both eligibility and in the level of pensions granted.[22] For example, a private with two years of service and two campaigns whose wound lost him the use of a limb would have received 180 livres in 1800, but under the new law of 1803 he received only 109 livres a year. Even without comparison to the long-gone egalitarian treatment of wounded soldiers under the Convention's law of June 1793, erosion occurred under Napoleon relative to the original reform of 1791–92. Thus if we take the ratio of the average private's pension to the average captain's pension, we find that under the law of 1792 the proportion was about 28 percent (227 livres to 800 livres). With the pensions paid out under Napoleon the proportion dropped to 19 percent in 1804 (200 livres to 1,057 livres), and to 17.6 percent by 1811 (178 livres to 1,011 livres). The "sacred debt" to veterans was still being honored, but in a much more grudging and paltry fashion for the rank and file. Even General Serrurier, Napoleon's handpicked governor of the Hôtel des Invalides, regarded prevailing pension rates for the lower ranks as "too niggardly," and thereby explained why even married veterans now sought to reside in the confining institutional atmosphere of the Invalides.[23]

Discretionary allocations reminiscent of the old regime also reappeared under Napoleon. With enormous rewards and endowments being granted to his marshals and favorite generals, the very line between veterans and active officers was blurred as it had been under the Bourbons. Occasionally, on the other hand, this same discretionary prerogative could work to the rank and file's advantage. Thus, with calculated éclat, Napoleon decided to celebrate his remarriage in 1810 by offering 6,000 dowries of 600 francs each to war veterans who would join him in a march to the altar of matrimony in towns and cantons all over France on the day of the imperial wedding. The response was enthusiastic, and despite the short interval of several weeks to select these veterans in local communities, over 4,000 weddings took place. A six-month delay in actually paying the money, however, produced a flood of agonized letters from the intended beneficiaries complaining of hardship, debt, and even lawsuits over unpaid bills.[24] The conclusion follows from this episode that while veterans' pensions helped meet the minimal expenses of subsistence, they did not generally suffice for needy veterans at the lower ranks to establish new households of their own, whereas this lump sum of 600 additional francs enabled them to do so.

Like any needy rural Frenchman, most veterans would have relished a substantial plot of land in the countryside. The notion of land as a proper recompense for war veterans surfaced during the egalitarian fervor of 1793–94 and after, but was never acted upon until Napoleon's expansionist policies opened up a new possibility. Perhaps reviving a Roman precedent, Napoleon proposed in 1803 to settle disabled French veterans in the annexed provinces of Germany and Italy in "veterans camps" comprising individual farms under the paternalistic scrutiny of a military ambiance. Coveting the land but rejecting the regimentation, the 400 veterans in the first two camps caused such contention that Napoleon sourly abandoned plans for additional camps, which he originally intended to accommodate 4,000 emigrating veterans. While his officers tried to convert these veterans back to a quasi-military life, the ex-soldiers clung to their rights and entitlements as citizens and ultimately undermined Napoleon's scheme. The emperor's notion of a quasi-military landed community (a bizarre variant in the annals of utopian social thought) aborted, but for the 400 disabled veterans who actually settled in the first two camps and more or less threw off military tutelage, the experiment was a boon. In Alexandria (Italy) and

Juliers (near Cologne) each veteran controlled his own substantial plot of land, which he could farm directly or lease out, and which would have been heritable, unlike his pension, had the Napoleonic empire endured.[25]

Having abandoned his plan for additional "veterans camps," Napoleon certainly did not abandon the Hôtel des Invalides, which could more readily be made to conform to military and paternalist norms. Under the Consulate the institution's future was secured when Napoleon ordered the establishment of two substantial annexes in Louvain and Avignon, effectively increasing its capacity by 50 percent. The transfer (or purge) of dissident veterans to Versailles in 1798 had already restored a traditional kind of order at the Hôtel in Paris, and thereafter Napoleon progressively placed his personal stamp on its ambiance. The commander once again took the title of governor, military routines were strengthened, religious worship restored. But despite the unconcealed distaste of Napoleon for the preceding decade of innovation, the legacy of 1793 had taken deep root. Indeed the popularity of *égalité des tables* worked against any attempt to end it by returning the lower ranks to a less generous regimen. Similarly, the status of the amputee as an honorary lieutenant was by now so ingrained (and cost so little relatively speaking) that it lingered on at the Invalides long after it had ceased to exist outside.[26]

In the full flush of imperial pretensions, however, Napoleon finally ordered an all-out transformation of the Invalides's ambiance to replicate the grandeur of Louis XIV's days. This involved physical renovation (more for display than for the residents' comfort); an endowment and administrative structure that would distinguish the institution regally; the end of *égalité des tables* by upgrading the menu and table service for officers; and the creation of distinctions in treatment (food, clothing, insignias, lodging) between commissioned officers and honorary officers—effectively downgrading the latter. Material gains from the revolutionary period for the rank and file remained, but by systematically elevating the status and material benefits of regular officers, the imperial regime extinguished the last echo of the egalitarian model.[27]

III

Without veterans benefits, disabled and retired soldiers would have swollen the ranks of France's indigent. Undoubtedly, however, they would have been classed among the "deserving poor," for their palpable need resulted from service to the fatherland rather than their own shortcomings—the presumed cause of poverty in eighteenth-century France in most contemporary thinking. With his moral claim to assistance—with his recompense declared a "sacred debt" by the republic of 1792 and every subsequent regime—the French war veteran was by far the state's most favored ward, and veterans policy was likely to form the outer limit of the state's social welfare commitments.

Initially the performance of the revolutionary state on this social welfare frontier was impressive and effective. The Hôtel des Invalides, after reforms began in 1792, is only the most obvious instance, but it bears underlining since it could be taken as a model public institution. Its nutritional regimen, for example, provided far more than the average Frenchman consumed, and even reflected the concept of a balanced diet that included meat and vegetables as well as wholesome, plentiful bread. Moreover it showed both realism and compassion in providing a substantial wine ration, available in equal measure to *invalides* of all ranks after 1793. The infirmary was probably as good a clinic as existed in that era and did not seem to have the aura of a charnel house that pervaded other hospitals. The dormitories for the rank and file were probably more salubrious and comfortable than the typical rural habitation or the crowded working-class lodging houses of large cities. Finally, the pocket-money allowance (raised from fifteen sous a month for privates before the Revolution to five livres a month in 1792) constituted an unprecedented element of liberality toward an institution's residents.

French veterans policy after 1792 was also a model of social welfare because it offered a real choice between institutional and independent assistance—between the Hôtel des Invalides and a pension. In fact most veterans far preferred to take their pensions and return to their own communities where (if they were able) they might marry, raise children, and find work suitable to their disabilities. But only after the reforms of 1790 and 1792 did pensions for the first time even begin to reach adequate subsistence levels at the lower ranks, and beginning in 1793 those most in need generally received relatively substantial amounts.

Having a choice of a pension or an institutional refuge served both the older retired veterans and the newly wounded ones. When an old royal veteran who had retired in the 1770s or 1780s could no longer care for himself, he was able—even at the height of the revolutionary mobilization—to gain admission to the Invalides. There he likely died 10 or more years later, totally bereft of worldly possessions, as poor as the poorest of Frenchmen. Analysis of the inventories of property left behind by 577 deceased *invalides* between 1799 and 1801 (only 9 percent of whom were younger than 50 when they died), shows that 82 percent left "estates" worth only 10 livres or less. Indeed 89 *invalides* had no personal property at all beyond their uniforms; 153 had possessions valued at less than one livre, while 112 were scarcely better off with property worth between one and two livres—mostly worn articles of extra clothing.[28] But in the Hôtel des Invalides such men received about 700 livres worth of provisions and services annually. They could finish their days with a measure of material security, comradeship, and personal dignity.

For the young disabled veteran even with family back home, the choice of pension or institution was helpful as well. The bulk of the rank and file were doubtless "devoid of resources," as the national Commission on Public Assistance believed in 1794, and depended on their pensions or the Invalides for sustenance. The Hôtel was undoubtedly useful as a way station for nursing the traumas of wounds and amputations. In this respect Brard's school for veterans was perhaps the Revolution's most useful innovation, almost prefiguring a concept of rehabilitation otherwise unknown.

The goal of social control is often seen as the obverse of social welfare policy. As Pierre Goubert puts it in his authoritative discussion of the old regime, there was a tendency for the impressive charitable institutions of that era to evolve into "correctional institutions." More sweepingly, Michel Foucault situated schools, hospitals, almshouses, orphanages, and prisons along with military camps as outcroppings of the "disciplined society, the society of generalized surveillance."[29] In certain respects French provisions for veterans conformed to this pattern, though in others they contradict it or stand as exceptions. Of course, the military is by definition a disciplined society in view of its primary function, and in the old regime the norm of brutal discipline was usually packaged in a rhetoric of paternalism. For veterans, when the discipline that combat demanded could no longer be invoked as a constraint, paternalism remained as a rationale for continued surveillance.

In the debate on the Invalides in 1790 this paternalism was still being expressed in the view that old-time royal soldiers could not make it on their own. If given pensions they would squander them improvidently and be reduced to pitiful or dangerous circumstances. Better to have them under the caring eye of an institution (so the argument went) than left to their own devices. Beneath this argument lay a traditional image of soldiers and ex-soldiers as antisocial types, if not potential brigands. This attitude could scarcely prevail after 1792 when the French nation called its citizens to arms, when citizens became soldiers and soldiers were citizens. But paternalism did linger on in various guises and revived strongly, as one would expect, under Napoleon. The successful opposition of Goulhot (a key veterans bureau functionary) to a lending bank for veterans because they would surely squander such loans of capital;[30] the opinion of the Invalides's governor urging stringent control over residents who left the institution and later reapplied for admission (presumably after spending their pension money); and Captain Marie's attitude toward the men under his command at the Juliers veterans camp in Germany all recall a type of paternalism commonplace under the old regime. Such thinking reflected assumptions that eighteenth-century elites were likely to make about the laboring poor in general: to pay high wages was to encourage slacking and absenteeism; to pay adequate relief allotments was to encourage idleness and vice.

But in the way it allocated veterans and war widows pensions, the Jacobin National Convention for once put this kind of thinking behind it and embraced a straightforward notion of entitlement and recompense—a breakthrough of sorts toward a new mind-set. The government preferred to steer veterans back home to their communities, where they would be completely free to dispose of their pensions as they saw fit. Indeed a veteran's pension was virtually inviolable. It could not be seized for debt, nor did the government ever try to deprive a dissident veteran of his pension. The only exception was where the ministry might attach a portion of a veteran's pension if he was proven to have abandoned the upkeep of his wife and children. Otherwise pensions were granted without strings attached and were not designed to promote regimentation or unusual surveillance. Veterans were free to move anywhere as long as they registered with the authorities, essentially a requirement for all Frenchmen, and in any case necessary for the disbursement of quarterly pension payments. Only veterans who registered elsewhere but in fact resided in Paris aroused attention under the empire.[31]

Paris was always a special case, and the Hôtel des Invalides was an obvious instrument of social control from the year of its founding under Louis XIV. The Jacobin regime was second to none in subjecting the *invalides* to republican proselytizing and symbolic politics. There was even pressure from the radical Cordeliers Club for a kind of indoctrination of old royal veterans to convert them heart-and-mind to republicanism—an impulse that was fortunately deflected into more constructive channels such as Brard's school.[32] Ironically, however, within a few years the institution was proving to be a notable source of dissidence rather than a convenient instrument of control. By clustering revolutionary veterans together, the Invalides eventually created a critical mass, helped to stimulate a new collective consciousness, and facilitated political activism under the Directory regime. Fervently embracing the ideals of republicanism, dissident *invalides* chal-

lenged the appointed commander and his staff over the institution's governance, attempted to influence the outcome of annual elections in their district, and even (in the government's view) threatened to "infect" regular
troops garrisoned in Paris. Astonishingly, for a few months in 1798 dissident
veterans became *the* police problem in the capital for both the civil authorities and military police. The Directory responded by transferring (or purg-
ing) dissidents to annexes outside of Paris, and by tightening the institution's
administration, eliminating meaningful self-government for the second and
last time. Thereafter the Hôtel des Invalides resembled other public institutions in the passivity of its residents, particularly after Napoleon restored a
hierarchical military regimen. Paternalism again became the norm.

The structures that the reformers of 1791 and the Jacobins of 1793 had
created in the area of veterans benefits briefly reached extraordinary heights,
but were soon toppled by a terrible jolt. The trauma struck in 1795–97
when France's paper money became virtually worthless. Veterans on pension or awaiting pensions on *solde provisoire* temporarily lost almost everything; those at the Hôtel des Invalides were more insulated from deprivation
but likewise suffered a drastic erosion of their living standard. The monetary
collapse created a totally unexpected situation, and if veterans suffered
severely in those years it is obvious that for other categories of the poor and
dependent it was a catastrophe. Veterans benefits were eventually salvaged
out of this debacle, and they remained impressive compared to other categories of public assistance in France or, as seems likely, veterans benefits
elsewhere. But the level of provision diminished substantially for those most
in need. That remarkable creation of 1793—the disabled common soldier
elevated to the status and recompense of an honorary lieutenant—disappeared in the revised laws. In the end, the republic's "sacred debt" was
devalued not simply by monetary catastrophe but by policy—by the wan-
ing of egalitarian attitudes, the reassertion of military professionalism and
hierarchy, and the revival of a condescending paternalism. Veterans benefits
remained the frontier of social welfare in France, but the brief and remarkable transformation of that frontier receded.

NOTES

This paper is adapted from my book *The French Veteran from the Revolution to the Restoration* (Chapel Hill, 1979). Since the audience for that volume consisted mainly of people
interested in the French Revolution or the history of the French army in the revolutionary-Napoleonic era, publication of the paper in the present collection gives me a
welcome opportunity to reach a new group of readers. The book, of course, provides

much greater detail and documentation on the matters discussed here, as well as a much fuller consideration of the experience of the veterans themselves.

1. A. Corvisier, *L'Armée française de la fin du XVIIᵉ siècle au ministère de Choiseul: Le soldat*, 2 vols. (Paris, 1964), 2:791–816, 901–47. See also Jean-Pierre Bois, *Les Anciens Soldats dans la société française au XVIIIe siècle* (Paris, 1980).

2. *Etat nominatif des pensions sur le Trésor royal, imprimé par ordre de l'Assemblée Nationale en 1789*, 4 vols. (Paris, 1790). A corrected version of this crucial document is reprinted in volumes 13 through 15 of the *Archives parlementaires*. Baron F. de Wimpffen, *Discours sur les pensions militaires prononcé le 31 Décembre 1789* (Paris, 1789); also Archives de la Guerre, Vincennes (hereafter AG) Yᵃ 77: Mémoire historique sur les pensions.

3. Wimpffen, *Rapport du Comité militaire . . . du 3 Juillet 1790* (Paris), 11–12; Dubois-Crancé, *Deuxième rapport du comité militaire sur les Invalides . . . Septembre 1791* (Paris), 7–9.

4. The archives of the Hôtel des Invalides (hereafter FHI) are now located at the Chateau de Vincennes. Key documents on the institution before the revolutionary transformation include FHI 96 (Conseil d'administration): Mémoire sur l'hôtel envoyé au Ministre le 29 Août 1791; FHI carton "Généralités: Rapport Général—Invalides," by a royal commission appointed to investigate the institution in Sept. 1789; AG Yᵃ 115: War ministry correspondence on the Invalides, 1784; A. Tournon, *Etat historique et critique des petits abus, des grands pensions et des jolies erreurs de Mm. les administrateurs de l'Hôtel des Invalides* (Paris 1790). The debate may be traced in *Archives parlementaires*, vol. 24. For lavish illustrations and a thorough bibliography on the Invalides see *Les Invalides: Trois siècles d'histoire* (Paris, 1974).

5. J. G. Lacuée, *Rapport fait à l'Assemblée Nationale au nom du comité militaire relatif aux Invalides . . . 17 Décembre 1791*. The final amended text of this landmark legislation, which runs to 53 pages, is *Loi Relative au Ci-devant Hôtel des Invalides, conservé sous la dénomination de l'Hôtel National des Militaires Invalides: 16 Mai 1792* in Archives Nationales (hereafter AN) AD VI 65. See also AN D XV 6: dossier 104, pièce 9: Observations présentées à l'assemblée nationale par les sous-officiers et soldats invalides pensionnés retirés dans le département de Paris, sur le Rapport fait à l'assemblée par le comité militaire.

6. On the republic's army as a democratic institution see Jean-Paul Bertaud, *The Army of the French Revolution*, trans. R. R. Palmer (Princeton, 1988); and Alan Forrest, *Soldiers of the French Revolution* (Durham, N.C., 1990).

7. For home-relief legislation, which was introduced as early as November 1792, see *Journal Militaire*, 1793, 294–97; an II (1), 413–15 and 417–26. On widow's pensions, I. Woloch, "War-Widows Pensions: Social Policy in Revolutionary and Napoleonic France," *Societas* 6 (1976): 235–54.

8. The text is in *Archives parlementaires*, 66:105ff.

9. See FHI, Archives administratives, carton 2: Pensions représentatives de l'Hôtel des Invalides 1793–94; AG Xˢ 212: Etats de pensions.

10. AN AF III 148a: Mémoire, brumaire IV–pluviôse V; AN F9 53a: Notes remises au Ministre. de l'Intérieur par les administrateurs municipales de Cambrai.

11. AN AF III 159: Rapport au Directoire, 16 messidor V. See also *Conseil des Cinq Cents: Motion d'ordre de Jourdan . . . 28 fructidor V* (Impr. Nationale).

12. AN AF IV 1159: Analyse des lois relatives aux pensions militaires, 25 Décembre 1790–28 fructidor an 7; *Bulletin des Lois*, 2ᵉᵐᵉ série, no. 310, law of 28 fructidor VII.

The debate over this issue (more revealing than the text of the law itself) can be reconstructed from about twenty published speeches and committee reports.

13. FHI 61: Table d'admissions, Ans III-VIII, and the more detailed alphabetical Registres des Invalides, FHI 211–34.

14. AN AD VI 65: *Adresse des militaires invalides à la Convention . . . 24 Février 1793* (Impr. Nationale); AN AF III 148a: Mémoire sur l'administration du département de la guerre, pluviôse an V; AN AF III 472: tableau annuel, pluviôse an VI.

15. These examples come from FHI 50: Registre matricule, lieutenants.

16. Numerous petitions, denunciations and reports, from which this episode may be reconstructed, are preserved in FHI carton "Généralités." For the attack see especially *Club des Cordeliers: Rapport sur l'organisation de la Maison nationale des Invalides, 4 Octobre 1793,* which is bound together with *Rapport de la Commission nommée par le directoire du département de Paris, fait le 12 brumaire II pour vérifier les différentes dénonciations* (Paris). For the suppression of the council see AN AF II 284, pl. 2366; and A. Aulard, ed., *La Société des Jacobins: recueil de documents pour l'histoire du club des Jacobins de Paris* (6 vols. Paris, 1897), 5:674–75, and 6:97–98, 142.

17. FHI 97: 9 and 15 floréal an II; FHI 152: Vivres.

18. Aulard, *Société des Jacobins,* 6:100; A. Aulard, ed., *Receuil des Actes du Comité de Salut Public,* 13:311, 341:17–18 floréal An II; AN F15 2653: Comité des secours, 22 frimaire an III; AN AF III 167, dossier pluviôse VII; AN AD VIII 28 for printed proceedings of the school's prize ceremonies in the years VI and VII.

19. On the deterioration of food service see AN F15* 10 and 11, an III, and AN AF II* 41 (Comité des secours), an III. On pocket-money allowances see FHI, Archives administratives, carton 5: *menus besoins,* ans IV–V. On death rates, FHI 136–37: Registres des décès.

20. For this extremely interesting episode and its aftermath see *The French Veteran,* chap. 6: "From Heroes to Dissidents." A collection of dissident pamphlets may be found in the Bibliothèque Historique de la Ville de Paris, no. 8486; for police reports see AN F7 3688/14 and AN AF III 167.

21. AG X^s 218.

22. Again my evaluation of this change is not based merely on the text of the law of 8 floréal an XI, but on the tenor of the discussion surrounding it in governmental circles, e.g., AN AF IV 1075: Conseil d'Etat: Rapport sur l'Armée morte aux Consuls par Lacuée, and AG X^s 218: Délibérations du Conseil d'Etat, 13 prairial XI.

23. FHI, Archives administratives, carton "Dispositions réglementaires": Serrurier to War Ministry, 3 July 1806, and AG X^s 192: letters of June 1810.

24. These moving letters are collected in AN F9 54b, along with prefectorial correspondence.

25. The inner history of the Juliers veterans camp near Cologne may be reconstructed from AG X^n 1, 3, and 4: Vétérans.

26. See *The French Veteran,* chap. 9: "The Invalides under Napoleon."

27. On the antiegalitarian sentiment see AG X^s 192 and AN AF IV 1153. Napoleon's call for a restoration to ancient grandeur is contained in a memo in his own hand in AN 138 AP 167, Daru Papers. The reorganization was announced in a published decree dated March 25, 1811. The antiegalitarian spirit in which the changes were carried out is apparent in FHI 109: Conseil d'administration.

28. FHI 341: Inventaire des effets délaissés.

29. Pierre Goubert, *L'Ancien Régime, II: Les Pouvoirs* (Paris, 1973), 101; M. Foucault, *Discipline and Punish: The Birth of the Prison,* trans. Alan Sheridan-Smith (New York, 1977).

30. AG X^s 218, fol. 102: Rapport fait au Ministre le 27 Mai 1808.

31. Ibid., *état* for the second quarter of 1811, noting that a total of 6,747 francs was being withheld. On surveillance of nonregistered veterans in Paris: AN AF IV 1160, February 19, 1812.

32. *Club des Cordeliers,* 68.

Robert I. Goler and Michael G. Rhode

From Individual Trauma to National Policy: Tracking the Uses of Civil War Veteran Medical Records

From the stump of the arm, the amputated hand,
I undo the clotted lint, remove the slough, wash off the matter and blood,
Back on his pillow the soldier bends with curv'd neck and side-falling head,
His eyes are closed, his face is pale, he dares not look on the bloody stump,
And has not yet looked on it.
> —Walt Whitman, "The Wound-Dresser"

Let Grover talk against the tariff tariff tariff
  And pensions too.
We'll give the workingman his due
  And pension the boys who wore blue.
> —Republican party campaign song, 1888

On September 19, 1998, 133 years after Lee's surrender at Appomattox one of three surviving widows of Civil War veterans died in Denver at the age of 97. Daisy Anderson met her husband-to-be when he was 79 years old: "I wanted a home," she recalled shortly before her death. "I didn't have anything. I didn't have but one dress. We ate standing up at the table." She was 21 years old. Robert Hall Anderson (1843–1930) had been born a slave and ran away to join the Union army and, while he never saw Civil War action, he served in the "Buffalo Soldiers" on the western frontier before marrying Daisy in 1922. Eight years later her husband died in a car crash, and for over 50 years Mrs. Anderson continued to receive pension benefits. The extraordinary length of the federal government's obligation to Mrs. Anderson underscores the extent to which the relations between the individual and the government were changed by the Civil War.[1]

This essay emphasizes the study and interpretation of a relatively unknown collection of materials—Civil War medical records, documentary photographs, and associated pension files—that point to the emergence of the relationship between the citizen and the nation-state in the United

States during the latter decades of the nineteenth century.[2] In contrast to the enormous literature on the Civil War—its causes, battles, leaders, equipment—and Reconstruction, scholarly investigation and popular interest in its veterans have been sparse.[3] This situation is beginning to change.[4] We believe that the records of the Pension and Records Department, in combination with the artifactual and photographic documentation at the Army Medical Museum, provide important and often overlooked contemporary evidence of the Civil War veteran experience. In addition to their value as documents of Civil War medicine, these records document the federal government's early attempts to undertake scientific research through the process of long-term longitudinal examination.

These materials also suggest new ways to explore the study of national memory and memorialization.[5] Where most scholars have woven arguments from parades and diaries, we have turned to bones and medical files. Our thesis is that the creation of a bureaucracy to compile, manage, and analyze medical records of Civil War veterans, augmented with the special visual components of innovative photographic techniques, led to an expanded federal recognition of public obligations to veterans. Furthermore, the public exhibition of Civil War soldiers' bones, tissues, and photographs at the Army Medical Museum in Washington, D.C., helped to shape a consciousness of reconciliation and civic purpose that hastened the formation of a national memory. It is possible to consider this essay as the beginnings of a forensic examination of memory.[6]

Medical Treatment and Documentation

The number of casualties and the scope of medical treatment in military conflicts was never so great as it was in the American Civil War. On the Union side alone, over 7 million cases of disease were treated and over 250,000 wounds were examined.[7] The need to study these wounds emerged from the unexpected violence of the Civil War, and the results of new technologies such as the minié ball, a conical bullet whose force and velocity dramatically changed the nature of gunshot wounds. Most notable were the 30,000 amputations where quick resolution of a shattered limb was essential if the soldier was to survive under the rough conditions of battlefield surgery. The majority of these procedures were of fingers or the hand; most operations were over within two minutes, including the time needed to close off arteries and prepare a covering skin flap. Large numbers of shoulder, elbow, knee, and hip amputations were performed with varying rates of fatality.[8]

The mortality figures for these amputations were tragically high. Mary Gillett has calculated that just one out of six (17 percent) of those with hip joint operations survived; the numbers for knee (just under one out of two, or 50 percent) and for lower arm amputations (four out of five, or 80 percent) were significantly better.[9] The incidence of medical complications is not surprising given the surgical conditions and the limited awareness of modern sanitary methods. The germ theory of disease was not to gain widespread acceptance until Robert Koch's experiments in the 1870s.

At the onset of the Civil War, medical authorities called for a systematic documentation of the battlefield injuries. Attempts at this scientific approach to documenting battlefield medical conditions had been attempted by both the French and British during the Crimean War, but both efforts had failed to follow postoperative conditions.[10] To remedy this deficiency in the scientific method, army doctors were enlisted to gather specimens to be sent to a central repository, the newly created Army Medical Museum, for preservation and future study. The army developed several overlapping means of compiling information, the first of which were the field notes of surgeons from their surgical tents.

Record keeping was an integral part of the Medical Department's efforts. Detailed records were compiled when possible in the field and were filed in Washington with the Surgeon General's Office for future reference.[11] Considering the difficult conditions under which these records were created and transcribed, it is not surprising that the methods of collecting information underwent various reforms during the war. Initial medical records, for example, listed gunshot wounds without accompanying information such as part of the body wounded or results of surgery. Patients also were being counted as new cases each time they were transferred from hospital to hospital. In late 1863, new forms, reports, and registers were designed by a special board of medical officers and included registers that were given to officers to use in the field. Two large ledgers, one for information on the sick and wounded and another for surgical operations, were used in hospitals with new quarterly report forms. These records frequently were supplemented by the medical entries from the attending surgeon and, in the case of amputation or excision, the severed limb was to be forwarded to the Army Medical Museum for study. Based partially on analysis of these records, disabled veterans were entitled to up to eight dollars a month and also had the option of being fitted for prosthetic devices.[12]

The effort to assemble a collection for medical research quickly took shape. Using the centralized bureaucratic methods of the army, Surgeon General William Hammond ordered the museum's curator, John Brinton, to collect specimens that had already been saved in military hospitals by interested surgeons for their own use. These specimens comprised limbs that had been severed, as well as various internal organs and tissues from surgical procedures. "Should any officer of the Army decline or neglect to furnish such preparations for the Museum," Hammond declared to Brinton, "you will report the name of such officer to this office."[13] The collecting project moved quickly, with Brinton writing to doctors at hospitals throughout the country and traveling the eastern battlefields, meeting surgeons and collecting specimens. Brinton documented this project noting that after removal from the patient the specimens would be cleaned, tagged, and then "would be packed away in a keg, containing alcohol, whiskey, or sometimes salt and water," until the keg was full and shipped to Washington. At the museum the specimens would undergo final preparation and would be organized

> so that they could take their place upon the shelves. The memoranda or histories of these specimens would in the meantime have been forwarded to the Surgeon-General's Office, and after having been fitted to objects and their truthfulness assured, would be entered in the books of *Histories of Specimens*.[14]

Within the first few months, 7,000 specimens were gathered in Washington, and, over time, the collection of amputated limbs and shrapnel expanded to include medical equipment, photographs, and weapons. As a result, for the first time in recorded history, a large body of scientific specimens from military battlefields was assembled complete with accompanying documentation.

In addition to the documentary and physical evidence of battlefield amputations, the museum initiated procedures to develop photographic records of specimens and of patients, including long-term follow-up documentation of postoperative veterans. Selected images of medical anomalies had been distributed in the antebellum years between physicians and medical societies, but the Civil War provided the first large-scale conflict to record medically significant numbers of injuries. A contributor to the *Photographic Journal* on the eve of the American Civil War observed that "the day is not far hence when the museum of every medical school will be furnished with photographic illustrations of the terribly diversified forms of disease [that] will not depend on the lively imagination of the lithograph."[15] With the founding of the Army Medical Museum at Washington in 1862, this new approach found a welcome home, and, indeed, the museum can be seen as the first institution to effectively combine medical photography with military conflict. The result was a body of images depicting the terrible cost of war in harsh, graphic realism. "Showing what was more difficult to see and acknowledge than the grisly remains of corpses soon transfigured into stone monuments," wrote one scholar, "these are the most unforgettable of the albums of war."[16]

The photographs were intended to provide a scientific record of visual specimens, not to honor individual veterans—whether general or of lower rank—nor as a polemic against the terrible ravages of war. The images accompanied various written documents, such as field surgery notes and examining physician observations. And, following their study at the Army Medical Museum, copies were distributed to medical schools and military installations to assist those in training for military medicine. Nevertheless, these images are haunting and powerful forms of memory. Unlike severed, cleaned, and cataloged limbs in the museum's cases, these documents retain an image of the whole individual and convey the "gaze" of the subject. The knowledge of both the subject and the viewer that these were to be used for scientific purposes partially blunted their visual impact, but one can hardly look at them without some visceral response.[17]

Research on Military Medicine

From 1862 to 1889 the Army Medical Museum served as the principal and innovative agent for the inventory and assessment of Civil War veteran injuries. Requests for federal pension benefits made to the Pension Bureau were routinely directed to the Surgeon General's Office for evaluation and confirmation. In addition, those veterans appearing in person at the Surgeon General's Records and Pension Division were generally sent to the museum, located on a different floor of the same building, where their photographs were taken. The result of this long-term collaboration with the Pension Bureau (and, after the turn of the twentieth century, the Office of Veterans Affairs) was the creation of a unique repository and database on American veterans.

Upon the conclusion of the Civil War, an exhaustive research project on the collection was undertaken by museum staff. The records collected by the museum during the war, and indeed the entire idea of the museum, were used to produce the *Medical and Surgical History of the War of the Rebellion* (hereafter cited as *History*). This gigantic undertaking was a triumph of medical research requiring 23 years and took the form of six folio volumes weighing in at 56 pounds with more than 6,000 pages. The principal investigators were Drs. George Otis and J. J. Woodward. They used every possible means at their disposal to ensure veracity and detailed thoroughness in documenting and recording the wounds and treatments for thousands of soldiers. Each entry contains basic identification information on the soldier (e.g., name, rank, military unit), a description of the wound including the battle in which it occurred, and a chronological outline of the medical treatment and patient response. Complicated cases were regularly reviewed, and information on subsequent treatments was included in the entry. In this respect the *History* has been cited as an innovative advance in the scientific method of a longitudinal patient study.

The six-book set attempted to discuss every aspect of military medicine encountered during the Civil War. The massive bureaucracy and organization of the North was replicated in a smaller scale in the Surgeon General's Office. Hammond, brought in to shake up the hidebound Medical Department, created his own, far larger, bureaucracy with its own policies, forms, and regulations. Reports were revised time and again to ensure the clear flow of knowledge back to Washington. A large, sometimes stultifying, bureaucracy was the only way the *History* could ever be done. By the time it was done, both printings are believed to have cost well over $100,000.[18]

Barnes credited Secretary of War Stanton with promoting the publication to Congress and cited these volumes as the first long-term follow-ups of surgical cases, setting the stage for the development of modern medical studies conducted on groups over a period of years:

> Through the liberality of the Government, in its beneficent pension laws, it has been found practicable to obtain accurate histories of many thousand wounded or mutilated men for years subsequent to their discharge from service. [Since] in the official returns of the casualties of the French and English Armies in the Crimean War, the cases were dropped when the men were invalided, pensioned, or discharged from service, this information [of army cases] was considered peculiarly desirable.

Otis also credited the "former medical officers of the Confederate army" for providing much information. He was also able to use Confederate hospital records that had been captured by the Union. Occasionally, Otis would even advertise in newspapers for information on specific cases. But the vast majority of information came from pension records, detailed verification procedures, and subsequent correspondence to the pension examiners.[19]

Impact of Medical Science

The *History* was a landmark in both publication and medical information dissemination. It was the single largest medical reference work in human history and provided fresh information on trauma injury and treatment to military surgeons. Copies of each volume were provided to major medical research and governmental offices around the globe. A comprehensive examination of individual entries in the *History* would reveal significant clues to the experience of injured veterans. From the 6,000 entries, it was possible to identify larger patterns of comparable outcomes and to suggest new medical procedures.

An investigation of the different approaches to operations on extremities taken by Civil War surgeons may help to explain the role of medical documentation in the generation of knowledge. Two central issues surfaced in conjunction with amputations: first, was it better to remove the full arm (amputation) or a portion of the limb (excision)? Second, should one operate immediately before the patient lost more blood and succumbed to possible infection, or wait until the patient regained his strength and was better able to fight postoperative infection? A critical finding of the study was that, for those soldiers in overall good health, immediate amputation led to lower rates of complication than occurred when the injured soldiers were transported to a hospital setting. "If a study of the histories of over twenty thousand major amputations, and of more than four thousand excisions of the larger joints, performed during the late war, may permit me to speak authoritatively on this point," responded Otis to critics of his aggressive surgical recommendations, "I would say that no doctrine in military surgery is supported by more ample evidence than that which teaches that in operations for traumatic causes, there is a wide difference in the results of those performed during the existence of an inflammatory action, and those done after the symptomatic fever and inflammatory symptoms have abated."[20] Otis hoped that the procedures outlined in the study would revolutionize the ways in which field amputations were managed throughout the modern world. And, in the most practical manner, of course, the Civil War produced one of the most proficient and capable generations of surgeons in America. "[W]hile before the war," remarked Otis,

> there were few surgeons who chose to undertake operations on the great vessels [arteries of the neck], there are now thousands who know well when and how a great artery shall be tied. . . . Without further

illustration, we may claim that the additions to surgical knowledge acquired in the war are of real and practical knowledge.[21]

From this generation of physicians emerged what has been characterized as the "heroic" age of surgery.

Woodward's statistical work led him to conclude that fewer troops died from disease in the Union army than during any previous war, but that the mortality rate for soldiers due to disease was more than five times higher than expected for a similar group of men during peacetime. The rate of deaths due to disease was also far higher than that from injuries. Facts like these enabled Woodward to state unequivocally the value of the *History:* "Such a publication, therefore, becomes one of the most important duties of the Medical Department of the Army; a duty the evasion or neglect of which would be a grave crime against the army of the United States, and against every American citizen who, in future wars, volunteers in the defence of his country."[22] Yet, the long-term impact of the *History* as a model for subsequent studies of American veterans seems to have been minimal. Less than a decade after the completion of the work, one of the medical profession's greatest scholars—Dr. John Shaw Billings—complained that the federal government had lost interest in tracking the effects of war on the veterans.[23]

In its time, the *History* was perceived as being akin to a monument of the valorous conduct of soldiers. Writing during a memorializing age when much of Washington was being filled with statues of war heroes, Barnes remarked on the similar role achieved by the publication of these findings:

> In carrying out the intentions of Congress, it has been my earnest endeavor to make this *Medical and Surgical History of the War,* not only a contribution to science, but an enduring monument to the self-sacrificing zeal and professional ability of the Volunteer and Regular Medical Staff; and the unparalleled liberality of our Government, which provided so amply for the care of its sick and wounded soldiers.[24]

Intended as a reference work and a monument, the *History* succeeded as both and remains a unique history, even now that advances in medicine and surgery have made much of its hard-won knowledge obsolete.

Veterans in the Antebellum Era

The extent of suffering experienced by so many tens, perhaps hundreds, of thousands of Civil War veterans was unprecedented. Nothing close to its intensity would occur for the remainder of the century. By the end of the Civil War, some 1.9 million Union veterans returned to their farms, towns, and cities to pick up the pieces of their lives. This number of veterans far exceeded anything the nation had known. Statistics may help to give a quantitative sense of this. There had been 286,000 survivors from the Revolutionary War, 285,000 from the War of 1812, and another 86,000 from the Mexican-American War. At the time of the attack on Fort Sumter, a total of roughly 80,000 veterans from all of these conflicts were alive.[25] By war's end the balance had shifted dramatically.

In the five years following the Civil War, the government spent more funds on veterans than they had in the preceding 80 years. As government benefits changed over the subsequent years, pension records were routinely checked to confirm new and revised applications.[26] The sheer number of claims in itself spawned a large workforce, for in the year ending June 1866, the division examined and classified 210,027 disability discharges and provided information on another 49,212 cases to the Pension Bureau and other offices. Ten years after Appomattox 43 percent of veterans who had been wounded, a figure equivalent to 6.5 percent of all surviving veterans, were receiving benefits.[27]

In the subsequent decades, congressional authorization for pension benefits increased substantially. Lobbying efforts of the Grand Army of the Republic played a significant role in the expansion of benefits with important changes coming in the 1879 Arrears Act, which provided lump sum payments to beneficiaries that were roughly 2.5 times the average annual income of American citizens. Despite these increased rates of compensation, individual requests by veterans to the Pension Bureau were often denied, leading claimants to exert political pressure.

This approach of using political influence to increase benefits was also taken up by individual veterans who chose to argue their cases directly before Congress. A prominent example of this was Major General Henry A. Barnum's appeal. Barnum had been wounded at Malvern Hill in 1862 by a musket ball, and, as the wound was considered fatal, he was left on the field. After being captured he was transported to Libby Prison, then exchanged and had part of his intestine removed before he returned to action only to be wounded two more times before the end of the war. Barnum's abdominal wound never healed, and following the war, he had pictures taken that documented this fact (fig. 4), as well as numerous affidavits of his military record, to include in a packet that was submitted directly to Congress. His doctor, for example, wrote, "The courage, will and determination of this man are something I have never seen equalled, and to them alone is he indebted for his present tolerably good physical condition." As a result of his

FIG. 4. Major General Henry Barnum, c. 1880, showing wound suffered in 1862 at Malvern Hill. (Pension File 78753, National Archives.)

aggressive strategy, Barnum's pension was raised to $100 per month by an act of Congress in 1890.[28]

With the increased physical needs posed by the aging of all Civil War veterans and the mounting evidence that their votes could prove influential in political elections, momentum to change the requirements of the pension system gained adherents in the 1880s. The 1890 Dependent Pension Act led the way to a benefit system based on military service of at least 90 days, as opposed to injury, and by 1910 over 90 percent of all veterans, or their legatees, were receiving federal checks that were equal to about one-third of the average American income. As a result, political appeals such as Barnum's were no longer necessary to obtain a pension. Thus, within 50 years of the war, veteran benefits had essentially been transformed from compensatory annuities to old-age support.[29]

Until the rise of a system of benefits in the 1890s requiring only evidence of military service, determination of general pension rates for medical conditions were made by Congress, but only after an assessment of the information had been processed by the museum. To meet this demand Woodward and Otis both oversaw large offices; Otis directed the Division of Surgical Records, while Woodward headed the Record and Pension Division. The Record and Pension Office occupied Ford's Theatre's first floor and shared the second floor with the Surgeon General's Library (which formed the core of what is now the National Library of Medicine), providing easy access to the most current medical information.

In the Record and Pension Division, a large staff reviewed and cataloged pension applications and documents. The processing of the papers corresponded with the physical design of Ford's Theatre, where work during the postwar years occurred. The first floor held some 16,000 folio volumes of hospital books including monthly sick reports, along with related correspondence. In the first decade of operation this unit indexed some 300,000 names of deceased soldiers in alphabetical registers and cataloged disability discharges for another 200,000 individuals. The surgical records were maintained on the building's second floor, documenting the treatment of some 200,000 wounds and 40,000 surgical procedures organized according to the nature of the injury.[30]

With the call for a comprehensive service-related system of benefits in the elections of 1884 and 1888, the criteria for awarding benefits shifted from the medical to the political arena. Reflecting this change and the ever-present desire to reduce military costs, Congress shifted the management and responsibility for veteran records to an independent department in 1888.[31] A massive brick structure, with an elaborate Civil War frieze cast in terra cotta about its circumference, was constructed under the supervision of Major General Montgomery Meigs (who also oversaw the completion of the Washington Monument at the same time) to house this department. The political symbolism of this event reflected the changing character of the pension system: the building constructed to process the pension claims that, in turn, influenced presidential elections was now host to the inaugural celebration.

Prostheses, Pensions, and Employment: Rebuilding the Wounded

In addition to financial compensation and housing, the federal government provided medical care for injured soldiers. Prostheses were routinely offered by the army to amputees. In many cases this required traveling to a major metropolis for fitting. Many veterans were sent to Dr. Erasmus Darwin Hudson in New York City, whose artificial limbs received a grand prize and gold medal at the 1867 Universal Exposition at Paris. Hudson, a graduate of the Berkshire Medical College (Springfield, Massachusetts) and activist in the antislavery movement, had manufactured artificial limbs in Springfield for five years before moving to New York City in 1855. There he began a long-standing commitment to provide artificial limbs to the federal government until his death in 1880.[32]

Finding a suitable position in civilian life was often difficult, and certainly many pensioners never returned to work in any meaningful way after the war. But the adoption of preferences by the federal government to hire those with disabilities had a significant impact on the opportunities available to this population. Pensions provided only partial income replacement, and several amputees found employment in federal government offices to supplement their income. "Colored laborers" at the museum were receiving $40 per month in 1867 at a time when skilled workers such as engravers were paid $150 per month; by comparison, the total disability pension for a veteran was as low as four dollars per month at this time.[33]

It has been estimated that roughly one-third of the veterans residing in the District of Columbia in the postwar years received a pension.[34] In 1866 John F. Reardon, a 25-year-old veteran of the Sixth New York Calvary whose arm had been partially amputated in October 1863 (fig. 5A), began working in the Army Medical Museum, where the curator noted Reardon's ability to "lift a weight of 200 pounds or more with the injured limb without pain."[35] More remarkable was the experience of Private Samuel Decker, Fourth United States Artillery, who had lost both arms in an explosion in October 1862 (fig. 5B). Thirty months later he designed his own prosthetics—"an apparatus hitherto unrivaled for its ingenuity and utility"—and moved to Washington, where he was appointed a doorkeeper at the House of Representatives to supplement his $300 per year pension. "With the aid of his ingenious apparatus," note his medical records, "he is enabled to write legibly, to pick up any small objects, a pin for example, to carry packages of ordinary weight, to feed and clothe himself, and in one or two instances of disorder in the Congressional gallery has proved himself a

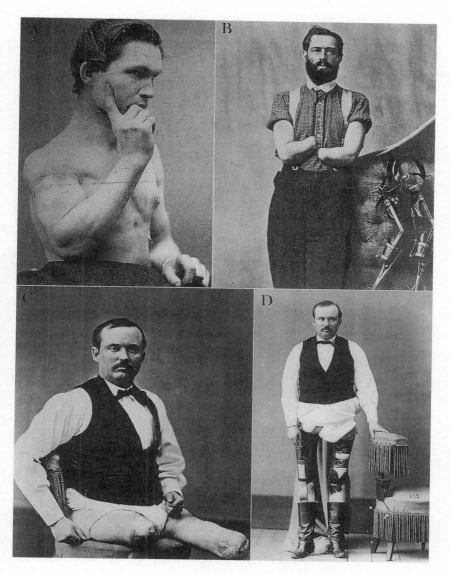

FIG. 5. *A*, John Reardon, 1874 (Surgical Photograph 6, reverse); *B*, Samuel Decker, 1867 (Surgical Photograph 205); *C, D,* Charles Lapham, 1865, without and with prostheses (Surgical Photographs 154, 155) (National Museum of Health and Medicine).

formidable police officer."[36] Private Charles Lapham, First Vermont Cavalry, lost both legs in 1863. Hudson made artificial limbs for him that he used to attend college (fig. 5C, D). Otis, notified by Hudson, wrote to Lapham asking to receive photographs of both his legs and prosthetics. Ten years later he was working in Washington at the Treasury Department.[37]

Veteran Applications to the Pension Office

Notwithstanding the benefits provided by the government, the pension applications of veterans illustrate that their lives often remained harsh and difficult. Evidence of the long-term and debilitating nature of wartime injuries was required by the Pension Bureau to assess the appropriateness of a requested increase in benefits. Over time information compiled by the Pension Bureau gave multiple perspectives on the injury and the veteran's life. Several examples drawn from these records document the types of evidence—generally presented in affidavits, testimonials, and photographs—used by veterans to make their cases.

The records for Private James M. Greenleaf, Company C of the 145th Pennsylvania Volunteers, who was wounded in the eye at the battle of Fredericksburg in 1862 when he was 32 years old, document his experiences for over half a century. In addition to fractures of his jaw and eye socket, Greenleaf lost his right eye and was discharged from the army in April 1863 with a monthly pension of eight dollars. Over the next 53 years Greenleaf made at least four appeals to have his pension increased. "My hip has pained very much," he wrote in 1872, "it still slips in the joint, and the joint has enlarged. It is so that it troubles me very much, so much at times that I cant [sic] walk without great trouble." Although he included two affidavits and asked friends to write, his application was rejected in 1874 with the note: "injury of left hip not proven." At age 47, his pension was increased to $18 when a pension examiner commented that pus continued to leak out of his eye. In fact, his wound never healed completely, prompting Greenleaf to have a lawyer apply for another increase in 1882:

> [His wound] has been constantly open, suppurating and discharging ever since with a fistulous opening back into the throat . . . that there is an increase of pain from year to year with loss of strength and increasing blindness in the left eye which is very weak & he is less & less able each year to do *any manual labor* or care for himself.

Greenleaf also submitted an affidavit signed by 24 acquaintances stating that his wound was worse than the loss of an arm or leg. While this request was rejected as well, an act of Congress in 1883 raised his pension to $24. In 1907, an insurance agent wrote,

> [I] simply will say Mr. Greenleaf attends to his wound himself, as it is in such condition that his wife and daughter can not attend it, it makes them *sick* so he does the best he can to wash it out and keep it from rotting. Mr. Greenleaf is confined most of the time to his house and bed. He is not able to do any kind of work whatever.

His examining surgeon added: "This claimant is so totally & permanently helpless from G.S.W. [gunshot wound] of face & loss of right eye that he requires the regular personal aid and attendance of another person." The 77-year-old Greenleaf's request for an increase was rejected again, and Greenleaf died without another review of his record.[38]

A similar example of the vagaries of making applications through the bureaucratic procedures of the Pension Office is evident in the experience of Private Patrick Hughes. Hughes, Company K of the Fourth New York Volunteers, was wounded at the battle of Antietam in 1862 by a bullet that went through his skull and part of his brain. Hughes seems not to have lost consciousness and left the battle himself. Following a limited hospital stay he was released from the army four months later and began receiving a pension of four dollars per month in 1865 for total disability. In 1870 two examining doctors summarized his condition:

> He is rather easily bothered and confused, and more irritable than formerly. The sight of his right eye, he thinks, is poor. Whisky affects him as usual. Sexual power undiminished. He has no paralysis. . . . When he coughs, even with moderate force, the depressed scalp instantly hedges up in a cone, which nearly reaches the general level of the skull and obliterates the depression, and then as suddenly subsides.

The following year he successfully applied to have his pension increased to $18. In 1876, Hughes married and subsequently fathered two children. He also returned to his former occupation as a stonecutter, presumably to supplement his pension, but "could only work about one day at a time after which he is compelled to lay off about 2 or 3 days on account of his head." His demeanor was peculiar, prompting a coworker "to believe the man might be deranged"; however, his 1886 request for an increase was rejected. His doctors wrote of his increasing paralysis in 1907 and, again, in 1910; at the time of his death in 1912 he was living with his cousin and was receiving $50 per month.[39]

The impact of pensions on the ability of a veteran to develop a family life was significant. Robert Hall Anderson, cited at the beginning of this essay, had to wait until he was 79 years old to marry, and the financial security offered by his pension was certainly a factor in Daisy's decision to marry him. And it may have not been coincidence that Hughes chose to marry after securing an increase in his pension in 1871. Rowland Ward, Fourth New York Heavy Artillery, whose jaw was removed by a shell and whose face was substantially reconstructed through surgery after the war, could only eat through a straw (fig. 6A, B). He married late in life in 1884 when he was getting a pension of $30 per month. Like Barnum, Ward had his pension raised to $50 per month by an act of Congress in 1889. His widow, Amelia, was still getting a pension of $40 per month when she died in 1934.[40]

Carlton Burgan, who died in 1914 at age 72, married and raised a large family in spite of his horrific wound. Burgan's commanding officer, Captain William Hogarth, Co. B., Purnell's Legion, made a pension declaration stating, "While encamped near Strausburg [sic], VA, Pvt. Burgan was taken sick with typhoid and being compeled [sic] to lay on the wet ground and from the incompetence of the Regt. surgeon who gave him mercury while thus exposed it took effect on the bone." Burgan's poisoning by his doctor led to a large portion of his upper jaw being surgically removed. His disability was rated complete and he began receiving eight dollars a month in 1865; the amount only increased to $30 per month by 1912. Burgan became a gardener and wore a mask over his face even after undergoing rudimentary, but successful, plastic surgery (fig. 6C, D). Notwithstanding his injury, he married in 1866 and had eight children, descendants of whom still live in the Baltimore area.[41] The process of building families was thus facilitated by the financial mechanisms of the pension system.

Memorializing Injuries: Museum Galleries

As the pension system assisted in the reconstruction of the lives of individuals, so the institutional study and display of battlefield injuries helped to reshape national attitudes and to bring reconciliation to those seeking to find meaning in the aftermath of the war. Above the Records and Pension Division, the exhibits of the museum physically documented the carnage recorded in the paperwork on the first two floors. These physical materials were called upon to furnish supporting information to veteran benefit claims. In the decades following the war, the galleries of the Army Medical Museum also served as a unique physical repository to the general public

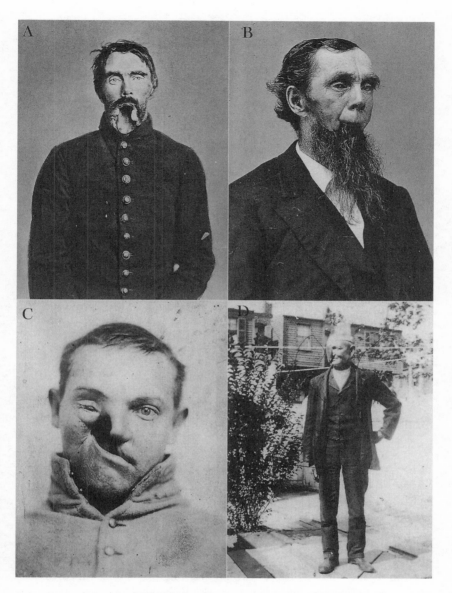

FIG. 6. *A,* Rowland Ward before his surgery, 1864 (Surgical Photograph 186, National Museum of Health and Medicine); *B,* Rowland Ward, 1876, 12 years after his injury (Contributed Photograph 1150, National Museum of Health and Medicine); *C,* Carlton Burgan, 1862, before his surgery (Contributed Photograph 1659, National Museum of Health and Medicine); *D,* Carlton Burgan, c. 1890 (National Museum of Health and Medicine, Courtesy of Mrs. Clara Ewell).

and contributed to the perception and memory of Civil War veterans in the United States. The museum's role in healing the postwar nation took primary shape in its graphic exhibits of shattered bones and severed limbs, which continued to place before the public examples of the terrible suffering of wartime. The museum, frequently visited by foreign surgeons and dignitaries, as well as veterans and their relatives, gave form to Victorian styles of mourning and reconciliation.

When the galleries were opened to the public in Ford's Theatre on April 16, 1867, a journalist for *Appleton's Journal* warned that it was "not such a collection as the timid would care to visit at midnight."[42] The large hall on the third floor contained rows of wooden cases facing framed photographs of injured soldiers and their specimens. But the first impression is "the peculiarly prevalent odor of carbolic acid" for the preservation of the physician remains that were carefully arranged by anatomical categories on the glass shelves. Atop the cases were stored models of Civil War ambulances, stretchers, and tents, and "in the ceiling are arranged, artistically, half a dozen flags and standards belonging to various ambulances during the war," complemented by an elaborate arrangement or swords, sabers, and the other weapons that caused the injuries so forcibly displayed.

Some soldiers felt that representation in the museum enhanced the veneration of their fallen comrades. For example, upon hearing of a "remarkable injury of a lower extremity" of a buried soldier, museum curator Brinton discussed the case with friends of the deceased:

> [I] dwelt upon the glory of a patriot having part of his body at least under the special guard of his country. . . . My arguments were conclusive; the comrades of the dead soldier solemnly decided that I should have that bone for the good of the country, and in a body they marched out and dug up the body.

However, this sentiment was not shared by all who survived an amputation. Brinton recalled one soldier on leave in Washington who had unexpectedly discovered his lost limb in the museum and demanded its return. The curator replied that he should come to the museum to collect it once he had completed the term of his enlistment.[43]

Residency at Ford's Theatre, where President Lincoln had been assassinated, certainly reinforced the museum's mission as a resource for the healing arts. "What nobler monument," commented the museum's curator, "could the nation erect to his [Lincoln's] memory than this somber treasure-house, devoted to the study of disease and injury, mutilation and death?"[44]

To general visitors, as recorded by a contributor to *Appleton's Journal* in
1873, the comparison of "the somber significance of the character of the
collection . . . and the late history of the building" was palpable.[45] Veterans
returning to survey the display of limbs must certainly have been powerfully
affected by the seemingly endless rows of bones lined up in cases. Even the
staff of the museum must have constantly recalled their sad duty in performing the autopsy on the late president.[46]

This museum was a cultural linchpin in the popular understanding of
death in the aftermath of the Civil War. Attendance in the nineteenth century was never large, but it was diverse. Veterans, medical practitioners,
interested members of the general public, and gawkers were certainly
among the audience. This fact alone made the museum noteworthy in the
eyes of those familiar with attendance at European museums. Furthermore,
the staff sent a representative selection of medical and surgical photographs
to the Centennial Exposition at Philadelphia as evidence of national scientific advances. Thus, while fulfilling its stated purpose of improving the
effectiveness of battlefield medicine, the museum also honored those who
had died in battle. It provided a reference point for those who wanted to
learn more about military medicine, and a memorial to those who wished
to come to terms with the horrible reality of the Civil War. Indeed, the
museum became what Edward Linenthal has called "sacred ground."[47]

The needs of, and obligations to, veterans were thus made visible as
governmental benefit programs evolved from the compensatory pensions
and hiring preferences in the 1860s and 1870s to the political patronage and
electoral issues of the 1880s.[48] Lincoln's Gettysburg Address exhortation that
the "living . . . dedicate [themselves] to the unfinished work" of the Civil
War, prefigures the astonishing survival and presence of Civil War veterans
who were to change the face of America. Following the war, the broken
bodies of disabled veterans could be found in most communities, constant
reminders of the loss of loved ones. In the national capital, veterans could be
seen at many government offices and were given an institutional presence at
the Army Medical Museum through photographs and the scientific treatises,
as well as skeletal and tissue remains.

NOTES

The opinions or assertions contained herein are the private views of the authors and are
not to be construed as official or as reflecting the views of the U.S. Department of
Defense. This piece is a U.S. government work and, as such, is in the public domain in
the United States of America. The photographs in this essay come from the collections

of the Otis Historical Archives, National Museum of Health and Medicine, Armed Forces Institute of Pathology, Washington, DC 20306 or the National Archives and are also in the public domain. Earlier versions of this essay were read by Goler for Indiana University's American Studies Program and the National Museum of American History (Smithsonian Institution).

1. "Daisy Anderson, Civil War Soldier's Widow, Dies at 97," *Washington Post,* September 27, 1998.

2. The general transformation of the United States from a network of agricultural communities and small-scale producers to industrialization and national structures has been outlined in Robert Wiebe, *The Search for Order, 1877–1920* (New York: Hill and Wang, 1967) and T. Jackson Lears, *No Place of Grace* (New York: Pantheon, 1981).

3. At the outset we should make clear that this paper focuses on the experiences of veterans from Northern states. The role of the Civil War and the attitudes of, and toward, its veterans took on a very different character in the Southern states (e.g., "The Lost Cause"), a topic covered quite effectively in Larry Logue, *To Appomattox and Beyond* (Chicago: Ivan R. Dee, 1996).

4. A recent comparative analysis of Civil War and Vietnam veterans has opened up new prospects for research. See Eric Dean Jr., *Shook over Hell: Post-Traumatic Stress, Vietnam, and the Civil War* (Cambridge: Harvard University Press, 1997).

5. For discussion of the role of memory in shaping national identity, see John Bodnar, *Remaking America* (Princeton: Princeton University Press, 1992), Michael Kammen, *The Mystic Chords of Memory* (New York: Knopf, 1991), Edward T. Linenthal, *Preserving Memory: The Struggle to Create America's Holocaust Museum* (New York: Viking, 1996), and James E. Young, *The Texture of Memory* (New Haven: Yale University Press, 1993).

6. Reference to Michel Foucault, *The Birth of the Clinic: An Archaeology of Medical Perception,* trans. A. M. Sheridan-Smith (1963; rpt. New York: Vintage, 1994).

7. Mary C. Gillett, *The Army Medical Department, 1818–1865* (Washington, D.C.: U.S. Army Center for Military History, 1987), 275.

8. Ibid., 286.

9. Ibid. The precise figures are hip joint (83.3 percent fatality), knee (57.2), lower arm (20.7).

10. For a discussion of the methods and extent of injuries see *Medical and Surgical History of the British Army which served in the Crimea . . . in the years 1854, 1855, 1856* (London, 1858), 2:259, cited in George Otis and J. J. Woodward, *Circular No. 6: Reports on the Extent and Nature of the Materials Available for the Preparation of a Medical and Surgical History of the Rebellion* (Washington, D.C.: Government Printing Office, 1865), 2.

11. John H. Brinton, *Personal Memoirs of John H. Brinton* (New York: Neale, 1914), 249–50.

12. Matthew Naythons, *The Face of Mercy: A Photographic History of Medicine at War* (New York: Random House, 1993), 61. The requirement for documentation of disabilities, which helped to create the body of photographic images, was lifted by Congress in the act of June 27, 1880.

13. Brinton, *Personal Memoirs,* 180–81. When he wrote his autobiography in 1891, Brinton commented on his personal collection, suggesting that he felt himself exempt from Hammond's order.

14. Ibid., 186.

15. Alison Gernsheim, "Medical Photography in the Nineteenth Century," *Medical and Biological Illustration* 11 (1961): 90.

16. Alan Trachtenberg, *Reading American Photographs: Images as History, Mathew Brady to Walker Evans* (New York: Hill and Wang, 1989), 116–18.

17. This argument is essentially an example of the corporal "gaze" described by Foucault by which pathology helped to usher in the modern world. See *Birth of the Clinic,* passim.

18. Woodward to Crane, July 29, 1875, "Curatorial Records: Letterbooks of the Curators," housed at the Otis Historical Archives, National Museum of Health and Medicine.

19. Office of the U.S. Army Surgeon General, *The Medical and Surgical History of the War of the Rebellion* (Washington, D.C.: Government Printing Office, 1870–88), Surgical 1:xix.

20. Otis and Woodward, *Circular No. 2, 6.*

21. *Medical and Surgical History,* Surgical 1:xxix.

22. Otis and Woodward, *Circular No. 6, 90.*

23. John S. Billings, "The Health of the Survivors of the War," *Transactions of the College of Physicians of Philadelphia,* January 1892, 652–58. Billings notes that the health of veterans in Massachusetts was significantly worse than that of comparably aged nonveterans and called for a comprehensive national study of veterans.

24. Barnes, "Prefatory," in Office of the U.S. Army Surgeon General, *Medical and Surgical History,* Medical 1:ix.

25. That translates to roughly 25 new individuals for every pre–Civil War veteran. Sar A. Levitan and Karen A. Cleary, *Old Wars Remain Unfinished: The Veterans Benefit System* (Baltimore: Johns Hopkins University Press, 1973), 8–9. This work forms the basis of much of the discussion on veteran benefits in the subsequent paragraphs.

26. Gillett, *The Army Medical Department,* 23. The rising cost of these benefits also reflected the expansion of veteran benefits in 1862 for death and disability for regular and volunteer soldiers. This system was augmented in 1864 by the addition of a list of specified disabilities graded to different rates of compensation. Donald L. McMurry and R. W. Daly, "Pensions, Military and Naval," *Dictionary of American History* 6:222.

27. Theda Skocpol, *Protecting Soldiers and Mothers: The Political Origins of Social Policy in the United States* (Cambridge: Harvard University Press, 1992), 109. Financial benefits to injured veterans date to the Revolutionary War and have remained a constant commitment of the federal government to its soldiers. These rates increased according to rank.

28. Barnum lived with his wound for 30 years before his death in 1892. *Surgical Photograph 93* (text); Pension Certificate 78753 on file at the National Archives; Dr. Lewis A. Sayre to Commissioner John C. Black, August 17, 1888 (accession file 1002020 on file in the National Museum of Health and Medicine).

29. Skocpol, *Protecting Soldiers and Mothers,* 107–30.

30. J. J. Woodward, "The Army Medical Museum at Washington," *Lippincott's Magazine* 15 (1871): 234.

31. Gillett, *The Army Medical Department,* 24.

32. Hudson was cited by a contemporary for his "philanthropic zeal and a thor-

oughness and conscientiousness which avoided the usual liberal profits of Government patronage." Blair Rogers, "Rehabilitation and Pension Payments for the Civil War Wounded," unpublished manuscript on file at Otis Historical Archives, 35–48.

33. Otis to Barnes, April 30, 1867, "Curatorial Records: Letterbooks of the Curators."

34. Skocpol, *Protecting Soldiers and Mothers*, 138.

35. George Otis, *Surgical Photograph 6* (text). Otis wrote 375 labels that appeared on the reverse of the surgical photographs that were distributed by the museum individually or in bound volumes.

36. George Otis, *Surgical Photograph 205* (text).

37. Otis to Lapham, May 25, 1865, "Curatorial Records: Letterbooks of the Curators"; George Otis, *Surgical Photographs 154–155* (text).

38. While several of Greenleaf's pension applications were rejected, general changes in the rate of benefits did increase the amount of his benefits somewhat, and, at the time of his death he was receiving $90 per month. Pension Application 18613, Certificate 14904, National Archives.

39. It seems that even death did not always settle pension disputes. Hughes's death engendered a dispute between his landlady and his cousin over who should collect his insurance and pay for his burial. *Medical and Surgical History,* Surgical 2:206–7; Pension Application 13596, Certificate 38452, National Archives.

40. George Otis, *Surgical Photographs 167–170* (text); Pension Files for Rowland Ward (Application 75706, Certificate 47031) and Amelia Ward (Application 679307, Certificate 469,264), National Archives.

41. George Otis, *Surgical Photograph 28* (text); Pension Application 50509, Certificate 49299, National Archives.

42. Louis Bagger, "The Army Medical Museum in Washington," *Appleton's Journal,* March 1, 1873, 9:206, 294–97. The subsequent description relies heavily on Bagger's account and on photographs in the Otis Historical Archive.

43. Brinton, *Personal Memoirs,* 190–91. As the names of the individuals associated with these stories are unknown, it is not possible to determine the fate of their remains.

44. Woodward, "Army Medical Museum," 242.

45. Bagger, "Army Medical Museum," 294.

46. General accounts of the museum during the period of its tenure at this location appears in Robert S. Henry, *The Armed Forces Institute of Pathology: Its First Century, 1862–1962* (Washington, D.C.: Office of the Surgeon General, 1964), 54–82, and Barbara Ann Ramlo-Halsted, "The Army Medical Museum and Its Roots in the American Natural History Museum: A Late-Eighteenth Century Paradox," M.A. thesis, Yale University School of Medicine, 1993.

47. For an extended treatment of the theme of "sacred ground" see Edward T. Linenthal, *Sacred Ground: Americans and Their Battlefields* (Urbana: University of Illinois Press, 1991).

48. Those receiving veteran pensions were distinguished by their service, not their economic standing. For an insightful discussion of this distinction see Skocpol, *Protecting Soldiers and Mothers,* 150.

Jeffrey S. Reznick

Work-Therapy and the Disabled British Soldier in Great Britain in the First World War: The Case of Shepherd's Bush Military Hospital, London

In May 1918, the French and Belgian ministries of war hosted the second annual international conference on the aftercare of soldiers disabled in the Great War. In London, leading medical authorities, voluntary-aid representatives, labor leaders, and politicians met to exchange views on two vital questions: How could the war's disabled be healed effectively and, following this healing, how could they be successfully reintegrated into civilian society? Officials at the previous conference had examined these questions in detail, but questions remained about the best approaches to rehabilitating the wounded serviceman, for the welfare of the man himself as well as for the benefit of his family and his nation.

In his introduction to the official conference proceedings, John Galsworthy, the British novelist and dramatist, offered a hopeful description of Britain's rehabilitation scheme for disabled servicemen. "In special hospitals," he wrote,

> orthopaedic, paraplegic, neurasthenic, we shall give [the crippled soldier] back functional ability, solidity of nerve or lung. The flesh torn away, the lost sight, the broken ear-drum, the destroyed nerve, it is true we cannot give back; but we shall so re-create and fortify the rest of him that he shall leave hospital ready for a new career. Then we shall teach him how to treat the road of it, so that he fits again into the national life, becomes once more a workman with pride in his work, a stake in the country, and the consciousness that, handicapped though he be, he runs the race level with his fellows, and is by that so much the better man than they.[1]

Galsworthy's sketch is revealing for the way in which it suggests how rehabilitating disabled soldiers involved not only conventional rest but also two
distinct yet interconnected kinds of work. Through supervised, postoperative manipulations of maimed limbs, using water, weights, and electricity, medical authorities sought to repair both the body and the mind. At
the same time, administrators of this program promoted another form of
rehabilitative work as a way to prepare disabled soldiers for reentry into
civilian life. Vocational labor, they held, helped to make them workmen
once again. As Galsworthy therefore suggested, providing disabled soldiers
with these kinds of work thus meant reconstituting them in three respects:
as healthy individuals, able-bodied male breadwinners, and productive citizens.

In the past decade, historians have devoted considerable attention to
the ways in which the mental and physical wounds of the Great War helped
to shape the identity of the British soldier and his perception by government
officials, care providers, and the public. Focusing on the curative program at
Chailey Heritage Hospital in Sussex, Seth Koven has demonstrated that
crippled boys, who were traditionally objects of rescue in orthopedic healing programs, became agents of healing during the Great War. By pairing a
disabled soldier with a crippled boy, medical authorities at Chailey intended
to help the soldier remember the value and hope of youth and his own
future promise as a productive member of civilian society.[2] Building on
Koven's work, Joanna Bourke has shown that crippled soldiers themselves
drew on traditional forms of masculinity, like male bonding, as means of
coping with their injuries and reconstituting their sense of kinship and their
lives after the war.[3]

This essay extends this literature by exploring the development of
Shepherd's Bush Military Hospital, Britain's premier orthopedic center,
established in 1916 at London's Hammersmith Workhouse Infirmary.[4]
Based on existing therapies for the physically disabled and the mentally ill,
as well as on occupational programs for convict prisoners, unemployed sectors of the working classes, and the urban poor, the rehabilitation scheme at
Shepherd's Bush reflected the persistence of Victorian modes of medical
care and social welfare into the twentieth century. At the same time,
wartime concerns among authorities about efficiency, economy, and postwar society helped to shape the development of this program. Analyzing
Shepherd's Bush in this way demonstrates that this institution was a site
where healing time overlapped with productive work time, creating arenas
of teaching and industry where medical authorities conceived disabled soldiers as able-bodied workers who could continue to "do their bit" for their

own welfare and for the benefit of wartime efficiency. Like munitions and metalworking factories, therefore, Shepherd's Bush was an integral component of the "war machine," the system of efficient organization, administration, and production that characterized nearly every facet of British society during the Great War.[5] Moreover, like the contemporary work environment, Shepherd's Bush simultaneously undercut and reinforced traditional gender roles. Factory work enabled women to take on men's roles as the producers of the weapons of war even as it deepened misogyny by highlighting the privileged status of most women as noncombatants and present or future mothers. Similarly, while therapeutic work at Shepherd's Bush was intended to "reclaim" disabled soldiers, it helped to remind these men of their emasculated condition.[6]

As Roger Cooter has demonstrated, Shepherd's Bush occupies an important place in the history of medicine. It represented the first large-scale mobilization in Britain of orthopedic and physiotherapeutic specialists. Never before had there been a single hospital set aside uniquely for the care of the adult disabled. And never before had a hospital staff faced such a multiplicity of physical injuries. But medical authorities at this hospital did not develop their curative scheme de novo. They drew extensively upon their experiences of caring for crippled children and injured industrial workers.[7] Moreover, as this essay contends, this endeavor reflected the broader contemporary shift in conceptions of work and the effect that work had on the human body.

Between the 1880s and the 1920s, as Anson Rabinbach has shown, authorities in scientific and industrial circles were becoming increasingly concerned about the "wastage" of labor in modern society. Applying metaphors of the machine to the human body to illuminate the extent to which it was becoming plagued, both mentally and physically, by modern "fatigue," these individuals suggested that the moral value of work, as virtuous and inherently good, was gradually being displaced by more scientific, measured evaluations of work. Although Rabinbach chiefly emphasizes this development on the Continent, a comparable shift in the conception of work simultaneously occurred in Britain, particularly in the fields of medicine and social and penal reform.[8]

During the last quarter of the nineteenth century, British surgeons began to recognize the value of work in surgical aftercare schemes for the physically disabled. Based on the long-established "moral treatment" of the insane and the poor, which sought to reform individual conduct according to ideas of self-discipline and moral self-consciousness,[9] the orthopedic surgeon—and later founder of Shepherd's Bush—Robert Jones used two kinds of work to help rehabilitate injured industrial workers and crippled children. At one hand, he followed what was essentially an early form of physio-therapy, emphasizing the so-called external movement of a patient's muscles by means of water, machine-mounted and directed weights, and electricity. Complementing this scientific evaluation of labor was "useful" work in the form of craftmaking, which helped the disabled patient to learn how to move his or her own wounded muscles alone, without external aid. This component of the treatment was especially vital, Jones held, because the successful rehabilitation of the disabled depended as much on their relationship to "social service" as on effective medicine and surgery.[10] It was important, he believed, to make disabled individuals aware of their potential abilities as newly functional and productive members of the community. This twofold view of work, as both morally and scientifically worthwhile, was central to Jones's efforts as medical supervisor of the Manchester Ship Canal project between 1888 and 1891, where he fitted splints on amputation cases that were the result of industrial injuries. It was also crucial to his subsequent work as surgeon at Nelson Street Hospital in Liverpool, where he aided the rehabilitation of shipwrights, ironworkers, boilermakers, and dockgatemen of Merseyside who had sustained severe physical disabilities from their work. Beginning in 1909, Jones's view of work also became integral to the healing scheme established at Baschurch Hospital for crippled children. Here, Jones continued his pioneering psychological treatment of physical injury, emphasizing not only the value of "useful" work but also that of open-air wards in promoting contentment and recovery.[11]

While Jones emphasized the orthopedic value of work, comparable evaluations of work appeared in sectors of the reform-minded individuals. This development reflected both the persistent moral valuations and the emergence of the new "scientific approach" to poverty and social indiscipline. In Toynbee Hall and Salvation Army classrooms, women organized and taught semiskilled work as a means of promoting personal edification, physical sturdiness, and a sense of civic service among the poor and working classes.[12] From the 1880s, workhouses also reflected this development. In those institutions established by Reginald and Mary Brabazon, women used semiskilled work to fulfill the principles of the 1847 Poor Law, to "save the inmates of the workhouse from the terrible monotony of an idle life" by teaching them how employ their idle hands usefully.[13] These venues later formed the institutional basis for the Soldiers' and Sailors' Workrooms for disabled veterans of the Boer War. This institution, in turn, became the Lord Robert's Memorial Workshops and aftercare clinic for disabled veterans. In both the workrooms and the workshops, handicraft instructors and medical authorities promoted the idea that semiskilled work was valuable in social terms as a means to reconstitute disabled persons' sense of individual and communal worth. Moreover, like the original Brabazon shops, the workrooms and the workshops were economically productive environments that attracted customers and extended the markets of items made by retrained disabled men.[14]

These new attitudes also informed contemporary debates among English prison authorities about the meaning and purpose of institutional punishment and the value of work in convict prisons. These debates stemmed from the application of new scientific measurements to physical and psychological suffering.[15] Having lost faith in the promotion of self-discipline through deterrence, penal reformers claimed that prisons should seek to promote self-realization among inmates through direct therapeutic action, namely various forms of productive work. Such activity, reformers believed, was also useful for the efficient functioning of the institution itself. Despite opposition by some authorities, including Edmund DuCane, chairman of England's Prison Commission, these views took hold among prison officers. By the 1880s, convicts in local and military prisons were put to work making their own uniforms as well as mailbags for the Post Office and mats, paperclips, packing cases, notice frames, and twine and gunny bags for the Admiralty and Office of Works.[16] Gladstonian penal reform at the turn of the century led to a further amelioration of the harsher aspects of penal servitude under the guidance of a more expansive yet less punitive state. Like the orthopedic center and the workhouse, therefore, the contemporary convict prison was also becoming a regimented arena of industry where reform-minded observers promoted work as not simply virtuous but also scientifically worthwhile in terms of advancing personal, institutional, and national standing.

Organized and administered by hospital authorities along simultaneously moral, medical, and scientific lines, the "curative workshops" at Shepherd's Bush functioned as productive work environments intended to heal and to retrain disabled soldiers while benefiting the economy of the medical service. Three groups constituted the support base of the Shepherd's Bush scheme: the War Office, the British Red Cross, and the public. An examination of how Jones and his colleagues mobilized the aid of each of these institutions reveals key features of the shops themselves and of the multifaceted official view of disabled soldiers.

From the outset of the Great War, the British government demonstrated little interest in providing comprehensive postoperative treatment to soldiers who sustained severe injuries in battle. Due to manpower needs and to limited finances, military policy dictated that disabled cases should receive short periods of treatment followed by either quick return to, or if the case warranted, discharge from, military service. Aftercare, the government insisted, should be prescribed only after military discharge and under the sponsorship of voluntary aid organizations like the British Red Cross.[17]

However, in the spring of 1915, when the military began to return increasing numbers of disabled men home for treatment, Robert Jones argued that the government's existing policy on wounded soldiers was inadequate. It provided for the discharge of disabled cases before proper surgical aftercare. Moreover, it exempted the state from the essential responsibility of rehabilitating men who could no longer serve their country. As Jones explained in a letter to Alfred Keogh, director general of Army Medical Services, there was essentially "a want of cohesion between departments of treatment, such as massage, physical exercises, electricity, and manipulative and operative groups of cases, all of which, properly controlled, make for success in orthopaedic surgery."[18] What was needed, Jones argued, was a comprehensive system of state-sponsored aftercare, one that could provide an extended period of recovery and continuity of treatment directed toward efficient and complete restoration of locomotor function. Jones concluded that the country required a central hospital where all existing resources could be brought together to bear on the problem of the war disabled.

In late 1915, the government accepted Jones's plan as a viable strategy for dealing with increasing numbers of wounded soldiers. Soon after this acceptance, however, Jones received word that while the government had approved his plan, it had insisted that finance of such a program had to remain the preserve of voluntary aid.[19] This policy, a turning point in the development of his scheme, led Jones to refashion the purpose of Shepherd's Bush and the identity of the disabled servicemen who were beginning to receive treatment at the hospital.

From late 1915, both the Joint War Committee and the British public became the foci of intense fund-raising efforts by the chief administrator of the Shepherd's Bush workshops, Manuel II, the deposed king of Portugal.[20] A key element of this campaign involved Manuel himself "travelling around the country, more or less like a missionary, to explain what it means for the wounded soldiers as well as for the nation to have orthopaedic centres established, with curative workshops attached to them."[21] In his travels, Manuel emphasized the practical potential of the hospital, essentially redefining the identity of disabled soldiers. Though still crippled in medical terms, he claimed, these men were nonetheless able-bodied individuals who in the workshops could learn new trades and how to regain productive lives after the war. Such appeals were successful in raising voluntary aid for Shepherd's Bush. In October 1916, the Joint War Committee awarded an initial £1,000 grant to Shepherd's Bush based on its agenda to cure and to retrain disabled soldiers. This sum was followed by a £10,000 grant in 1918. Supplementing these funds throughout the war were thousands of pounds donated by the public directly both to Shepherd's Bush and to its associated orthopedic facilities in the provinces.[22]

Voluntary aid helped to open Shepherd's Bush and keep it operational. However, Jones and his colleagues knew that in order to extend the scope of their work both within the institution and around the country they needed to gain further military authorization and even greater financial support. To achieve these goals, they further manipulated their rehabilitative scheme and the role of disabled soldiers in it. Appealing to the government's concern about the financing of medical service, they constructed an image of the hospital as a factory and identified soldier-patients in this environment as able-bodied and efficient workers. As Jones explained in a 1917 speech to the Royal Institute of Public Health, disabled soldiers were "an essential part of the economic manpower of the nation, independent producers and wage-earners, and not helpless dependents."[23] Playing on the view of women held by the government and the industrial sector of the war economy, Jones thus aligned his conceptualization of retrained disabled soldiers to address concerns about the wartime paucity of labor generally and the economic state of the military medical system in particular.[24]

This approach helped to win Jones the official authorization he needed to expand the Shepherd's Bush program itself and to establish associated regional orthopedic centers. In October 1916, he received a £500 grant from the War Office to support the maintenance of new shops at Shepherd's Bush.[25] Subsequently, in November 1918, he received from the War Office "an unlimited sum for maintenance" of all shops that were part of or associated with the Shepherd's Bush plan, including those established at 16 regional orthopedic facilities,[26] which by the end of 1918 were caring for nearly 15,000 disabled servicemen.[27]

From the perspective of government officials, this network of orthopedic centers was an essential component of postwar reconstruction. As a War Cabinet secretary suggested in a March 1917 memorandum to Prime Minister David Lloyd George, it was an effective way to prepare a soon-to-be-enfranchised population for participation in local and national political life. If the "whole local machinery for the registration and supervision of the disabled" is not "carefully thought out," the secretary wrote, the government "risk[s] opportunities for training being lost and the country being saddled with thousands of untrained idle pensioners, who will ever be available as object lessons to which political wire-pullers can appeal."[28] Like the People's Budget of 1909, therefore, which sought to rekindle enthusiasm for further liberal social reform in part by providing better pensions scheme to veterans,[29] government policy toward disabled soldiers was intended to make these men healthy citizens for the benefit of postwar reconstruction.

An analysis of the curative function of the Shepherd's Bush program underscores the connections between the rehabilitation of disabled soldiers and official concerns about health, society, and economy. In a 1941 speech to the British Association of Occupational Therapists, G. R. Girdlestone, one of Robert Jones's colleagues at Shepherd's Bush, recalled that in the early summer of 1916, when bedside occupations like embroidery, raffia work, and basketwork were introduced to make daily hospital life more pleasant for the disabled soldier-patients, authorities at Shepherd's Bush began to realize the value of such occupation in "preserving men's mental and physical fitness."[30] In the summer of 1916, this realization ultimately resulted in the construction on the hospital quadrangle of what authorities called the "curative workshops."

The first three of these shops opened in October 1916, becoming the nucleus of the hospital's rehabilitation strategy. They included a direct curative shop, in which disabled soldiers received various forms of mechanical therapy; a central shop, which contained a smithy fitted with an electric forge and anvils; and a site for commercial photographic work. The rapid growth of these sites attests to their great success. Within less than a year, hospital authorities used soldier-patient labor to help construct and maintain 15 additional shops. In engineering shops disabled soldiers repaired motorcar engines, enameled frames, relacquered fittings, and reupholstered seat cushions. In artistic shops, they made decorations for the hospital chapel and wards. In the carpentry shops, soldiers made hospital furniture, shelves, and cupboards for the institution. And in other shops there were materials for them to learn tailoring, cigarette making, French polishing, sign writing, and fretwork.

Three related criteria determined the kind of work done in the shops. Above all, work that was primarily vocational in character had to move muscles and limbs in ways comparable to work intended strictly as medical therapy. Moreover, the trades taught in the shops were those that authorities saw as growing and nonseasonal, that is, work that could provide long-term employment and a decent wage. What was important in this regard was not specialization in any one trade, but work in a number of "standard trades." This was the best means of increasing the chances of disabled men at gaining fruitful employment upon discharge. Finally, authorities considered the previous occupations and personal preferences of the men to be vital in what trades were taught in the shops.[31]

Authorities believed that surgery was vital in the uninterrupted system of care offered at Shepherd's Bush, but from late 1916 they consistently held that the curative shops were the centerpiece of the program for the way in which they gave attention to the physical and psychological conditions of disabled men. The shops were "a priceless therapeutic boon," Jones claimed, because they established an atmosphere of activity and usefulness, which counterbalanced the monotony of hospital life generally and that of physiotherapeutic activity in particular.[32] The shops, Jones added, effectively rearranged the daily routine and spatial environment of the hospital. From their opening in 1916 until their period of full development in late 1918, they were part of the daily routines of an average of half of the patients resident in the hospital.[33] Delineating specific periods of work during each planned five-hour hospital day, Jones explained, this arrangement "enabl[ed] convalescent patients who were still receiving one or two treatments to work regularly . . . and cases [who] were receiving three treatments a day to work for shorter hours."[34] The workshops also became prominent features of the architecture of the hospital. Designed to "create an atmosphere of contentment among the men," they effectively extended the traditional healing arenas, the ward and operating room.[35]

Jones was proud of the fact that the shops set Shepherd's Bush apart from most hospitals in the country. "Those of us who have any imagination, cannot fail to realize the difference in atmosphere and *morale* in hospitals where the patients have nothing to do but smoke, play cards, or be entertained, from that found in those where for part of the day they have regular, useful, and productive work."[36] Jones's rationale for the shops was thus straightforward. Work broke up the monotony of hospital life and the physical and mental healing process generally. It also gave social value to rehabilitation.

The workshops at Shepherd's Bush involved two kinds of active curative treatment in mechanical-therapeutic terms, direct and indirect.[37] Direct mechanical therapy was used "when we give a man with a stiff shoulder paper-hanging or whitewashing, in order to loosen [his shoulder]; or screwing to pronate or supinate his arm, or a plane to mobilise his wrist." Indirect therapy was used in the case of patients with stiff limbs that they were not likely to use. As Jones put it:

> He may be given a job to do with his hands. In the interest which the work inspires he forgets to nurse his foot, which almost unconsciously and often very rapidly becomes again mobile. A knee joint which could not bear the continued strain of working a treadle will, perhaps, improve in function quickly, which the patient, forgetful of his injury, is working with a saw.[38]

Jones called this indirect therapy "psychological curative treatment." It involved disabled soldier-patients literally working their own bodies to the end of "reeducating" their own muscles. The right balance of work had to be maintained so that the activity did not "fatigue [the disabled limb] and so impede recovery."[39]

Like therapeutic work, vocational work helped to define a disabled soldier as a functional individual. "He is like a great schoolboy," Jones observed, "and with tact and sympathy he can be led by a silken cord." For all disabled cases, Jones argued further, "'From hospital to industry,' should become their aim. They should be pulled back from the 'blind alleys' of labour. Unless this is done, a great tragedy will occur when the war ends and the wounded soldier is displaced by a more competent worker."[40] This moralistic configuration of the disabled soldiers thus identified them as members of an undifferentiated working class whose energy could be harnessed to help him build their own "bridges" from military to civilian life.[41]

By mimicking a classroom environment where disabled soldiers could feel and be productive and useful, the workshops also served to counter the idea among many patients that they would never again be able to work, or that they would never again be able to earn their living when they were discharged from the army.[42] The shops were intended to be productive centers that sought to help men realize for themselves how wrong they were about their disabled bodies, their usefulness to their communities, and their role as productive workers. As Jones explained at the 1918 Inter-Allied Conference, these sites helped to "create a more complete atmosphere of satisfaction amongst them, and to give them every possible chance of again becoming useful citizens to their country."[43]

The fact that authorities actually conceived disabled soldiers as workers for the institution underlines the socioeconomic value that authorities attached to the hospital's rehabilitation scheme. In many shops, soldiers produced basic hospital supplies and essential medical equipment, including surgical splints and boots, artificial limbs, operating tables, and "Sinclair" and "Balkan" surgical frames. Between October 1916 and March 1917, disabled servicemen who were either largely cured of their injuries or already skilled at using their artificial limbs produced over 1,600 splints of two dozen different varieties. During the same period, in workshops for patients who still required treatment by prescribed work therapy, over 2,000 splints were made, and over 1,000 were repaired and altered.[44] This arrangement, as the commanding officer of Shepherd's Bush observed, allowed disabled men to "profit" from their own work in the shops, as "they have in many cases been able to suggest improvements in older patterns of splints."[45] Here, then, was soldier-patient labor that benefited not only the man himself but also his immediate community and the wartime medical service generally. Further emphasizing the economic value of this labor, Manuel pointed out that shops "had the enormous advantage of being, not only a more speedy means of obtaining the necessary articles than would have been the case if we had to produce them outside, but also a very considerable economy to the State."[46] Authorities at Shepherd's Bush underscored this message in hospital publicity literature, which plainly depicted the workshops as factories and soldier-patients as efficient workers.[47]

The similarity between these photographs and those of contemporary factories suggests that authorities intended to represent the hospital to the government and to the public not as a place of rest and healing but rather as an efficient workplace and an arena of retraining. Fitting with the rhetoric of curative and vocational work extolled by Jones and his colleagues, these images demonstrate that officials visually shaped the identity of the disabled soldier as a self-healing machine, a mechanism to be retrained for personal and familial welfare, and an efficient human motor for the state at war.

But even as Shepherd's Bush exemplified these factory-like characteristics, it distinguished itself from the wartime workplace in two ways. First, whereas munitions work was directed primarily toward achieving sufficient production of the weapons of war,[48] labor in the Shepherd's Bush was intended to help "remedy the general discipline problems of the orthopaedic institution," where interesting activity was limited to "breaking rules," experiencing "the mild excitement of coming before the commanding officer," and "having a grievance to grumble about."[49] Authorities thus intended hospital work to stem these potentially disastrous situations and to deter disabled men from becoming "foci of seething discontent and . . . a menace to successful recruiting."[50]

Hospital work also distinguished itself from factory work on the grounds of remuneration. While women workers in munitions factories

Curative Workshops, Special Military Surgical Hospital, Shepherds Bush, W

FIG. 7. Publicity postcard, one of a series of 10 that authorities used to depict the "curative shops" at Shepherd's Bush and the industry of disabled soldiers in these environs. These cards were themselves products of soldier-patient industry, being made by disabled men in the hospital's printshop. Authorities sold these cards to raise money for the hospital. (Image courtesy of Hammersmith and Fulham Archives and Local History Centre.)

were paid for "doing their bit," albeit under circumstances of "dilution,"[51] soldiers at Shepherd's Bush received no remuneration for shop work beyond either soldier's pay or pension. In addition, all hospital work was theoretically mandatory.[52] As Jones explained, "No rigid lines are drawn round the work, but it is constantly enlarged and adapted, giving full play to the initiative and freewill of the patients . . . depending largely upon the psychological element to help in the recovery. By this "psychological component," Jones meant an arrangement that involved specific measures designed to compel participation in workshop work. These included "gentle methods of persuasion" like "sympathy and patience" to build a "spirit of trust" between staff and patient, and "certain privileges, such as permission to wear khaki instead of the hospital blue or grey; [and] more frequent passes out of the hospital."[53] Promotion of work in this way, Jones believed, helped to create an environment in which authorities could effectively heal and retrain the disabled while stemming potential disenchantment among them.

Significantly, British authorities looked to "mandatory" Continental rehabilitation schemes as a means of differentiating the "voluntary" work schemes at Shepherd's Bush and its associated regional hospitals. I. G. Gibbon, a War Cabinet secretary, observed that in France and Germany, "special measures have to be adopted to induce the disabled generally to take advantage of the opportunities of restoration and training which may be available for them. So great is the difficulty that compulsion has been suggested in some quarters."[54] Similarly, in his speech to the first Inter–Allied Conference on After–Care of Disabled Men, Arthur Boscawen, MP and parliamentary secretary to the Ministry of Pensions, criticized Continental schemes as a way of praising the British efforts. In French and Belgian hospitals, Boscawen explained, "the man himself appears to have little voice in deciding his future, while a battle royal between the doctor and the technical expert often rages over his mutilated body."[55] The fact that British authorities were themselves torn between carrot and stick approaches to making their patients work suggests that both Gibbon and Boscawen could well have been describing the approach taken by Jones and his colleagues. These reports testify to the battle that was indeed being fought in Britain over the disabled soldier's body, one that was intimately connected to official concerns about health, society, economy, and politics.

Evidence suggests that soldier–patients viewed hospital work with resentment at best. Despite assurances by government and military–medical authorities to the contrary, soldiers feared that their well–deserved, albeit meager, pensions would be reduced or taken away completely because they were making efforts to compensate for their disabilities.[56] Thus, soldier–patients often refused work altogether, rebelling when work time in the hospital impinged on what they saw as well–deserved recreational time. As an instructor at the Roehampton shops suggested in a report to the executive committee of the hospital, patients consistently refused to attend his classes, preferring to take advantage of fresh–air cures and riverboat outings on the Thames.[57]

Many disabled soldiers also saw hospital work to be a "kind of charitable action," comparable to being sent to the workhouse.[58] This view had been articulated by medical authorities and newspaper columnists since early 1915. It became more pronounced after early 1917, when many local pensions committees were still sending disabled cases to the workhouses, despite the existence of regional orthopedic facilities.[59] Even when this was not the case, disabled men and their families "loathed" government relieving officers who visited orthopedic hospitals, regarding them as "the front–door step to the Workhouse."[60]

This animosity became more pronounced toward the end of the war even as the British Legion lobbied the government for a law that would oblige employers to hire retrained disabled soldiers.[61] As it had done throughout the war, the government insisted that employment schemes for the disabled should remain the preserve of the voluntary sector.[62] The outcome of the Legion's efforts, the King's National Roll scheme, only encouraged employers to take on disabled ex-servicemen to a minimum of 5 percent of their workforce.[63] By 1926, 28,000 firms were participating in this scheme, employing 365,000 disabled ex-servicemen.[64] But the National Roll was not as successful as these numbers suggest. For the most part, it provided temporary work schemes that became vulnerable to elimination as the economy became more depressed and unemployment rates soared. Moreover, the roll failed to stave off the tendency of government and private employers to prefer able-bodied men in the postwar workforce. Disabled veterans thus found it difficult to compete with the able-bodied for an ever-shrinking pool of jobs.

The publications of veterans' groups clearly registered these concerns. From 1916, the Association of Ex-Service Civil Servants, which represented the interests of many disabled veterans, fiercely supported "the principle of the right of ex-servicemen to priority and consideration for permanent posts in Government offices, and to something more than a mere struggle for existence."[65] And from 1917, the Association of Disabled Sailors and Soldiers leveled harsh criticism against women workers who took jobs from deserving veterans.[66] Veterans' groups also accused trade unions of ruining any chances of the retrained disabled veteran's gaining decent employment.[67]

Like the King's National Roll, Shepherd's Bush ultimately failed to achieve its goal of successfully rehabilitating those men who "did their bit." The hospital provided comprehensive aftercare to disabled soldiers until 1922, when government authorities transferred the facility from the possession of the War Office to the Ministry of Pensions. This transfer did not go smoothly. Since the establishment of the ministry, government officials had been increasingly "uncertain where the duties and obligations" of this department and the War Office "began and ended."[68] At the same time, the Council of the Royal College of Surgeons raised concerns about orthopedic specialists continuing to claim an area of surgical aftercare that had traditionally been the territory of the general surgeon.[69] Between 1922 and 1924, Jones made numerous appeals in the *Times* for public support to help save the hospital. His efforts ultimately failed, and in April 1925 Shepherd's

Bush ceased to exist when the government returned the building to the control of the Hammersmith Board of Guardians.

In light of the promising rhetoric of work extolled at Shepherd's Bush, disabled men, like many working women, ultimately found themselves being swept out of the labor market. But whereas women could reclaim their roles as mothers, sisters, daughters, and wives in a "land fit for heroes," the disabled heroes of war faced substantial difficulty in reclaiming their roles as breadwinners. As one veteran explained, disabled men found themselves in a "waste land" where they "searched for work" with "sickening heartbeats while being driven to prison or to beg for bread in the streets."[70]

NOTES

The author would like to thank David Gerber, Margot Finn, Kathryn Amdur, Walter Adamson, Laura Callanan, Chris Warren, and Jonathan Lewis for advice and encouragement on drafts of this essay. Earlier versions of this work were presented at the Institute of Historical Research's Modern Social History Seminar, the Northeast Conference on British Studies, and Emory University's British Studies Workshop.

1. John Galsworthy, foreword to *The Inter-Allied Conference on the After-Care of Disabled Men (Second Annual Meeting, Held in London, May 20 to 25) Reports Presented to the Conference (by various authors)* (London: HMSO, 1918), 14–15.

2. Seth Koven, "Remembering and Dismemberment: Crippled Children, Wounded Soldiers, and the Great War in Great Britain," *American Historical Review* 99, no. 4 (1994): 1167–1202.

3. Joanna Bourke, *Dismembering the Male: Men's Bodies, Britain, and the Great War* (Chicago: University of Chicago Press, 1996).

4. I am indebted to Roger Cooter's pathbreaking study of Shepherd's Bush in *Surgery and Society in Peace and War: Orthopaedics and the Organization of Modern Medicine, 1880–1948* (London: Macmillan, 1993), 113ff. Cooter is chiefly concerned with the implications of Shepherd's Bush for orthopedics; in contrast, I focus here on how this institution and its work-oriented rehabilitation program helped to shape the wartime and postwar identities of disabled soldiers.

5. Daniel Pick, *The War Machine: The Rationalisation of Slaughter in the Modern Age* (New Haven: Yale University Press, 1993).

6. On the implications of wartime factory work for gender see especially Laura Lee Downs, *Manufacturing Inequality: Gender Division in the French and British Metalworking Industries, 1914–1939* (Ithaca, N.Y.: Cornell University Press, 1995); and Angela Woollacott, *On Her Their Lives Depend: Munitions Workers in the Great War* (Berkeley and Los Angeles: University of California Press, 1994).

7. Cooter, *Surgery and Society*, 105ff. On these points of continuity see also Koven, "Remembering and Dismemberment," 1186–88; and Bourke, *Dismembering the Male*, 31–75.

8. Anson Rabinbach, *The Human Motor: Energy, Fatigue, and the Origin of Modernity* (Berkeley and Los Angeles: University of California Press, 1990), 38.

9. Andrew Scull, Charlotte McKenzie, and Nicholas Hervey, *Masters of Bedlam: The Transformation of the Mad-Doctoring Trade* (Princeton: Princeton University Press, 1996).

10. Frederick Watson, *The Life of Sir Robert Jones* (London: Hodder and Stoughton, 1934), 50.

11. Ibid., 114ff. See also Cooter, *Surgery and Society*, 53–78.

12. Gertrude Himmelfarb, *Poverty and Compassion: The Moral Imagination of the Late Victorians* (New York: Vintage Books, 1992), 226–43.

13. "The Brabazon Employment Society," *Times,* January 26, 1899, 7.

14. "Employment for Disabled Soldiers and Sailors," *Times,* July 26, 1905, 8.

15. Martin Wiener, *Reconstructing the Criminal: Culture, Law, and Policy in England, 1830–1914* (New York: Cambridge University Press, 1990). Significantly, Victor Bailey has questioned the trend toward therapeutic work in English prisons. See "English Prisons, Penal Culture, and the Abatement of Imprisonment, 1895–1922," *Journal of British Studies* 36, no. 3 (1997): 285–324.

16. PRO WO 33/47, Paper A.88, "Report of Committee on the Employment of Military Prisoners" (1887), which acknowledged the economic benefits of productive work programs in both military and civilian prisons.

17. *Reports by the Joint War Committee and the Joint War Finance Committee of the British Red Cross and the Order of St. John of Jerusalem of England on Voluntary Aid Rendered to the Sick and Wounded at Home and Abroad and to British Prisoners of War, 1914–1919, with Appendices* (London: HMSO, 1921), 248–53 and 732–44. Hereafter cited as *Reports.*

18. Jones to Keogh, as quoted in Watson, *Robert Jones,* 164–65. This correspondence also implied criticism of the general surgeon, who, as Jones saw it, could not effectively treat severe physical injuries. This criticism later prompted the Royal College of Surgeons to oppose Jones's naming of Shepherd's Bush a "Special Military Orthopaedic Hospital." From the perspective of the college, Shepherd's Bush represented a "hoarding of disabled cases" and an attempt to "break up surgery into sections. See "Report of Orthopaedic Committee," July 16, 1918, in *Royal College of Surgeons, Minutes of the Council of the Royal College of Surgeons, 1917–1919* (London: Taylor and Francis, 1919), 159–60.

19. *Reports,* 732.

20. The Joint War Committee consisted of the British Red Cross and Order of St. John. These organizations combined in 1914 for the duration of the war in an effort to provide the best possible aid to the country. Manuel had been a longtime supporter of the International Red Cross. After being deposed by republican forces during the Portuguese civil war, he emigrated to England, where British Red Cross officials placed him in charge of the organization's effort to establish curative programs for soldiers.

21. *Reports,* 734.

22. Ibid., 733.

23. Robert Jones, "The Problem of the Disabled," lecture delivered at the Royal Institute of Public Health, November 14, as reprinted in *American Journal of Orthopaedic Surgery* 16, no. 5 (1918): 273–90.

24. Of the first 1,300 men who entered the hospital and passed through its workshops, no fewer than 1,000 were sufficiently rehabilitated to return to military action. See Cooter, *Surgery and Society,* 118.

25. *Reports,* 733.

26. Ibid.

27. Robert Jones, "Orthopaedic Outlook in Military Surgery," *British Medical Journal*, January 12, 1918, 41–45, 42.

28. Thomas Jones, "Notes on the Arrangements for the Treatment and Training of Disabled Soldiers," a War Cabinet memorandum dated March 5, 1917 lodged in the Lloyd George papers, House of Lords, F/79/15.

29. See David Powell, *The Edwardian Crisis: Britain, 1901–1914* (New York: St. Martin's Press, 1996), 44–48.

30. G. R. Girdlestone, *Occupational Therapy for the Wounded,* lecture given at the Annual General Meeting of the Association of Occupational Therapists, March, 1941 (London: Association of Occupational Therapists, 1941), 7.

31. Jones, "Problem of the Disabled." See also Douglas C. McMurtrie, "The Rehabilitation of War Cripples," *Medical Review of Reviews* (1918): 409–85.

32. Jones, address to the Inter-Allied Conference on the After-Care of Disabled Men, Second Annual Meeting, as quoted in *Reports,* 253.

33. "Meeting the Problem of the War Cripple: Fighting in the Front-Line Trenches of the Army of Reconstruction is the American Red Cross," *American Red Cross Bulletin* (London: American National Red Cross, 1918), 6–7. At its opening in 1916, Shepherd's Bush contained 800 beds and roughly as many patients. By the following year, approximately half of this number were working in the curative workshops. See *Hammersmith Hospital and the Postgraduate Medical School of London: A Short History, 1905–1955* (London: Hammersmith Hospital, 1955), 9. Evidence suggests that when the number of patients at the hospital increased to nearly 1,200 in 1918, participation in the shops also increased to half this number. See "Meeting the Problem."

34. Jones, *Notes on Military Orthopaedics* (New York: British Red Cross Society and Cassell and Company, Ltd., 1917), preface.

35. Manuel II, "Scheme and Organization of Curative Workshops," in Robert Jones, ed., *Orthopaedic Surgery of Injuries* (London: Oxford Medical Publications, 1921), 629–44.

36. Jones, *Notes on Military Orthopaedics,* preface.

37. Watson, *Robert Jones,* 164–68.

38. Jones, "Problem of the Disabled."

39. Jones, "The Orthopaedic Outlook in Military Surgery," lecture delivered at the Hunterian Society on June 2, 1918, as reprinted in *British Medical Journal,* June 12, 1918, 41–54.

40. Jones, "Problem of the Disabled."

41. Jones, address to the Inter-Allied Conference on the After-Care of Disabled Men, Second Annual Meeting, as quoted in *Reports,* 253.

42. Jones, "Problem of the Disabled."

43. Jones, *Notes on Military Orthopaedics,* preface.

44. *Reports,* 253.

45. Major Walter Hill, "The Training of the Disabled: The Military Orthopaedic Hospital, Shepherd's Bush," *War Pensions Gazette,* no. 41, August 1917, 40–41. Red Cross reports similarly noted that hospital workshops "had the enormous advantage of being, not only a more speedy means of obtaining the necessary articles than would have been the case if we had to produce them outside, but also a very considerable economy to the State." *Reports,* 1921, 248–53.

46. *Reports,* 734.

47. The American Red Cross used similar images in it publicity pamphlets. See, for example, Douglas C. McMurtrie, *Reconstructing the Disabled Soldier* (New York: Red Cross Institute for Crippled and Disabled Men, 1918), especially 26.

48. Woollacott, *On Her Their Lives Depend,* 72.

49. Jones, "The Orthopaedic Outlook," 42.

50. Letter from Jones to Sir George Makins, as quoted in Watson, *Robert Jones,* 147–48.

51. See Downs, *Manufacturing Inequality,* 33–43 and 82–85; and Woollacott, *On Her Their Lives Depend,* 27–30.

52. See clauses 16 and 17 of Ministry of Pensions, *Instructions and Notes on the Treatment and Training of Disabled Men* (London: HMSO, 1917), 8. Authorities certainly realized that this policy might well court disciplinary problems. Jones himself believed that it wasn't proper to link hospital work to the soldier's receipt of a pension. See official memorandum on the care of disabled soldiers written in November 1916 by Knowsley Derby, undersecretary of state for war, to Lloyd George, which reveals Jones's position on this matter early in the development of Shepherd's Bush. Lloyd George Papers, House of Lords, E/1/1/9.

53. Jones, *Notes,* preface. Manuel similarly observed that although the work in the shops was "ordered by the surgeon directly, and can therefore be considered as theoretically compulsory, it is still voluntary." On the privileges use to promote work, see *Reports,* 250.

54. I. G. Gibbon, "Confidential Report to the War Cabinet from Intelligence Department, Local Governments Board: Care of Disabled Soldiers in France and Germany," Lloyd George Papers. House of Lords, F/79/15.

55. Arthur Boscawen, in *Report on the Inter-Allied Conference for the Study of Professional Re-Education and Other Questions of Interest to Soldiers and Sailors Disabled by the War (Paris, 8 to 12 May 1917)* (London: HMSO, 1917), 3–10.

56. Gerard J. DeGroot, *Blighty: British Society in the Era of the Great War* (New York: Longman, 1996), 257–58. The meager pension offered to disabled soldiers itself promoted grievances among disabled veterans. See, for example, "The Plight of Disabled Soldier," *Labour Leader,* August 10, 1916, 2; and A. A. Watts, "Disabled Heroes: Pensions or Pittances," *Call,* July 27, 1916, 1.

57. J. M. Andrew, "Employment Bureau and Instruction Classes, Queen Mary's Auxiliary Convalescent Hospital, Roehampton, Reports for May and June 1917," London Metropolitan Archives, Ref. H02/QM/A.

58. This was the observation of T. J. Passmore, a member of the Birmingham Citizens' Committee, who spoke at the Inter-Allied Conference on the After-Care of Disabled Men, Second Annual Meeting. See *The Inter-Allied Conference on the After-Care of Disabled Men (Second Annual Meeting, Held in London, May 20 to 25) Supplement to the Reports Presented to the Conference (by various authors)* (London: HMSO, 1918), 57. Passmore also pointed out that this view was widespread among the families of disabled soldiers.

59. *Hospital,* July 9, 1917, 267; and *Times,* April 9, 1917, 8. The *Hospital* also reported that the "discharged soldier, technically capable of work, but really incapacitated and thrown aside [was] once more knocking at the infirmary door." See *Hospital,*

June 9, 1917, 180. Public complaints about this phenomenon had been occurring since early in the war. See *Poor Law Officers Journal,* October 22, 1915, 1229.

60. Captain W. G. Wilcox, organizing secretary of the British Legion, Appeal Department, in a draft speech on "raising funds for the relief of distress among ex-servicemen and their dependents," accompanying letter to General Haig, dated January 16, 1926, Haig Papers. National Library of Scotland, Acc. 236/H/C.

61. DeGroot, *Blighty,* 260ff.

62. The Ministry of Labour, for example, provided retraining centers for ex-servicemen in its "Government Instructional Factories," but it left the subsequent hiring of these men to the initiative of civilian employers. For an excellent description of how these government-run factories sought not to "produce component or finished goods, but [rather] skilled men," see Ministry of Labour, *Memories: The Magazine of the 19th London Old Comrades Association,* June 1920, 23. Why the MOL took such a position is made clear in the Minutes of the Cabinet Committee on Unemployment, which explained that it would be "unwise" to do more than "train" ex-servicemen, since "owing to Trade Union objections and trade depression, there was a likelihood that the men trained would be unable to find employment." PRO CAB 27/114, Minutes of September 14, 1920 Meeting.

63. For an excellent description of the debate surrounding the King's Roll, whether it should be voluntary or compulsory, see the King's Roll National Council, "Memorandum on Compulsory Employment of Disabled Ex-Servicemen," Item 3 on the Council's Agenda for May 20, 1924, Haig Papers, Acc. 3155/236s, National Library of Scotland.

64. DeGroot, *Blighty,* 260.

65. "The President's Message," *The Live Wire: Official Organ of the National Ex-Service Men's Union of Temporary Civil Servants,* June 1, 1920, 2.

66. For criticisms of women, see especially the series of poems, entitled "Fit For Heroes," in the first volume of the *Live Wire.* See also National Association of Discharged Sailors and Soldiers, Proceedings of the First Annual Conference, held in Blackburn, October 6, 1917, Imperial War Museum, Department of Printed Books.

67. See, for example, J. Paterson Bryant, "Are We Trade Unionists?" *Live Wire,* May 1921, 2.

68. Watson, *Robert Jones,* 210–12.

69. See note 18 above and J. Trueta, *Gathorne Robert Girdlestone* (Oxford: Oxford University Press, 1971), 27. For further details on this debate see "Report of Orthopaedic Committee," July 16, 1918, in *Royal College of Surgeons, Minutes of the Council of the Royal College of Surgeons, 1917–1919* (London: Taylor and Francis, 1919), 159–60.

70. "How You Were Fooled," in J. Snooks, *To Hell with War* (London: National Committee for the Declaration of Ex-Servicemen Against War/Holborn Labour Party Rooms, 1927), 3–4. On this phenomenon see especially Arthur Marwick, *The Deluge: British Society and the First World War* (Boston: Little, Brown, 1966), 284.

R. B. Rosenburg

"Empty Sleeves and Wooden Pegs": Disabled Confederate Veterans in Image and Reality

"Truly it seems to me that the time has come when 'No Maimed Confederate Need Apply,'" observed 41-year-old Charles Moore Jr., of Alexandria, Louisiana, during the summer of 1880. For some time after the war, Moore, a former corporal in Company F, Fifth Louisiana Infantry (Hays' Brigade), had done remarkably well for himself and his family of five, despite being shot and having his leg amputated on the second day of fighting at Gettysburg more than a decade earlier. Yet in 1877 Moore lost his clerking job, and for the next few years he applied for positions all over Rapides Parish, only to be told that the job had been offered to some "Planter's Son or Relative." Although feeling "Very Delicate about the Matter," he had no choice but to request assistance from his former comrades. Having appeared in New Orleans with only four dollars in his pocket, his health completely broken, and his family evicted from their home, Moore appealed for help with the "Extremest Delicasy Imaginable." "Pride and Hunger are not Mutual Friends," Moore averred. Besides, it is not "Manly in Me to see My wife, Children and Myself in want any longer."[1]

John Newton Sloan of Pontotoc, Mississippi, knew firsthand the desperation Moore described. As a captain in a Mississippi regiment, he was horribly wounded and disabled at Chickamauga on September 20, 1863, by a shell fragment that smashed through his lower jaw, shot away his tongue, shattered his upper teeth, and terribly mutilated his face. The regimental chaplain vividly recalled years later: "Four surgeons pronounced his case hopeless. The chin dangled in front of his breast. The shell made a gash from the outer edge of the right eye to the corner of the mouth." He lingered in a field hospital untreated for three days, in agony, without water, until doctors from Ringgold, Georgia, arrived on the scene, cut away Sloan's chin, and sewed his nose to his face. Ever since, Sloan had had to lie on his back three times a day in order to be fed by others with fluids, since he could not chew any food. Nevertheless, he had managed to support himself and his wife and two daughters for over 25 years, but could do so no longer. On December 27, 1893, he pleaded: "Comrades, I dislike to beg. I had rather that it was different, but I cannot help it. I received this ugly and unfortunate wound in a just and honorable cause . . . defending our beloved Sunny Southland, homes, property and firesides." Accompanying his letter was the endorsements of two other Confederate veterans who knew Sloan to be a "very poor, a good, moral man, a law-abiding citizen, [who] merits all that can be done for him."[2]

The sad reality was that Moore and Sloan were not alone in their suffering and shame. Wherever ex-Confederates resided there were disabled veterans who found themselves unable to recover from the ravages of the war. John Smith Watson, antebellum Georgia planter, slaveowner, and father of seven, returned from the war twice wounded and penniless. Forced to sell his plantation at a fraction of its value, he turned to drinking and to gambling and suffered periodic depressions, causing his fortunes to sink even further. By 1878 he had fallen into a "hopeless stupor," leading a broken life in a "miserable shanty." J. H. Allen, ex-captain, Fifteenth Virginia Infantry, lay confined in his bed in Richmond, owing to wounds received more than 20 years earlier at Sharpsburg, Maryland, with "all the means which I possesed [sic], eather [sic] in money, or properity [sic] . . . wrenched from my grasp." Excruciating pain still plagued Nathan J. Lewis of Bullock County, Alabama, a former sergeant in the 38th North Carolina Infantry, whose right leg had been amputated at Petersburg and was unable to work years later. James H. Eubank, Company K, 34th Virginia, was "shot through right wrist" at Hatcher's Run in March 1865, rendering his hand and fingers "useless" ever since. By 1893 William J. McNairy of Aberdeen, Mississippi, still had not fully recuperated from the wound he had received at Gettysburg, nor had he been able to hold down a decent job. Samuel J. Spindle, formerly of Harpers Ferry, spent nearly 20 years in Mexico, before showing up in Austin, Texas, penniless, unemployed, and agonized by an old war wound. And then there was William E. Todd, who trekked from New Orleans to Birmingham in search of "honest" work. "I came here to leave behind my faults & follies, to start afresh & build myself up. *I have acted like a man,* but been deceived & disappointed." Evidently, so had Todd's comrades. He has lost "all sense of manhood," remarked F. A. Biers, who had encountered Todd on the streets of Birmingham some weeks earlier, hungry, poorly clad, broke, and drunk. Todd was fed, given clothing and a dollar for a bath and some tobacco, as well as introduced to a gentleman who promised to find him work. But Todd began to drink again. The last time Biers saw him was in front of the Post Office "sure enough as drunk," "sitting on the steps with a crowd of boys around him," taunting him.[3]

The postwar careers of these veterans typify the lives of thousands of disabled and indigent ex-Confederates who were compelled to apply to relief agencies for help. They appeared on the scene in significant numbers in the countryside, a familiar sight, plodding along dusty roads. Moving from place to place, as homeless, unemployed drifters, they sought to satisfy their hunger and to seek shelter. Standing hat in hand at the kitchen door to seek a handout, they were forced to perform a chore or two in exchange for food. In the cities they hoped to find work and the necessities of life for themselves and their families. The city served as a delta of rivers of depression, unemployment, and displacement. And the sheer mass of these pathetic men who, in the prime of their lives, found themselves disabled, out of work, and impoverished posed a problem. The number of three-year Confederate enlistees who survived the Civil War is estimated to have been 881,875. Of these, 220,469 (or one of every four) had been disabled by disease or wounds.[4] For tens of thousands of Confederate veterans who returned to civilian life suffering from the long-term physical and psychological consequences of battlefield wounds or wartime disease, the war never ended. How might their suffering best be abated?

Dealing with badly injured and potentially helpless soldiers did not wait until war's end. The Confederate Congress had recognized the need to do something. Beginning in April 1862 permanently disabled soldiers (but not sailors or marines) were granted honorable discharges and allowed to return to their homes without monetary assistance from the government. A second act in December 1863 entitled discharged Confederate soldiers, who "by reason of wounds or injuries received in the service" were prevented from earning a livelihood, to continue drawing their service pay. In February 1864 Congress created the Invalid Corps, in which all soldiers who were disabled would be "retired or discharged from their respective positions . . . but the rank, pay and emoluments . . . shall continue to the end of the war." The Confederate government also created a system of orthopedic hospitals intended for "the exclusive treatment of old injuries and deformities from gunshot wounds." In addition, on March 9, 1865, Confederate hospitals were authorized to admit *all* veterans who were disabled, owing to "unhealed or imperfectly healed wounds, necrosis, sloughing, false joints, ununited dislocations, local paralysis, hernia, stone of the bladder," and other postoperative complications, provided the patients had "reasonable prospects of responding to skilled surgical attention." Lawmakers in Richmond, however, stopped short of providing artificial limbs to needy soldiers, as the federal government had begun doing early in the war. And despite the passage of a measure that would have created a national Confederate "Veteran Soldiers' Home" for "wounded and disabled officers, soldiers, and seamen," President Jefferson Davis, on February 11, 1864, vetoed the bill on constitutional grounds.[5]

Private relief agencies were also formed during the war in an attempt to meet the needs of disabled veterans. One such organization was the Association for the Relief of Maimed Soldiers (ARMS), founded at the African Church in Richmond, Virginia, on January 22, 1864. Its purpose: to "appeal principally to benevolent and patriotic Confederate citizens to unite and present to each of those deprived of their limbs, an artificial limb not as an act of charity, but of esteem, respect, and gratitude." ARMS estimated that more than 10,000 men had lost their limbs in battle during the war, and "the sight of empty sleeves and of men hobbling on wooden pegs, or swinging on the galling crutch" underscored the necessity for such an organization. Despite its clever acronym, ARMS aimed to collect money for and to distribute only artificial *legs* by way of membership dues ($10 per year or $300 for life memberships). From the time of its founding until the end of the war, ARMS received $113,464 and distributed as many as 75 artificial legs each month to men from 14 different states. The prostheses came from 11 Southern or foreign manufacturers. Five of the artificial leg manufacturers were located in Virginia, two each in Alabama and in Georgia, and one in each of the Carolinas. Never had prostheses manufacturing possessed such a commercial value as the artificial limb industry of the postwar South, where numbers of needy veterans far exceeded those who had been maimed in prewar farm accidents.[6]

With the fall of the Confederacy it was up to other private charities and individual states to aid ex-soldiers who were incapable of caring for their families and who were not otherwise eligible for Federal pensions. One such benevolent group that distributed food, money, and clothing to deserving and disabled veterans was the Washington Light Infantry Charitable Aid Association, which contributed over $20,000 from 1865 to 1900.[7] Public support for those with wartime disabilities, especially returning amputees, remained a subject of wide concern in the immediate postwar years. As a disabled ex-Confederate in North Carolina, who identified himself as "One Arm," summarized the situation in November 1865:

Our public men say much and promise to do much if elected for the [ex-slaves]—but not a syllable . . . is said to comfort the poor unfortunate man who has his feeble scarred body suspended on crutches—or the poor creature who has hanging by his side an empty coat sleeve. Is it right to pass this class by and do nothing to aid them in their dark future? . . . These are hard times on the maimed of the land. Give us a chance and we will not be a burden to the country.[8]

Some Southern state governments formed after the war under President Andrew Johnson's relatively lenient plan of restoration of the Union did the best they could with limited resources to aid disabled Confederate veterans such as "One Arm." By act of February 19, 1867, for example, the Alabama legislature appropriated $30,000 and authorized the governor to contract with some manufacturer of artificial limbs to furnish such products to the "large number of men" then residing within the state who had "suffered bodily mutilation" while in military service. The manufacturer was required by law to deliver the limbs (furnished at a price not to exceed $70 for a prosthesis above the knee and $50 below the knee) to some central point in the state and to ensure that limb(s) properly fit so as to ensure the "ease, security and comfort" of the amputee. Any needy veteran who was so seriously disabled that an artificial limb would be of no value could collect a $100 commutation (onetime appropriation approved by the General Assembly). During the first year of this program, some 218 artificial limbs were distributed by the firm Strasser and Callahan of Montgomery. Among the veterans who received a free prosthesis was C. J. Armstrong, Company C, 33rd Alabama, who had been wounded at New Hope Church, Georgia, on May 27, 1864. Armstrong received another of "Strasser's legs" in 1872, and three years later he was fitted for a "Hawkins" peg leg, wearing it every day, "until [he] wore it completely out."[9] Virginia's first attempt in supplying artificial legs at public expense "to every citizen of the commonwealth who lost a limb in the late war" was a January 25, 1867, act that appropriated $20,000. Before receiving a substitute limb the veteran had to satisfy residency requirements and to prove that the limb had been lost during the war.[10] South Carolina's legislature set aside $20,000 for limbs and gave free passes on railroads to and from the place where the limbs were fitted. Similar veterans' aid programs were initiated in Florida, Georgia, North Carolina, Arkansas, and Mississippi, which devoted a fifth of its entire 1866 revenues to artificial legs. In addition to spending approximately $32,000 from 1866 to 1869 on its maimed veterans, Georgia also offered free education to disabled veterans to attend public colleges.[11]

"The war veterans who received as holiday presents artificial legs and arms, may be said to have been truly re-membered," quipped the *New*

Orleans Daily Picayune.[12] In addition to allocating $20,000 to purchase prostheses for its veterans, Louisiana also appropriated in March 1866 an extra $20,000 to establish a soldiers' home for all indigent, wounded, and maimed men who served in Louisiana commands. Nowhere in the enabling act did the term "ex-Confederate" appear, though the measure was obviously intended to benefit the state's veterans. After Governor J. Madison Wells signed Act No. 103 into law, he appointed eight members of the legislature (five of whom were ex-Confederate officers) to serve as a board of directors, who made it clear from the outset that the planned institution was not a charity but a "happy home" prepared by a proud and grateful people. Within a few months the board leased the widow Doussan's Lake Shore Hotel, described as a "large and commodious" building "healthily and pleasantly situated," overlooking Lake Pontchartrain, at Mandeville, St. Tammany Parish. What was then a two-and-a-half-hour boat ride from New Orleans, the temporary home was fitted up with "every comfort," including "bathing houses and places of recreation." Of the 96 inmates who eventually resided there, almost all were native Louisianians, and over one-half suffered from chronic disabilities. The home managed to receive an additional $10,000 the following year, before a Republican-dominated government, which had no sympathy for ex-Confederates, rescinded the act in 1868. With no further operating capital, the institution had to be abandoned.[13]

No other Southern state, for the time being at least, attempted to provide "indoor relief" to its disabled ex-Confederate populations. But what happened to the soldiers' home in Louisiana was by no means unique. Other state veterans' programs established during the Presidential Reconstruction era (1865–67) also ended or were seriously curtailed. Not long after the war, Georgia had one of the most comprehensive veterans' benefits programs of all the Southern states. In early 1866 the state appropriated $200,000 to purchase corn for the families of deceased soldiers, and later that fall disabled veterans specifically received another $100,000 for corn. In addition, the legislature provided $50,000 to furnish artificial limbs to maimed ex-Confederates, and it inaugurated a program that paid more than $100,000 to assist "many indigent maimed soldiers, . . . who, by reason of loss of limbs, are deprived of the ability to perform physical labor" to attend any of the state's five public colleges. Furthermore, before the year was over, the state authorized each county to levy an annual tax to provide for the basic needs of disabled veterans and the indigent families of deceased Confederate soldiers. But these programs survived for only two years, becoming victims of "bloody shirt" politics in which Republicans sought to preserve the memory of Civil War divisions by associating both ex-Confederates and Democrats with rebellion and disloyalty in order to garner votes. By 1869, Republican-dominated sessions had either repealed these acts or discontinued funding them.[14]

After the reestablishment of Democratic rule, new (or newly funded) programs for veterans gradually came into being as states offered war-disabled ex-soldiers an expanded array of social benefits. For instance, in 1871, when Democrats again controlled the state government, Georgia Redeemers immediately reinstituted an artificial limbs program for Confederate amputees. Despite their reputation for fiscal conservatism or retrenchment, the so-called Bourbon Democrats in 1875 reauthorized each county to pay maimed and indigent soldiers $100 annually, provided that the intended beneficiaries had lost two limbs during the war and that they now possessed less than $1,000 of taxable property (a law passed in 1885 removed the property requirement). A measure enacted on September 20, 1879, appropriated additional funds for artificial limbs; upwards of $60,000 was finally distributed. The 1883 legislature authorized commutations in lieu of artificial limbs and exempted disabled Confederate veterans from the poll tax. And a constitutional amendment ratified in 1886 empowered the Georgia legislature for the first time to provide pensions to disabled veterans. Under this provision, by act of October 24, 1887, any disabled, maimed, blind, or deaf Confederate veteran then residing in Georgia was eligible to receive an annual pension ranging from $20 to $100, depending upon the type of disability. Two years later Georgia lawmakers extended pension benefits to include "diseased" veterans.[15]

A similar pattern of aid to disabled veterans can be observed throughout the post-Reconstruction South. The artificial limb program that began in South Carolina in the fall of 1866 ended in early 1869 but was continued by the Redeemers in 1877, after the last federal troops had withdrawn from the capital in Columbia and the Republican government had collapsed. The program expanded in 1879 to include commutations and broadened beginning in 1881 to provide for veterans who suffered from all war-related injuries.[16] In Virginia, commutations also replaced artificial limbs in 1872, and over the next decade thousands of ex-Confederates who were disabled in ways other than amputation gradually became eligible for veterans' benefits.[17] Redeemed in 1874, Alabama recommenced buying artificial limbs for its veterans in 1876 and offering commutations the following year. More than $150,000 had been appropriated by 1889.[18] Beginning in 1880 and for the next three successive biennial sessions, Louisiana's lawmakers appropriated funds for artificial limbs. By 1888 pro rata cash payments were being made for veterans whose wartime injuries involved the loss of limbs, sight, hearing, voice, or mobility. In addition, Louisiana Act No. 96, signed on July 10, 1884, by Governor Samuel D. McEnery, a veteran himself, offered 160 acres of public land to ex-Confederates whose service-related disabilities disqualified them "from active vocations of life" and to widows of soldiers in "indigent circumstances." By 1886, some 226 veterans and widows had been granted 123,103 acres of public lands.[19] Meanwhile, in 1881 the Texas legislature had been able to offer disability compensation in the form of land scrip certificates of 1,280 acres to every permanently disabled and indigent Confederate veteran and Confederate widow residing in the state. Land certificates could be sold and purchased for between $5 and $400. The act had to be repealed in 1883, after some 1,979,852 acres had been awarded and the public domain was declared "virtually exhausted."[20]

By the 1880s the plight of disabled veterans across the South aroused attention. Even though nearly half of all Confederate veterans who had returned from the war were no longer living, those who had survived were still a visible problem.[21] C. F. Beauregard, formerly of the New Orleans Light Horse, but now an invalid and entirely destitute, was "sadly in need of attention." N. E. Edmundo, a veteran of the 56th Virginia wounded at Gaines Mill, was "bankrupt and homeless" in Texas. Having lost his right arm at Spottsylvania, A. B. Carter of Memphis was no longer able to work and was now beginning "to feel very dependent" and despondent. J. B. Clark of Bowling Green, Kentucky, who had lost a leg while riding with John Hunt Morgan, was now destitute, his health entirely broken and feeling "acute humiliation." R. B. Clements's boss informed him that he could no longer keep his job as temporary mulewatcher and janitor for the Richmond armory because he had only one arm. "My soul is lost," uttered Samuel Vaughn Corbell, who had enlisted in the Sixth Virginia Cavalry when he was only 14 years old and was wounded nine times and taken prisoner twice. His health impaired and his property destroyed by the war, he became a "wanderer," drifting aimlessly from Virginia to Maryland to Texas and finally back east to North Carolina. George W. Grant was "utterly helpless," as was another old veteran from Alabama who was in an Abingdon, Virginia, almshouse and was "now verry week [sic] and has the consumption." Auriel Aimard had contracted dysentery during the war, and it continued to plague him, rendering him a "perfect invalid" without the resources or kin or friends to help him. J. Medlock had "lost all my property and my health in the late war" and had "wandered from North Carolina to Texas trying to make a living." Daniel Daly of New Orleans needed money to purchase a pair of crutches, owing to the loss of use of his leg while a prisoner of war. Fifty-five-year-old R. R. Johnston, a former private in the 154th Tennessee, wounded at Shiloh and now "incapacitated for work," was "Homeless, friendless & destitute."[22]

In the urban areas impoverished men such as these and thousands of others like them appeared on the scene, jobless, half-starved, weary, ragged, excessively dirty, and sorrowful. There one sat with shoulders sagging in a vacant doorway, desperately waiting for someone to pass by and offer him a job, a meal, or some spare change and perhaps another drink. Elsewhere another huddled next to his meager fire in a vacant lot by the railyard, reflecting on painful memories. Down the street still another lay dying of disease amid the foul conditions of the city almshouse. The economic outlook for unskilled and permanently disabled veterans was bleak. Thousands who appealed for medical and monetary assistance from various fraternal groups, private charities, and relief agencies in the 1880s claimed that the wounds they had received in the course of the fighting had not yet healed. In each case, the loss of a limb, blindness, or the inability to stand upright without flinching had seriously curtailed a veteran's postwar economic activity and his ability to care for family. Forced into desperate circumstances, a number turned to begging, and the disturbing sight of battle-scarred veterans appealing for money on city streets became depressingly familiar in the postwar years. Wherever they were, realization of the suffering of the South's poor boys pricked Southern consciousness and moved it to action.

Whether viewed annually, by decades, or as a percentage of total state expenditures, Confederate disability compensation programs enacted after Reconstruction in response to the perceived need of poor veterans were significant long-term consequences of the Civil War. By the early 1920s, when the number of intended beneficiaries had dwindled to fewer than 80,000, 20 percent of all Southern state revenues went to Confederate relief measures. Why this level of commitment?

Many people were motivated not only by a sense of comradeship and humanitarianism, but also by what they themselves defined as being their often repeated "sacred duty." For it was not only a matter of regional pride for Southerners to take care of their less fortunate brethren of a glorious cause; it was a matter of honor to praise the "supreme manliness" of the "devoted" Confederate soldier, who by virtue of self-discipline had attained "moral perfection." The Confederate private soldier "bore so large a share of hardship" during the war. They were poorly armed, barefooted, hatless, and had clothing "often the more ragged than any beggar." Despite Johnny

Reb's sometimes "picturesque, grotesque, unique" appearance, he was the "model citizen soldier, the military hero of the nineteenth century!" Confederate veterans are "the men who made the grandest fight that the world has ever seen," exclaimed Governor E. W. Rector of Arkansas. "The whole world was their enemies—they fought the universe!"[23] Surely men of such caliber merited special attention. "These old soldiers cannot be with [us] much longer," wrote General Joseph Wheeler in 1902. "They are rapidly nearing the sunset of their lives, and the present generation must be saved the remorse which in after years they will feel, if, looking back, they see that during the short time these brave heroes were with them, they were allowed to spend their last days in want and suffering."[24] To many, Johnny Reb symbolized valor, obedience to duty, and self-sacrifice—true Southern values. The empty sleeve was a badge of courage, and the disabled veteran stood as testimony to the violence and pain caused by the war. Clement J. Moody, a legislator from Middle Tennessee, certainly agreed:

> When the Southern Confederacy had been wrapped in her bloody winding sheet, and the formally cherished hope of the South had gone down in darkness and in death, when our boys in sorrowful silence had stacked their guns at Appomattox and began their lonesome journey home, some came home with empty sleeves, some came hobbling home on one leg, some left both legs on the battlefield, some with sightless eyeballs groped their way home in blindness, in darkness—all came in tatters and rags to look upon the ashes of their ruined homes. . . . All of them are rapidly going and will soon be gone.[25]

It was this image of the Confederate soldier, someone rendered physically disabled by war who was fast approaching extinction, that Southerners wanted to protect, preserve, rehabilitate, and (as some critics would charge) exploit. The image of Johnny Reb was persistently conjured up, nurtured, and promoted, as a means of advancing a host of causes. Gaunt forms in ragged shirts and torn pantaloons and empty sleeves or wooden pegs became the image's most dominant features. The visibly disabled veteran was an important symbolic repository of Southern identity. A powerful illustration that appeared in the *Atlanta Constitution* in 1903 best captures this image. Here an old, one-legged Confederate hero, with a laurel wreath draped over his shoulders and with the aid of a crutch, a peg leg, and a cane (all symbols of both disability and independence) totters past a banner that suggests lasting camaraderie, courage, and defiance, as well as the South's continuing emotional investment in fulfilling its sacred duty. "The old brigades march slower now— / the boys who wore the gray," the banner reads. "They hear their comrades callin' from the white tents [heaven] far away; And answer with the ringin' roll of 'DIXIE!' " Proponents of public relief for the disabled Confederate veteran were moved largely by the popular icon of Johnny Reb as depicted in this drawing. His form and likeness dotted the Southern postwar landscape on countless courthouse lawns, as a visible reminder of those who had long frequented these places.[26] To the men and women who sought to perpetuate his memory, Johnny Reb served as a living relic from a mythic past to be preserved and enshrined.

One of the most tangible and long-lasting attempts to preserve and enshrine Confederate veterans came in the form of soldiers' homes. It will be recalled that the first such institution, chartered in Louisiana in 1866, was soon abandoned. The Confederate Soldiers' Home and Widows' and Orphans' Asylum, founded in 1881 in Georgetown, Kentucky, for the relief of the "crippled and indigent Confederate," likewise failed two years later.[27] But on March 14, 1884, when the Camp Nicholls Confederate Soldiers' Home in New Orleans officially opened its doors, they were destined to remain open for nearly 60 years. Named for Governor Francis T. Nicholls, a one-armed, one-legged, one-eyed, ex-Confederate brigadier, the second soldiers' home of Louisiana was made possible through the combined efforts of two strong veterans' societies headquartered in New Orleans: the Association of the Army of Northern Virginia (AANV) and the Association of the Army of Tennessee (AAT).

Like most fraternal orders of the period, each group functioned primarily as a benefit society, preferring to identify itself as "benevolent" and incorporating the word as part of its official title. Benevolence assumed two forms. First, each association aimed to provide its own dues-paying members and their dependents with assistance during personal and unavoidable crises: sudden unemployment, poverty, and "extreme cases of want and sickness." Nonmembers, but comrades nonetheless, received second priority. In response to the yellow fever epidemic that devastated New Orleans in 1878, each association created and maintained for many years veterans' benefits and relief committees that supervised the distribution of funds and other donated items of clothing, food, and medicine to "worthy" recipients. The AAT Relief Committee in New Orleans received hundreds of requests for aid. The committee filled prescriptions for veterans, paid funeral expenses (until 1905) and provided cash relief (until 1903). During and after the 1878 yellow fever epidemic the AAT paid for nurses, incidentals, and groceries. The $1,202 paid to 103 veterans for the month of October 1878 is typical: October 1–5, $110 distributed to 16 veterans, $147.75 to 11 vet-

FIG. 8. Johnny Reb. Images such as this one not only helped inspire Southerners to respond to the physical and emotional needs of disabled Confederate veterans, but also provided testimony to the veterans' pride and manliness. (*Atlanta Constitution,* May 21, 1903.)

erans; October 5–11, $388.45 to 23 veterans, widows, and families; October 11–16, $176 for 24 veterans; October 17–24, $248.95 for 28 veterans; October 24–31, $279.15 for 25 veterans. In 1881 $270 was distributed among 11 veterans and widows, with the most any one veteran received being $7.50 per month. In 1882 $449 was handed out to 13 veterans and widows. In the depression era of the mid-1890s several prominent members of the AANV founded a job agency in order to assist able-bodied comrades (and their spouses and children) in finding work. Headed by James Y. Gilmore, a journalist, and Hamilton Dudley Coleman, a local plantation machinery manufacturer and dealer, the Confederate Veterans Employment Bureau of New Orleans published and circulated a small pamphlet containing the names, addresses, and occupations of hundreds of "exemplary and lawabiding" applicants. Owing largely to the lobbying efforts of the AAT and AANV, the State of Louisiana had supplied artificial limbs or commutations and had granted a quarter section of land to disabled and indigent Confederate veterans and widows. Also among the first homes founded for "invalid and infirm" Confederate veterans was the R. E. Lee Camp Soldiers' Home in Richmond, Virginia. Dedicated on February 22, 1885, the home was established by a veterans' group that was primarily dedicated to "minister[ing] . . . to the wants of" disabled comrades languishing in poorhouses throughout the South.[28]

Inspired by the success of these two examples in Louisiana and Virginia, Confederate veterans' organizations in several other states soon joined the soldiers' home movement. Numerous ex-Confederate generals—including Joseph E. Johnston, E. Kirby Smith, James Longstreet, Clement A. Evans, Fitzhugh Lee, John B. Gordon, and Joseph Wheeler, as well as the wives and daughters of Generals Robert E. Lee, Thomas J. ("Stonewall") Jackson, and A. P. Hill, among others—participated in and gave their pledges and influence to the benevolence activity. By 1929, 16 Confederate soldiers' homes were founded, one in each of the 11 states of the Confederacy, plus Maryland, Kentucky, Oklahoma, Missouri, and even California. Originally, only honorably discharged and poor Confederate veterans (and in some cases veterans' wives, but only when accompanied by their husbands) were admitted as inmates to Confederate soldiers' homes. Funding for the homes came from private contributions and, predominantly, state revenues, but never from the federal government, though there were several aborted attempts to secure such funding; and unlike their national counterparts, the Union veterans' homes in 28 different states from Vermont to California that augmented the network of national homes for disabled volunteer soldiers (NHDVS), Confederate soldiers' homes from the outset excluded veterans from other wars.

In all, an estimated 20,000 Confederate veterans resided in the 16 homes, where they were given food, medical care, shelter, entertainment, and companionship. Although the homes were relatively few in number, more disabled Southern veterans received institutional care in the homes than in any other locations. Soldiers' homes were largely places for poor, single, wounded men to mend their broken lives or to spend the remainder of their days. Roughly one of every four of these veterans had suffered from a visible war wound, such as the loss of a limb, a broken back, or a fractured skull, the most dramatic examples of wartime disability. More than one-half of all ex-Confederates who resided in such institutions had either been yeoman farmers, agricultural workers, or other unskilled laborers both before and after the war. Many of these same men had always lived on the margin, with the bare minimum of land, education, and worldly goods. Nearly 20 percent were confined in poorhouses, while another 20 percent had been out of work for at least five years prior to entering the homes. Ninety percent of these men were on the dole, and fully two-thirds reported having no family to support them. Nearly one-third of all inmates were single or never-marrieds, and about half of them applied for admission before the turn of the century. Estimated annual income among those who were employed ranged from one dollar a day to five dollars plus board a month. Low body weight and poor health were further indices of the debilitating consequences of their poverty.

There is also evidence to support the contention that some Confederate veterans may have suffered from lingering service-related social and psychological problems that significantly reduced the ability to adapt to a stress-inducing institutional environment, thereby increasing vulnerability and heightening mortality rates. A number of veterans were expelled from the Confederate homes for acts of violence against staff members or their fellow inmates, while administrators fought ceaseless battles against inmates' intemperance and recalcitrant behavior, and several others were ordered transferred to state insane asylums each year. Sometimes the homes' statistical reports also had to account for veterans who committed suicide, a problem that persisted in Confederate soldiers' homes well into the twentieth century. But these acts may have been adaptive techniques employed by inmates in coping with institutional life rather than symptoms of any serious and debilitating mental problems. Medical case histories from the state asylum in central Georgia reveal several Confederate veterans who had attempted suicide or had threatened kin or had become mentally deranged. Two veterans suffered from night terrors and panic attacks reportedly stemming from their war experiences, while another had turned to alcohol too often for relief. Although not committed to any institution, Tom Watson's father, John Smith Watson, portrayed above, who is reported to have suffered chronic bouts of depression and remained in bed with his face to the wall for two or three weeks at a time, appears to have developed periodic insomnia, absence of feeling, acute depression, and paralysis of mind and body, all symptoms of what today one may regard as post-traumatic stress disorder (PTSD). Kathleen Gorman, in "When Johnny Came Marching Home," concludes that one of her Confederate subjects, William Armstead of Walton County, Georgia, who was victimized, committed to an insane asylum against his will by a woman who was only after his pension, and abandoned by his former comrades who were either embarrassed or ashamed of his behavior, probably suffered from PTSD. Similarly, John Simpson's disturbing and dark portrait of S. A. Cunningham, editor and publisher of the *Confederate Veteran Magazine,* a man who seems to have been deeply frustrated and dissatisfied with himself all of his life, offers a solid case for perhaps yet another Confederate veteran who may have suffered from mental paralysis, anxiety, and depression ("hypochondria" or the "blue devils," as some soldiers referred to their condition), in much the same way that veterans of other wars experienced shell shock, battle fatigue, or the "thousand-yard stare."[29]

Caring for poor, disabled, and elderly ex-Confederates proved to be an elaborately expensive endeavor. Total expenditures for all 16 homes, from the time of their establishment beginning in the 1880s and 1890s until their closing by the 1960s, when the last veterans had died and their widows had been transferred to other institutions, were in the tens of millions of dollars. From 1884 to 1898, for instance, the Lee Camp Home of Virginia received $428,056, nearly two-thirds of which represented state appropriations, the remainder being city and private contributions. From 1899 to 1914 the state of Tennessee paid an estimated quarter of a million dollars in per capita allowances alone. Annual appropriations for the Texas home from 1910 to 1920 ranged from $90,000 to $225,000, while total operating expenses for the Arkansas home for the period 1923–24 were $163,013.62. The total cost for all 15 Confederate homes in 1914 (excluding California's, which was not founded until 1929) amounted to $518,000.[30]

That figure was truly a bargain, compared to Confederate pension payments by Southern states, which totaled $7.4 million during the same year. North Carolina had been the first Southern state to make permanent provision for pensions, by an act passed by the legislature and approved on March 12, 1879. Veterans who were blind or limbless were entitled to $60 per year. By 1907 the basic entitlement had been increased to $120. Tennessee first granted a modest disability pension in 1880. By 1898 it provided $10 per month until death to limbless veterans and $25 per month to those who had been totally disabled "while engaged in battle." Arkansas's pension grew from $25 per year in 1891 to $100 per year in 1917. Georgia's first pension enacted in 1886 granted as little as five dollars per year for veterans who returned from the war minus a finger or a toe and up to $150 for those who were missing both an arm and a leg. By 1929 Georgia had paid more than $43 million in Confederate pensions. Beginning in 1888 and continuing until 1927, Virginia's pension expenditures would nearly surpass $16 million. Texas and Louisiana became the last former Confederate states to enact a pension. Texas created a special tax for its disabled and indigent soldiers, sailors, and their wives and widows. In order to do so, however, the state's constitution had to be officially amended. Ratified in the election of November 6, 1894, the amendment was proclaimed adopted six weeks later. Finally enacted in 1900, Louisiana's Confederate pension provided $8 per month. By that time nine Southern states spent over $100,000 each on pensions; by 1914 all of the states were paying above the 1900 level. By 1929 the total annual amount spent on pensions in the 11 former Confederate states exceeded $19 million.[31]

State funding for pensions came from general revenues, special property taxes, and the sale of bonds. In 1891 Alabama started a pension program, funded by a tax of one-half mill (five cents) on the dollar; before the decade had ended the tax had been doubled. The 1901 Virginia Constitutional Convention authorized a special five-cent tax for every $100 in personal property to fund $300,000 in pensions for "disabled and deserving" Confederate veterans. In addition to providing some financial relief to "maimed, disabled, aff[lict]ed, and indigent" Confederate veterans and widows, Virginia's pension program beginning in 1924 allowed a $25 annual payment for "any person who actually accompanied a soldier in the service and remained faithful & loyal as the body servant of such soldier, or who served as cook, hostler or teamster or who worked on breastworks under any command of the army and thereby rendered service to the Confederate States of America."[32] Much of the money for Georgia pensions—which accounted for 21.5 percent of state expenditures by 1897—came from cigarette taxes, while Florida was able to increase its Confederate pensions four times from 1897 to 1904, funded by the convict lease system. By 1923, when there were more than 10,000 Confederate pensioners, $2 million pensions were being funded via property taxes.[33]

No matter how much state governments spent on veterans, their Confederate pension programs could hardly match federal pensions, a discrepancy that deeply disturbed some Southerners. Compared to what the federal government was doing for its veterans, the pensions, homes, and other forms of relief provided by the Southern states were miniscule indeed. Beginning in 1862 the federal government awarded free prostheses to amputees, with a refitting every three years. This benefit entitled a veteran to an allowance of $50 for the purchase of a prosthetic arm and $75 for a prosthetic leg, as well as a free trip to and from the location of his fitting. Other benefits included back pay for time spent in service, preference in government jobs, domiciliary and medical care in the many state homes and the NHDVS system, and federal pensions, which provided eight dollars per month in 1862 and additional funds in the coming years. Every year between 1885 and 1897, federal pensions were the single largest expenditure in the annual budget, excluding service on the debt. Between 1865 and 1930 Federal pensioners received on average $165 per year compared to the annual allotment of $38.50 to the typical Confederate pensioner.[34]

To equalize federal and Confederate pensions and other veterans' benefits, various proponents argued that Uncle Sam should come to the aid of Johnny Reb. Representative Peter J. Otey of Virginia, a veteran, introduced just such a bill in 1895, and other congressmen from both Southern and Northern districts also sponsored similar, bipartisan legislation from time to time. Did not the Southern states pay billions of dollars in federal taxes each year? Were not veterans of the Southern army and their families entitled to their fair share? In December 1898, again in 1902, and still later in 1904, Congressman John F. Rixey of Virginia introduced legislation calling not only for the government to allow ex-Confederates to be admitted to the national soldiers' homes, but also for the Confederate homes to receive the "same financial assistance" as those in the North and West. "We do not suggest or ask this as a charity," Rixey maintained, "but as an act of justice, equality and right, just as we insisted, when the South re-entered the Union, that the Confederate soldier should have the ballot, with the right to hold office. In this light I, as a Southern Repesentative, not only suggest, but demand it." Representatives from various Northern states endorsed Rixey's proposal. Washington Gardner of Michigan, for example, declared that it was "better to feed the hungry and shelter the living Confederate than to care for the graves of the immortal dead." He added: "This Government is great enough and rich enough to care for *all* the men who suffered in its defense or at its command." Granting federal pensions to ex-Confederates, as Richmond P. Hobson of Alabama proposed doing in 1908, would "do much to break down any lingering sectional animosities still existing," a group of Tennessee veterans maintained. In 1916 John H. Tillman of Arkansas invoked an oft-repeated claim and forlorn hope for the return of an estimated $100 million illegally collected by the federal government through the confiscation and sale of captured and abandoned property and the collection of taxes placed on cotton and sugar cane. The House Committee on Invalid Pensions held a committee hearing on a measure that would do just as Tillman suggested. Later that summer the Senate Committee on Military Affairs held a hearing in Washington on a bill that would provide homes for Confederate veterans, this time introduced by Union veteran and Senator John D. Works of California. George M. Jones, of Springfield, Missouri, did not think it was possible that anybody could have thought it wrong for a wounded Confederate soldier to accept a drink of water from the canteen of a Union soldier. Therefore, it seemed strange to him that there should be "any opposition to the passage" of a law granting a pension to worthy and needy ex-Confederates. Isaiah Rusk, a Confederate veteran who had lost his arm at Vicksburg, assured his senator in Washington that the majority of his comrades in Texas would accept a federal pension, adding: "In accepting it . . . I think they would . . . by this act show no dishonor or disrespect for their dead comrades or the cause for which they fought." A Georgia veteran in 1914 echoed Rusk's sentiment: "99 percent of the veterans would gladly accept such a pension. . . . What is the hitch or stumbling block?"[35]

There were several hitches or stumbling blocks. Certain Southern members of Congress kept such proposals bottled up in committee. Bolstered by letters of protest from their angry constituents, the Southerners argued that acceptance of such gifts would undermine the poor Confederate soldiers' "pride and self-esteem" and especially their sense of honor. The Benjamin F. Cheatham Bivouac in Nashville, a Confederate veterans group founded in the 1880s, renounced any claim to federal pensions and condemned "sending committees north to beg aid for indigent Confederate soldiers." Accepting such aid, the veterans believed, "would be placing a money value on the patriotism of those who were willing to give their all, and their lives, if necessary, in defense of their Southern country." The editor of the Nashville *Christian Advocate* wrote that federal pensions for Confederate heroes who are "ennobled by their poverty" would be "bartering much manhood for a little money." A "Limping Confederate" in Richmond observed that while his Northern friends received large pensions, his reward for being on the losing side is "much more valuable than all the pensions Congress can appropriate." H. H. Carleton of Athens, Georgia, said he and his former comrades would "rather . . . suffer and endure honorable discomfort than become humiliated pensioners. . . . To make our gallant Confederate veterans dependent for their future . . . upon piteous charity of a former foe, would not be in keeping with the southern manhood [he and others] so gallantly and heroically illustrated." Dr. R. L. Johnson, a former private in the Moultrie Guards who had surrendered at Appomattox, viewed offers of federal pensions as "kind and generous" but "unreasonable and illogical." It is "inconsistent with our self-respect," contended the R. E.

Lee Camp No. 1, a veterans group in Richmond, for it "stains the record of those whose purity we devote and consecrate ourselves, our lives, and our sacred honor."[36]

The strong sentiments Confederate veterans expressed about receiving federal benefits were similar to their aversion to aid of any kind. Apparently nothing aroused an ex-Confederate's indignation more than a perceived assault on his manhood, regardless of the source. Many Confederate veterans (like most nineteenth-century Americans) opposed pensions and other forms of welfare (both outdoor and indoor relief), even if it came from local sources. Such handouts were demoralizing and demeaning, even effeminate. Moreover, few persons entertained the notion of entitlement, firmly believing that it was the individual's responsibility for success, not the government's. To be "taken care of by the government" was to become dependent upon someone else. And to become dependent upon others was to admit failure, which people were reluctant to do. In other words, *true men are responsible for their own lives and should never look to others for assistance*. In fact, fewer than 20 percent of all Confederate veterans and widows received pensions, while an even smaller percentage ever applied for admission to a soldiers' home. Given the overwhelmingly negative attitude that many veterans and the public at large held concerning institutional relief and pensions, opposition to veterans' benefits was understandable. As one veteran revealed, he felt a certain "humiliation" in applying for admission to a home, because one invariably "loses caste" when entering it. "The thought of having to go to the Paupers Home is a horor & a dread to many of us old vets," an ex-Confederate stated, which "to beg [for] we are ashamed; to except [sic] the charity of friends in case we have them, is humiliating." For these reasons, charity carried with it a nasty stigma that compelled many proud veterans to renounce pensions.[37]

There were many "maimed, tottering helpless men" in this state "too proud to accept pity," remarked Texas governor James Stephen Hogg, in his inaugural message of January 21, 1891. More than any other conflict in American history, the Civil War wrought unprecedented and unexpected human devastation and left a legacy of maimed and disabled veterans too proud to accept pity. Thousands lost an arm or a leg to the wounds of battle, while thousands of others were injured so severely rendering limbs useless. Still more lost eyes or received debilitating wounds. "Deep in the heart of Texans lie smouldering sympathies, mingled with tender feelings of love for those men," Hogg remarked. "They obeyed the State's command. If a state orders her men to fight, it accepts the obligation to care for them to protect them. She can no longer bear the shame of standing mute witness to their miseries." Hogg's words are reminiscent of those of an observer who witnessed a Memorial Day service that took place in Albany, Georgia, in 1905. At the conclusion of the ceremony, more than a dozen feeble Confederate veterans arose and marched down the aisle. The scene "brought tears to hundreds of eyes." "Every head was white or streaked with gray and nearly every form was bent. Here was an empty sleeve, there was a leg of cork." The audience stood in reverent silence, a "spontaneous tribute of a Southern audience to Southern heroes."[38]

Southerners obviously did more than stand in silence in respect for Johnny Reb. These men were not forgotten or rendered obsolete. Rather they became heroes, the subjects of admiration and enthusiastic press. They were mobilized into a collective social consciousness that developed during the war and after, which led to both public and private attempts to aid these men. This philanthropy was continued by state legislatures with a series of policy initiatives intended to repair the veteran's damaged body. Small-scale programs to provide artificial limbs and land grants to amputees expanded to include disabled veterans of all types. Commutations replaced artificial limbs, while pensions replaced commutations and soldiers' homes were established in lieu of pensions. As the years passed and death thinned the pension rolls and soldiers' home wards, individual pensions and annual home budgets increased, providing financial aid well into the twentieth century. Such homage paid to ancient warriors was a natural and proper act for a civilized people. Yet response to this aid by its intended beneficiaries was overdetermined by Southern pride and a sense of history. While Charles Moore of Alexandria, Louisiana, and John Sloan of Pontotoc, Mississippi, and thousands of other proud Confederate veterans like them, bore the marks of unquestionable valor and certainly merited help, persuading them to accept such aid freely was another matter altogether. Many disabled Confederate veterans rejected the very notion that their heroism and sacrifice should be remembered and rewarded. As the drawing in the *Atlanta Constitution* attested, there remained "life an' battle-spirit in a host" of these men despite their disabilities. And, ironically, it was precisely this same quality that endeared Johnny Reb to those who wanted to comfort and to preserve him.

NOTES

1. See Moore's letters of August 26, 1880, June 6, 1881, and October 7, 1887, in Association of the Army of Northern Virginia (hereafter AANV) Papers, Veterans Benefits, Louisiana Historical Association Collection (hereafter LHAC), Howard-Tilton Memorial Library, Tulane University, New Orleans.

2. *Confederate Veteran* 2 (1894): 37. Sloan died four years later; he was 68 years old.

3. C. Vann Woodward, *Tom Watson: Agrarian Rebel* (New York, 1938), 2, 9–14, 18, 32, 43; Dixon Wecter, *When Johnny Comes Marching Home* (Cambridge, 1944), 155; J. H. Allen to R. E. Lee Camp, March 26, 1884, Grand Camp Confederate Veterans, Department of Virginia, R. E. Lee Camp No. 1 Records, Correspondence, Virginia Historical Society, Richmond. Nathan J. Lewis to "Managers of Confederate Soldiers Home," February 3, 1885; S. J. Spindle to "Secretary, R. E. Lee Camp," August 30, 1885, Lee Camp Soldiers' Home, Board of Visitors, Correspondence, Library of Virginia, Richmond. See also McNairy's application for admission, Tennessee Soldiers' Home, Tennessee State Library and Archives, Nashville. William E. Todd to Association of the Army of Tennessee (hereafter AAT), August 11, 1889; F. A. Biers to Nicholas Curry, August 28, 1889; AAT Papers, Veterans Benefits, LHAC. For information on Eubank, see Jeffrey R. Morrison, "'Increasing the Pensions of These Worthy Heroes': Virginia's Confederate Pensions, 1888 to 1927," M.A. thesis, University of Richmond, 1996, 69.

4. The exact number of persons who served in the Confederate armed forces is open to speculation. In 1900 Thomas L. Livermore of Boston estimated the number of three-year enlistments in the Confederate army to have been 1,082,119. *Numbers and Losses in the Civil War in America, 1861–1865* (Boston, 1901). This total is the same as cited by William H. Glasson, "Professor of Economics at Trinity College, N.C.," in "The South's Care for Her Confederate Veterans," *American Monthly Review of Reviews,* July 1907, 42 (cf. Theda Skocpol, *Protecting Soldiers and Mothers: The Political Origins of Social Policy in the United States* [Cambridge, 1992], 597–98, who employs Glasson's estimate in her calculations). Cornelius B. Hite, "The Confederate Army," *Confederate Veteran* 31 (1923): 221, settles on a much smaller figure of 605,250. Relying upon Livermore's data, Donald S. Frazier, in *Encyclopedia of the Confederacy,* ed. Richard N. Current (New York, 1993), 338, estimates that 54,000 Confederates were killed in action; 40,000 died of battlefield wounds; 140,000 died of disease; 26,000 died in prison. Although Hite may have underestimated the total number of enlistments, his casualty figures are similar to (and more detailed than) Livermore's: 52,954 Confederates killed in action; 21,554 died of battlefield wounds; another 59,297 died of disease, 26,439 died in prison; and 40,000 died from "other" causes. Subtracting Hite's total battlefield and nonbattlefield casualties (or "hits") from Livermore's total for three-year enlistments, I arrived at the figure of 881,875. Of this number, an estimated 220,469 (25 percent) were wounded but survived the war. I chose this percentage based on research that suggested that approximately 25 percent of inmates of Confederate soldiers homes—where more than 20,000 veterans eventually resided—had been afflicted with a "war wound." Rosenburg, *Living Monuments: Confederate Soldiers' Homes in the New South* (Chapel Hill, 1993), 165. By 1900 one out of four residents in the National Home for Disabled Volunteer Soldiers (NHDVS) listed battlefield wounds as the source of their disability. Patrick J. Kelly, *Creating a National Home: Building the Veterans' Welfare State, 1860–1900* (Cambridge, 1997), 130, 133. Frazier places nonmortally wounded at 226,000. In *To Appomattox and Beyond: The Civil War Soldier in War and Peace* (Chicago, 1996), 107, Larry M. Logue estimates that "at least" 200,000 Confederate soldiers had been wounded during the war, and of the "thousands" who endured amputations, mortality rates were staggeringly high. See also Wecter, *Johnny Comes Marching Home,* 209, who places the number of Confederate

amputations at 25,000. These estimates also compare favorably to the 281,881 Union soldiers who received gunshot wounds and the 29,980 who experienced amputations. Kelly, *Creating a National Home,* 3, 15, 208.

5. By Act of July 14, 1862, the federal government passed a General Pension Law (retroactive to March 1, 1861) establishing uniform pension rates for soldiers disabled from military service. A second measure enacted two days later directed the U.S. Surgeon General to provide artificial limbs to needy veterans (Kelly, *Creating A National Home,* 18); Wecter, *Johnny Comes Marching Home,* 213. For a discussion of disabled veterans' benefits authorized by the Confederate government, see W. Jackson Dickens Jr., "An Arm and a Leg for the Confederacy: Virginia's Disabled Veteran Legislation, 1865 to 1888," M.A. thesis, University of Richmond, 1997, 11–15. Ironically, it was Senator Jefferson Davis who in the early 1850s introduced legislation that resulted in the founding of the U.S. Soldiers' Home, with branches in Louisiana, Mississippi, Kentucky, and Washington, D.C. *Journal of the Congress of the Confederate States of America,* 7 vols. (Washington, D.C., 1905), 6:808–10.

6. Dickens, "Arm and Leg," 16–19. Note that ARMS resisted reliance upon Northern limb manufacturers, both a political and economic necessity. There is anecdotal evidence that this resistance continued long after the war. One Southern veteran insisted on trying a collection of European manufacturers and a "Confederate leg" before grudgingly conceding that a "Yankee leg was the best." Laurann Figg and Jane Farrell-Beck, "Amputation in the Civil War: Physical and Social Dimensions," *Journal of the History of Medicine and Allied Sciences* 48 (1993): 464.

7. Another organization, the Confederate Relief and Historical Association of Memphis, started in 1866 but accomplished little and soon disappeared. Gaines M. Foster, *Ghosts of the Confederacy: Defeat, the Lost Cause, and the Emergence of the New South, 1865–1913* (New York, 1987), 50. See also Logue, *To Appomattox and Beyond,* 107–8.

8. *Raleigh Daily North Carolina Standard,* November 22, 1865.

9. Alabama *Acts* (1866–67), 695–98; "Surviving Confederate Pensioners," *Alabama Historical Quarterly* 2 (1940): 208–16.

10. Under this legislation 225 veterans received limbs at a cost of $13,700 in 1867 (Dickens, "Arm and Leg," 27–29).

11. E. Merton Coulter, *The South during Reconstruction, 1865–1877* (Baton Rouge, 1947), 14; William W. White, *The Confederate Veteran* (Tuscaloosa, 1962), 107; Dickens, "Arm and Leg," 35, 37; Kathleen L. Gorman, "When Johnny Came Marching Home Again: Confederate Veterans in the New South," Ph.D. diss., University of California, Riverside, 1994, 37–38.

12. *New Orleans Daily Picayune,* March 20, 1866.

13. Ibid., March 10, 11, 14, April 6, May 4, 10, 26, 1866; Coulter, *The South during Reconstruction,* 352–53; White, *The Confederate Veteran,* 110; Louisiana *Acts* (1866), 194, 196, 198.

14. Peter Wallenstein, *From Slave South to New South: Public Policy in Nineteenth Century Georgia* (Chapel Hill, 1987), 138–39, 161, 192.

15. Georgia *Laws* (1875), 107–8; (1878–79), 41–42; Wallenstein, *Slave South,* 191; Gorman, "Johnny Came Marching Home," 67–68. The interpretation presented here, that Bourbon Democrats were relatively generous when it came to providing relief to disabled ex-Confederates, challenges the traditional viewpoint enunciated by William White, who argued that state aid was not immediately forthcoming owing to the

retrenchment policies following Reconstruction, "despite any social consciousness on the part of state legislators who wanted to help their unfortunate comrades. . . . Parsimonious as the state governments might have been, they could not long afford to ignore the veterans' pleas" (*The Confederate Veteran,* 107).

16. Dickens, "Arm and Leg," 16–19, 35, 37, 71.

17. Between 1867 and 1886, despite being chronically in debt and hobbled by a bitterly divisive political crisis that pitted Readjustors against Democrats, the Virginia state government gave a total of $302,300 in aid for disabled veterans. Deceptively impressive at first glance, the $83,000 appropriated in 1886 (the largest amount awarded in any one year) represented only 2.63 percent of all state appropriations. Ibid., 84; Morrison, "Increasing the Pensions," 37.

18. "Surviving Confederate Pensioners," 208–16.

19. Louisiana *Acts* (1880), 65–66; (1882), 94; (1884), 56, 123–24; (1886), 212–15; (1888), 23–24; (1888), 53–54; White, *The Confederate Veteran,* 108.

20. Often the grantee had to forfeit half of their land in order to pay to have it surveyed in west Texas. H. P. N. Gammel, comp., *Laws of Texas, 1822–1897,* 10 vols. (Austin, 1898), 9:122. House Bill No. 25, passed on January 11, 1881, appropriated $2.5 million for artificial limbs. But the Senate narrowly defeated the measure by a 39-to-29 vote, on the grounds that it violated Section 51, Article 3 of the Texas constitution that prohibited a grant of public money to an association of individuals. Texas *House Journal* (1881), 14, 45, 151–53.

21. The 1890 census reveals 432,020 living Confederate veterans. The largest percentage (15.5 percent) lived in Texas (which in 1860 ranked sixth in population among Confederate states), followed by Virginia (11.3 percent), Georgia (10.9 percent), North Carolina (8.9 percent), Alabama (7.9 percent), Tennessee (7.4 percent), Arkansas (6.2 percent), Mississippi (6.2 percent), South Carolina (5.5 percent), Missouri (4.1 percent), Louisiana (3.7 percent), Kentucky (2.6 percent), Florida (1.9 percent), and Maryland (1.9 percent). Some 382,089 (88 percent) of the veterans were still employed, and most of them (294,521) worked in agriculture. U.S. Bureau of the Census, "Soldiers and Widows," *Compendium of the Eleventh Census: 1890,* pt. 3, Population (Washington, D.C., 1897), 593; Gorman, "Johnny Came Marching Home," 35.

22. The plight of these veterans is documented in the following: D. F. Dunn to Judge W. H. Rogers, October 7, 1885; John B. Glynn to F. A. Ober, June 16, 1886, AANV Papers, Veterans Benefits, LHAC; Auriel Aimard to W. H. Rogers, November 11, 1887, Camp Nicholls Soldiers' Home, Board of Directors, Correspondence, LHAC; John P. Breland to Nicholas Curry, February 28, 1891; Daniel Daly to [AANV], March 10, 1891; P. M. McGrath to Joseph A. Charlaron, September 12, 1882, AAT Papers, Veterans Benefits, LHAC; J. B. Clark to Fitz Lee, May 23, 1885; N. E. Edmundo to C. W. Williams, June 17, 1883; A. B. Carter to Fitzhugh Lee, February 11, 1885; John C. Sims to John R. Cook; May 5, 1885; S. V. Corbell to W. H. Terry, April 26, 1886; F. Charles Stainback to "Lee Home," September 4, 1885; Charles W. Green to [Norman V. Randolph], October 20, 1886; Lee Camp Soldiers' Home, Board of Visitors, Correspondence, Virginia State Library; R. B. Clements to James McGraw, June 6, 1885; Thomas W. Colley to Lee Camp, April 11, 1887; Thomas Rudd to Lee Camp, May 29, 1891, R. E. Lee Camp Records, Correspondence, Virginia Historical Society, Richmond. See also William Thomas Allen, Co. H, 53rd Virginia Infantry, who "served all during war, was wounded in head & never recovered from effects of wound," and James

A. Cridlin, Co A, 2nd Virginia, wounded at Five Forks "by a Minnie ball through the Fibula of the left leg," who was among the first to apply for a Virginia pension in April 1888, which he continued to receive through 1902 (Morrison, "Increasing the Pensions," 60, 69).

23. For Rector's comments, see *Arkansas Gazette,* May 9, 1889.

24. For Wheeler's comments, see Wheeler to Jefferson M. Falkner, December 29, 1902, *Montgomery Advertiser,* January 4, 1903. See also Foster, *Ghosts of the Confederacy,* 122–26; White, *The Confederate Veteran,* 37; Charles R. Wilson, *Baptized in Blood: The Religion of the Lost Cause, 1865–1920* (Athens, Ga., 1980), 37–54, 127, 189.

25. *Nashville Daily American,* March 16, 1889.

26. See G. Stephen Davis, "Johnny Reb in Perspective: The Confederate Soldiers' Image in Southern Arts," Ph.D. diss., Emory University, 1979. Edward Ayers writes that by 1880 "Confederate veterans at the court house . . . bore empty sleeves and blank stares." *The Promise of the New South: Life after Reconstruction* (Oxford, 1992), 3.

27. *Georgetown Weekly Times,* July 13, November 30, 1881; November 14, 1883; *Southern Historical Society Papers* 11 (1883): 432.

28. Although no complete published histories of either the AANV or AAT exist, their papers form the nucleus of the LHAC. For an introduction, see Herman Hattaway, "The United Confederate Veterans of Louisiana," *Louisiana History* 16 (1975): 5–7. The word *worthy* appears in William Kinney to AANV, April 17, 1895, AANV Papers, Veterans Benefits, LHAC, and is used in reference to relieving the "distress" of nonmembers. The palm-sized pamphlet *Confederate Veterans Employment Bureau,* printed by Gilmore's Sugar Planters publishing firm, contains the names of more than 200 individuals. For related correspondence, see: J. Y. Gilmore to AANV, October 12, 1895, AANV Papers, Veterans Benefits, LHAC; Gilmore et al. to "The People of Louisiana," November 16, 1895; H. Dudley Coleman to AAT, May 11, 1897, AAT Papers, Veterans Benefits, LHAC. White, *The Confederate Veteran,* 100, tells of a Nashville Confederate organization—Benjamin F. Cheatham Bivouac No. 1—that sponsored an identical enterprise initiated in that city about the same time. The John B. Hood Camp of Austin, Texas, and the Confederate Veterans Association, Fulton County, of Atlanta, also had relief committees to "minister as far as practicable to the wants of all needy and worthy [maimed and disabled] Confederate soldiers and sailors." Robert L. Rodgers, comp., *History of Confederate Veterans Association, Fulton County, Georgia* (Atlanta, 1890), 6–14. The earliest reference to a relief committee for the R. E. Lee Camp No. 1 in Richmond was September 7, 1883.

29. Simpson, *S. A. Cunningham and the Confederate Heritage* (Athens, Ga., 1994). While it is possible that Confederate veterans may have suffered from acute delayed stress after the Civil War, as Eric T. Dean has argued in *Shook over Hell: Post-Traumatic Stress, Vietnam, and the Civil War* (Cambridge, Mass., 1997), the evidence is at best sketchy and anecdotal. Without extant case files that could be examined, one may never know why inmates behaved the way they supposedly did.

30. White, *The Confederate Veteran,* 113–14, estimates that from 1865 to 1962, the 11 states that comprised the Confederacy (together with Maryland, Oklahoma, Missouri, and Kentucky) spent approximately $500 million on pensions and homes for veterans and widows.

31. Ibid., 109; Gammel, *Laws of Texas,* 10:42–44; Louisiana *Acts* (1900), 124–26; *Confederate Veteran* 2 (1894): 73, 262; 24 (1916): 390; Vance R. Skarstedt, "The Confed-

erate Veteran Movement and National Reunification," Ph.D. diss., Florida State University, 1993, 200; Morrison, "Increasing the Pensions," 101, 103; James R. Young, "Confederate Pensions in Georgia, 1886–1929," *Georgia Historical Quarterly* 66 (1982): 47–52.

32. In 1926 there were 289 black pensioners in Virginia. South Carolina, Tennessee, Mississippi, and North Carolina also provided pensions for African-American veterans who remained loyal to the Southern cause. Charles Kelly Barrow et al., comps. and eds., *Forgotten Confederates: An Anthology about Black Southerners* (Atlanta, 1995), 109–12, 113–20, 121–22, 123–24.

33. Gorman, "Johnny Came Marching Home," 72; Skarstedt, "The Confederate Veteran Movement," 201–3; "Surviving Confederate Pensioners," 208–16.

34. Kelly, *Creating a National Home,* 56–57; Dickens, "Arm and Leg," 8. In 1880, Union soldiers who had lost an arm received an annual pension of $432, while the same disability suffered by an ex-Confederate in Georgia was compensated $50. The 1890 census counted 26,538 Confederate veteran and widow pensioners, who received $1.02 million in pensions, or $38.50 per person. M. B. Morton, "Federal and Confederate Pensions Contrasted," *Forum* 16 (1893): 68–74.

35. *Confederate Veteran* 10 (1902): 173–75; 16 (1908): 128–29, 259, 353; 26 (1918): 255–56; *Montgomery Advertiser,* April 27, 1902; Skarstedt, "The Confederate Veteran Movement," 198–99; Morrison, "Increasing the Pensions," 23–24. For Rixey's proposals, see *Congressional Record,* 55 Cong., 3d Sess., vol. 32, pt. 1: 268; 57 Cong., 1st Sess., vol. 35, pt. 1: 627, 632, 637; and 58 Cong., 2d Sess., vol. 38, pt. 2: 1873. For reaction to the Virginian's bills, see *Congressional Record,* 57 Cong., 1st Sess., vol. 35, pt. 1: 628–34; and pt. 8, appendix: 91–92. Neither Works's nor Tillman's measures ever made it out of committees. See *Homes for Confederate Veterans Hearing,* and *Claims of Confederate Soldiers Hearing.* See also *Confederate Veteran* 23 (1915): 102–3; 24 (1916): 8, 56, 90. *Congressional Record,* 64th Cong., 1st Sess., 24, 83.

36. Skarstedt, "The Confederate Veteran Movement," 195–96, 199; Wilson, *Baptized in Blood,* 82–83; *Atlanta Constitution,* April 10, 1889; *Confederate Veteran* 3 (1895): 228; 16 (1908): 210. The Fourteenth Amendment specifically prohibited Confederate veterans from receiving federal benefits, a provision that was not changed until May 23, 1958, when Public Law 85–425 symbolically granted federal pensions of $135.45 per month to two Confederate veterans: 112-year-old John B. Salling of Virginia and 116-year-old Walter Washington Williams of Texas. The last Confederate survivor, Williams died on December 19, 1959. Jay Hoar, *The South's Last Boys in Gray* (Bowling Green, Ohio, 1986), 510–11.

37. Theda Skocpol concludes that less than 20 percent of all Confederate veterans were ever pensioned, while some 90 percent of all Union veterans received pensions in 1910. *Protecting Soldiers and Mothers,* 132, 597. See also Jeffrey Morrison's suggestive findings that widows constituted over half of all Confederate pensioners in Virginia ("Increasing the Pensions," 73).

38. Texas *House Journal* (1891): 110–11; *Confederate Veteran* 13 (1905): 313.

Gregory Weeks

Fifty Years of Pain: The History of Austrian Disabled Veterans after 1945

Generally, soldiers who are part of a defeated army anticipate little sympathy from their captors but a great deal of support and understanding from their countrymen and their government. In the case of the Republic of Austria, both because of its annexation by Germany in 1938 and because of the special role its citizens played as soldiers in the German Wehrmacht during the Second World War, neither of the foregoing was really the case. Austria's veterans were treated by the occupying powers, France, Great Britain, the United States, and the Soviet Union, as the soldiers of a defeated army but with less of the harshness accorded veterans in Germany. This was in part due to the Moscow Declaration of 1943 signed by all four powers, which proclaimed Austria to be "the first victim of National Socialism." After the war, Austria's portrayal as a victim by both the Allies and its own provisional government continued. The tacit agreement of the Allied powers to Austria's victim status meant that Austrian citizens who had fought and been severely disabled in the German Wehrmacht were an unwelcome reminder to the provisional government that Austria might not have been as guiltless as was heretofore presumed. Thus, disabled Austrian Second World War veterans were shunned not only by the occupying powers, who viewed them as a defeated but "friendly" enemy, but also by their own government for the role they had played in the National Socialist dictatorship. Despite their role as pariahs, disabled veterans began organizing and fighting to get treatment for injuries they had sustained in the war.

This essay will sketch the history of Austria's disabled Second World War veterans first by examining the number of disabled veterans and their needs at the end of the war, then by presenting a picture of the chaotic nature of the Austrian and Allied administrative system in the postwar period, and finally, by looking at the lobbying efforts of Austria's disabled veterans up to about 1990.

By the end of the Second World War, Vienna and large portions of Austria had been reduced to rubble and ashes. Public services had stopped functioning, and the population was suffering proportionately as a result. On April 17, 1945, retired Austrian general Theodor Körner was named by the Allied occupation powers to the post of interim mayor of Vienna. On the same day, a new disabled veterans' organization, the Central Organization for Austrian War Victims (Zentralorganisation der Kriegsopfer Österreichs), was founded. In the midst of almost total destruction, veterans made their way through the rubble to meet, exchange addresses, and begin rebuilding their lives. But the founding of the disabled veterans' organization was the easy part. Rebuilding broken lives and learning to cope with destroyed bodies would take these disabled veterans much longer.

One woman recounts with regret how she and her family suffered as a result of her husband's war injuries:

> My husband, who went to war with total enthusiasm (unfortunately I have to say that), returned home an entirely different man. Before the war, he was a handsome athlete, a nondrinker and nonsmoker; afterward, the cranky opposite. The last days of the war in Russia (February 1945) got him; he lost his right upper thigh. After a year in various hospitals, he returned heavily disabled. Admittedly, we did not suffer any material need because I was always employed, and really, everything humanly possible was done for those disabled in the war. But what could make good the suffering of the war casualty and the consequent suffering of his family? Not money in any case. My now nicotine-addicted and alcoholic husband only felt himself to be, according to his own statements, a real human being when he could drive his car. And he did that in every condition. The number of incidents was great. There was always some sort of excitement. And so, this war ruined not only one human being but also his entire family.[1]

Other disabled veterans reacted quite differently. A Viennese veteran who was wounded in the leg and back by an air attack in southern France said simply, "I was lucky. It could have gotten me in the head." He had no complaints about his injury or his treatment after the war. "It was war, and that's the way it was." According to him, one moment a comrade was there, and the next he was gone, blown to bits by a bomb.[2] The sentiment expressed by this man that it "could have been me too" was repeated by the majority of veterans with whom I spoke. Most of them were glad simply to be alive at the end of the war.

Hans Hirsch, director of the Austrian War Blind Association (Kriegs-blindenverband) and a First and Second World War veteran, in a speech on December 4, 1948, greeting schoolchildren from Vienna who were sent to the Waxenburg Palace in the Mühlviertel for a vacation, expressed perhaps best the pain and suffering experienced by blind and disabled Austrian veterans. Hirsch raised the stumps of his amputated arms and pointed them toward the empty sockets where his eyes should have been and said, "Remember this well! This is war!"[3] This sort of antiwar sentiment was a common reaction from all the veterans interviewed for this essay, and it influenced greatly their readiness to be integrated into disabled veterans' advocacy groups that, like Hirsch's War Blind Association, worked not only to secure better treatment for the disabled but also to teach the younger generation in Austria the dangers of war.

Veterans like Hirsch who had been involved with disabled veterans' organizations since the end of the First World War played an important role in the establishment of new war victim associations following the end of the Second World War. That the Austrian veterans were able to organize themselves so quickly after the war was due in no small part to the presence of disabled First World War veterans like Hirsch, who had been organized in the prewar period and who were still active at the collapse of the Third Reich. In the interwar period, the motto of the Austrian War Victims' Association (Österreichischer Kriegsopferverband) had been simply:

Loyalty to the homeland,
far away from party politics,
for the well-being of the war victims.[4]

This motto held true until the NSKOV, the National Socialist War Victims' Organization, headquartered in Vienna, was formed as an umbrella organization for all of the various existing disabled veterans' organizations and the Austrian War Victims' Association was dissolved during the Third Reich. After the end of the Second World War, however, veterans who had been members of either the NSKOV or the War Victims' Association saw the necessity of organizing anew and the advantages that could be gained as a result. Thus, they had already begun preparing for the long road ahead while Russian troops were still in the process of capturing Vienna.

The prewar dedication to the task of taking care of the needs of disabled veterans and staying away from party politics, an axiom that was even more important after the years of National Socialist dictatorship, continued after the Second World War, and the newly established Central Organization for Austrian War Victims served not only as an umbrella organization but also lobbied for the interests of disabled veterans and, later, the handicapped in general.

The Second World War changed the way Austria approached the treatment of disabled veterans significantly. The number of Austrians disabled in the Second World War was estimated by the provisional Austrian government to be 38,100 in 1945, not including those victims who had failed to register with the authorities. Ultimately, this number turned out to be overly optimistic. Statistics calculated by the War Victims' Association in the province of Upper Austria (Oberösterreichischer Kriegsopferverband) listed the number of Austrian Second World War disabled veterans who were receiving partial payments in 1949 as 116,313. To this, the surviving First World War disabled veterans, another 51,996, must be added. Thus, the total number of war victims requiring support actually must have been much greater when one includes civilian bombing victims and those veterans who had not yet made the authorities aware of their disability. The Austrian government estimated in 1945 that nearly 79,200 surviving dependents of those soldiers killed in the war as well as approximately 7,500 bombing victims had a legal right to pensions from the Republic of Austria based on German law, which was still in force at this time.[5] This number also turned out to be low since, according to the Upper Austrian War Victims' Association, 339,803 parents, widows, and orphans of soldiers killed or missing during the war as well as those injured as a result of wartime events were receiving pensions in 1949. Compensation of these civilian hardship and personal injury cases combined with the responsibility for providing pensions to disabled former soldiers made the situation in Austria difficult because state finances were not sufficient to provide for all of those disabled as a result of the war.

The position of the provisional Austrian government at this time with regard to the differences between soldiers disabled in the First World War and those disabled in the Second World War was made quite clear in a paper drafted by the State Office for Social Administration (Staatsamt für Soziale Verwaltung) and presented to the Cabinet Council in June 1945. Ironically, the paper was supposed to introduce preliminary measures to help Austria's war victims, but it stated in part: "The new compensation law will not be able to avoid a certain varied treatment of war victims from the First and Second World Wars for the time being, [especially] when one considers that it is the continuing duty of the Austrian people to be grateful to the victims of the First World War, while the victims of the Second World War suffered their injuries in a war of exploitation for foreign interests that shook the very foundations of the Austrian state."[6] Despite this lack of compassion, these victims could expect at least minimal assistance from the provisional Austrian government, although it was much less than that received by the victims of the First World War. In this way, the stage was set for the future lobbying efforts of the Austrian disabled veterans' organizations, which will be described in the third section of this essay.

Administrative and Political Chaos, 1945–1950

Disabled veterans were confronted with all sorts of difficulties following the war. The greatest of these problems was the administrative and political chaos that reigned in Austria during the immediate postwar years. Because of disputes about property ownership, many facilities for the treatment and advising of disabled veterans had to be closed or moved, adding to the already daunting difficulties confronting the war disabled and those trying to provide them with care. For the most part, the administration of facilities and the management of property that previously had belonged to the German Reich was handled in one of two ways: Whenever possible, the provisional Austrian government assumed the operation of public facilities, and if this was not an option, then the seized or stolen property was returned to its original owners. This liquidation of "German" facilities and furnishings was the first major task confronting the provisional government under Dr. Karl Renner, Austria's first federal president following the war, in 1945. Since all Austrian veterans' organizations had been *gleichgeschaltet* (streamlined) under the NSKOV after the annexation of Austria in 1938, there were great difficulties in determining how property that had been confiscated by the Nazis and given to the veterans' organizations should be treated. Generally, property that had belonged to the Austrian state before 1938 automatically returned to state ownership. More difficult, however, was the problem of property that had been confiscated from Jews, opponents of the regime, or other private citizens. The Austrian state did not have title to these buildings before 1938 and, thus, had no legal right to them after the war.

No less a personality than Dr. Renner himself wrote the draft of a law to remove the German *Reichsversorgungsverwaltung* (care administration) in Austria.[7] The problems involved were great. Not only the buildings and property had to be returned from German ownership to Austrian but also the administrative files regarding the running and costs of the wartime *Versorgungsämter* (care offices) and individual patient medical files had to be taken over by the Austrian State Invalid Offices (Landesinvalidenämter, or

LIAs). Sorting out this mess required reams of paper, and even then it was not always entirely clear who was responsible for which area.

Besides the closure of facilities, the other difficulties confronting former soldiers who sought treatment for their disabilities in the post–Second World War period were numerous. First, the destruction of hospitals and deficiencies in the medical system and medical care, not to mention the lack of physicians and medicine, had to be overcome. Second, a severe shortage of pension funds made it difficult to provide adequate pensions for those disabled who were unable to earn a living themselves and who could not find a friend or family member to support them.

Moreover, disabled veterans were a blunt reminder that Austrians had been involved in a war for National Socialist aims and that many of them had fought side by side with the Germans in a war of territorial conquest and ethnic murder. Thus, merely because of their presence, disabled veterans came to be regarded as an irritation by Austrian politicians after 1945. Austrians wanted to forget the war, but disabled veterans were visible everywhere, and this made forgetting difficult.

Added to this was the problem of denazification. Many doctors had either fled or were no longer allowed to practice medicine due to their involvement with National Socialism. Despite this, a few incriminated doctors remained and continued to help out wherever they could even though their medical licenses were often close to being revoked.[8]

The catastrophic situation in Austria throughout 1945, especially in the Soviet occupation zone, meant that war disability pensions could only be paid in reduced amounts because the Austrian government did not have the necessary financial means.[9] This is evidenced by requests from the LIAs to extend the year loans for the payment of war victims' pensions, for the procurement of prostheses, for social insurance for surviving dependents, and for the operation of the individual Landesinvalidenämter. In 1947, the total for these services amounted to approximately 67.5 million Austrian schillings.[10]

The bleak picture, above all in the areas occupied by the Soviets, left little hope that the Austrian government would be able to obtain the necessary funds for emergency measures to aid the war disabled. To make matters worse, in an order dated July 5, 1946, General Kurassov, the Russian commander, ordered all "German property" in the Russian zone of occupation to be confiscated and sent to the Soviet Union. What was to be viewed as "German property" was determined by the Soviets themselves. Among the property confiscated was the entire crude oil industry and the Danube Steamship Line DDSG. Not only were entire factories dismantled and sent across the border but also the oil reserves in the east of Austria were taken to repay "war debts" and reparations. In this way, the Soviets bled Austria of much of its capability to rebuild quickly after the war. In the Allied occupation zones, the situation for disabled veterans was not much better. Due to administrative and funding difficulties, veterans' pensions also could be paid out only in limited amounts, and getting adequate treatment for injuries was difficult.

In addition, since virtually every Austrian family with a disabled veteran had suffered some form of hardship as a result of the war, it was nearly impossible for the Austrian government to determine who should be awarded benefits on the basis of need. Thus, as is often the case, those who were already receiving pension payments and those who took the initiative and filed pension requests almost immediately after the war had ended received their money sooner than those who waited longer to file, since later filers were given lower priority. This chaotic and unfair situation continued until the first law especially designed to meet the needs of those disabled in the war was passed on July 14, 1949. This law, known as the Kriegsopferversorgungsgesetz (KOVG, or War Victims' Care Law), made a fair and routinized treatment of disabled veterans possible for the first time. The law went into effect on January 1, 1950, and regulated the pension payments, rights, and care of disabled veterans and the surviving dependents of those killed in the war.[11] In addition, the law made possible a fair and uniform handling of disability cases by making the LIAs responsible for all questions regarding the handicapped, whether they had been disabled in the war or in some other way. This law established the LIAs permanently as the central authority in questions regarding the handicapped, a system that continues today in Austria but in which the LIAs now have been renamed Federal Offices for Social and Handicapped Affairs, or Federal Social Offices (Bundesämter für Soziales und Behindertenwesen, or Bundessozialämter). The KOVG eliminated inefficient, competing jurisdictions once and for all and helped to improve the care provided to Austria's disabled veterans throughout the postwar period.[12]

As far as employment for disabled veterans was concerned, the severe shortage of workers immediately following the war meant that disabled veterans usually were able to find jobs with relatively little trouble. However, the health and psychological consequences resulting from their wartime injuries were another matter. Many veterans never recovered their former health and were plagued by pain. Immediately following the end of the war, work was begun by the Austrian Social Ministry to insure that disabled veterans would be reintegrated into the Austrian economy and that they would be given meaningful positions in which they could earn their own living. In the new Invalid Employment Law of July 25, 1946, a revision of the laws that had existed in Austria both before the Second World War and in the period of National Socialist dictatorship after 1938,[13] private employers were required to employ a minimum of one handicapped person for the first 15 employees and an additional disabled person for every 20 additional employees. For public employers, the requirement was that handicapped workers had to make up at least 5 percent of their total workforce. If a company failed to employ a handicapped person, the Austrian Employment Service was authorized to assess a charge based on the number of employees. Additionally, the law gave handicapped personnel special protection against being fired.

Austrian companies that did not employ disabled war veterans or civilians were required to pay a compensation charge, assessed on the basis of profits, which was fed into a fund used to help needy war victims. The law was enforced, too. In one instance, the Danube Chemical Stock Company complained about having to pay a compensation charge of 4,022 schillings, because it had no records with which to figure its profits. The reason given for the missing paperwork was the occupation of the Danube Chemical factory in Moosbierbaum by the Red Army. Despite the poor financial situation of the company, it was required to pay the full compensatory amount.[14]

Other difficulties arose from the membership of many disabled war victims in National Socialist organizations such as the SS or the SA, the stormtroopers. In one case, six severely disabled employees of the Suben Detention Center, part of the Austrian prison system, had to be moved to other jobs because of their previous membership in the Nazi Party or its organizations. Based on a rumor that started in the Upper Austrian War Victims' Association that these employees were to be fired, the Central Organization for Austrian War Victims lodged a protest with the Federal Ministry for Social Administration, and this protest most certainly helped these Nazi veterans to defend their status as war-disabled employees.[15] Conflicts of this nature were not unusual in the period after the war, since many former National Socialists attempted to avoid "atonement" for their crimes by using their war injuries to obtain better treatment. Thus, at the beginning of 1948, the Federal Ministry for Social Administration was forced to issue a memorandum to the governors of the Austrian provinces detailing how the cases of war disabled who had been members of the Nazi Party or its organizations should be handled.[16]

Unfortunately, Austria's disabled veterans never formally confronted their Nazi past, and the Allied powers and the provisional Austrian govern-

ment never forced them to do so. Cases like that of the employees of the
Suben Detention Center, although common, generally were handled in a
manner that did not arouse too much attention and permitted veterans to
continue receiving their pensions no matter what their political leanings.

While many former Nazis were receiving pensions in this manner,
other residents of Austria who were not Austrian citizens but who had been
wounded in Austria during the war were being denied war victims' and veterans' pensions and compensation. In the case of Hungarians living in Austria, the Hungarian Political Representation in Vienna in a verbal note on
March 17, 1947, requested that all aid possible be given to its citizens who
had suffered personal injury as a result of military service or wartime events
in Austria.[17] However, this did little good since Austrian citizenship was still
a prerequisite for receiving compensation benefits for war injuries from the
Austrian government.

A special political and administrative problem for the Austrian government in this regard was the citizenship of those veterans living in the South
Tyrol and in the Canal Valley. These areas had been ceded to Italy under
pressure following the First World War and reintegrated into the Third
Reich under an agreement between Adolf Hitler and Benito Mussolini following Austria's annexation by Germany in 1938. Thus, residents of the
South Tyrol and the Canal Valley who had served in the German armed
forces were entitled to benefits from the Austrian state even though they
were now actually citizens of Italy based on their place of residence.[18] By
providing pensions to these veterans, Austria risked upsetting the Italian
authorities, who could see such actions realistically as meddling in their affairs
and who might feel threatened by them. In the end, the Austrian State Office
for Social Administration, later renamed Federal Ministry for Social Administration (Bundesministerium für soziale Verwaltung), provided pensions to
all Italian citizens entitled to them but only after it had informed the responsible Italian authorities about the payments it was making.

Besides pensions and funding of rehabilitation centers, various other
methods were used by the Austrian authorities to either reduce the pain and
suffering of disabled war victims or to help in their rehabilitation. Frequently, the disabled were sent to recuperative facilities in the countryside
to undertake a cure or to treat their tuberculosis. There were several such
facilities, and they were often state-owned. The costs of the treatment for
disabled former soldiers were paid by the Austrian government.[19]

The use of seeing-eye dogs for the war blind was another method of
rehabilitating disabled veterans. However, this created a problem because of
a lack of government funding to purchase the dogs. Due to pressure put on

the ministries by the War Blind Association, this situation was improved, but requests for seeing-eye dogs and complaints about the lack of trained canines were a frequent occurrence in the files of the responsible Ministry for Social Welfare in the years immediately following the end of the war.[20]

The question of rehabilitation of Austria's disabled civilians and veterans also took on political overtones. This was especially true with regard to the state-run prosthetics factories that had existed both before 1938 and under National Socialist rule. These factories manufactured artificial limbs at low cost.

The prosthetics industry was very interested in getting the state ministries to support its work. Individual manufacturers and designers of artificial limbs often sent descriptions of their new developments or patent applications to the Federal Ministry for Social Administration in hopes that their patents would be used in the treatment of disabled war victims.[21]

Dealing with the invoices for prosthetics delivered to the German Wehrmacht toward the end of the war also became the responsibility of the new Austrian government, which paid 21,967 schillings, nearly 50 percent of the total of 49,541 schillings paid, to 14 prosthetics specialists, rather than the minimal compensation of 20 percent that was required.[22]

The state-run prosthetics factories also allowed the Austrian government to set prices and with great success implement price controls, not only for the material needed to make prostheses, such as leather, metal, and rubber, but also for the prostheses themselves. The Viennese and Lower Austrian Guild of Bandagers, Orthopedic Mechanics, and Surgical Instrument Makers (Wiener- und Niederösterreichische Innung der Bandagisten, Orthopädienmechaniker und Chirurgieinstrumtenmacher) took part in negotiations to establish prices for orthopedic supplies and reached an agreement with the Austrian Social Insurance Work Group on September 20, 1946.[23]

The Central Organization for Austrian War Victims was also contacted with regard to the regulation of prices for orthopedic materials by the Federal Interior Ministry (Price Control Department/Preisbildungsstelle). In a statement summarizing the situation, the Referat K (responsible for War Disabled Health Care/Kriegsbeschädigte Heilfürsorge) pointed out that the main difficulty with price regulation was that "the Greater German Reich concluded an agreement with the [prosthetics] suppliers that expired for this group with the reestablishment of Austria because the position had to be taken that Austria is not the legal successor of the Greater German Reich."[24] The suppliers naturally wanted a price increase for prostheses that was equal to the amount they were receiving from their private customers, and, of course, the war disabled sought refunds for the payments they had made as private customers to the orthopedists from the LIAs. However, the LIAs could or would only refund the amount set in the contracts from the Third Reich. This, in turn, led to unhappiness on the part of the war disabled or in the case of some suppliers, who still felt bound to the old prices, to an unwillingness to deliver finished prostheses. This, combined with the post-war shortage of raw materials, led to a standstill in orthopedic care.[25]

By August 1945, meetings were already being held to determine how best to reintegrate the war wounded and disabled into the Austrian economy and Austrian society. A meeting on August 9 of that year suggested a long list of jobs for those who had been disabled in the war. Among the suggestions were baker, bookbinder, chassis and wheel maker, electrician, butcher, hairdresser, glazier, belt maker, engraver, men's tailor, plumber, electrician, pipefitter, jeweler, mechanic, furrier, painter, miller, horse butcher, blacksmith, chimney sweep, carpenter, cabinetmaker, watch-maker, agricultural machinery producer, embroiderer, photographer, and graphic artist.[26]

For those who had been blinded, a different set of professions was suggested than for those who had been physically wounded in other ways: broom maker, telephone receptionist, piano tuner, or basketweaver. For example, a limited number of spaces were made available in March 1946 for a basketweaving course to be held by the Austrian Blindenindustrie at its workshop in Vienna and financed by the Austrian Federal Ministry for Social Administration. The participating war blind had to fulfill certain conditions and were then accepted for the course.[27]

Another example of reintegration of disabled veterans is provided by the efforts of the United States Military Government in Lower Austria. There, in St. Florian near Linz, the LIA with the help of the Lower Austrian state government, established a State School for the Blind. The Americans brought all the necessary medical equipment and furniture from the former War Blind Field hospital in Castle Engleiten. Those participating in the course learned such subjects as Braille reading, typing, basketweaving, broom making, massage, and music. By April 1946, the first course for broom makers was already completed.[28] By 1948, in eight different courses, 230 vision-impaired veterans had completed courses to ready them for their future careers.[29]

Another method of hastening the reintegration of disabled veterans and civilian victims was the introduction of scholarships making it possible for them to learn new professions or trades either at the university level or through training in manual jobs. These scholarships helped provide the physically handicapped with the knowledge and skills necessary to obtain meaningful jobs and smoothed their reintegration into civil society following their hospitalization.[30]

Because reintegration and retraining were so expensive, the Austrian government and its ministries also developed innovative methods for raising money for the care of disabled veterans and civilian war victims. One was a tax on gasoline at filling stations that benefited these groups. Another was the licensing of tobacconist's shops to the disabled so that they could earn their own livings. The main goal of these licensings was reintegration rather than pension or disability payments. This was not only the goal of the Austrian state but also of the Central Organization of War Victim and Disabled Associations.[31] A blind tobacco shop proprietor named Bartak offers just one example of how well this type of reintegration process could function. Bartak had everything in his shop in a specific place so he could quickly hand the proper newspapers and cigarette packages to his customers. In this manner, he made himself almost entirely self-sufficient. This from a man who was unable to find a job anywhere else.[32] Training of this nature was supported not only by the government but also by private associations and organizations for the disabled and was carried out at schools specially equipped to provide such training.

Yet another method used by the Austrian state to raise money to pay the health care costs of those disabled in the war was special-issue stamps. The first special-issue printing was in 1945, and the concept functioned so successfully that its use was continued. Today, the main beneficiaries from the sales of these stamps are homes and schools for the blind.[33] Another method that both the War Blind Association and the Central Organization for Austrian War Victims used to raise money was lotteries. The concept of running a lottery to benefit the disabled was not new. The war blind had used this method with great success during the economically turbulent First Austrian Republic from 1918 to 1938. Beginning in 1947, the War Blind Association held its first postwar lottery. During the previous two years, this had not been possible due to the chaotic conditions and the daily struggle for survival and food. An envelope with tickets for the lottery was sent to each member of the War Blind Association, who could then either purchase them or attempt to sell them. The industriousness of some members can be seen in the records of the War Blind Association. For example, in 1953, the blind Viennese war veteran Theodor Kozel sold an impressive 3,335 tickets.[34] This record held until 1959, when Karl Stadelmann sold 4,985.[35] The first war blind lottery had a total capital of 200,000 schillings. By 1967, in the twentieth lottery, the total capital had increased to 4.8 million schillings, and the profit was over 1.6 million schillings.[36]

The Central Organization for Austrian War Victims held its first lottery three years later in November 1950 with prizes totaling 250,000 schillings.[37] The success of the War Blind Associations' lottery most certainly had an effect on the Central Organization for Austrian War Victims' decision to begin conducting a lottery itself, and this became a powerful fund-raising tool for both organizations and supplemented voluntary contributions and yearly membership dues. The inability of the Austrian central state to provide adequate funding to care for disabled veterans played a significant role in encouraging such independent lotteries and provided the impetus for the use of such methods by all disabled organizations in the postwar period.

With regard to the question of gathering the resources to assist the disabled, the importance of Austria as a "neutral" nation during the Cold War had a significant impact on the economic aid it received, both for its disabled veterans and for its industry and commerce. One also must see the treatment of disabled veterans in this context, at least during the occupation period in Austria. The Americans, British, and French were very interested in keeping Austria on their side, and the Soviet treatment of Austrians, especially of disabled veterans, was of great help to the Western propaganda cause. The less able and willing the Soviets were to help suffering disabled veterans, the more the sympathy of these groups shifted toward the Western powers. At the beginning of the Cold War in 1948, one specifically sees the use of exhibits touting the Marshall Plan and its aid for the Austrian economy. U.S. Army photographers documenting visitors to a Marshall Plan exhibit in Vienna made a special priority of showing disabled veterans visiting the exhibit and photographed several disabled men. It appears that this was an attempt to appeal to this group and to build support for the Marshall Plan by showing that all Austrians would be included and benefit from the plan (see fig. 9).

On June 25, 1947, a foreign aid agreement was signed between the United States and Austria. This, of course, was not a disinterested act by the Americans since limiting Soviet influence in Austria was the goal. Although several countries were included in the overall aid program of which this agreement was a part, Austria was the first nation to receive aid. At this same time, the U.S. Senate passed a bill to aid areas devastated by the war, including Greece, Italy, Austria, Hungary, Poland, and China. On July 2, 1948, Austria was included in the Marshall Plan. Despite these aid efforts and the accompanying propaganda barrage, however, the situation of Austria's dis-

FIG. 9. Disabled veteran at a Marshall Plan exhibit in Vienna in 1948. The
United States and its allies were particularly interested in getting Austrian
veterans involved with the Marshall Plan in order to make them feel a part
of Western Europe and to gain their loyalty in the Cold War. The economic reintegration of Austria's numerous disabled veterans and war
wounded was also considered an important part of national recovery.
(Photo Collection, Austrian National Library.)

abled veterans did not improve dramatically, since the aid sent to Austria
was mostly in the form of food and other material goods for the rebuilding
of industry, rather than for assisting disabled individuals.

Because Austria and Germany were both important to the United
States during the early years of the Cold War, Secretary of State George C.
Marshall was involved heavily not only in beginning the program of aid to
relieve the economic hardship and suffering in Europe but also in the early

discussions regarding Austria's independence. Austria, and especially Vienna, was an important bulwark for the Allies against perceived threats from the Russians.[38]

Another factor that must be considered, in addition to the high number of Austrians disabled as a result of the war, was a large number of returning POWs (approximately 500,000). In the Western zones, the release of POWs and their return home from detention camps was largely completed, with some exceptions, by October 1946. In the Soviet zone, however, the process was not nearly as rapid. Transports of returning POWs, the so-called *Heimkehrer,* continued up until 1955. Large numbers of POWs, both those who had been injured in the war and those who had suffered at the hands of the Russians, returned from Soviet camps with psychological trauma and physical injuries.[39] The disabled among these returnees also had to be treated following their return to Austria and placed additional strain on an already burdened health care system. Although the transports were greeted enthusiastically by the population at large,[40] there is some doubt about the joy of the personnel in the state and government ministries, especially the Social Ministry, whose duty it was to arrange care for these returnees. The large influx of new cases taxed the physical capabilities of the Social Ministry's civil servants as well as the financial resources of the ministry itself. Thus, there was a scramble to find solutions for the hundreds of individual cases that threatened to break the social insurance system.

Despite its status as an occupied nation, Austria's government and its ministries were given a great deal of autonomy in dealing with handicapped civilians and disabled veterans by the Western occupying powers. The Soviets maintained tighter control, but the situation improved gradually throughout the 1950s since the example of the Western zones helped spur the Soviets to do more in their zone.

In contrast to occupied Germany, the Allies did not systematically dismantle the system of war disability benefits in Austria.[41] Austria's status as "victim" of German aggression, which was established by the Moscow Declaration of 1943, allowed the Austrians much more freedom in determining how their pension and disability system would be organized than was allowed in Germany. The Western Allies, of course, viewed Austrians as less of a potential military threat than the Germans, among whom they wished to destroy all traces of military culture, including pensions. Thus, Austria was given substantially more political autonomy in minor affairs such as the treatment of disabled veterans and the awarding of pension payments. For example, Austrian veterans who had already been receiving pension payments during the Second World War generally continued to receive these same payments under Allied occupation, whereas veterans in Germany often had to wait months. In Austria, control was less strict, and hospitals and treatment centers as well as administrative offices merely changed hands from the National Socialists to the provisional Austrian government. Of course, the Austrian ministries were required to obtain approval for any changes they made to the system in their area from the Allied power responsible for their zone of occupation. That meant that the system of care for disabled veterans was by no means unified, and this created a number of problems for individual veterans who sought treatment.

In fact, many veterans who had been wounded, but not severely, did not qualify for a pension. Despite injuries that would pain them for the rest of their lives, these men received no disability or pension payments and had to content themselves with being happy that they had survived the war relatively unscathed.[42] The determination of disability was often decided at the whim of Austrian civil servants without medical degrees in the Social Ministry or in the Landesinvalidenämter and was based on criteria about what constituted a severe injury established by the Social Ministry. Very often a government bureaucrat with no knowledge about what constituted a functional limitation determined the range of ability of an injured veteran and, thus, the percentage of his disability and the amount of his future pension. In Germany, the general rule in the Soviet zone of occupation was that a veteran had to be at least two-thirds disabled in his "vocational ability" to receive any sort of a pension.[43] Thus, veterans who were less than two-thirds disabled and able to work, even when they had a disability of over 50 percent, often were denied pensions in the Soviet-occupied zones of Germany and Austria. This situation, although less common in Austria than in Germany, was still a problem and was exploited fully by the Western Allies in their Cold War propaganda against the Soviets.

Throughout the decades following the war, the main task of the veterans' organizations was political lobbying in order to get compensation and treatment for veterans with severe war injuries like the ones mentioned above who had not been granted pensions. In the immediate postwar period, several laws were passed as a result of pressure from veterans. Ultimately, however, these laws alone were not enough to ease the pain and suffering of Austrian veterans.

A major step to better the situation of Austria's disabled war veterans was taken in 1956. In that year, the upper house of Austria's parliament passed a two-stage law to increase the amount of pensions to those disabled by the war. The first stage went into effect on January 1, 1957, and the second exactly one year later. This law replaced the previous fifth amendment to the KOVG from February 29, 1956, which had garnered much criticism from the Central Organization for Austrian War Victims. In this amendment, only those war victims who had received food payments were to receive increased pensions. Naturally, this angered those who had received no increase, and the Central Organization for Austrian War Victims voiced this anger to Social Minister Anton Proksch in a meeting on June 24, 1956. As James M. Diehl says in a study of disabled German war veterans, "the vanquished were not voiceless."[44] In many cases, they were able to influence their governments to make changes. The unusual pattern of combined civilian-veteran advocacy in Austria under the auspices of the Central Organization for Austrian War Victims certainly helped to give disabled veterans a greater voice in Austrian politics. The situation of civilian-veteran advocacy is unique to Austria and Germany and arose out of social democratic traditions as well as the forced demilitarization of these two nations by the Allied powers at the end of the First World War. However, of these two nations, only the Austrians had been able to establish a single central organization representing all civilian and military disabled. In Germany, by contrast, the formation of such a group had fallen victim to ideological differences and political conflicts among rival organizations, which were often affiliated with the major political parties. The ability of Austrian organizations to agree on common lobbying goals and to prioritize helped the Central Organization for Austrian War Victims to gain recognition as a lobbying force and to improve care for both disabled veterans and civilian handicapped.

An excellent example of the continuing efficacy of the less politicized Austrian tradition of advocacy was the War Victim Fund Law, which was passed in 1960, and which the Central Organization for Austrian War Victims had actively supported.[45] The law provided interest-free loans to war victims and disabled veterans to help them obtain housing, to get or keep a job, to make possible a professional education for their children, or to remedy a financial crisis. The loans were granted up to an amount 60 times greater than the monthly disability pension and were repaid by deducting the monthly payment directly from the pension check before it was sent to the recipient.

Yet the difficult situation caused by insufficient laws regulating social assistance to disabled veterans continued throughout the 1960s despite lobbying efforts on the part of the Central Organization for Austrian War Victims. The organization by this point represented not only disabled veterans but also all those who had been injured as a result of the war: disabled female factory workers, children injured in bombing attacks, and those civilians blinded by phosphorus bombs or by grenade fragments. In contrast to the United States, Europe had many victims among those who had not fought on the front. These civilian victims of the war could not be blamed for having served in a foreign army, but they, like the disabled veterans, were a strong reminder of Austria's role in the war and an irritation to politicians intent on portraying Austria as a victim of Nazi Germany.

Throughout the 1960s and 1970s, the Central Organization of War Victim and Disabled Associations in Austria—its name changed to reflect its larger constituency of both military and civilian war victims—continued its lobbying efforts for better pensions and treatment for those who had been disabled in the war. Due to its efforts, many needy and suffering war victims received help from Austria's federal ministries that they otherwise would have been denied.

In 1966, the organization called for its members to protest the refusal of Finance Minister Wolfgang Schmitz to negotiate with them about an increase in funding for the betterment of war victims' care. Only 88 million schillings were earmarked for this purpose, and without additional funding, the situation of former military and civilian war disabled most certainly would not improve. After several unsuccessful attempts to convince Dr. Schmitz to negotiate with the Central Organization of War Victim and Disabled Associations, it was decided to stage an Austria-wide protest in each of the state capitals on Saturday, October 15, 1966. The turnout was impressive: 2,000 in Innsbruck, 2,500 in Graz, 4,000 in Klagenfurt, 6,000 in Linz, and over 14,000 in Vienna. The final outcome was negotiations with the finance minister and an increase in funding for the needs of those disabled in the war.[46]

Other changes were made in the late 1970s, perhaps due to a decrease in the membership of the war victims' organization, resulting from a large number of deaths. In 1975, a major change was made to the by-laws of the organization, allowing all Austrian citizens with a disability of 50 percent or more to become members. In conjunction with this change, widows, orphans, and parents of those war disabled with a 30 or 40 percent disability were allowed to join following the death of the veteran, even though they no longer had legal right to benefits from the Austrian government. As an open example of these changes, the name of the War Victims' Association for Vienna, Lower Austria, and Burgenland was changed to the War Victims' and Disabled Association in 1978.[47]

On April 29, 1987, at a mass rally of the Central Organization of War Victims and Disabled Associations in the town of Eisenstadt, a resolution was passed that established the social policy of the organization for the coming years, the so-called Eisenstadt Declaration. One of the central points of this declaration was that the compensation of war and military service victims was seen as a "fundamental right" and that compensation laws should be required of the Austrian government. A second point was a right of war disabled to work, including protection from being fired and the opportunity for further education to keep or advance their present jobs. The representatives in Eisenstadt also proposed an increase and additional support for the construction of handicapped-accessible facilities, especially public buildings and housing, as well as public transportation to increase the mobility of the handicapped. Because of the additional costs incurred by those who were handicapped, the members also affirmed their support for the tax advantages granted to the disabled. Here again affirmed was the principle that work was always preferable to a pension. The members also stated their unhappiness with the inequality within divisions of the systems of social insurance and of socialized medicine, for example, Farmers' Social Insurance and Tradesmen's Insurance. Each of these systems permitted different benefits for the handicapped and thus, according to the disabled veterans and handicapped, violated the equal rights granted to all Austrian citizens in their constitution.[48]

The Eisenstadt Declaration was the culmination of many of the political goals first set by disabled veterans immediately following the Second World War, but it was also a summary of unfinished work remaining after years of lobbying efforts, a blueprint for future lobbying by the Central Organization of War Victims' and Disabled Associations.

The Eisenstadt Declaration shows clearly how far Austria's war-disabled and handicapped veterans had progressed in organizing themselves and influencing the passage of laws to better their situation in the four decades following the war. The rehabilitation and reintegration of disabled war veterans and the war wounded was made a priority by these organizations, which wielded a great deal of power and exerted pressure on the Austrian authorities to better their situation.

The historian Manfred Rauchensteiner has argued that postwar Austria, forgiven its alliance with Nazi Germany and, as a neutral, courted by both sides, was a "special case" in the Cold War years.[49] Austria's singular international position, as we have seen, did have an impact, too, on its war-wounded veterans, for it influenced the gathering of the resources to assist them. But, as their persistent efforts over many decades to denounce the inadequacies of government assistance and to strengthen the social commitment to such assistance suggest, the suffering of many of Austria's veterans continued. They still had to live with the injuries incurred in a war that many of their fellow Austrians would just as soon have forgotten, and this meant, for many of the war disabled, 50 years of both physical and mental pain.

NOTES

The author would like to express his sincere thanks to Berthold Konrath of the Austrian State Archives in Vienna for his help in obtaining primary source material for this study.

1. Contribution by Karoline Fritsch, "40 Jahre Ehe mit einem Schwerstkriegsversehrten," quoted in Theo Fischlein, "Lebensgeschichten österreichischer Kriegsopfer," in *Schicksal Kriegsopfer*, ed. Michael Svoboda (Vienna: Kriegsopfer- und Behindertenverband für Wien, Niederösterreich und Burgenland, 1995), 80. All translations are the author's.

2. Interview with Franz Mustermann (name changed to protect privacy) on November 16, 1998, in Wien-Penzing.

3. Otto Jähnl, *Die österreichischen Kriegsblinden der beiden Weltkriege* (Vienna: Böhlau, 1994), 164.

4. "Die Gründung des österreichischen Kriegsopferverbandes," *Öffentliche Sicherheit*, August 1934, 18.

5. Österreichisches Staatsarchiv (Austrian State Archives), Archiv der Republik, Group 03 (hereafter cited as AR3), Carton 89, "Kriegsbeschädigte 1947, 1–13000," Document II AV-120.005 11/45, "Vorläufige Maßnahmen zur Entschädigung der Kriegsopfer" (Staatsamt für Soziale Verwaltung), sheet 2.

6. Ibid., sheets 2 and 3. The original German reads as follows: "Das neue Entschädigungsrecht wird zunächst an einer gewissen unterschiedlichen Behandlung der Kriegsopfer des 1. und des 2.Weltkrieges nicht vorbeigehen können, wenn man bedenkt, daß gegenüber den Opfern des 1.Weltkrieges die Pflicht der Dankbarkeit des österreichischen Volkes fortbesteht, während die Opfer des 2. Weltkrieges ihre Schädigung in einem für fremde Interessen geführten, die Grundlagen des österreichischen Staates auf das tiefste erschütternden Raubkrieg erlitten haben."

7. AR3, Carton 29, "Kriegsbeschädigte 1945 120.000–Ende," Document III AV-120.012 11/45, "Entwurf eines Gesetzes über die Aufhebung der Reichsversorgungsverwaltung in Österreich."

8. In Styria where between 70 and 75 percent of the doctors had been members of the National Socialist German Workers' Party (NSDAP) before the annexation of Austria, the situation was particularly drastic. Dr. Helmut Hammer, who had not been in the NSDAP but in the German Wehrmacht, is a case in point. He returned to Graz after being released from a British POW camp and worked as a volunteer in the state hospital *(Landeskrankenhaus)* in Graz. For more information on this subject, see Alfred Ableitinger, Siegfried Beer, and Eduard G. Staudinger, eds., *Besatzungszeit in der Steiermark 1945–1955, 4. Geschichtswerkstatt Graz 1991* (Graz: Andreas Schnider Verlags-Atelier, 1994), 53–57.

9. Karl Ernst, "50 Jahre Kriegsopferversorgung in der Zweiten Republik 1945–1995," in Svoboda, *Schicksal Kriegsopfer*, 233.

10. AR3, Carton 90, "Kriegsbeschädigte 1947 13001–Ende," Document IV-

150.302–15/1947, "Überschreitung der Jahreskredite des Bundesvoranschlages 1947 bei Kap.15, Titel 4 (Kriegsbeschädigtenfürsorge)." The same situation was also true for the months August, September, October, November, and December 1946. See AR3, Carton 30, "Kriegsbeschädigte 1946 100–11000," Documents IV-41.727–15/1946, IV-49.954–15/1946, IV-58.945–15/1946, IV-708020–15/1946, IV-82.932–15/1946.

11. *Bundesgesetzblatt für die Republik Österreich,* no. 197 (1949).

12. Ernst, "50 Jahre Kriegsopferversorgung," 251.

13. *Bundesgesetzblatt für die Republik Österreich,* no. 163 (1946).

14. AR3, Carton 31, "Kriegsbeschädigte 1946 11001–Ende," Document IV-11.415–15/46, "Donau Chemie Aktiengesellschaft; Beschwerde gegen Vorschreibung der Ausgleichstaxe."

15. AR3, Carton 90, "Kriegsbeschädigte 1947 13001–Ende," Document IV-27.270–15/1947, "Entlassung von Schwerkriegsbeschädigte aus dem Justizdienst," sheets 4, 5, and 6.

16. AR3, Carton 90, "Kriegsbeschädigte 1947 13001–Ende," Document IV-24.896–15/1947, "Nationalsozialistengesetz; Regelung für die Entschädigung von Personen in der Versehrtenstufen III und IV."

17. AR3, Carton 90, "Kriegsbeschädigte 1947 13001–Ende," Document IV-31.185–15/1947, "Rechtsverhältnisse der Kriegsfürsorge geniessenden Personen," sheet 3.

18. AR3, Carton 169, "Kriegsbeschädigte 1948 1–40.000," Document IV-1400–15/48, "Behandlung der Südtiroler und Canaltaler."

19. AR3, Carton 19, "Volksgesundheit," Document V-17879–21/46, "Heilstättenbehandlung der Kriegsbeschädigten in den Landeslungenheilstätten in Enzenbach und in der öffentlichen Lundentuberkulösenheilanstalt Buchberg-Traunkirchen."

20. AR3, Carton 19, "Volksgesundheit," Document V-17879–21/46, "Ausbildung von Blindenführhunden für Kriegsblinde."

21. AR3, Carton 90, "Kriegsbeschädigte 1947 13001–Ende," Document IV-42.382-K/1947, "Leichtmetall-Oberschenkelprothesen nach schwedischem Patent"; IV-44.464-K/47, "Simplex Sitzprothese; Patent Gottfried Hadl (für Oberschenkelamputierte)."

22. AR3, Carton 19, "Volksgesundheit," Document V-9967-K/1946, "Wiener- und Niederösterreichische Innung der Bandagisten, Orthopädienmechaniker und Chirurgieinstrumentenmacher; Forderungen an die ehemalige deutsche Wehrmacht," May 17, 1946.

23. AR3, Carton 19, "Volksgesundheit," Document V-60523-K/45, "Orthopädische Versorgung der Kriegsversehrten," letter from the Wiener- und Niederösterreichische Bandagisten, Orthopädienmechaniker und Chirurgieinstrumentenmacher to the Bundesministerium für soziale Verwaltung from October 5, 1946.

24. AR3, Carton 19, "Volksgesundheit," Document V-43.074-K/46, "Orthopädische Versorgung der Kriegsbeschädigten im Bereiche des LIA Wien.— Anfrage des LIA Wien bzw. der Zentralorganisation der Kriegsopfer wegen der Preisgestaltung," sheets 2 and 3. The original German for this passage reads as follows: "Das großdeutsche Reich hatte mit den Lieferanten eine Vereinbarung abgeschlossen, die mit dem Wiedererstehen Österreichs für dessen Bereich erlosch, weil der Standpunkt eingenommen werden mußte, daß Österreich nicht der Rechtsnachfolger des großdeutschen Reiches ist."

25. Ibid.

26. AR3, Carton 29, "Kriegsbeschädigte 1945 120.000–Ende," Document III-120.206 11/45, "Wiedereinführung Kriegsbeschädigter in das gewerbliche Erwerbsleben—Sitzung am 9.8.1945."

27. AR3, Carton 30, "Kriegsbeschädigte 1946 100–11000," Document IV-10.546–15/46, "Berufsausbildung der Kriegsblinden; Korbflechterei."

28. "Eröffnung eines Kriegsblindenschulungsheimes in St. Florian," *Mitteilungen der Kriegsblindenvereinigung*, May–June 1946, 1.

29. *Nachrichten des Verbandes der Kriegsblinden Österreichs*, May–July 1948, 16.

30. *Bundesgesetzblatt für die Republik Österreich*, no. 164 (1952), secs. 21 and 22.

31. Ernst, "50 Jahre Kriegsopferversorgung," 255.

32. Jähnl, "Grete Bartak freute sich: Mein Mann ist vollbeschäftigt," in *Die österreichischen Kriegsblinden*, 174–76.

33. Verbal information from the Austrian Post Office, Vienna.

34. *Nachrichten des Verbandes der Kriegsblinden Österreichs*, July 1953, 50.

35. *Nachrichten des Verbandes der Kriegsblinden Österreichs*, July 1959, 85. See also Jähnl, *Die österreichischen Kriegsblinden*, 154–60.

36. Jähnl, *Die österreichischen Kriegsblinden*, 155.

37. Elfriede Sengstschmied, "50 Jahre Kriegsopferverband—ein Stück österreichischer Sozialgeschichte," in Svoboda, *Schicksal Kriegsopfer*, 342.

38. For a detailed history of the occupation period in Austria, see Manfred Rauchensteiner, *Der Sonderfall. Die Besatzungszeit in Österreich 1945 bis 1955* (Graz: Styria-Reprint, 1995).

39. For more on the Austrian *Heimkehrer*, consult Stefan Karner and the Ludwig Boltzmann Institut für Kriegsfolgenforschung in Graz, Austria. Especially interesting is Karner's book *Im Archipel GUPWI: Kriegsgefangenschaft und Internierung in der Sowjetunion 1941–1956* (Vienna: Oldenburg, 1995).

40. Franz Wolf, "Einer unter vielen," in Svoboda, *Schicksal Kriegsopfer*, 219.

41. James M. Diehl, "Change and Continuity in the Treatment of German *Kriegsopfer*," *Central European History* 18 (June 1985): 177.

42. Gustav Klier, telephone interview on November 16, 1998. Dr. Klier, born in 1923, served on both the Eastern and Western fronts, was wounded twice and eventually captured by the Americans in Normandy (1944) and spent the rest of the war in a POW camp in Trinidad, Colorado.

43. James M. Diehl, *The Thanks of the Fatherland: German Veterans after World War II* (Chapel Hill: University of North Carolina Press, 1993), 75.

44. Diehl, "Change and Continuity," 182.

45. "Kriegsopferfondsgesetz," *Bundesgesetzblatt für die Republik Österreich*, no. 217 (October 19, 1960).

46. Sengstschmied, "50 Jahre Kriegsopferverband," 404–6.

47. Ibid., 439.

48. Ernst, "50 Jahre Kriegsopferversorgung," 292–95.

49. Rauchensteiner, *Der Sonderfall*, "Vorwort zur Neuauflage," 2.

Ethel Dunn

Disabled Russian War Veterans: Surviving the Collapse of the Soviet Union

Finding information about the disabled in Russia is not easy, because Soviet and Russian statistical handbooks until recently tended to lump pensioners and disabled into one category. There was also a tendency to deny that any problems existed among the disabled, which kept them even further from view. In the 1990s, a diligent researcher could nonetheless dig into printed books, scholarly journals, and newspapers and construct a picture of what life on a pension in present-day Russia must be like. There are a few basic questions for which there are no clear answers when it comes to these veterans: how many disabled Russian war veterans are we talking about, and which category of pension, a key to discovering their disabled status, do they receive? The different ministries and agencies that administer pensions divide all of the disabled into three groups: Group I, the most disabled and supposedly unable to work; Group II, those able to work under certain conditions; and Group III, the least disabled. The population of these cohorts is hardly stable. A Medical-Social Expert Bureau reviews the health status of the disabled, including veterans, every two years, unless the person's condition is judged unlikely to change. People receiving old-age pensions may also now qualify for a disability pension, but it is almost impossible to know whether the result is an increase in the total number of disabled or simply a redistribution of the disabled population. I will be discussing three groups of Russian disabled veterans: those who served in World War II; those who were drafted during peacetime, including those who served abroad in various conflicts; and the so-called Afgantsy, soldiers who served in the war in Afghanistan. Some sociological studies have been made of the Afgantsy, and I will be discussing these studies in this essay.

World War II, called the Great Patriotic War in Russia, resulted in 20 million dead, 7.5 million of them in the armed forces.[1] At the end of World

War II there were 11,365,000 officers and troops in the Soviet armed forces, including 800,000 women. Demobilization started toward the end of 1945, and in a few years there were fewer than three million troops.[2] Not only was this a huge population loss, a flood of men and women needing jobs, services, and health care were released into a ruined civilian economy. World War II remains vivid in the memories of most of the older generation of Soviet and Russian citizens, because every family and every village suffered some loss. The disabled and veteran pensioners still pose a huge problem in terms of health care for the Russian government. Disabled veterans of World War II numbered 659,200 in 1989, but their numbers increase as those veterans who survived the war without crippling injuries (2,660,000 in 1994, and another 13 million who, because they worked in the rear of the army, are entitled under law to the same benefits) age and acquire multiple disabilities.[3]

The Soviet Union was also involved in a substantial number of other conflicts, before and after 1945. The soldiers called up to serve in these conflicts were called "internationalists," but they never achieved the same status as the veterans of World War II, who were fighting in defense of their invaded fatherland. The "internationalists" were doing their socialist duty to help defend other countries from Western imperialism, according to Soviet definition, but by the late Soviet period, there was considerable skepticism and cynicism about the motivating ideology in Soviet society. There was a Soviet military presence in these other conflicts:

Afghanistan (April 1978–February 1989)
Algeria (1962–64)
Angola (November 1975–November 1979, 1985)
Bangladesh (1972–73)
Cambodia (April–December 1970)
China (1920s–1953)
Egypt (October 1962–1975)
Ethiopia (December 1977, November 1979)
Laos (1960, 1975)
Mongolia (1939)
Mozambique (1967–69, 1975)
North Korea (1950–53)
Spain (1936–39)
Syria (1967, 1970)
Vietnam (January 1961–December 1974)
Yemen (October 1962–December 1967, March–December 1969).[4]

All of these conflicts presumably have produced their own disabled veterans. In addition, Soviet troops were stationed in Czechoslovakia, Hungary, and East Germany, with massive concentrations of troops in East Germany, but their roles apparently did not involve combat. After the breakup of the Soviet Union, there was the war in Chechnya (1991–96), which many Russians considered almost a civil war,[5] and which Russia essentially lost in the first round of fighting.[6] The Russian army recently has also served as peacekeeper in other areas of the former Soviet Union, with varying degrees of success and probably significant injuries and casualties.[7]

In this essay, I will be discussing the benefits given to veterans who served in wartime and to veterans of labor, who are mostly, by Russian government categories, the same cohort as veterans of World War II, and will describe the difficulties encountered in collecting the benefits today. These difficulties are a result of transition to a market economy since the collapse of the Soviet Union and of the Russian government's decreasing investment in the public health sector. This is not an easy story to tell, because of the difficulties getting consistent information and data on disabled veterans in the former Soviet Union and in contemporary Russia. But the story is very much worth telling, especially when it may be developed utilizing Russian language sources, such as the publications of disability and veterans organizations, that are little known in the West.

According to Bernice Madison, under the Soviet regime, World War II veterans and their survivors got substantially higher pensions than the rest of the Soviet population. They have always been a favored cohort of the population. Moreover, veterans were also eligible for impressive supplementary benefits, such as a nursing care allowance for those in Group I (severely disabled). They also received a Zaporozhets automobile free of charge, which was replaced every seven years, though at present, the automobile is in such short supply that the veteran may receive a onetime monetary supplement instead. Service for the automobiles was free, and there was also a payment for gasoline. Public transportation was free, and trips to health resorts were free to the veteran and one companion. Veterans were first on waiting lists for housing, although at present the lines are still impossibly long. They were eligible for no-interest loans to build homes for themselves, and to make major repairs, which did not have to be paid off in 10 years. They got telephones installed free and were entitled to buy groceries at special stores and to have them delivered, and they were first in line to purchase scarce goods.[8]

World War II veterans who could walk and were able to work appear to have reentered Soviet society and received education and jobs. Their government discouraged dwelling on their disabilities, but they could enjoy these relatively impressive benefits. The benefits they received supplemented relatively small pensions and gave them a measure of security. Much more severely disabled veterans also received benefits, but they were also kept out of sight, some even segregated in remote locations, and there was little public discussion of them except for occasional references in literature. Vera Dunham quotes from passages of Yurii Nagibin's novella *Patience,* in which two lovers are reunited on an island called Bogoyar, where the man, legless from injuries received in World War II, lives with other disabled veterans.[9] Bogoyar may have been Nagibin's fictional name for the island of Vaalam in Lake Ladoga, near St. Petersburg. In 1992, the chairman of the Subcommittee on the Affairs of Veterans and the Disabled of the Supreme Soviet of the Russian Federation, Vladimir S. Zinov'ev, gave an interview in which he said that while he was still a medical student, he saw the Home for War Disabled on the island of Vaalam, in Lake Ladoga, where veterans without arms and legs were housed.[10] There are also a few extraordinary, if in some instances sentimentalized, pictorial representations of Vaalam. The artist Gennadii Dobrov has published some drawings of the patients on Vaalam, the most haunting of which is *The Unknown Soldier,* who lost his arms, legs, speech, and hearing as the result of war wounds. Only sight remains, and he lies on his bed, a neatly swaddled package, his eyes burning with pain and anger. *Wounded in the Defense of the USSR* shows another resident of Vaalam, Alexander Podosenov, who volunteered at age 17, became an officer, and received a paralyzing head wound in Karelia. His medals do not comfort him as he sits, almost tearful, one hand clutching a surrounding pillow. Another drawing, *The Family,* shows Vasilii Lobachev, a defender of Moscow, and his wife Lidia. They have two sons. Lobachev's legs and arms were amputated because of gangrene, and Lidia too lost her legs during the war. Her hands rest on his shoulder as he sits in his wheelchair. In one hand there is a telephone, which Lobachev holds to his ear by hunching up the other shoulder. He looks straight at the viewer, smiling slightly, but engaged by his telephone conversation; Lidia looks up and to the right, her lips pressed determinedly together. *Letter to a Comrade-in-Arms* shows Vladimir Eremin, a resident of the village of Kuchino, near Moscow, wearing his medal and ribbons, sitting cross-legged and barefoot. He lost his arms and so holds a pen between the toes of a huge foot, lips pursed in concentration. Not only did he teach himself to write in this fashion, after the war, he completed a legal *tekhnikum* (specialized secondary school). Noncombatants are represented by *Tears,* in which a pretty fair-haired child without arms wipes away tears with her foot.[11] The impression I got from these drawings is that

Soviet medical personnel when faced with injuries to limbs in wartime conditions may well have lopped off the limbs and sent the patient out the door. In any case, putting the severely disabled out of sight with others of their kind kept the rest of society from reflecting on what in different ways the war and the Stalinist bureaucratic system had done to them, but it may also have been a way of trying to deal with their needs. We do not have much evidence, however, that they were consulted about their needs.

Certainly Russia has always had severely disabled people, particularly in rural areas, where medical care was poor and tolerance for people with disabilities was probably higher in proportion to their numbers and where, one gets the impression, people had to get on with their lives as best they could, without much medical assistance. But life for people in Russia who cannot walk is extremely limited. Most never leave their apartments, and what education they receive is acquired at home or in institutions. Until recently, it was thought that those who could not walk, also could not work.[12] It is important to keep in mind that what the disabled get often has to be in competition with able-bodied veterans, and the rest of Russian society. In present-day Russia dissatisfied able-bodied veterans represent a potentially destabilizing force in Russian society, because the safety net that all Russians utilized under the Soviet system is disappearing.

Most of the veterans' benefits that applied during the Soviet regime are supposed to be in force at the present time. However, transition to a market economy has left the welfare system unable to pay for them. Veterans' pensions are currently small, and there seem to be problems implementing them. For instance, veterans of World War II were supposed to have had their pensions increased in 1995 at the time of the 50th anniversary of the end of the war in Europe, but the increase depended on a review of the veterans' monetary allowance, and the review did not occur on time.[13] Those veterans who can do so supplement their income by selling produce raised on their private plots or, in extreme cases, their personal belongings,[14] but most veterans, and many Russians generally, have a hard time buying enough food to eat. One reporter writing in 1992 compared the daily ration of a prisoner in a Soviet labor camp with the daily ration of a pensioner and found that the prisoner ate better, because he at least got meat and milk. In any case, the pensioner gets mostly bread, tea, and sugar.[15] Another reporter labeled the situation in 1993 "social genocide." He compared the price of potatoes, for example, in 1985 (10 kopeks a kilo) with 1993 (50 rubles); milk (32 kopeks a liter in 1985, 110 rubles in 1993). Consumer services have also risen in cost: washing clothes was 20 kopeks per kilogram in 1985, 115 rubles in 1993.[16] Still another commentator reported that a person with a

minimal pension in October and November 1993 could afford food
amounting to 1,713 calories per day—28 percent less than the norm.[17] In a
1998 interview, an auditor with the rank of minister in the Accounting
Office of the Russian Federation put the blame for the food situation
squarely on the Russian government, saying that "30 percent of the population lacks the means to acquire food at a minimal physiological level of
consumption," and he likened the situation to that of Leningrad during the
blockade in World War II.[18]

Such conditions probably bear down most heavily on people with disabilities, but there are some special sources of assistance to war veterans,
including those with disabilities. Private philanthropy is making some grants
to improve the lives of war veterans. For instance, the Russia Fund for Philanthropy and Health decided in 1995 to pay the neediest World War II veterans a monthly supplemental grant.[19] On April 20, 1995, 75,000 war veterans received coupons through the Moscow Soviet in connection with the
50th anniversary of victory (end of World War II) as a gift from Montazh-
SpetsBank and the Moscow Production Unit, which has 150 shops for auto
service in Moscow.[20] Free telephones are part of veterans' benefits, but
there are a variety of problems obtaining and using them that give insight
into the difficulties that bureaucratic ineptitude and insensitivity pose for
people trying to claim benefits. There are long waiting lists for installations.
In Krasnodar, in September 1991, the Communist Party of the Soviet
Union gave 150 telephones to veterans of World War II.[21] In other cases,
the law on telephones is ignored. For example, a 75-year-old married couple in a small town in Moscow Oblast, both of them Group II decorated
disabled veterans of World War II and veterans of labor, waited a long time
for their telephone. Finally, their local telephone company installed one for
them in February 1997, and then sent them a huge bill of 1,662,080 rubles
(at present this would be 1,662 rubles), much more than their pensions. It
turned out that someone using their number had been calling America three
times a day. After trying to straighten things out over the phone, the couple
went to the office to try and resolve matters. The person listening pounded
the table and said, "Pay up, or we cut off your phone and take you to
court." Understandably upset, the couple asked *Izvestiia* for help, a not
uncommon practice in the former Soviet Union and present-day Russia
when all else fails. *Izvestiia* replied that in Russia today, the bill owed is
more compelling evidence than age, length of service, or character. The
editors hoped, without being able to promise, that the regional authorities
would intervene. The resolution of this problem is not known.[22] Other
benefits are proving just as elusive. Free trips to sanatoriums, even when

they are available to veterans, are not being used because the veteran does not have the money to pay for his travel ticket.[23] Even small perks are being cut back. In 1995 the regional administration in Krasnodar gave veterans six free stamped envelopes for writing congratulations and greetings to comrades-in-arms—a measure of the relative poverty of local resources, but by 1998 even this small benefit, part of a long-cherished tradition among veterans, had to be dropped by the federal government.[24]

Retrenchments in care for disabled veterans represent much more serious difficulties. The nursing care allowance for Group I disabled appears to have been cut back, and the Red Cross, which provides the care, experienced staff cuts of 50 percent in Krasnodar Krai, allegedly due to a transition to a market economy (and decreased government investment in the health care system).[25] Some new approaches to elder care are being tried, for example, in the city of Dubna. A home health care program was started in early 1992 as a result of the Dubna-LaCrosse (Wisconsin) Hospital Partnership. The team approach to caring for the elderly is quite new for Russia, since it relies on social workers interacting with the patient-client. An example of how it operates is given by the case of Georgii, a 72-year-old World War II veteran who was living alone in a two-room apartment on a small pension. After a 20-year struggle with diabetes, he was told that his left leg would have to be amputated. He was given a team of social workers, nurses, psychologists, and doctors who helped him to learn to walk on his new prosthesis, and to take better care of himself. After five years of such attention, he has graduated to only a twice-weekly visit from his social worker and a nurse. Since April 1997, Georgii has paid 25 percent of his $115 pension for ongoing home health care.[26] The supply of free medicine has been shrinking for some time, and the cost of medicine has been rising, although the effect varies in different regions. Those regions of Russia that were doing relatively well were able to use local resources, such as taxes received from efficiently operating factories.[27] Among recently demobilized veterans, more than 60 percent were unable to get the medical care to which they are legally entitled, and only 7 percent used trips to sanatoriums.[28] These statistics suggest that many recently demobilized veterans should be considered disabled to some degree, even if only temporarily.

The lack of adequate housing seems especially critical for war veterans, disabled or not. Municipal authorities in Krasnodar promised to have housing for all disabled war veterans in 1990, but there was a list of more than 1,600 veterans and more than 200 disabled veterans.[29] In Khabarovsk, Primorskii Krai, the regional government saw to the building of a nine-story brick apartment house with phones in every apartment.[30] However, this meets the needs of a relatively small population. There is also a large group of recently demobilized soldiers and officers with their families who lack housing, and it seems unlikely that many of the disabled veterans will receive attention until this group has been served. In 1993–95 only a little more than 30 percent of the planned housing for veterans was completed, and the Ministry of Defense had 125,000 officers and warrant officers in need of housing, and 40,000 who needed improved housing, with 150,000 men and their families waiting for housing in the places where they have chosen to live.[31] The mayor's office in Krasnodar, in view of the failure of the federal government to provide housing for the families of the Afghan war and for relief workers from the Chernobyl nuclear site, announced plans in January 1998 to build an 80-apartment complex in the suburb of Yubileinyi. The mayor has requested 10 million rubles from the Krasnodar Krai administration.[32]

The same pressures from competing groups of veterans exist with respect to retraining for civilian life, and especially for life as a disabled individual. Although centers have been set up to retrain demobilized military personnel, many remain unemployed. In St. Petersburg, for example, 2,953 (78.3 percent) of the officers with permanent residence in the city went to the employment department looking for work; 1,631 (43.2 percent) were placed, and 1,294 (34.3 percent) were sent for retraining. Because of a complex indexing system, military pensions in 1994–95 were lower than civilian pensions, putting most of those demobilized on the edge of poverty.[33] Among recently demobilized military personnel, 85 percent are under 45 years of age, 43 percent do not qualify for pensions, and 70 percent have no civilian skills. In Samara Oblast, there are 150,000 former military personnel, and the fact that they need housing has been recognized by devoting 22 billion rubles to construction; 510 apartments were assigned, with a waiting list of 5,400 veterans. These veterans have returned home to a society officially recognizing unemployment for the first time. Only 17 percent of the veterans applied to the department of employment, allegedly because the jobs offered were mostly low-skilled. In areas with high unemployment, however, there are six applicants for every job, and in Ivanovo Oblast, where textile factories are the main employers, there are 88 applicants for every position.[34]

Anyone who is disabled and wants to work or needs to apply for disability pensions is literally at the mercy of the certifying body, the Medical-Social Expert Bureau, which replaced the older Physician-Labor Expert Commission (VTEK) in 1996.[35] These commissions and other governmental agencies often pose seemingly insurmountable difficulties for disabled veterans. The following three stories illustrate the problems that disabled veterans face, especially if they are not in the well-defined, socially valorized category of World War II veteran and have not been injured in combat conditions.

A soldier who had been serving in Germany since 1966 in a construction brigade was called up to "fulfill his internationalist duty" in Czechoslovakia in 1968. In the course of attempting to stop a fellow soldier from taking poisoned candy offered by a local resident, he fell and hit his head so severely that he almost lost consciousness. He was not then treated in any way, but since 1969, he has been a patient of the Psychoneurological Dispensary No. 20 in Moscow with a diagnosis of epilepsy. Beginning in 1991, when he wanted to establish his right to a military pension, he was told repeatedly that Czechoslovakia was not a region in which Russia engaged in military actions. Nevertheless, he wrote to the Moscow City Military Commissariat (which had jurisdiction over him) and to the chief specialist of the Moscow VTEK, as well as to People's Deputies and the President's Coordinating Commission for the Affairs of the Disabled. The commission told him that he needed to get a certificate from his military unit, but the Military Commissariat did not answer his letters. In September 1992, the Committee for Social Security and Aid to Pensioners and Disabled in Moscow told him that cases like his were handled by the Ministry of Defense. In December 1992, the Military Commissariat told him they would look into his case, but nothing happened. Because of his epilepsy he had to change jobs several times. He had a certificate from VTEK saying that he could work as a machinist, but not on heights or moving equipment or with heavy lifting. For the previous five years, he had been working at a factory as a machinist-plumbing technician in the position of dispatcher. He lived on a Group III pension for epilepsy, which in February 1993 was 2,800 rubles (280 rubles today), and on what he earned. His wife and son had long since left him.[36]

Military personnel who are injured as a result of peacetime service are also ineligible for pensions. Veterans in rural areas who, because of their location, have reduced access to jobs and medical care seem especially vulnerable. *Ogonëk* published a letter from a man living in a village in Voronezh Oblast who was called up for army service in September 1958, was hospitalized in October with "a bouquet of illnesses," but who nonetheless served until November 1960, when he received leg wounds in the course of duty. By March 1961, he was released from the hospital to rejoin his unit. Now, 34 years later, his health has been undermined, but he apparently cannot turn to the Ministry of Defense, or any other ministry, for help.[37] It is not clear why he cannot apply for an old-age pension, but possibly his status as a rural resident puts him outside presently established pension categories, since until recently, the collective farm pensions were separate from the state pension system.

Finally, there is the case of Evgenii Demkin, which illustrates many of the problems veterans disabled in peacetime face in Russia today. Demkin entered the army in 1983 with scoliosis and was assigned to a construction unit as a consequence. Demkin's service-related injuries were the result of the well-known,[38] brutal hazing to which all Russian army recruits are subjected. His case is complicated by the fact that he lives in a rural area without adequate public transportation and cannot walk without crutches, and even then only with great difficulty. He had to appear before the VTEK for certification,[39] and he came into the town of Khot'kovo (Moscow Oblast) with his elderly mother, who dragged him the five kilometers from his home village of Antipino on a sled.

> The polyclinic is a three-story building with stairs too high for a man with bad legs. One doctor is taking patients on the second floor, another on the third. Another doctor, the one that they must see, won't be in till tomorrow. So the son had to stay with relatives while his mother returned home to the village. If she did not fire up the oven, the potatoes stored in the basement would freeze. At the crack of dawn she again dragged her son to the polyclinic, and there, more dawdling: he's not here, he'll come later, wait here, wait there . . . Raisa Dmitrievna didn't wait. At the Medical-Labor Expert Bureau she spoke her mind: "Why should a sick person be forced to suffer? Your treatment doesn't help, you call us in for nothing, only for him to appear before a committee. I haven't got the strength of a grown man to carry him; I'm a pensioner already!" This time, the committee, confirming that her son is Group 1 disabled in connection with the injuries he received in the army, wrote "indefinite" on the registration for his stay in the polyclinic [meaning that he was ineligible for a hospital stay]. . . . They returned home on the train. The driver helped Zhenya [diminutive of Evgenii] take a seat in the carriage. Raisa Dmitrievna dragged her son from the station back to the village on a sled, but she could never make it up a certain small hill. She had to make a detour through Antipino, on a different road, three miles further.[40]

These mobility problems obviously would have been helped if Demkin could have gotten a wheelchair or an automobile. VTEK would not authorize an electric wheelchair because of the poor state of his health. His mother, who was a tractor driver before her retirement, was willing to be his chauffeur, but everywhere they got the same answer: he could not have an automobile. Personal health insurance for servicemen and their families and a onetime payment have been available since the early 1990s, but Demkin could not qualify because he served before the resolutions and orders were implemented. He would have had to serve in the army for 15 years or be currently serving in order to be hospitalized.

Russians living in the "near abroad" (newly independent states of the former Soviet Union) also pose a problem for the Russian government, which has said that it wants to protect them. A 70-year-old World War II veteran wrote to *Ogonëk* in 1998 from Riga, Latvia that he gets a pension from the Interior Department as a former colonel in the militia (police). He is a citizen both by birth and by passport of Russia, although he is a permanent resident of Riga. He asked why the government of Russia could not have foreseen when it signed an agreement with Latvia about the status of Russians in the newly created nation that Latvia would not pay Russian veterans a pension, but instead only a subsidy. When pensioners of the Soviet Union Ministry of Internal Affairs were given over to the Department of Social Security in the Ministry of Internal Affairs of Latvia, there was nothing in the agreement stating that the established pension level could not be changed. The result was that this veteran gets 10 times less than he did originally.[41]

This veteran probably does not intend to return to Russia, but after the breakup of the Soviet Union, thousands of Russians did, putting a further strain on the system of social protection. One such veteran, a deputy commander of a combat engineering unit during the war in Afghanistan, lost his left foot and an eye and sustained other injuries to his arms and torso when a mine exploded. When he came home, it was to Uzbekistan, and with the breakup of the Soviet Union, he needed to choose a place in which to live and educate his son. For a time he moved between Uzbekistan and Ukraine, rejecting both, because of the requirement that he and his family learn the native language, and because of growing anti-Russian sentiment in each of the new republics. In Moscow, on the other hand, he had comrades he could turn to. The 345th Army Regiment contained members who would come if called at night, to help talk away dark memories of Afghanistan. His comrades were beginning to be retrained and to move up in the world, and he could have done the same if he had had permanent residence. Finally he was given a temporary residence permit in a suburb outside Moscow, and the 345th Regiment took up a collection for the more than $10,000 needed for his rehabilitation in Mexico.[42] In view of the opinion of some Afgantsy that the officers who commanded them were brutes who remained largely immune to the war in Afghanistan, this man's tribulations prove that at least some officers suffered as much as the men they commanded.

Veterans' organizations do what they can to help members, but they appear to be underfunded and relatively inactive politically.[43] There are exceptions: the Voronezh branch of the Committee of Veterans from Special Forces in February 1998, appealed to President Boris Yeltsin to pass a law officially recognizing veterans of special forces. The committee has also brought suit in the Constitutional Court, claiming that their members' rights have been violated.[44]

The status of Afghan war veterans differs in some significant respects from that of veterans of World War II, and still more from drafted soldiers engaged in ordinary tours of duty. The data that I have to report on the Afghan war veterans are fragmentary, and in some cases, contradictory, but can still be used to illuminate the situation of contemporary, younger Russian war veterans. The official language of the 1980s described them as brave internationalists, but when they returned home, they found neither jobs nor benefits nor respect. The Soviet economy was collapsing, and the war in Afghanistan was increasingly viewed by the Soviet intellectual community as criminal and by the Russian public as a mistake. There was no state-sponsored campaign to awaken a sense of responsibility for the further fate of the Afgantsy, and this led to general indifference, exemplified in the statement made by one member of an agency supposed to help veterans: "Well, I didn't send you to Afghanistan."[45] Even a carefully planned and adequately funded rehabilitation center in a Moscow suburb was opposed by local residents because it would damage the greenery and create unfavorable social conditions in the vicinity.[46]

How many Afgantsy are there, and how many are disabled? A statistical handbook listed 372,700 Afgantsy in the USSR as of 1989, 167,700 of them in Russia. Three percent of the total (11,181) were disabled, almost half of them classified for pension purposes as Group I and Group II disabled—Group I including those presumed unable to work, and Group II considered able to work under certain conditions.[47] In 1989, some 2,000 of the Afgantsy were in need of prostheses.[48] (The number of shops producing prostheses has for many years remained at 66, according to Deputy Minister of Social Protection A. I. Osadchikh, and is inadequate to supply the need for prosthetics.)[49]

Something obviously needed to be done to break through the hostility and indifference that greeted these men at the end of the war. In 1991 President Boris Yeltsin issued a decree creating a Russia Fund for Veterans of the Afghanistan War, which held over a billion tax-free rubles.[50] Foreign organizations, including veterans groups, also offered assistance. According to the chairman of the Union of Afghan Veterans, the veterans were eventually so well supplied with wheelchairs from foreign donors that they gave some to World War II veterans and people disabled from childhood.[51] Two prosthetics shops, in Moscow and St. Petersburg, were established by the veterans, as well as two-year training courses abroad. Veterans have also contributed equipment to various hospitals to aid in rehabilitation. When asked where the money came from, the chairman said that in 1993, their 184 regional organizations had 2,500 enterprises bringing in money.[52] One of the most successful is a Pacific coast fish-processing enterprise, which rents part of the local fleet and earned $340,000 in the early 1990s.[53] Whether this is a lot or a little is hard to say. Other enterprises were not doing as well, apparently due to the lack of management skills.

Moreover, the existence of such large sums of money has exposed the leadership to temptations to steal and to turf wars over control of funds, and there have been several instances of assassination—proof that disabled people are not free from the pervasive corruption and violence in Russian society today. On November 10, 1994, in Moscow, at No. 11 Orekhov Street, the leader of the Afghan War Disabled, Mikhail Likhodei, and his bodyguard were killed by fragments of an exploding bomb. Likhodei's wife and a second bodyguard were seriously injured. The reason for the killing appears to have been a struggle between the original founder of the organization, Colonel Valerii Radchikov, and his competitor Likhodei over the use of the money in the fund. Radchikov, a paratrooper who lost his legs in Afghanistan, continued to operate from Moscow, and Likhodei launched a criminal case against him in September 1993. In 1993 the Russia Fund had been granted very lucrative tax breaks, including exemptions from the payment of duties on goods imported into Russia (at the time mainly alcohol and tobacco). In 1995, Radchikov was badly injured in a shooting in Moscow. *Literaturnaia Gazeta* reported that Radchikov was treated in the United States for his injuries and voluntarily returned to Moscow.[54] On November 10, 1996, as Afghan veterans and their families were gathered for a memorial service to honor Likhodei, a bomb exploded. The fund's chairman, Trakhirov, and 13 other leaders were killed, with 50 wounded.[55] The Ministry of Internal Affairs conducted an investigation that questioned 430 people and imprisoned 11, including Radchikov, who allegedly instructed others to plant the bomb near a large gas pipeline.[56]

While the leadership fought it out, individuals struggled as best they could with the problem of housing. Neither job training nor schooling nor medical care can be given to people without a permanent residence. In a particularly egregious case, special-forces personnel took control of a recently privatized apartment complex in Moscow and designated for five Group I disabled Afgantsy, 11 veterans, and 16 Russia Fund staff members, including families of soldiers who died in Afghanistan. The Moscow Military Commissariat favored the special forces and did nothing. The matter was proceeding through the courts, but in 1994 only one decision had been handed down (to return one apartment to the original owner).[57]

This decision aside, the Russian government itself has seemed frequently to hope that veterans' organizations and other nonprofit groups would find solutions to these social problems and, at the least, take up the burden of benefits. A group of disabled Afgantsy formed an association called Hindukush, a reference to the mountainous region of northeastern Afghanistan, in 1992 with the help of administrators in the Southwest District of Moscow. The group set as its goals social security, work, and medical rehabilitation of the disabled; helping them to achieve participation in public life; and raising their standard of living through economic activity. By 1994, Hindukush qualified as an interregional association and joined the Russia Fund for the Disabled by the War in Afghanistan, which has about 60 member organizations. They also have contacts with similar groups in Ukraine and Uzbekistan and, in fact, hope to set up a museum devoted to the history of veterans in all wars. One of their planned economic activities was to set up a car service shop to put hand controls on cars. Their leader, Sergei Ponomarev, thinks that they may have outgrown their status as a purely Afghan group, since there are many veterans of the Chechen war in the Moscow district Hindukush serves.[58]

Greater willingness to confront the legacy of the Afghanistan war developed by the mid-1990s. In 1995 in St. Petersburg there was a well-publicized conference sponsored by the Academy of Military Medicine, devoted to the topic Medical-Biological and Psychological-Psychiatric Problems of the Rehabilitation of the Participants in Local Wars and Armed Conflicts, and of Persons Participating in the Liquidation of the Consequences of Radiation Accidents. Part of the conference report that dealt with the Afgantsy was published in the widely circulated *Literaturnaia Gazeta,* under the general title, "War Is an Epidemic of Amorality."[59] Mikhail Reshetnikov, director of the East European Institute of Psychoanalysis, noted the familiar symptoms of post-traumatic stress disorder—suicide, violence against others, isolation from family, and withdrawal from social relations. Reshetnikov noted the attraction to violence as a way of life among some Afgantsy: "War negates many laws, primarily the prohibition against murder, theft, and sexual assault. Therefore war often seems too attractive an occupation. As many as 12 percent of the former participants of military action in Afghanistan (in a survey of 2,000 men in 1991) would have liked to devote their life to military service on contract as part of any fighting army, no matter what country presented the opportunity. Thus, war is in equal measure a crime against the personality and against culture, since it lays bare our deepest (and if we are Darwinists) animal nature." Valerii Nechiporenko, chief psychiatrist at the Ministry of Defense of the Russian Federation, noted that 15–20 percent of military personnel who fought in local conflicts like Afghanistan, Karabakh, Abkhazia, Tadzhikistan, and Chechnya suffer some form of borderline personality disorder, but it was only in Chechnya that the Russian army made use of psychologists to treat temporary psychic disorders caused by stress before they became chronic. V. Lytkin and I. Garasim note that between 1989 and 1995, the Military Medical Academy's inpatient clinic saw 104 Afgantsy, 92 percent of whom thought that the government and society were doing "disgracefully little" to solve the problems of the veterans. When asked about the consequences of participation in the war, 76 percent thought it was time to stop talking about war and start giving real aid to those who had returned from it. On the other hand, existing benefits were characterized as "clearly insufficient" and "only paper benefits" by fully 82 percent of those questioned. Their most pressing problems, according to these men, were the restoration of health and psychic equilibrium (59 percent) and money difficulties (37 percent). Still, 61 percent considered the Afgantsy to be one of the few groups that could be counted on—presumably not to buckle under pressure (suicides and murders to the contrary), and to do the correct thing as patriots.[60]

The war in Afghanistan was brutal and dehumanizing. Not only were the soldiers fighting a skilled and ruthless enemy for reasons they did not clearly understand, but their own officers enforced discipline by a well-entrenched system of abuse and indifference called *dedovshchina,* by which more experienced, senior soldiers hazed younger draftees, exemplified, as we have seen, in the case of Evgenii Demkin. Mikhail Reshetnikov was of the opinion that only those who had actually served in Afghanistan could understand the problems of the veterans. Public opinion at the time was deeply divided, running the gamut from an "I didn't send you to Afghanistan" indifference to the angry "This war was criminal."

Among the veterans of the conflict, there was also a wide range of opinion about the war. One soldier concluded an interview with inquiring reporters by saying, "Even though I had to see a lot of cruelty in Afghanistan, I nevertheless believe that there was something good in the experience. I learned to endure the feeling of uncertainty of the present moment and the unpredictability of the future. At this moment it is important to me to be able to tell my family and strangers that we who wound up going there aren't evil. Even though we did some things wrong, still we aren't evil. We aren't bad."[61]

Other veterans, however, carried much anger and bitterness into civilian life and had great difficulty adjusting to it. A surviving buddy of one such soldier who committed suicide said that if he had known that he would never see his friend Igor again, "I would have put handcuffs on our hands so that we would never be separated. . . . I got a telegram saying that Igor had died. He'd been in a mental hospital. When he got out of hospital, he'd tried to go to work. His mother said that he hadn't talked about anything except Afghanistan. He broke the television, constantly tore up newspapers, and yelled that everything that was written was a lie and you couldn't believe in anything and that the war had been useless." In a letter to his friend, Igor has said, "Aleksandr! When I remember Afghanistan, the question always bothers me about where the dividing line is between a man and an animal."[62]

Another theme that emerges in the testimony of the Afgantsy is the brutality of life inside the Soviet Army. Another veteran said that what had bothered him about the war was not the harsh climate or the missions he was sent out on, but the hazing within the army itself. "It took away all your strength. Strength that every person has received from God. In order to stay alive in that environment you had to use up so much physical and mental energy that there wasn't anything left for the rest of your life. The worst thing in the Afghan War wasn't the guerrillas' bullets, but rather the people that I served with. I didn't think of the guerrillas as monsters. They were quite ordinary people. Our own troops seemed inhuman. The juniors were all subjugated; the older soldiers, for their part, were as savage as animals. It was hard to find one human being in that group."[63]

The Institute of Sociology, Russian Academy of Sciences, carried out a research project called "Social Rehabilitation of a Lost Generation: Social Protection of the Veterans of the War in Afghanistan" in 1991–92.[64] While the study does not focus directly on disabled veterans, it can be assumed that the views expressed by the subjects were also typical of the disabled. The factor of disability is most crucial for the question of job retraining, and on this point, there are almost no data. Russia is still a country in which many people think that the disabled cannot work, and the idea is reinforced by the physical inaccessibility of educational institutions and of the workplace and by the heavy manual labor still involved in many jobs in the less developed Russian economy. The locations in which the small-scale survey on social adaptation under the conditions of the current economic reform was carried out were two regions in Moscow, the suburb of Balashika, and the first youth cooperative set up under the Moscow Union of Afgantsy. To begin with, they found a relatively good adaptation to the market among 27 percent of those questioned, but 46 percent were dependent upon the state budget, or temporarily not working (6 percent), or disabled (2 percent). When compared with a general all-Russia survey of public opinion conducted by B. Grushin, the Afgantsy showed a higher level of adaptation than average Russians in this age group. At the same time, 28 percent felt threatened by unemployment, and 3 percent had already lost their jobs. About 52 percent of respondents wanted to have either lower taxes, or both a complete remission of taxes and credit and loan benefits. Only 4 percent were using their government benefits, which in any case were being provided at a very minimal level.

Relatively few (29 percent) were connected with any organization for Afghan veterans, but 35 percent kept in close touch with other Afghan veterans, and 38 percent contacted comrades from time to time; 26 percent said that they were always helped by those they contacted, 35 percent said sometimes, and 36 percent said they never asked for help. As concerns their psychological and physical health, about 40 percent of those surveyed had wounds and contusions; nearly 7 percent had experienced severe injuries. About 8 percent of the sample were disabled, but fully 45 percent suffered from chronic diseases (malaria and stomach disorders, for example) acquired in Afghanistan. Even so, 83 percent were still judged fit for military service. When asked to evaluate their own state of health, 42 percent said that they needed physical therapy, 40 percent psychotherapy, 11 percent surgery, and 8 percent orthopedic care. Concerning the possibility of getting such aid, 59 percent thought they could, 21 percent said there was no possibility, and 19 percent were confused about the sort of assistance that might be available to them. The authors of this study were interested in the question of how post-traumatic stress syndrome manifested itself: 17 percent of those surveyed fought with their family almost every day; 10 percent had not very good relations with colleagues at work; and 16 percent had conflicts with neighbors. At least part of the reason for these conflicts, according to the respondents themselves, was haunting memories from Afghanistan: 85 percent spoke of such memories, and nearly 9 percent spoke of having such memo-

ries constantly. More than 10 percent said that there was no way to avoid or
to get rid of these memories, though 7 percent resorted to alcohol to relieve
them.

Perhaps the best conclusion to make is that war is hell on the survivors.
The Russian army today is ragged, hungry, ill-trained, poorly housed, and,
most importantly, in poor health. Perhaps the situation will improve if the
army becomes a professional one. For the disabled veterans, who are least
likely to be able to fend for themselves (and the data adduced above appear
to show that most veterans left Afghanistan sick or physically or mentally
injured in some way), their present hope seems to lie with the economic
strength of their veterans organizations. However, the Russian government,
which has cut back its investment in social services and which should be
glad that private organizations are providing benefits to members, was considering revisions to the tax code that would deprive more than 150,000
noncommercial enterprises, including hundreds of organizations of disabled,
of important tax benefits.[65]

While I was writing this paper, I wondered, as I have many times since
the fall of the Soviet Union, what it is that keeps the Russian people, veterans and nonveterans alike, from marching on the Russian White House and
tearing it down stone by stone. The answer surely lies in their reliance on
family and a network of friends and fellow workers, which allows them to
function on a subsistence level without state intervention for long periods of
time. Most of the data used here were collected in the early 1990s, and I was
more than a little surprised to the extent to which the deterioration of the
quality of Russian life started before the collapse of the Soviet Union and
only accelerated under the Yeltsin regime. Making do with little and without help has been an increasing requirement of Russian life for a long time.
But such conditions make life very difficult for people with disabilities. To
some Russian commentators, the policy of the current regime toward the
disabled is one of "social genocide." My impressions, however, do not suggest that every link in state and society has sunk into indifference and apathy. People are trying to bring social problems into the open and perhaps—
rather than raging about either the problems or those who have created
them—trying to change their situation using their own resources. There is
hope in that, but no one reading these words should think that disabled veterans, and disabled people in general, in Russia do not need Western help.
They certainly do, but we need to learn to give the right kind of help, assisting the Russians in establishing quality medical care, housing, job training
and jobs, and in empowering the Russian disabled to take greater control of
their lives.

NOTES

1. John Paxton, *Encyclopedia of Russian History from the Christianization of Kiev to the Break-up of the U.S.S.R.* (Santa Barbara, Calif.: ABC-Clio, 1993), 437.

2. *The New Encyclopedia Britannica, Micropedia* (15th edition, 1994), 9:981. *Golos* (Novosibirsk), October 22, 1994, 1. In 1994, Novosibirsk Oblast had 1,870 women veterans out of a total of 53,500.

3. *Sotsial'noe obespechenie* 1995, no. 3: 2.

4. *Russkii invalid* 1993, no. 7 (January): 11.

5. Valery Tishkov, *Ethnicity, Nationalism, and Conflict in and after the Soviet Union: The Mind Aflame* (London: Sage, 1997), 183–227.

6. A second round of fighting has been in progress in 1999–2000.

7. Tishkov, 287–89.

8. Bernice Madison, "Programs for the Disabled in the USSR," in *The Disabled in the Soviet Union,* ed. William McCagg and Lewis Siegelbaum (Pittsburgh: University of Pittsburgh Press, 1989), 185–89.

9. Vera S. Dunham, "Images of the Disabled, Especially the War Wounded, in Soviet Literature," in McCagg and Siegelbaum, *Disabled in Soviet Union,* 161–63.

10. *Nadezhda* 1992, no. 17 (December): 8. We are not told whether the young women were thought to have weaker stomachs, or whether the attempt was to shield the shattered men from embarrassed thoughts of sexual inadequacy.

11. *Golos* 1993, no. 1: 23–29.

12. For further details, see Ethel Dunn, "The Disabled in Russia," in *Russia's Torn Safety Nets: Health and Social Welfare during the Transition,* ed. Mark G. Field and Judyth L. Twigg (New York: St. Martin's Press, 2000).

13. *Izvestiia,* February 3, 1995, 5.

14. Ibid.

15. *Russkii invalid* 1992, no. 4 (August): 2.

16. *Russkii invalid* 1993, no. 6 (June): 6.

17. *Nadezhda* 1994, no. 4 (March).

18. *Literaturnaia gazeta,* June 8, 1998, 5.

19. *Krest'ianskie Vedomosti,* 1995 No. 14, 2.

20. *Izvestiia,* April 20, 1995, 1.

21. *Rassvet* 1991, no. 6 (September): 2.

22. *Izvestiia,* November 16, 1997, 4.

23. *Sotsial'noe obespechenie* 1997, no. 7: 10.

24. *Izvestiia,* April 20, 1995, 5.

25. *Rassvet* 1991, no. 2 (June): 1.

26. Joanne Neuber, "Dubna's Social Workers Reorient Care for Elderly," received as e-mail, April 3, 1998.

27. *Sotsial'noe obespechenie* 1997, no. 5: 11–12.

28. *Sotsial'noe obespechenie* 1997, no. 3: 10.

29. *Rassvet* 1991, no. 7 (September): 3.

30. *Izvestiia,* April 21, 1995, 2.

31. *Sotsial'noe obespechenie* 1997, no. 3: 36.

32. *Agency for Social Information Bulletin* 1998, no. 3 (January 23–29) (received as e-mail).

33. *Sotsial'noe obespechenie* 1996, no. 12: 16–17.

34. *Sotsial'noe obespechenie* 1995, no. 7: 22–23, 27.

35. *Sotsial'noe obespechenie* 1996, no. 9: 4, 8.

36. *Russkii invalid* 1993, no. 5 (May): 13.

37. *Ogonëk* 1994, no. 52: 13.

38. Apparently many young men have been drafted into the armed forces who should have been granted medical exemptions. The parents of a dead soldier, killed in Grozny, during the first round of the war with Chechnya, learned of his death only from his comrades. His body was finally located in Mozdok. His commanding officers took no further responsibility for the body or the parent-survivors. To add to the tragedy, he was ill with liver disease before he was even inducted. See, *Izvestiia*, March 18, 1995, 2.

39. People who receive disability pensions had to appear before VTEK every two years unless they are unlikely to improve, but VTEK's decisions were often arbitrary. A man wrote to *Pravda* that his brother, who served in Afghanistan and lost his legs there, was lucky enough to find a job without the military card he needed as documentation, and then his disability rating was changed from Group II to Group III, meaning that he was considered minimally disabled and could work under the same conditions as anyone else, "although," the brother wrote, "during this time my brother's legs hadn't grown a millimeter." "Soviet Afghan War Veterans," *Station Relay* 3, nos. 1–3, September, November 1987–January 1988, 47.

40. *Sel'skaia Nov,* March 1994, 7–9.

41. *Ogonëk* 1998, no. 13: 2.

42. *Izvestiia*, September 6, 1996, 4.

43. A veterans' conference in Krasnodar in September 1991, about three months before the collapse of the Soviet Union, speaks of lobbying only People's Deputies who are veterans (*Rassvet* 1991, no. 7 [September]: 3).

44. *Agency for Social Information Bulletin,* February 27–March 5 1998 (received as e-mail).

45. See A. V. Kinsburskii and M. N. Topalov, eds., *Problemy sotsial'noi reabilitatsii uchastnikov voiny v Afganistane (1979–1989)* (Moscow: Institute of Sociology, 1993), 8, 31; and "Soviet Afghan War Veterans," 47.

46. *Sotsial'noe obespechenie* 1992, no. 5: 33.

47. *Okhrana zdorov'ia v SSSR,* Moscow, 1990, 163.

48. See *Station Relay* 4, 1988–89, 93; *Sotsial'naia zashchita invalidov* (Moscow: Goskomstat Rossii, 1994), 114–15.

49. *Sotsial'noe obespechenie* 1995, no. 3: 4.

50. *Izvestiia*, November 8, 1994, 2.

51. Nonetheless, there is a brisk trade in donated wheelchairs such that when a Finnish businessman sent two dozen wheelchairs purchased with his own money to Leningrad for the Afgantsy, he insisted on a full accounting of how and to whom his present was distributed: *Sotsial'noe obespechenie* 1991, no. 1: 25.

52. *Literaturnaia gazeta,* September 8, 1993, 5.

53. *Nadezhda* 1992, no. 10 (July): 4.

54. *Literaturnaia gazeta,* May 14, 1997, 2.

55. *Izvestiia,* November 8, 1994, 2, November 12, 1994, 2; Penny Morvant, "Death in a Moscow Cemetery," *OMRI Analytical Brief,* no. 456, November 11, 1996; *Izvestiia,* May 17, 1997, 6.

56. *Izvestiia,* May 17, 1997, 6.

57. *Izvestiia,* August 24, 1994, 4.

58. *Sotsial'noe obespechenie* 1998, no. 3: 24–25.

59. *Literaturnaia gazeta,* July 5, 1995, 12.

60. Ibid.,12.

61. Anna Heinämaa, Maija Leppänen, and Yuri Yurchenko, *The Soldiers' Story: Soviet Veterans Remember the Afghan War,* trans. A. D. Haun (Berkeley and Los Angeles: University of California Press, 1994), 47.

62. Ibid., 65–66.

63. Ibid., 88.

64. S. V. Eremin, A. V. Kinsburskii, M. K. Titov, and M. N. Topalov, "Sotsial'-naia adaptatsiia uchastnikov voiny v Afganistane v usloviiakh ekonomicheskoi reformy" (Social adaptation of the participants in the war in Afghanistan in conditions of economic reform), in *Problemy sotsial'noi reabilitatsii,* ed. A. V. Kinsburskii and M. N. Topalov (Moscow: Institute of Sociology, Russian Academy of Sciences, 1993), 98–120.

65. E-mail posted by Andrei Blinushov, August 10, 1998, with a subject heading of "Danger for the Nonprofit Organizations of the Country."

III. LIVING WITH
A DISABILITY:
ADJUSTMENTS AND
MALADJUSTMENTS

James Marten

Nomads in Blue: Disabled Veterans and Alcohol at the National Home

On a Saturday evening in late March 1878, amid the glades and glens surrounding the Milwaukee's Civil War soldiers' home, a veteran named
Henry Ives died. Ives had spent all of Friday afternoon and most of the
night drinking at Brady's, a nearby saloon. By Saturday morning he was in
the guardhouse sleeping off what the home's surgeon would later call his
"recent debauch" and charged with absence without leave from his post
as a home police officer. During the day the surgeon prescribed several
doses of chloral hydrate to steady his nerves, and by suppertime he was
well enough to eat a hearty meal. Shortly afterward, however, he collapsed and died.

The surgeon's postmortem, which discovered a damaged heart, liver,
and spleen, an inflamed stomach, and "very much congested" kidneys, concluded unequivocally that Ives had died of the "muscular exhaustion of the
heart" brought on by "chronic Alcoholism." The brief investigation that
followed, which included testimony from doctors, the keeper of the guardhouse, and fellow veterans, came to the same conclusion. Two of the wit-
nesses were also being held for drunkenness. One admitted that he had
"been in the Guard-House, with Ives, several times before"—once for
more than two weeks—for drinking offenses and had, in fact, been with
him at Brady's on the fateful night. The other rather forlornly reported that
he had still been drunk when Ives died, and went on to describe his own
Friday evening: "I met some old friends; and drank too much; and, then,
left the Home; without permission; and, then, got drunk again."[1]

Residents of Milwaukee—a half-hour's carriage ride from the home—
no doubt preferred to think of the men living there as the colorful, kindly
old gents they saw strolling around the grounds or occasionally glimpsed on
streetcars going into Milwaukee. Yet, like Henry Ives, many of those men
struggled to adapt to the aftermath of the bloodiest war in American history.
This essay will explore that struggle from a very specific point of view: the

role alcohol played in their lives.[2] Alcohol abuse was the most serious health and disciplinary problem at the National Home; it became, in a sense, one of the chief disabilities of the already disabled men who lived out years, even decades, at the home. After briefly describing the origins of the home and its place in the larger community, I will show how alcohol hindered the well-being of the veterans and the orderly administration of the institution; explore attempts to combat alcoholism at the home; and offer several suggestions about why these men turned to drink. No single factor can explain the descent of these men into alcohol abuse. Some were scarred by battle, some by mental handicaps, others were worn down by old age. But a significant number of these sad, battered men turned to the bottle for relief. It must be acknowledged that there were obviously men living outside these institutions—veterans and nonveterans alike—as well as inmates of the home who faced similar personal challenges and did not become alcoholics or alcohol abusers. But administrators identified alcohol as perhaps their most serious problem, and this essay will undertake to show why.[3]

As the United States Army quickly demobilized following the defeat of the Confederacy, a host of social problems faced returning veterans. Many soldiers, especially those discharged late in 1865, were unable to find work, while homelessness and addiction to painkillers like opium and laudanum plagued others. Many Americans believed that ex-soldiers were disproportionately represented in the growing prison and jail populations. In Lancaster County, Pennsylvania, a postwar increase in crime was fueled largely by returned veterans, who committed nearly half of all offenses, especially "moral" and property crimes. These conditions were exacerbated by well-publicized incidents of rioting, lawlessness, and general misbehavior by mobs of ex-soldiers and a fairly generalized fear among employers that veterans, used to the "wild life of the army," in the words of future president James A. Garfield, would make poor and untrustworthy workers. Some veterans were actually reduced to begging, while newspapers frequently described their destitution and reported despondent veterans' suicides. Perhaps 200,000 were fully or partially disabled by wounds or disease.[4]

The federal government responded to the financial and health crises facing the saviors of the Union with a pension system for disabled and, later, aged veterans that by 1885 comprised 18 percent of the total federal budget. But first, in the spring of 1865, Congress established a system of federal "asylums" for disabled veterans. Over the next several years, the Board of Managers of the National Asylum—later Home—for Disabled Volunteer Soldiers created branches in Milwaukee, Wisconsin; Dayton, Ohio; Togus, Maine; and Norfolk, Virginia, with five more added in subsequent years. A key element in the successful proposal put forward by advocates of locating the northwestern branch of the federal facility in Milwaukee was their offer of the $100,000 raised at a fair to benefit the local soldiers' home. In May 1867, the first company of men moved out to a ramshackle collection of farmhouses on a 400-acre site west of Milwaukee in rural Wauwatosa.[5]

Initially, the National Homes housed disabled, single, primarily foreign-born veterans who either died there or eventually left when they were well enough to earn their own livings. Men applied directly to the branch in which they wanted to live, where surgeons determined their eligibility based on rather loose criteria of how likely it was that they could earn their own livings. While popular images of the veterans residing in the homes exaggerated the number of men who had lost limbs or suffered severe injuries, according to a recent history of the National Homes, most inmates were "fully ambulatory." Yet they suffered from such chronic illnesses as arthritis or rheumatism, diseases of the eye, exhaustion, or other painful conditions that inhibited their ability to live independently. Congress dropped the requirement that veterans have disabilities due to wartime injuries in 1884, and by late in the century the National Homes had become havens for elderly veterans.[6] The number of men housed in the several branches also rose. The 212 men cared for as residents and as outpatients in 1867 rose to 2,347 in 1884–85; the number of men actually living there in 1900 was 2,113. As many as two-thirds of the veterans were foreign-born (chiefly in Germany and Ireland); a handful had served in the War of 1812 or the Mexican War; only two or three at any time were African-American; most were literate; "farmer" and "laborer" were the dominant peacetime occupations; perhaps one-fourth had wives or minor children; by late in the century a large majority were between the ages of 50 and 70.[7]

The National Home quickly established itself as a prominent feature of the landscape of Milwaukee County. Guides to the city traditionally featured illustrations and detailed descriptions of the beautiful grounds. In 1877, *Milwaukee Illustrated* described the home as "one of the most attractive sights Milwaukee affords." Most descriptions of the home focused on the beautiful hills and groves that surrounded the sprawling physical plant. Summer or winter, it was, as a newspaper article gushed, "a place of great beauty by nature, vastly improved upon by the work of man." The grounds were "enchanting" on summer days, with its "far blue vistas, the wide stretches of high-way, velvety turf, odorous shrubbery and variegated beds of flowers."

Even on cold days in late fall, the brightly colored leaves and "tantalizing effects of light and shade" in the distance made for a stimulating and gracious ambiance.[8]

Officials nurtured the home's parklike elegance. In 1871, for instance, they invited city residents to come out and enjoy the home's new pleasure boat, while in 1875 alone, a dance hall, a bandstand, three summerhouses, two "outside water closets, for use of pic–nics," and a new street gate were built, new and existing roads were graveled and graded, and 600 shade trees were planted along the paths and drives crisscrossing the grounds. The home's governor acknowledged that this "judicious betterment and tasteful adornment" not only benefited the old soldiers by beautifying their surroundings, but also made their lives less monotonous by attracting "large numbers of visitors."[9]

For many residents of the nearby city, one of the attractions of the home was its sober gentility. "No more suitable and attractive situations for pastimes of this kind can be found anywhere in this region," boasted the *Milwaukee Sentinel,* in an apparent reference to the sometimes rowdy beer gardens and private parks in the city. "Here are tolerated none of the riotous worshippers at the sickening shrine of Bacchus. Here the lovers of order and innocent amusements can while away a leisure hour, with no apprehension of disturbance from the interference or the clamorous babblings of the vulgar and dissipated." Those words were written in 1871, only a few years after the home was founded. By the 1880s and 1890s, as the home's officials grappled with the issue of alcohol abuse among the veteran inmates, such sentiments would have rung hollow.[10]

The 60,000 visitors who thronged the grounds of the soldiers' home every year seem to have maintained their distance from the residents, although they may literally have tripped over a few of them lying about on the grass. Elizabeth Corbett, who grew up at the home in the 1890s and early twentieth century, reported that their reclining bodies littered the grounds on most fair days. If visitors had looked more closely, they would have noticed the colorful core to the genteel institution: the old men Corbett compared to Dickens's characters, in whom, she wrote, "eccentricity ran riot." They rarely bathed and frequently swore, but also fondly offered visiting youngsters tasty Smith Bros. cough drops. Corbett cataloged their offbeat hobbies: collecting burned matches, manufacturing and wearing counterfeit medals, "curing" deadly diseases, and proposing to women visitors, inevitably claiming to have run away to become drummers in the Union army as little boys.[11]

And, as Corbett recalled years later, many filled their empty hours by drinking, a habit she called "that great resource of veterans." The men could buy beer at the home saloon, but for hard liquor they turned to the establishments located just outside the grounds that Corbett compared to "the lowest type of waterfront saloon." In 1896, for instance, over 30 clustered near the northern and southern entrances, with 17 crowded into a two-block stretch of National Avenue. Veterans may have been attracted to dives boasting familiar names like Lincoln, Sheridan, and Sherman, or to bars employing fellow veterans like August Miller, a member of the Grand Army of the Republic, or George Eagan, an inmate who moonlighted as a bartender. A *Milwaukee Sentinel* correspondent claimed that "the baser sort from the city" haunted these saloons, shrewdly getting veterans to buy them drinks and then, after the old men were "stupidly drunk on vile whiskey," robbing them in the street.[12]

The convenience of these drinking establishments had rather inevitable consequences. Being "drunk" and "under the influence of liquor," two separate violations of home regulations, were among the most commonly broken rules. In 1881, for instance, they accounted for over 800 of the 1,840 offenses committed (behind only absent without leave with 858) and for over one-fourth of the 3,195 arrests in 1887–88. The offenses listed in a ledger book that covered disciplinary actions for roughly the years 1888 to 1899 revealed that over half—55 percent—were connected to drinking. Most men ran afoul of the rules rarely or not at all, while others seemed to be in trouble all the time. Frederick Richards, for instance, was charged with 13 alcohol-related offenses in less than three years. On separate occasions he was caught drunk off the home grounds, in the main building, in the cemetery, and in his quarters. Another, John O'Brien, racked up nine offenses between late 1888 and the fall of 1889.[13]

The most severe sanctions imposed by home officials punished behavior committed while under the influence of alcohol. Although most violators ended up in the guardhouse, performed 30 or 60 days' labor without pay, or lost their right to leave the grounds, a few were discharged from the home. One man picked exactly the wrong time to show up drunk. When the board of managers for the National Home, led by former general Benjamin Butler, met in Milwaukee in 1879, James Ford appeared before them "in a drunken condition." Butler ordered him put in the guardhouse. A few days later, he attacked the provost-sergeant with a club and was booted out of the home within a day. In fact, each year about 1 to 2 percent of the inmates in the entire system were expelled for drunkenness; in Milwaukee, the multiple offenses of six out of the nine men dishonorably discharged in 1908 included drunkenness. Many were later readmitted to the system, although some made fresh starts at other branches of the home.[14]

The most serious—and rare—offenses were sexual and were nearly always alcohol-related. Several inmates were charged with "exposing" their "persons" on National Avenue or at the train depot; others did so in their quarters or outside in the presence of visiting women. In addition to swearing at guards or other inmates, they sometimes "insulted . . . ladies on Home grounds" or used "indecent language in presence of ladies in depot." After several drinking incidents, William Armour was charged with exposing himself and using obscene language "in the presence of ladies." Even more serious was the behavior of Rollin Black, who was once charged with "repeatedly insulting schoolgirls & following them on Home grounds while they were going to and from school" and, on another occasion, of "insulting a young girl & putting his hand under her clothes."[15]

While drinking was obviously a discipline problem, it was also one of the worst health problems facing officials at the home. Hospital records from the 1880s suggest that at least 14 percent of all cases of disease or injury were related to drinking.[16] Attending physicians sometimes merely wrote "alcoholism" to describe a patient's condition, but most cases were more complicated. Patrick King came into the hospital with double pneumonia on November 3, 1883, after a "protracted debauch of 7 days" and died less than three days later. The surgeon blamed his death on "long continued periodic sprees." Drinking exasperated existing conditions such as heart disease, asthma, insomnia, and digestive problems; resulted in falls down stairways, on sidewalks, and in quarters; caused sudden, outdoor blackouts that led to frostbite during bitter Milwaukee winters; and caused psychological problems so severe that some men—suffering, perhaps, from "softening of the brain," as the home surgeon liked to put it—had to be put in restraints, placed in the "insane ward," or transferred to the asylum for insane veterans in Washington.[17] John Van Gent, "being a constant drinker," jumped out of a two-story building on Spring Street (just north of the home), suffered a compound fracture of both bones in his lower right leg, had it amputated, and died of infection a week later. Walking home late one night after spending the evening drinking on National Avenue, George F. Conn died when he fell, hitting his head on the porch of a house. Other alcohol-related injuries were less serious but no doubt painful. Gustav Johnson, was once treated for "contusion of [the] scrotum from a kick in a beer saloon brawl."[18]

It was no secret that drinking was a problem among veterans. Administrators of the state-sponsored homes for Confederate veterans had to deal with the same alcohol-related discipline and health issues. In fact, officials of the northern state veterans' homes who convened in Milwaukee late in 1894 believed that "habitual drunkards" were the biggest challenge they faced. The convention resolved that the National Homes should accept "such persons" who had been discharged from state homes immediately—there was at the time a six-month waiting period to get into National Homes for men kicked out of state homes—and that Congress should build a special asylum just for drunken veterans. "I have come to believe," thundered a delegate from Michigan, "that there is such a thing as the old soldier who has forfeited every right he had to the protection of the state . . . when he goes so far as to lose all manhood, punish him just as you would a criminal." Perhaps, he suggested half-seriously, the new institution should be labeled "This is the Drunkards' Home."[19]

Despite such expressions of concern, the board of managers for the National Homes virtually ignored the issue of alcohol use at the homes. But a hint of a policy did emerge. Temperance was to be encouraged, but not required, among inmates, and in 1872, the board announced that furloughs would be "refused to inmates addicted to intemperance." Yet the board consistently shrugged off protests by the Women's Christian Temperance Union about beer sales at one of the branches. Beer was widely believed to be less addictive and less harmful than hard liquor, and at a nickel a pint, it was far less expensive than the high-priced liquor sold at neighborhood dives. For these reasons, and because the earnings from beer sales helped pay for entertainment and recreational facilities at the homes, the board declared that beer would continue to be sold. In addition, the availability of relatively harmless and inexpensive beer right on the home grounds had produced "excellent results . . . both as to the morals and the discipline of the men" and had helped the men save more of their pension money. Although they never seemed enough to satisfy Milwaukee teetotalers—newspaper debates in the form of editorials and letters to editors broke out in the *Milwaukee Sentinel* over the sale of beer at the home in 1879 and in 1901—temperance efforts were certainly encouraged. In 1903, for instance, the Protestant and Roman Catholic chaplains at the Milwaukee branch of the National Home told the board that they had between them enlisted nearly 200 men to the cause of temperance. The priest also assured the board that he "occasionally admonished them in my sermons to shun saloons and the use of alcoholic liquors." The effectiveness of such temperance efforts is, of course, hard to measure. The number of temperance men claimed by the chaplains represented under 10 percent of the total membership of the home at the time. Most old soldiers were probably no more likely to respond to pleas to stop drinking than they had been as young soldiers. Despite the thousands of pamphlets distributed to them by the American Temperance Union, the American Tract Society, and the Christian Commission, Civil War armies were hardly models of temperance.[20]

The National Home's policy of firm lenience and understanding toward alcohol abuse matched the attitudes held by many Americans late in the nineteenth century. Even absolute temperance advocates like the Women's Christian Temperance Union favored rehabilitation and sympathy for victims of alcohol. This was also reflected in physicians' growing acceptance of alcoholism as a disease. Heredity, a weak moral backbone, and the social and psychological pressures arising from the rapid industrialization and urbanization of the United States continued to be blamed for the apparently growing number of drug and alcohol addicts (sensationalistic and unconfirmed estimates reached a million by 1900). Yet the medical community instinctively turned to the idea that addiction—to opium, to heroin, to alcohol, to sex, to tobacco—was a curable pathology.[21]

Perhaps wisely, the board of managers allowed physicians in the several homes to "use such remedies as they, in their professional opinion, may deem proper." In the sometimes terse notes they kept whenever a veteran was admitted to the hospital, surgeons at the Milwaukee branch seemed to refer to "alcoholism" as a kind of temporary state, a short-term infection that, once the effects wore off, was gone. By 1903, surgeons actually listed "alcoholism" as a separate condition, divided into "acute" and "chronic"; the 62 men suffering from alcoholism in that year had grown to 284 four years later. Withdrawal symptoms were treated with small doses of whiskey, bromide solutions, morphine injections, and, as in the case of Henry Ives, chloral hydrate. Surgeons followed up in a few cases by prescribing special diets.[22]

But these treatments merely coaxed addicts through isolated crises. Physicians and entrepreneurs around the United States, building on the developing theory of addiction as disease, sought permanent cures to the scourge of alcohol or opium. They hoped to instill discipline and order in the lives of their patients, to eliminate the craving for consciousness-altering stimulation, to cure the side effects of addiction—the muscular, respiratory, and digestive problems that inevitably accompanied long-term drug use. Most of the best-known "cures," however, focused on relieving patients of the pain and exhaustion of withdrawal. "Cold turkey" cures, while briefly popular in the 1870s and early 1880s, expected too much of patients. As a result, a number of self-proclaimed experts designed treatments that substituted different substances—codeine or heroin, for instance—or gradually weaned patients from narcotics or alcohol with slowly decreasing doses of comforting drugs. Less respectable entrepreneurs offered "plant specifics" refined from oats or flowers. Most of these "cures," like their patent medicine cousins, did more harm than good in that they contained high concentrations of morphine or other narcotics. For instance, the nerve-steadying, sleep-inducing chloral hydrate administered during the 1880s and 1890s to many of the men consigned to the guardhouse at the Milwaukee home was highly addictive in its own right. Many products, such as those widely advertised in popular magazines and newspapers, were supposedly effective with home use, but the most respectable—and expensive—cures were designed to be administered over a several weeks in private sanatoriums, which were all the rage by 1900.[23]

In its most comprehensive effort to treat alcoholism, the Northwestern branch experimented with just such a sanatorium in the mid-1890s. In 1894, Cornelius Wheeler, governor of the home, devoted a full page of his brief report to the board of managers to "Temperance." He boasted that "the Home seems almost a model community when compared, or rather contrasted, with its character" three years before. Wheeler had reason to be happy, for the number of disciplinary cases at the home had plummeted from over 5,000 in 1890–91 to fewer than 1,600 for the 1893–94 fiscal year. He obviously believed that at least a part of reduction was due to the establishment of a Veteran Keeley League and of a Keeley Institute at the home, in which nearly 400 members were enrolled.[24]

The Keeley Institute at the Milwaukee home was only one of dozens of franchises established around the country. The original had been created in Dwight, Illinois, by Dr. Leslie E. Keeley. First marketed as a home remedy, the Keeley cure became part of a much more comprehensive several-week-long course of therapy and the inspiration for a nationwide Keeley League, which held annual conventions and sponsored a "Keeley Day" at the Columbian Exposition in Chicago in 1893. Every year, thousands of people from all walks of life—although primarily members of the middle and upper classes—flocked to Dwight, where they submitted to injections of a secret compound four times a day and took less powerful doses of medicine every two hours. Otherwise, the treatment consisted of kind words, sympathy, and freedom; the patients could stroll around the grounds and the streets of Dwight. Ultimately, their addictions would be broken, their self-respect restored, and their lives put back on track. Keeley claimed that his "simple and mild, but thoroughly effective" treatment had proven "uniformly and almost miraculously successful," with only 5 percent of his patients backsliding into addiction, although Wheeler admitted the much higher rate of nearly 30 percent at the Milwaukee branch.[25]

Keeley had spent years developing his formula. His service as an army surgeon at Jefferson Barracks during the Civil War exposed him to the effects of drink on the men under his care. He eventually came to believe that drunkenness was a disease rather than a sin and that he could find a way to cure it—sentiments quoted on promotional pamphlets for his institute. His research protocol seemed to have been simply to try anything, and in the 1870s he came up with what he called the "Double Chloride of Gold," the medicine injected into and swallowed by thousands of patients all over the country. He never divulged the exact nature of the cure, other than to affirm that gold was the key component.

The National Home in Milwaukee established its own Keeley Institute in 1892. One of Keeley's biggest supporters was the Milwaukee newspaperman Charles S. Clark, who wrote a memoir of his own addiction to alcoholism and the lasting cure he found at Dwight. In fact, the *Milwaukee Telegraph* gave Clark credit for facilitating the founding of the Milwaukee franchise in 1892. Clark alluded to the connection between old soldiers and drinking in his dedication to, among others, the "Grand Army of American Inebriates"—a sly play on the Grand Army of the Republic, the leading Union veterans' organization. Keeley himself prominently displayed the adoption of his program at the National and State Homes for Disabled Volunteer Soldiers in his promotional literature. The institute in Milwaukee gained a measure of notoriety at the meeting of the Northwestern Soldiers' Association that toured the National Home grounds and listened enthusiastically to Governor Wheeler's speech on a number administrative issues, including "the drink habit and the Keeley cure."[26]

Even before Keeley died in 1900, his methods were controversial. Critics blasted his secrecy and his assertion that he had found the single, "perfect" cure for a wide variety of addictions. The significant number of relapses among his patients called his credibility into question, and his far-flung empire eventually crumbled. Although the original institute in Dwight continued to clear a profit well into the twentieth century, the cure had been thoroughly discredited long before. A backhanded compliment showing how far the Keeley cure's fortunes had deteriorated appeared in a famous exposé (of the patent drug industry) in 1907, in which the muckraker Samuel Hopkins Adams said that, since the institutes had modified their "extravagant claims," he could not now "include them in the swindling category." A hint that the board of managers may have had some doubts about the use of the cure at the National Homes appeared in their minutes late in 1894, when they passed a motion to "strike out certain lines touching the cure of drunkenness in the various Branches." The institute may also have created hard feelings among the hundreds of inmates who refused to take part. When an old sailor named Michael Butler was brought into the guardhouse for being "drunk & disorderly," he called the attendant "a Keely [*sic*] Son of a Bitch & other vile names."[27]

The "Keeley cure" obviously failed to solve the problem of alcoholism at the Northwestern branch. During 1907, the year in which Congress banned beer sales at the homes, disciplinary offenses rose 28 percent, with bringing liquor into the home and drunkenness accounting for well over a third of the total. As the annual report commented dryly, "the closing of the canteen has not proven beneficial to the members of this home." Veterans kept on drinking, and Americans continued to ponder the causes of this major disability among the disabled.[28]

No one explanation can account for the alcohol abuse of a widely diverse population, and the men living at the National Home—those who developed drinking problems as well as those who remained sober—differed in a number of ways. Although many, especially those admitted in the 1860s, were severely disabled, others had only mild disabilities. This was particularly true of the men admitted after the 1884 loosening of the disability requirements, when old age became the most common form of "disability." In addition, although a large percentage of the men had endured heavy combat, others had never had to duck enemy bullets. Even if one could divide the men into categories reflecting their conditions, it would be difficult to construct cause-and-effect sequences for individual men with absolute confidence. But a trio of conditions facing veterans offer plausible—at least from the standpoint of current scholarship on veteran populations and on addiction—causes for their alcohol abuse.

The most obvious explanation, of course, has to do with the injuries veterans received in the line of duty. In fact, the common practice of using morphine and opiates to relieve the pain and suffering of egregiously injured or ill soldiers has frequently been blamed for the rise of addicts in American society after the Civil War. Physicians prescribed countless medicines containing opium and morphine derivatives. Severely wounded veterans—the kind most likely to be admitted to the National Home system in the early days—may have been as likely to succumb to alcohol as to narcotics. A cursory look at the records kept by the surgeon examining men requesting admission to the home shows the severity of many of their wounds. A few reported disabilities stemming from disease or accidents such as falling into latrines, getting kicked by mules, or being poked in the eye during a night march. But on nearly every page of the hospital ledger one can find violent echoes of the great battlefields of the Civil War. During a single week in October 1867, for instance, applicants included soldiers who had lost an arm at Chancellorsville, a lower leg at Cold Harbor; and an arm at Pleasant Hill, while another was partially paralyzed at Chickamauga.[29]

Not every man with a drinking problem suffered from daily physical pain, and not every painfully crippled veteran became an alcoholic. But they may well have suffered from a different kind of pain. Disabled or chronically ill people, suffering from depression over their isolation, frustrating helplessness, and simple boredom, often turn to alcohol or narcotics to speed their long, empty hours. Elizabeth Corbett maintained that the monotony of life at the home caused some of her beloved veterans to seek release in the bottle, and her amateur diagnosis certainly accounted for at least part of the problem. The men may have been well cared for—they were surrounded by beautiful grounds and had plenty to eat, a clean bed to sleep in, all the clothes they needed, a little spending money, and the grateful respect of the community in which they lived—but their lives had climaxed decades before. Oliver Wendell Holmes Jr., might proudly say that his life had been "touched with fire"—but Holmes enjoyed a long and famously productive life. For some veterans, particularly those who were disabled in some way, that fire had left ashes rather than pride. Their curse was to live for many years as wards of the nation. In the late nineteenth century, the vast majority of male Americans over the age of 65 were still gainfully employed; indeed, the 1890 veterans' census found that, as Union veterans moved into and past middle age, 93 percent still reported occupations, compared to 90 percent of all men over the age of 45. Yet few of the thousands of veterans living in the National Homes held steady jobs. To be sure, veterans were hired to do much of the menial and some of the skilled labor at the homes, but even in the 1870s, only about a third of all inmates were employed, with most earning only a few dollars a month. Their inability—some critics would no doubt call it their failure—to support themselves no doubt contributed to the malaise that clearly infected some residents of the home.[30]

Years earlier, as the Civil War still raged, the United States Sanitary Commission had warned against creating a class of dependent veterans. Organized by northern philanthropists to provide medical and social services to Union soldiers, the USSC had begun studying how to deal with disabled soldiers as early as 1862. Based partly on an extensive examination of European institutions, but also on the USSC leaders' own very typical attitudes about work, class, and government, they had discouraged efforts to establish national asylums, except for the very small number of truly disabled survivors without home, family, or prospects. In their correspondence and their official reports, USSC officials argued that veterans should, whenever possible, be "reabsorbed" into their own communities and assigned to light labor (or even, in one recommendation, be mustered as a permanent "invalid corps" in the army). They should never be put into a situation that "renders them . . . independent of public opinion, or segregate them from friends, kindred, or fellow-citizens"; nor should they be granted such large pensions that they could "live in absolute idleness." Stephen H. Perkins, who toured the leading European soldiers' homes, including the famous Hôtel des Invalides in Paris, concluded in his 40-page report that purpose-lessness and drunkenness characterized many inmates. In his final recom-mendations, Henry W. Bellows, the president of the Sanitary Commission, declared that European homes were "costly failures," urged pensions rather than institutionalization for the overwhelming majority of veterans, and estimated that only two thousand men would be "so homeless, so helpless, so utterly disabled by sickness or wounds" that they would require perma-nent care.[31]

At least some spokesmen for veterans agreed. As the Civil War ended, the editor of a leading veterans' newspaper urged all veterans, including the disabled, to seek gainful employment as soon as possible. They must not, argued *The Soldier's Friend,* "sit down at street corners, as you have seen some of our number in the metropolis, and depend upon the charities of people for support." Nor should they think that "because you have suffered so much in your country's service, the world owes you a living." The paper suggested that there were "many branches of business in which a man with an artificial leg, or with only one arm, can be advantageously employed." To that end, *The Soldier's Friend* advertised jobs for disabled and convales-cent soldiers selling engravings of war pictures and peddling subscriptions to *The Soldier's Friend.* In addition, the monthly promoted "The Left-Armed Corps"—men who had lost their right arms—and sponsored a penmanship competition among disabled soldiers learning to write left-handed; the entries were exhibited in Washington.[32]

Clearly, in the immediate postwar period, even disabled soldiers were expected at least to try to support themselves. That officials in the National Home system agreed that even disabled soldiers must maintain at least a semblance of manliness is demonstrated by the military style discipline insti-tuted at the homes, which was designed to encourage self-reliance and self-respect, as well as their attempts to keep the men busy. Members performed maintenance work, clerked, minded a few cattle, tended the home garden; a few served as patrolmen or assisted in the hospital. They were entertained by the home band, treated to traveling stage shows and lectures, enjoyed the use recreation halls, bowling alleys, and libraries, organized baseball teams, and formed their own clubs and societies. And yet one is left with images of men with little to do, with no families to support, with no purpose to their daily lives.[33]

Veterans resigned to living at one of the branches of the National Home could not have escaped the prevailing turn-of-the-century notion among state and local poorhouse officials as well as the general public that men should support themselves as well as their dependents, and that aged males who had failed to put up money for their old age deserved whatever degraded and hopeless situation in which they found themselves. Alarming similarities link the residents of late-nineteenth- and early-twentieth-century poorhouses and soldiers' homes: the populations of both were rapidly growing older, many had never married, three-fourths had one or no children, and very few had any way of supporting themselves. By 1900, poorhouses had become old-age homes, mainly for men, that had not quite escaped the stigma attached to institutions widely believed to shelter lazy, shiftless, alcoholic vagrants. Henry Bellows had captured the attitudes of most Victorians—as well as a potent cause for veterans' ennui—when he stated in his report that one of the reasons that Union veterans would not require permanent care was that Americans shared "a spirit above dependence."[34]

Those experts of a later generation who urged that disabled survivors of the First World War not be reduced to idleness and dependence might have looked no further than the men who lived at the National Home to find evidence of just the kind of debilitating uselessness they warned against.[35] Inmates could accomplish and enjoy none of the standard goals of Victorian manhood. They obviously could not pursue careers in commerce or the trades. They could accumulate virtually no possessions; inventories of deceased veterans listed pitifully little property: John Dugan left clothes, towels, postage stamps, a pen, a razor, a looking glass, and a shaving mug and brush worth a total of 90 cents. Farrell Mitchell owned $1.40 worth of property, mostly in a pair of good trousers worth half a dollar. Henry C. Miller owned exactly one handkerchief, one pair of gloves, and a package of miscellaneous papers worth, all together, a dime. The men had no families. Wives were not allowed to live at the home, of course, and although a few men reported wives and dependent children, most were alone in the world. The loneliness of some of their lives is starkly symbolized in the pages of the hospital records, where, next to an occasional entry recording the death of an inmate, is pinned a letter from the attending surgeon to the veterans' next of kin. The letters were returned; sons, brothers, friends had moved without informing the veteran or the home.[36]

Somewhat more speculative as a possible cause of veterans' alcoholism is the notion that many of the veterans who lived out their years at the National Home suffered from what twentieth-century psychologists have termed post-traumatic stress disorder. Thousands of veterans of service in Vietnam have, of course, been diagnosed with this disorder, and their experiences and responses are instructive in piecing together the nature of Civil War veterans' postwar lives. Eric T. Dean has recently explored the ways in which some Civil War soldiers responded to the stress of combat: boredom with peacetime lives, a propensity for violence, and serious, long-term psychiatric problems ranging from depression and anxiety to "social numbing," irrational fears, and cognitive disorders. Many found it difficult to get along with family members and old friends, had trouble sleeping, and experienced "flashbacks," while others turned into loners ill at ease with other men and women. Family members in Dean's sample of Indiana veterans admitted to the state asylum for the insane reported that veterans had lost ambition, had become irritable, and could no longer concentrate or think clearly and that nearly 30 percent turned to alcohol or narcotics. Moreover, substance abuse remains a frequent companion to veterans suffering from post-traumatic stress disorders (PTSD); one recent study suggests that the most important psychiatric distinction between Vietnam veterans suffering from PTSD and the general population is the former's dependence on alcohol or drugs, while another argues that drug and alcohol abuse is a key "coping behavior" of PTSD victims, who also tend to withdraw from people who have not shared their combat experiences.[37]

The disabling mixture of social isolation, uselessness, psychiatric maladjustment, physical infirmity, and alcoholism surfaces in the records of the Northwestern Branch of the National Home, where the desperation in the lives of some of the veterans emerges from the slivers of evidence that have survived. It can be seen in Hannibal Hopkins, who got into trouble 19 times in two years and received a total of 65 days in the guardhouse—at least twice, he begged to be locked up after "suffering from a debauch." The desperation can be seen in the decision of Simon O'Kane, who had twice in a two-week period in 1891 requested to be confined in the guardhouse so he could sober up; he ended his torment by committing suicide. It can be seen in the men who, despite chronic misbehavior, found themselves at loose ends when finally freed from the home on furlough—and came back weeks before their leaves expired. Between the parades and the Grand Army of the Republic meetings, between the infrequent celebrations and the occasional touring company of actors or singers, the lives of many institutionalized veterans were empty and lonely.[38]

Ironically, the pension system implemented by the federal government between 1865 and the turn of the century attempted, in the words of a recent study of the issue, to "reconstruct" families in the Union. It did so by establishing pension eligibility based on patterns of familial dependence: orphans, widows, and parents could collect pensions if the men who would normally have supported them were unable to do so. Yet the system of National Homes established to care for and to honor the veterans who had sacrificed the most removed them from their families and eliminated the possibility of establishing "normal" lives. Already considered less than whole because of their disabilities, they were further emasculated, within the conventions of Victorian manhood, by their dependence, their isolation, their uselessness.[39]

Oddly enough, Leslie Keeley provided a point of comparison to the lives of these men in his book *Opium: Its Use, Abuse, and Cure,* with his eloquent, if fanciful and more than a little ethnocentric, account of opium use among the nomads of Arabia. He painted a startlingly attractive picture of the way opium swept away the "poverty and toil" of their daily lives. "Wearied with the long, fatiguing march across desert wastes, or maddened with the cravings of unappeased hunger and thirst," a nomad could submit to the "magic spell" opium "weaves around him," with its "visions of gorgeous splendor and princely state."

Keeley accepted the Arabs' urgent need to escape what he imagined to be the squalor of their empty desert lives with condescending understanding. "The sluggish nations of the Orient may be content to let to-day be as yesterday, and to-morrow as to-day." Nomads such as these "do not live— they only exist. As their fathers were thousands of years ago, so they are now." The monotony, the static—to Westerners—nature of desert life, had "become a part of their very souls." Who could blame them, Keeley seems to be saying, if they turn to opium. Moreover, he implies, what difference will it make to their lives or to the world if they retreat to opium dreams? Of course, in the bustling West, "so full of life and movement and throbbing energies," such a choice was unthinkable.[40]

Keeley obviously failed to realized how similar were the daily lives of Bedouin nomads and Union veterans waiting to die at the National Homes.

The latter were, in some ways, psychological nomads, doomed to wander from bunk to mess hall, from Main Building to recreation hall to library, from home grounds to saloon. Over and over again, looking at the same sights, the same men; their days blending together. Damned by wounds, by well-meaning government policies, by the nature of the Gilded Age economy, to live unusual, dependent, and unproductive lives in a place and a time that prized convention, independence, and productivity, many turned to the fleeting distractions of the bottle, the shallow and temporary communities of barrooms, and the slippery degradation of alcoholism. Americans proved their sincere reverence for Civil War veterans in their commitment to building them grand structures in which to live, in their enthusiasm for sharing the sacred spaces created by beautiful grounds and granite-studded cemeteries, and in their willingness to pay billions of pension dollars to veterans and their dependents. Yet the institutions thus created turned veterans into artifacts rather than artisans, patients rather than patriarchs, symbols of a glorious, even nostalgic past rather than symbols of strength and perseverance. These men were being honored and cared for because of something they had done over a few years in their youths. As disabled veterans, the long years that stretched before them mocked that brief past, and many could only bear that empty future if they shared it with a bottle.

NOTES

1. Henry Ives File, Sample Case Files, Box 1, Record Group 15, Records of the National Home for Disabled United States Soldiers and the National Homes Service of the Veterans Administration, 1866–137, National Archives and Records Administration—Great Lakes Region, Chicago.

2. Nineteenth-century physicians did not distinguish between addiction to, and abuse of, alcohol. For modern definitions of alcohol-related pathologies, Jack H. Mendelson and Nancy K. Mello, eds., *Medical Diagnosis and Treatment of Alcoholism* (New York: McGraw-Hill, 1992), 5–8; and David A. Knott, *Alcohol Problems: Diagnosis and Treatment* (New York: Pergamon Press, 1986), 21–25, 40–43.

3. For brief but useful accounts of the disciplinary problems caused by neighboring saloons and the economic benefits they provided to local entrepreneurs, see Patrick J. Kelly, *Creating a National Home: Building the Veterans' Welfare State, 1860–1900* (Cambridge: Harvard University Press, 1997), 164–66, 175–79.

4. Richard Severo and Lewis Milford, *The Wages of War: When America's Soldiers Came Home—from Valley Forge to Vietnam* (New York: Simon and Schuster, 1989), 130–31, 138–41, 176; Robert L. Hempel and Charles W. Ornsby Jr., "Crime and Punishment on the Civil War Homefront," *Pennsylvania Magazine of History and Biography* 106, no. 2 (1982): 223–44; James A. Garfield to Lucretia Garfield, December 6, 1863, in *The Wild Life of the Army: The Civil War Letters of James A. Garfield,* ed. Frederick D.

Williams (East Lansing: Michigan State University Press, 1964), 301; Larry M. Logue, *To Appomattox and Beyond: The Civil War Soldier in War and Peace* (Chicago: Ivan R. Dee, 1996), 85–89; Judith Gladys Cetina, "A History of Veterans' Homes in the United States, 1811–1930," Ph.D. diss., Case Western Reserve University, 1977, 61–83.

5. Kelly, *Creating a National Home*, 77–88, 128–30; Robert J. Neugent, "The National Soldiers' Home," *Historical Messenger* 31 (autumn 1975): 88–96.

6. Theda Skocpol, *Protecting Soldiers and Mothers: The Political Origins of Social Policy in the United States* (Cambridge: Harvard University Press, 1992), 140–41. Nearly 30 states also established homes for Union veterans, subsidized in part by federal funds. By 1910, 31,830 veterans—about 5 percent of those still living—lived in federal or state homes.

7. *Milwaukee Sentinel*, December 26, 1870; *Annual Report of the Northwestern Branch, National Home for Disabled Volunteer Soldiers, 1874* (Milwaukee: National Soldiers' Home Printing Office, 1875), 1–4; *Annual Report of the Northwestern Branch, National Home for Disabled Volunteer Soldiers, 1875* (Milwaukee: National Soldiers' Home Printing Office, 1876), 1–3; *Milwaukee Sentinel*, February 14, 1878, August 10, 1881, August 4, 1885, and March 14, 1887; *Report of the Board of Managers of the National Home for Disabled Volunteer Soldiers* (Washington, D.C.: Government Printing Office, 1903), 81.

8. *Milwaukee Illustrated* (Charles Harger, 1877), 28–31; *Milwaukee Sentinel*, September 16, 1869, and October 28, 1888.

9. *Milwaukee Sentinel*, November 27, 1870, December 24, 1868, February 14, 1878, and July 15, 1871; *Annual Report, 1875*, 7–8; *Annual Report, 1874*, 6.

10. Milwaukee *Sentinel*, July 17, 1871. For parks and beer gardens in Milwaukee, see Harry H. Anderson, "Recreation, Government, and Open Space: Park Traditions in Milwaukee County," in *Trading Post to Metropolis: Milwaukee County's First 150 Years*, ed. Ralph M. Aderman (Milwaukee: Milwaukee County Historical Society, 1987), 256–63.

11. Elizabeth Corbett, *Out at the Soldiers' Home: A Memory Book* (New York: D. Appleton, 1941), 38, 102–3, 18, 103–4, 100–101, 78–79, 60–61.

12. Elizabeth Corbett to Enos Comstock, September 8, 1943, Elizabeth Corbett Papers, Milwaukee Public Library; Corbett, *Out at Soldiers' Home*, 74–75, 156–57, 186–91; *Wright's Milwaukee County and Milwaukee Business Directory, 1896* (Milwaukee: A. G. Wright, 1896), 323–29; Descriptive Book, Robert Chivas Post No. 2, Records of Milwaukee, Wisconsin, GAR Posts, 1865–1943, Milwaukee County Historical Society; "Record D, National Home N. W. B.," Clement J. Zablocki VA Medical Center Library, 729; *Milwaukee Sentinel*, June 29, 1884.

13. *Milwaukee Sentinel*, August 10, 1881 and March 14, 1887.

14. "Record D," 819; James Ford File, Sample Case Files, Records of the National Home; Larry M. Logue, "Union Veterans and Their Government: The Effects of Public Policies on Private Lives," *Journal of Interdisciplinary History* 22 (1992–93): 416; *Northwestern Branch, National Home for Disabled Volunteer Soldiers, General, Special, and Circular Orders, 1908*, VA Medical Center Library; Kelly, *Creating a National Home*, 144.

15. "Record D," 550, 177, 731, 179, 254, 883, 552.

16. A fairly random sample from hospital records revealed 83 out of 591 cases related to alcohol. Hospital Record, Northwestern Branch, National Home for Disabled Volunteer Soldiers, Record Group 90, Records of the Public Health Service, National Archives and Records Administration, Great Lakes Region, 1:1–155, 4:1–78, 281–90, and 391–400, and 5:1–10, 101–10, 201–10, 301–10, 401–10, and 501–10.

17. Ibid., 1:8. "Softening of the brain" was a popular term for paralytic dementia, but could actually refer to a softening of the brain tissue, or encephalomalcia. *Dorland's Illustrated Medical Dictionary* (Philadelphia: W. B. Saunders, 1988), 1540.

18. Hospital Record, 1:126, 135, 5:205.

19. R. B. Rosenburg, *Living Monuments: Confederate Soldiers' Homes in the New South* (Chapel Hill: University of North Carolina Press, 1993), 88, 112–15; *Proceedings of the Northwestern Soldiers' Home Association* (Fullerton, Nebr.: Nance County Journal, 1895), 25, 24.

20. *Minutes of the Proceedings of the Board of Managers of the National Asylum for Disabled Volunteer Soldiers* (Zablocki Medical Center Library), 1:170, 2:279, 102, 328; Kelly, *Creating a National Home,* 165; *Minutes of Proceedings,* 3:91–92; J. C. Furnas, *The Life and Times of the Late Demon Rum* (London: W. H. Allen, 1965), 209–10.

21. Mark Edward Lender and James Kirby Martin, *Drinking in America: A History,* rev. ed. (New York: Free Press, 1987), 116–22; H. Wayne Morgan, ed., *Yesterday's Addicts: American Society and Drug Abuse, 1865–1920* (Norman: University of Oklahoma Press, 1974), 9–10, 16–23; David F. Musto, *The American Disease: Origins of Narcotic Control,* expanded ed. (New York: Oxford University Press, 1987), 73–77.

22. *Report of Board of Managers,* 89; *Annual Report of the Board of Managers of the National Home for Disabled Volunteer Soldiers* (Washington, D.C.: Government Printing Office, 1907), 158; Hospital Record, 4:12, 449.

23. H. Wayne Morgan, *Drugs in America: A Social History, 1800–1980* (Syracuse: Syracuse University Press, 1981), 65–74; Musto, *The American Disease,* 77–79; "Abuse of Chloral Hydrate," in Morgan, *Yesterday's Addict,* 145–46.

24. *Report of the Board of Managers of the National Home for Disabled Volunteer Soldiers* (Washington, D.C.: Government Printing Office, 1894), 208–9.

25. Morgan, *Drugs in America,* 74–83; Lender and Martin, *Drinking in America,* 122–24; Charles S. Clark, *The Perfect Keeley Cure: Incidents at Dwight and "Through the Valley of the Shadow" Into the Perfect Light,* 3d ed. (Milwaukee: C. S. Clark, 1893), 17–18; Leslie E. Keeley, *Opium: Its Use, Abuse, and Cure; or, From Bondage to Freedom* (Chicago: Banner of Gold, 1897), 79.

26. Clark, *The Perfect Keeley Cure,* iii (the *Telegraph* quote is from a clipping glued to the back of the copy of Clark's book in the Milwaukee Public Library); Morgan, *Drugs in America,* 74; *Proceedings of the Northwestern Soldiers' Home,* 19.

27. Lender and Martin, *Drinking in America,* 123–24; Samuel Hopkins Adams, *The Great American Fraud* (Chicago: American Medical Association, 1907), 121; *Proceedings of Board of Managers,* 2:599; "Record D," 548.

28. *Annual Report, 1907,* 155, 145.

29. David T. Courtwright, "Opiate Addiction as a Consequence of the Civil War," *Civil War History* 24 (June 1978): 101–11; "Surgeon's Daily Records, 1867–1877," Zablocki VA Medical Center Library, 29, 11, 24, 16–17.

30. Donna R. Falvo, *Medical and Psychological Aspects of Chronic Illness and Disability* (Gaithersburg, Md.: Aspen, 1991), 326–27; Corbett, *Out at Soldiers' Home,* 74–75; quoted in Mark de Wolfe, ed., *Touched with Fire: The Civil War Letters and Diary of Oliver Wendell Holmes, Jr., 1861–1864* (Cambridge: Harvard University Press, 1946), v; Jane Range and Maris A. Vinovskis, "Images of Elderly in Popular Magazines: A Content Analysis of *Littell's Living Age,* 1845–1882," *Social Science History* 5 (spring 1981): 137–38; Kelly, *Creating a National Home,* 159–60; Logue, "Union Veterans," 431–32 n. 41).

31. John Ordronaux, "Proposed Scheme of Relief for Military Invalids," no. 58, in *Documents of the U. S. Sanitary Commission,* vol. 1 (New York, 1866), 6–8; Stephen H. Perkins, "Report of the Pension Systems, and Invalid Hospitals of France, Prussia, Russia, and Italy, with Some Suggestions upon the Best Means of Disposing of Our Disabled Soldiers," no. 67, ibid.; Henry W. Bellows, "Provision Required for the Relief and Support of Disabled Soldiers and Sailors and their Dependents," no. 95, ibid., 5, 10.

32. *The Soldier's Friend* 1 (June 1865): 2; 1 (May 1865): 3; 2 (February 1865): 2; 2 (April 1866): 3; 1 (May 1865): 3; 1 (June 1865): 2; 2 (June 1865): 2.

33. Kelly, *Creating a National Home,* 158–66.

34. Michael B. Katz, *In the Shadow of the Poorhouse: A Social History of Welfare in America,* rev. ed. (New York: Basic Books, 1996), 88–102; Bellows, "Provision Required for the Relief," 10.

35. Douglas C. McMurtrie, *The Disabled Soldier* (New York: Macmillan, 1919); *Your Duty to the War Cripple* (New York: Red Cross Institute for Crippled and Disabled Men, [1918]), n.p.

36. John Dugan, Farrell Mitchell, and Henry C. Miller Files, Sample Case Files; see, for example, 5:5 and 508, for a letter from Surgeon Leighton to Adolph Schneider, June 1, 1890, informing him that his father, Charles, had died. The letter was sent to Columbus, Ohio, but never delivered.

37. Eric T. Dean Jr., *Shook over Hell: Post-Traumatic Stress, Vietnam, and the Civil War* (Cambridge: Harvard University Press, 1997), 87, 98–108; Charles R. Figley and William T. Southerly, "Psychosocial Adjustment of Recently Returned Veterans," in Charles R. Figley and Seymour Leventman, eds., *Strangers at Home: Vietnam Veterans since the War* (New York: Praeger, 1980; rpt. New York: Brunner/Mazel, 1990), 167–80; Richard A. Kulka et al., *Trauma and the Vietnam War Generation: Report of Findings from the National Vietnam Veterans Readjustment Study* (New York: Brunner/Mazel, 1990), 86–138, 139–88; Dean, *Shook over Hell,* 168–70. Of the more than 100 PTSD veterans examined by Herbert Hendin and Ann Pollinger Hass, three-fourths abused alcohol at one time or another after their return from Vietnam. See *Wounds of War: The Psychological Aftermath of Combat in Vietnam* (New York: Basic Books, 1984), 183–84. Evidence suggests, not surprisingly, that disabled persons who "misuse" alcohol, prescription drugs, or illicit drugs are those who are "less accepting" of their disabilities and more likely to be depressed over their condition. Allen W. Heinemann et al., "Prescription Medicine Misuse among Persons with Spinal Cord Injuries," *International Journal of the Addictions* 27 (March 1982): 301–16.

38. "Record D," 1, 187, 231, 333.

39. Megan J. McClintock, "Civil War Pensions and the Reconstruction of Union Families," *Journal of American History* 83 (September 1996): 456–80.

40. Keeley, *Opium,* 7–9.

Deborah Cohen

Will to Work: Disabled Veterans in Britain and Germany after the First World War

The First World War was murderous without precedent. More than nine and a half million soldiers died over a period of 52 months; on average, the war claimed the lives of 5,600 men every day that it continued.[1] Twenty million men were severely wounded; eight million veterans returned home permanently disabled.[2] They had suffered the worst injuries ever seen. Shrapnel from exploding shells tore a ragged path through flesh and bone, leaving wounds, one British surgeon acknowledged, "from which the most hardened might well turn away in horror."[3] Under the threat of constant shell-fire and ubiquitous death, some men lost their minds. After months of exposure in rat-infested trenches, others contracted debilitating illnesses that stole their breath and shortened their lives. As many as six million children lost their fathers in the war; perhaps another three million watched them die at home.[4] Few families were spared mourning.

Throughout Europe, the care of disabled veterans posed one of the most important challenges to reconstruction. Although the war's chief belligerents faced the same dilemma, each, strikingly, sought to resolve the problem in very different ways. In Britain, the reintegration of disabled men was left largely to voluntary effort. In Germany, on the other hand, the state embraced the care of disabled veterans as its highest duty, and charities for ex-servicemen were all but eliminated. In the latter half of the 1920s, Germany's first democracy spent approximately 20 percent of its annual budget on war victims' pensions; in Britain, by contrast, war pensions occupied less than 7 percent of the annual budget from 1923 onward.[5] Yet the British state's neglect, and the German state's attentiveness, had paradoxical effects. Despite comparatively generous pensions and the best social services in Europe, disabled veterans in Germany came to despise the state that favored them. In contrast, their British counterparts remained devoted subjects, though they received only meager compensation.

Why did those who had profited from a state's generosity become its implacable foes? Why did Britain's heroes, treated so shabbily by successive governments, never force the state to pay for its negligence? The answers to these questions are complicated. The consequences of victory and defeat, on the one hand, and the broader political cultures of interwar Germany and Britain, on the other, frame my inquiry. However, the war's resolution and political culture cannot fully account for the very different responses of veterans in Britain and Germany. Veterans' attitudes toward their fellow citizens left an indelible imprint on ex-servicemen's political movements. In Britain, broad public participation in the resolution of disabled ex-servicemen's problems—through voluntary organizations and charities—led veterans to believe that their fellow citizens had honored their sacrifices. Voluntarism brought about a reconciliation between the war's most visible victims and those for whom they had suffered.

This essay will examine the reintegration of disabled veterans into the workforce in postwar Britain and Germany. Specifically, I will consider the consequences of two very different systems of reintegration. The first part of this chapter explores parallel developments: in Britain, the evolution of a voluntarist system for the employment of disabled veterans; in Germany, the development of a system of preferential hiring for the severely disabled. Inaugurated in 1918, the British King's Roll scheme appealed to employers' patriotism to induce them to offer disabled men jobs. Businesses that voluntarily employed the disabled as 5 percent of their labor force received preference in government contracts. In Germany, by contrast, the pathbreaking Law for the Employment of the Severely Disabled (1920) mandated the compulsory employment of badly incapacitated men. The state required firms that employed more than 25 people to hire the severely disabled as 2 percent of their workforce.

As the second part of this essay demonstrates, compulsion generally succeeded where voluntarism failed. Surveying the question of employment for the disabled in 1923, the International Labour Office resolved that compulsion "would alone seem capable of achieving lasting results."[6] In Britain, the King's Roll sufficed to employ fewer than half of the nation's disabled. Perhaps as many as 15 percent of severely disabled veterans in Britain joined the long-term unemployed. In contrast to their British counterparts, approximately 90 percent of severely disabled veterans in Germany held down jobs throughout the 1920s and 1930s. Under the Law for the Employment of the Severely Disabled, it was almost impossible to fire a disabled man. At the height of the Great Depression, severely disabled workers were twice as likely as their able-bodied counterparts to retain their jobs.

And yet, contrary to historians' expectations, the state's largesse did not secure the loyalty of its veterans. In contrast to previous studies, which have explained veterans' attitudes as a product of state policies, the final part of this chapter will direct attention to disabled men's attitudes toward their fellow citizens. What was distinctive about German veterans was not their anger toward the state, but their antipathy toward the public. Disabled veterans in Germany complained that their fellow citizens had neglected, even scorned, their sacrifices. Even as disabled men demanded special consideration because of their suffering, ordinary Germans came to resent veterans' privileged position. While state-secured employment served to reintegrate the German disabled into the workforce, it also alienated the disabled from the general public. This antagonism between the German disabled and their fellow citizens contributed to veterans' hostility toward the new Weimar Republic. By contrast, British veterans, in part because they were never systematically integrated into the labor force, retained a purchase on the public's affection. Although individual ex-servicemen suffered terrible deprivation as a result of long-term unemployment, they nevertheless regarded the public as their allies. Veterans' confidence in the goodwill of their fellow citizens bound British disabled veterans closer to their society, diminishing their rightful claims on the victorious state.

I

Because it defined the nation's obligation to its heroes, the question of employment for badly disabled ex-servicemen became one of the more contentious social issues that European polities faced in the immediate post-war years. The problem rested on an assessment of responsibility: what were the state's obligations to the victims of the war? Was a pension fair compensation for permanent disability even if, as in the majority of cases, the rates paid were not sufficient to support a man and his family? Or was the state's responsibility more profound, as most people seem to have believed, extending to an obligation to return the man to the position in civil life he had occupied before the war? The discussion was a theoretical, an economic, and finally a moral one, but its consequences for disabled veterans were eminently practical. Either the state would secure the compulsory employment of tens of thousands of injured men, or it would subject those who had suffered on the nation's behalf to the vagaries of the marketplace and the pity of their fellow citizens.

In comparison with the Continental states, the British government proved notably reluctant to institute programs that provided disabled men with a chance at gainful employment. Where the sole British wartime report on the subject advocated only "public or private appeals to employers to hire ex-servicemen," most of the German states had, by 1916, established employment bureaus for disabled men, as well as a number of retraining programs. Despite the burdens the war had exacted, the French and Belgian states had begun even earlier; experts in the field cited as models the settlements at Port-Villez that prepared men to return to work. For the delegates who attended the Inter-Allied Conference on the After-Care of Disabled Men rehabilitation, training, and employment, not pensions, were of central concern.[7] Yet in Britain, the end of the war found the Coalition government with practically no plans for this purpose, a state of affairs that led one philanthropist to warn of the "formation of an army of cripples in the country."[8]

As the 1919 Royal Warrant made clear, the state would provide ex-servicemen with pensions and, for a limited time, an "out-of-work donation," but guaranteed little else. Although the minister of pensions acknowledged the amount of the pension "could never really be sufficient" to allow men to return to the standard of living they had enjoyed before the war, neither the central office nor the local war pensions committees had taken the necessary steps to develop the retraining programs they knew were required.[9] The local employment committees set up alongside the pensions committees in early 1918 had accomplished next to nothing.[10] By February 1919, the Ministry of Pensions had trained only 11,000 men.[11] That month, the Ministry of Pensions transferred responsibility for this area to the Ministry of Labour, but with little apparent improvement. The civil servants there were completely unprepared to carry out the task. As its chief officer James Currie acknowledged in his testimony before the Select Committee on Pensions, progress in the program's first 10 months had been "disappointingly slow," a fact that he blamed on the Treasury's obstruction, noting that with all of the paperwork the government could not act quickly enough to buy suitable buildings.[12] In July 1919, Currie reported that of the 80,000 places the Training Department required, they had only 15,000 at their disposal.[13] Nearly four months later, the ministry was training a mere 13,000 men, 20,000 stood on its waiting lists, and there were at least an additional 40,000 eligible who Curry estimated would come if the department advertised vacancies.[14] As demobilization proceeded apace and hospitals closed their doors, tens of thousands of disabled ex-servicemen returned home uncertain how they would earn a living.

While the next two years witnessed improvements in Britain's retraining program, the Ministry of Labour could not restore lost time. Between

1919 and 1921, the ministry's Training Department established 52 instructional facilities. Yet hardly had the training scheme been implemented before the country sunk into a severe trade depression in the autumn of 1920. Fearing an influx of disabled workers into already ravaged trades, union representatives restricted the numbers of new men admitted for training, arguing that the state should pay pensions sufficient to ensure that badly injured men need not work.[15] With so many healthy men out of work, the Ministry of Labour could not place those men who had already been trained in the apprenticeships necessary for employment. While the ministry eventually trained 82,000 men (most of whom were not severely disabled), it is doubtful that more than half of these found work in their trades. Citing the difficulty in placing men in improverships and employment, the Ministry of Labour closed the waiting list for training in September 1921, with an estimated 100,000 disabled ex-servicemen unemployed.

Although administrative disarray and the heavy hand of the Treasury undoubtedly contributed to what the chairman of the Select Committee on Pensions, Sir Montagu Barlow, called this "sad if not alarming state of affairs," the immediate postwar years illustrate what tasks—the employment of severely disabled men primary among them—the government preferred to pass off to the public and voluntary organizations.[16] Scholars have rightly faulted the Treasury, and especially the budgetary restrictions imposed by the Geddes Committee in 1922, for the failure of British reconstruction programs, but civil servants within the individual ministries also bore responsibility.[17] The civil servants who made policy in the Ministry of Pensions viewed it as their duty to avoid those commitments that could be handed over to charitable institutions. Their counterparts at the Ministry of Labour, recipients of "this heritage of woe," recognized that the state could not rely on "enthusiastic peeresses" alone, but found their hands tied by the Treasury's reluctance to incur capital expenditure, as well as "the awful mess and chaos" they had inherited from the Ministry of Pensions.[18] As a result, the Ministry of Labour, too, came to depend on voluntary organizations far more than originally planned.

In an era often characterized in terms of the expansion of the central state, care for disabled ex-servicemen demonstrates that the ethos and practice of voluntarism remained important far longer than generally acknowledged. Not only did the institutions founded by the charitable public serve as models for the government's own programs, but they also bore a substantial portion of the burden of treatment, training, and employment, especially for the severely disabled. In many cases, those ex-servicemen to whom the state ostensibly owed the most—the paralyzed, the armless, the insane, the tubercular—instead found themselves dependent on the public's generosity. At the Armistice, there were 6,000 charities for the disabled registered with the Charity Commissioners, including a number of sheltered workshops and settlements for the severely incapacitated.[19] In 1936, the Ministry of Pensions compiled a directory listing more than 500 war charities still operating on behalf of ex-servicemen and their dependents.[20]

Unlike in France, Germany, or Italy, where the state mandated the compulsory employment of severely disabled veterans, successive British governments largely disavowed responsibility. Other than the voluntary King's Roll scheme, there was no comprehensive state program for the employment of disabled veterans.[21] While the King's Roll enjoyed indisputable success—in 1926, the roll boasted 27,592 employers, in 1936, 23,586—it was the "lightly disabled" who most often profited.[22] The King's Roll offered employers little incentive to hire badly incapacitated men: any man who received a pension or a gratuity in respect of disablement, no matter how minor, counted toward the roll's 5 percent quota. Even those men who had passed off of the pension rolls, but were hired when still in possession of a pension, qualified.[23] Frustrated by the difficulty of placing severely disabled men in work, the secretary of the Edinburgh Local Employment Committee in 1921 condemned the roll's wide definition of disability as "capable of much misconstruction, and even abuse," adding that "it is probable that, if all the cases operating under the present arrangement of the Scheme were classified, only a trifling percentage of really disabled men would be found."[24]

In Britain, the rehabilitation of the disabled remained largely the business of voluntarists. In postwar Germany, it became a cornerstone of the Weimar Republic's welfare state. In contrast to British civil servants in the Ministry of Pensions, who deemed disabled veterans an unnecessary burden for the state, German officials regarded the "war victims problem" as an opportunity. They envisioned programs for wounded soldiers, alongside those for youth and the unemployed, as showpieces of social policy.[25] Intent upon preserving the new Republic's monopoly on benevolence, German civil servants viewed charities for the disabled as a threat to the state's own claim to legitimacy. The state required charities that sought to raise funds or solicit new members to secure the permission of the authorities. Only a handful of charities were granted such a permit, and only on the condition that they submit to government control of their expenditures. As Germany's authorities gained unprecedented control over the private, charitable sector, many new or small philanthropies folded, while their more prestigious counterparts entered into junior partnerships with the state. In

Germany's largest state, Prussia, the newly appointed state commissioner for the regulation of charity refused more than 300 charities for the war's victims permission to collect in the years 1919–24.[26] By 1924, nearly every charity for the disabled had been shut down or forced to submit to governmental control over its expenditure.

The central objective of German welfare programs for the disabled was rehabilitation. Unlike the British government, which largely limited its responsibilities to the distribution of pensions, German authorities sought to return even the most severely disabled to work, preferably to their former occupations. The nation's debt to its wounded, experts agreed, could not be discharged by cash payments alone. Disabled veterans were entitled to the restoration of self-sufficiency. The Weimar Republic's National Pension Law accorded the disabled more than a right to pensions; they were also entitled to an occupational retraining course and free medical care for their service-related ailments. In 1920, there were over 300 separate welfare offices charged with the implementation of the Labor Ministry's war victims' program.

Duty as well as right, work was theorized as the necessary condition for membership in a society.[27] "Even the best care cannot replace the blessing of one's own act of labor."[28] For the disabled, work was not to be simply a means of material subsistence or a general constitutional right. Employment promised therapeutic benefits. At work, a disabled man became self-reliant and fulfilled, secure in his sense of purpose.[29] He no longer "dwelt morbidly" on his injury or succumbed to depression. The "pleasure of working," claimed the Labor Ministry's Otto Wölz, "would change their state of mind and restore to them the feeling of their usefulness and the consciousness of their dignity."[30] According to one rehabilitation expert, only employment could make a man feel "whole" again: "For the war-disabled man, work is an especially exquisite and valuable life-property."[31] The ability to earn a living dignified a man—in his own eyes as well as those around him. No matter how badly disabled, the working man received his fellow citizens' regard. Work ensured a man's integration into his community.

The significance accorded work predated the Republic.[32] Even before the war ended, rehabilitation efforts were well under way. By 1915, military lazarets were outfitted with workshops intended to revive "an interest in productive occupation" and fill idle hours.[33] In a voluminous pamphlet literature, experts on the subject demonstrated how men without arms could be taught to operate machines, and the tubercular reinvigorated at the plough. The exhortation of the renowned orthopedist Konrad Biesalski, head of the German Organization for the Care of Cripples, became dogma:

"When we muster the iron will to overcome it, the era of cripples will finally be behind us."[34] At the end of the war, every German city and most towns could boast bureaus for career counseling, in addition to special retraining schools for amputees, the epileptic, and the blind—many of them the work of voluntary effort.[35] By 1919, local authorities in the Rhineland had provided 14,500 disabled men with career counseling, 3,600 with a retraining course, and 647 with small plots of land.[36]

Yet as welfare experts recognized, retraining alone would not suffice to return men to work. Although most wounded had found jobs easily because of wartime labor shortages, employers made clear their preference to hire able-bodied men after the demobilization.[37] Without compulsion, few of the disabled would be able to work steadily. At the new Labor Ministry's urging, the Republic's National Assembly sanctioned a fundamental intervention into private enterprise. From 1920 onward, the Law for the Employment of the Severely Disabled required businesses and government offices that employed 25 or more people to hire the incapacitated as 2 percent of their workforce.[38] Not only did the law establish hiring quotas, but it provided local welfare authorities with the means of enforcement. Businesses that failed to comply voluntarily with the law's provisions could be forced to hire extra workers. Without the welfare office's consent, no severely disabled man could be fired.

II

Never reintegrated into the economy, disabled men existed figuratively, as well as literally, on the margins of British society. Throughout the 1920s and 1930s, tens of thousands of disabled veterans waited on live employment registers. The number of men on special registers for disabled ex-servicemen never dropped below 24,000 in the interwar period and, in 1923, rose as high as 65,000. After falling, the total climbed again to 41,000 in 1931; how many were placed upon the ordinary register cannot be traced.[39] Countless men, having exhausted their unemployment benefit, failed to sign on.[40] According to the government's conservative estimates, there were at least 20,000 "unemployable" disabled veterans. Local committees had little to offer them. Speaking at a conference of London King's Roll Committees in 1927, G. H. Heilbuth, deputy mayor of Westminster, admitted that though his committee "had been working for some four years, very little had been done towards solving the problem of the disabled ex-Service man who found difficulty in securing employment."[41] Most employers were reluctant to hire the severely disabled, given the large numbers of able-bodied men out of work.[42] It was not simply a matter of the bottom line, though few firms were willing to hire an unprofitable worker. Businesses also feared that disabled employees might injure themselves further, or endanger their coworkers.

Denied the state-secured employment provided their German counterparts, disabled ex-servicemen were thrown upon their own devices. Some could return to their prewar employers, albeit on the understanding that they might have to accept a demotion and salary cut.[43] On his return from France, Bill Towers found that concrete had rendered his stone-masonry trade nearly obsolete.[44] Fitted with an artificial leg at Roehampton, Samuel Peers returned home to his guaranteed job only to hear from his employer that "there was nothing to suit him."[45] When he wrote to the minister of labor in 1921, George Ayling had lost the temporary pension granted him upon discharge because of deafness and waited upon training in the vehicle-building trade: "I have made an application for training as a disabled soldier in a trade last March and have called at Whitehall Gardens every week since and receive the same answer that I shall be called the end of the month now some months have past and I am still waiting I cannot get any nearer I am absolutely destitute. . . . I should not appeal in this manner if I was earning ever so little instead of sheer poverty."[46]

Men who managed to secure a trainingship through the Ministry of Labour felt lucky. However, because of the postwar depression, only a minority could actually be placed in the trades they had learned. Thousands of others were consigned to waiting lists. On the recommendation of his local employment committee, Bill Towers enrolled in a yearlong course in hand-tailoring. It was for naught. There were no more jobs. Like Towers, John Bennett completed one course of training; sent down to London from the Ministry of Pensions' Plymouth Convalescent Center, he discovered that his chosen career was closed to him because there were no more apprenticeships available. Although he received the one-pound out-of-work donation granted ex-servicemen, he wanted to work: "I am steady, willing, active, abstainer, etc. . . . I cannot stand the awful depression much longer; surely I can be of use to somebody."[47]

Despite the obstacles, some men persevered, found employment, and made careers for themselves. Those who stayed healthy had the best chance, though even for them, the future was anything but smooth. To find work, men had to walk very long distances, sometimes four or five miles in a day. In London, only blinded ex-servicemen received discounted fares on public transportation; all other disabled were expected to pay their own way.[48] Among the most fortunate were those who secured employment in government offices, replacing the women workers who had staffed wartime posts; in 1928, nearly 15 percent of the total staff in government departments were disabled ex-servicemen.[49] After a trade turned obsolete and one useless training course, Bill Towers, an economic as well as military casualty, found work in an engineering firm. The manager warned him that he would receive no special treatment. "And I said that would suit me fine. Just treat me as a normal person." To retain his post as a milk inspector, the one-armed Jack Hogg agreed to work for only a partial wage.[50] Gassed in France, repeatedly denied a pension, Arthur Pool struggled to keep his job as a chartered surveyor despite difficulties in breathing and worsening eyesight. So that he would not be absent from work, he ruled out all leisure activities, and "systematically tried to regain as much strength as possible by spending week-ends in bed."[51]

Not every disabled man could accommodate himself to the labor market. Some were too ill; others lacked training. As the economy slowed down, employers hired the disabled only reluctantly. For six years, William Parrott worked as an elevator attendant. In 1926, the stump of his amputated leg broke down, and he had to return to hospital. When he returned, his job was gone. He found another position later on but lost it when the firm went bankrupt. In 1932, after four years on the dole, he applied for training at Lord Roberts Workshop. The Ministry of Labour denied his petition on the grounds that he had once held "normal employment."[52] Another four months of fruitless job-hunting convinced civil servants to approve Parrott's application. Many others were denied.[53] In 1921, George Foote applied to the Ministry of Pensions for training, "but they informed me that owing to my wounds I was not fit to learn anything whatever, so for the next four years I was out of work."[54]

In contrast to Great Britain, unemployment among the badly incapacitated remained low during the Weimar Republic.[55] Despite the massive upheaval caused by the hyperinflation and the Depression, the Labor Ministry and its local welfare offices succeeded in returning the disabled to self-sufficiency and family life. In state-sponsored rehabilitative training programs, they learned the skills they needed to return to their prewar occupations, or if necessary, to embark on another career. Local welfare offices ensured that their severely disabled clients secured and kept jobs. In 1922, the Labor Ministry reported that more than 250,000 severely disabled veterans had found work. Only 17,000 (or 6.2 percent) were unemployed, a percentage similar to that recorded in 1928.[56] In cities, the number of jobs reserved for invalids consistently exceeded the supply of eligible workers. Although a number of disabled men received nothing more than "invalid posts," there were others entrusted with considerable responsibility.[57] Government offices took on a disproportionate share of the severely disabled. In Germany's welfare offices, more than 8 percent of all civil servants—and 34 percent of white-collar workers—were disabled veterans.[58] At the Labor Ministry, the severely disabled comprised 10 percent of all employees, and 6 percent of its civil servants.[59]

The Law of the Severely Disabled provided steady jobs for men who would otherwise have suffered extended bouts of unemployment. Evidence from welfare offices indicates that compulsion, while reluctantly invoked in many areas, was necessary to maintain the severely disabled in work.[60] As the historian Ewald Frie has documented, Westphalian officials resorted to compulsion only rarely, forcing the placement of only six severely disabled men in the years 1927–29, as opposed to 239 such interventions in Social Democratic Saxony during the same period.[61] While the Saxon policy undoubtedly antagonized some employers, it produced results. During the Depression, there were half as many unemployed disabled in Saxony as in Westphalia.

Although employers often complained about the law, most adhered to its principles. Meeting in 1925, welfare officials "unanimously expressed their satisfaction with the Law for the Employment of the Severely Disabled, which had passed the acid test."[62] By most accounts, businesses and government offices treated their severely disabled workers fairly.[63] According to a 1929 study by the Zentralverband, private employers complied with the law and attempted to accommodate their disabled workers with additional breaks and sickness leave.[64] The vast majority of the School for the War-Blinded's graduates reported satisfaction with their employers. Several noted that they and their comrades were paid more than the average rate, while others related with pleasure the consideration that their bosses showed them.[65] Treated as a "seeing person," Erich Heinen expressed his gratitude: "One feels like a human being once again." Hermann Kramer remarked on his supervisor's tact in seating him near a graduate civil servant instead of the lowly lady typists. "They treat me not simply as a typist, but rather as a kind of colleague."[66]

At its apex, in 1931, more than 350,000 severely disabled men profited from the law's protection.[67] For most men, as for the graduates of the School for the War-Blinded, work was not simply a means of sustenance. More than marriage or even physical recuperation, they credited employment with the restoration of their well-being. Employed by a "humane government office," Karl Noack wrote: "Now that I have steady work again, I feel happy and fortunate. It's hard for me to understand that I could have been idle for so long. Work is the only thing that can help us to over-come our hard lot." Returned to his classroom, one primary-school teacher reported that his "difficulties were now all overcome. My old balance has returned, so that I'm no longer the pitiable invalid of last summer." As a telephonist wrote: "With this job I've finally regained my sense of happi-ness. I feel best and most content when I'm at work."[68]

Like the civil servants responsible for their welfare, disabled veterans subscribed to the restorative value of work. In contrast to the largest British veterans' organization, the British Legion, which argued that the severely disabled should be exempt from work, German veterans' organizations agreed that employment was the best remedy for disability. The Social Democratic Reichsbund approved the priority accorded state-secured employment over pensions as a "thoroughly sound notion."[69] For the con-servative Zentralverband, work was "our reason for being. Only work can restore us."[70] At work, men like Karl Junghanns, whose "greatest wish was to be a useful member of humanity despite [his] blindness," could be like anyone else. Newly hired as a typist, the 23-year-old Willi Hemeyer exulted that he "worked as though he wasn't blinded at all." Employment mitigated blindness, for "work is the only thing that makes a person forget his fate." With work, the disabled man could "look with full confidence in the future." He had overcome his disability. "Ever since I've had a job like everyone else I've felt like a complete person."[71] Unemployed for four months, a Leipzig man delighted in his newfound occupation: "Since the day I began work I've become an entirely different person. I feel so well and carefree as never before, freed from tedium and boredom."[72]

With the law's protection, many of the severely disabled retained the social position they had achieved before the war. In 1926, the Hamburg welfare office's Dr. Gustav Tonkow undertook an investigation into the social conditions of severely disabled veterans resident in the city and the surrounding countryside. Based on a sample of 500 men chosen to reflect national averages, Tonkow demonstrated that 60 percent of the severely dis-abled had maintained or improved their prewar social standing, while 40 percent—8 percent of whom were "unemployable," 5 percent of whom were unemployed—had suffered a decline in status. Civil servants and office workers fared best, with 75 percent of their number in the same position as before the war. Worse off among the severely disabled—as in the country as a whole—were artisans and the prewar self-employed, most of whom had been forced to abandon their old occupations amid the turbulence of hyperinflation.[73] Unskilled laborers faced mixed prospects. Most remained in their prewar social position, a small minority (12.4 percent) succeeded in improving their lot, and 35 percent suffered a reverse.

For the study's author, the Hamburg statistics proved "less promising" than experts had hoped. The hopes that Biesalski had raised were disappointed. The age of cripples could not be overcome simply by an iron will. "All of the legal measures cannot restore a severely disabled man's full capacity to work."[74] Despite the millions of marks spent on rehabilitation, those men whose jobs required little physical effort had the best chance of keeping them. While most white-collar employees were able to return to their business jobs, half of all unskilled workers were forced to find other means of support. Before their enlistment, 36 percent of Hamburg's severely disabled had been artisans; in 1925, only 10 percent were so employed.[75] To remain employed, formerly skilled workers in many cases had no choice but to leave their trades. In 1925, 23 percent of Hamburg's severely disabled were employed as civil servants and office workers (as opposed to 5.6 percent before enlistment), while 12 percent held invalid posts.

Despite its successes, the law could not help everyone. Formerly highly skilled workers could not always content themselves with menial positions, and some employers proved reluctant to entrust a badly disabled man with important jobs. War victims' associations complained that private employers often placed the severely disabled "where they would not be so disruptive," as doorkeepers or elevator attendants.[76] Even the School for the War-Blinded's fine reputation did not prevent disappointments. Idle most of the day, the blinded Hans Weber quit his job as a stenographer because he could not find "the necessary satisfaction" in his work. To his chagrin, the blinded typist Kurt Neuwiller discovered that his supervisors considered him only a "50 percent worker" because he could not read the incoming mail. "With such a salary . . . a war-blinded man can never ever attain his highest goal—to have a wife and a home of his own."[77]

As welfare officials acknowledged by the mid-1920s, they could not return every man to his prewar social position. In a defeated and bankrupt society, their goal was unattainable.[78] That a majority of war-disabled men retained their prewar social position was an accomplishment. As many as one-quarter of disabled veterans returned to their prewar workplaces, if not to their old occupations. They changed jobs infrequently and, until the Depression, were rarely unemployed—security unknown in Great Britain. Although the severely disabled were not entirely spared layoffs in the public sector, they were much more likely than their able-bodied colleagues to retain their jobs.[79] As the Hamburg welfare office noted with pride, only a handful of severely disabled had been discharged from government jobs during the 1923 cutbacks, most of whom had been reemployed.[80]

Even during the Depression, the Law for the Severely Disabled continued to provide most of the badly incapacitated with steady work.[81] While the number of out-of-work disabled more than doubled from 1929 to 1933, their rate of unemployment was a fraction of that suffered by the able-bodied population.[82] In 1933, only 12 percent of the severely disabled were unemployed, as opposed to nearly 30 percent of German workers as a whole.[83] In Bavaria, Brandenburg, Hamburg, the Rhineland, Thuringia, and Württemberg, welfare offices persuaded many employers to retain their severely disabled workers. In 1931, Nuremberg businesses employed 690 more severely disabled than required by law.[84] Despite half a million unemployed, Berlin's welfare office maintained 30,000 of the severely disabled in work. In 1932, 28 percent of the capital's male workers were unemployed, as opposed to 15 percent of its severely disabled.[85]

There was a limit to what welfare offices could do. Where plants closed down, or industries went bankrupt, as in Saxony during the years 1930–31, local officials were powerless to stem the tide of layoffs.[86] Words of comfort meant little to those affected. Unemployment devastated the able-bodied, but it was still worse for the severely disabled. According to Bruno Jung, mayor of Göttingen and a former Westphalian welfare official, unemployment "embittered the severely disabled more than other workers, for in addition to his physical suffering, he now has the uneasy feeling that his remaining capacity for work is undervalued."[87] Independence was hard-won, its sacrifice deeply resented. In an appeal to President Hindenburg, the unemployed war-disabled August Cook deplored his lot: "Formerly young, a nature-lover, filled with the joy of life, today—shut off from others—I burden myself. Even in my family's eyes, I am not a full person."[88]

The National Pension Law and the Law for the Employment of the Severely Disabled shielded the war's unfortunates from some of the worst postwar economic hardships. They retained jobs when millions of their able-bodied contemporaries lost them. With work, many otherwise "unemployables" became in their own estimation "full men again," able to provide for their families, even to return to their prewar occupations. "I've now been a stenotypist for eleven years, and know to appreciate what it means to be equal to others in professional life."[89] The state's programs gave veterans the chance to prove their worth. The war-blinded teacher Herr Becker found the return to the classroom more difficult than he had imagined. He confused boys and girls and could not always match names to voices. Nonetheless, he wrote, "No one here should be able to say that I'm pitied because of my disability. Respect is what I want, the highest respect."[90]

III

British ex-servicemen never received the "land fit for heroes" that Lloyd George had promised them, but they blamed that on the government, not the public at large. The King's Roll and the many charities for the disabled testified to the public's appreciation. Scholars have often written of British ex-servicemen's hostility toward their fellow citizens, drawing on the writings of the war generation's literati, Robert Graves and Siegfried Sassoon among them. My research does not support that conclusion. However much the disabled ex-serviceman distrusted the Ministry of Pensions or the government or the state, he believed that members of the public had done their best by him. Disabled men directed their anger at the state, usually the Ministry of Pensions, rarely against their own families, and almost never against the public at large. The home front could not understand what soldiers had endured in the trenches. However, that did not prevent the public from helping disabled veterans to rebuild their lives. Most men appreciated the distinction. They had not wanted charity, of course, but voluntarists conveyed the public's gratitude.

The British Legion, founded 1921 as the country's largest veterans' organization, raised the public's gratitude to one of its foremost principles. According to the Legion's ethos, disabled veterans occupied an honored position in their society, a result not only of their own role in the war, but also their fellow citizens' appreciative response to soldiers' sacrifices. The Legion filled the pages of its *Journal* with praise for voluntarism. As one commentator noted, "What would these poor fellows do but for the help of the various voluntary associations?"[91] Delegates at the Legion's annual conferences invoked the "generous public" in near-reverential tones. Urging that the Legion's financial transactions be disclosed, a delegate in 1929 referred to the importance of "keeping faith" with the public: "It was impossible to tell the public too much, and the more they were allowed to know the more they would help." The Duncannon delegate reminded his fellow veterans, "When the public failed them, the Empire, and not only the Government would fall."[92]

As the Legion's leaders recognized, the knowledge that the public was on their side defused veterans' anger toward the negligent state. According to the Legion's officials, the problem of obtaining fair compensation was not "social" in nature. It did not, in other words, reflect the country's denial of disabled men's suffering, but had to be attributed to administrative failure, bureaucratic red tape, and official hard-heartedness. The Legion's diagnosis of the problem implied its solution. Demonstrations, boycotts, and veterans' candidates would not improve ex-servicemen's lot because, as the Legion's officials emphasized, bureaucratic failings required bureaucratic remedies. The best that ex-servicemen could do was to put their faith in the "generous public." Only if veterans defended their society's well-being in peace as in war—by refraining from demonstrations and proclaiming their "apoliticism"—could they maintain the privileged status gained between 1914 and 1918. Ex-servicemen owed the British public "Service, not Self," as the Legion's motto proclaimed. Instead of mere interest politics, then, the Legion promised ex-servicemen something higher: a moral and patriotic community.

In Britain, voluntarism—expressed through charities and the King's Roll—fostered a sense of belonging among the war's most visible victims. In Germany, by contrast, the disabled grew alienated from the rest of society, depriving the Weimar Republic of a much-needed source of support. Disabled veterans were among the most embittered of the Weimar Republic's discontented. In the years 1918–21, they formed scores of local associations to represent their interests. In 1922, there were six national organizations of disabled veterans with an estimated total membership of 1.4 million, largest among them the Social Democratic Reichsbund.[93] In the cities, thousands of disabled marched to secure their rights, but even the smallest towns witnessed protests. Demonstration followed on demonstration—for higher pensions, for secured employment, for free or reduced fares on public transportation. Even as pensions costs swelled to 20 percent of the Republic's total expenditure, veterans' organizations took to the streets to protest the state's neglect.

Veterans' bitter discontent requires explanation. Although the German disabled received pensions that were as good as their European counterparts, if not better, superior social services, and secured employment, most came to despise the republic that favored them. While lauding the state's material provisions as "exemplary," historians have blamed Weimar's welfare bureaucracy for veterans' alienation.[94] If the state succeeded in the realm of material compensation, it failed, in Robert Whalen's words, "to show human sympathy," to consider men's psychological needs, as James Diehl has argued, and to incorporate its intended clients in decision making, in Michael Geyer's formulation.[95] Yet judged by any criterion, the British state was just as inflexible, bureaucratic, stingy, and inhuman as its German counterpart, if not more so. Moreover, successive British governments not only dodged their responsibilities to the disabled, but remained largely immune from veterans' protests.

What was significant about German veterans' attitudes was not their anger at the state, but their antipathy toward the public. At the war's end, many disabled veterans in Germany still believed in the goodwill of their fellow citizens. The public might have to be "enlightened," but once people realized how soldiers were suffering, they would respond sympathetically. In 1920, the conservative Zentralverband observed that "the widest sections of the population have full sympathy for the situation of war disabled and war dependents," commenting particularly on the public's "sense of honor and obligation, and their will" to help war victims.[96] By the mid-1920s, hope had turned to hostility. The public, or so veterans believed, was not merely ungrateful, but it grudged war victims their rightful due. "It will not be much longer," warned one severely war-disabled man, "and we will be complete outcasts and pariahs, although it was this ruthless society that sent our bodies to be smashed up."[97]

By consolidating welfare programs for the disabled within the state's control, Weimar's civil servants had institutionalized benevolence. Yet however secure the job, however generous the pension, it was never enough to compensate for a leg, the loss of vision, or a disfigured face.[98] Disabled veterans in Germany wanted public recognition of their losses. They wanted an honorary place in society. Defeated in the field, they sought respect and gratitude at home. Instead, the regulation of charity forced philanthropists and the public out of the field of social welfare. Disabled veterans became convinced of the public's ingratitude, and turned in desperation to the state. If the state could deliver legitimation in the form of improved benefits, the peace it bought was fragile, dependent upon the Republic's financial prosperity.

Whereas the British disabled could take pride in their fellow citizens' gratitude, German veterans complained that the public did nothing to help them. When the disabled and widows of the town Fraustadt gathered in 1924 to protest their lot, they blamed the public as much as the state: "People have forgotten the solemn promises they made in 1914. They've absolved themselves of all responsibility."[99] At the same time, the perceived privileges of the disabled turned their fellow citizens against them. However dissatisfied the disabled might be, at the very least they had something, or so many people seemed to think. By the end of the decade, it was possible to believe that the disabled had profited from their injuries. By the early 1920s, what began as admiration and respect had been replaced by apathy, and later distrust. Disabled veterans had gone from being the honored victims of the nation to just another of the Weimar Republic's many supplicants.

Neither the war's resolution nor different national traditions fully explain the divergence of veterans' politics in Britain and Germany. Veterans' attitudes toward their fellow citizens, more than state policies, determined the course of ex-servicemen's movements. In response to state indifference, British philanthropists reconciled the disabled with those for whom they had suffered. The public's gratitude limited veterans' anger against the negligent state. In Germany, by contrast, the state suppression of charity eliminated most avenues for the country's citizens to demonstrate their gratitude. Convinced of the public's ingratitude, veterans demanded that the Republic recognize their sacrifices with improved benefits. The German state's monopoly of welfare for the disabled veteran jeopardized the very achievements its civil servants had aimed to protect.

Charity was no substitute for rights. As the state's favored wards, German veterans received secured employment and the best social services the Weimar Republic had to offer. By contrast, the British disabled faced chronic unemployment and, if they married, destitution. Under the watchful eye of the Ministry of Pensions' senior civil servants, the state took only the bare minimum of responsibility for the disabled; pension expenditure remained at levels acceptable to the Treasury. Victors of the Great War, British ex-servicemen pled in vain for the rights accorded their former enemies.

NOTES

This essay provides an overview of an argument developed in my forthcoming book, *The War Come Home: Disabled Veterans in Great Britain and Germany, 1914–1939* (University of California Press, 2001). An earlier version of this essay was published as "Civil Society in the Aftermath of the Great War," in *The Development of Civil Society in Great Britain and Germany,* ed. Frank Trentmann (London, 1999).

    1. Martin Gilbert, *The First World War* (New York, 1994), 541; Robert Whalen, *Bitter Wounds: German Victims of the Great War, 1914–1939* (Ithaca, N.Y., 1984), 38.

    2. Francis W. Hirst, *The Consequences of the War to Britain* (London, 1934), 295; International Labour Office, *Employment of Disabled Men: Meeting of Experts for the Study of Methods of Finding Employment for Disabled Men* (Geneva, 1923), 16.

    3. Henry Souttar, *A Surgeon in Belgium* (London, 1915), 22.

    4. Jay Winter, *Sites of Memory, Sites of Mourning: The Great War in European Cultural History* (Cambridge, 1995), 46; Eugen Weber, *The Hollow Years: France in the 1930's* (New York, 1994), 13.

5. Approximately 752,000 British men (from a total prewar population of 45,221,000) and 1,537,000 German (from a total prewar population of 67,800,000) were permanently disabled in the First World War. See Boris Urlanis, *Bilanz der Kriege* (Berlin, 1965), 354; J. M. Winter, *Great War and the British People* (Basingstoke, 1985), 73, 75; International Labour Office, *Employment of Disabled Men,* 15; Katherine Mayo, *Soldiers, What Next* (London, 1934), 555; L. Grebler and W. Winkler, *The Cost of the World War to Germany and to Austria-Hungary* (New Haven, 1940), 78. On budgets: for Germany, Peter-Christian Witt, "Auswirkungen der Inflation auf die Finanzpolitik," in *Die Nachwirkungen der Inflation auf die deutsche Geschichte,* ed. Gerald Feldman (Munich, 1985), table 9, 93; Whalen, *Bitter Wounds,* 16; Reichstag, Reichshaushaltsetat für das Rechnungsjahr 1932. For Britain, Sir Bernard Mallet and C. Oswald George, *British Budgets: Third Series, 1921–2 to 1932–3* (London, 1933), 558–59. These figures represent the total pension budget for disabled veterans and war dependents.

6. International Labour Office, *Employment of Disabled Men,* 233.

7. *Inter-allied Conference on the After-Care of Disabled Men, 1917* (Paris, 1919). From the International Labour Office, Compulsory Employment of Disabled Men Series and Reports, Series E, no. 2, April 25, 1921: "Work is an absolute necessity for the majority of the disabled. Before the war the vast majority of them lived on their wages. Now, as disabled men, they receive pensions which in no country are adequate for their maintenance without work, even if they are very seriously injured" (3).

8. Dr. Fortescue Fox, "The Origin, History, and Ideals of the Village Centres Movement for the Restoration of Disabled Men," address given to the staff at Enham, April 21, 1920. Ministry of Pensions (hereafter PIN) 15/34, Public Record Office (hereafter PRO).

9. Quoting Laming Worthington Evans's speech, "Village Centres," *Morning Post,* October 30, 1919, Cutting Book I, Enham Archive.

10. The Ministry of Labour complained about "the heritage of woe that the W.P.C.'s have left us." Minute Note [Foegamy?], November 18, 1919, Lab 2/522/TDS 3970/6/1919, PRO. See also E. Marlow's Minute Note to A. G., November 22, 1919: "When one remembers the awful mess and chaos which has been transferred to this Ministry by the Ministry of Pensions, the proposal made by the Training Department is, I think, quite reasonable."

11. International Labour Office, *Training of Disabled Men,* appendix 2, "Employment of Disabled Ex-Service Men," report submitted by J. R. J. Passmore, Ministry of Labour, 134.

12. James Currie's evidence before the Select Committee on Pensions, November 11, 1919, 449, PIN 15/381, PRO; J. A. Flynn to Matthew Nathan, August 9, 1918, PIN 15/1838, PRO. For the Treasury's role, see James Cronin, *The Politics of State Expansion: War, State and Society in Twentieth-Century Britain* (London, 1991); P. B. Johnson, *Land Fit for Heroes: The Planning of British Reconstruction, 1916–1919* (Chicago, 1968); B. B. Gilbert, *British Social Policy, 1914–1939* (London, 1970).

13. James Currie to the Minister of Labour, Minute Note of July 26, 1919, Lab 2/523/TDS 5354/1010, PRO.

14. James Currie's evidence, November 11, 1919, 449. For a harsh assessment of the Ministry of Labour's retraining programs, see Peter Reese, *Homecoming Heroes: An Account of the Reassimilation of British Military Personnel into Civilian Life* (London, 1992), 96. See also British Legion Planning Committee [World War II], *Training of Disabled*

Men, Confidential, British Legion Archive. David Englander's judgment is more optimistic: "an absolute failure cannot be spoken of." David Englander, "Die Demobilmachung in Grossbritannien nach dem ersten Weltkrieg," *Geschichte und Gesellschaft* 9 (1983): 203.

15. On unions and the disabled, Charles Kimball, "The Ex-service Movement in England and Wales, 1916–1930," Ph.D. diss., Stanford University, 1991, 83, 85–87, 105.

16. Select Committee on Pensions, November 11, 1919, 449, PIN 15/381, PRO.

17. See Johnson, *Land Fit for Heroes,* esp. 444–99; Cronin, *Politics of State Expansion,* chap. 5, esp. 87–92; José Harris, "Society and the State in Twentieth-Century Britain," in *The Cambridge Social History of Britain, 1750–1950,* ed. F. M. L. Thompson (Cambridge, 1990), 3:76–80.

18. Minute Note, Foegamy [?], November 18, 1919, Lab 2/522/TDS 3970/6/1919, PRO; James Currie, Select Committee on Pensions, November 11, 1919; Minute Note, E. Marlow to A. G., November 22, 1919, Lab 2/522, TDS 3970/6/1919, PRO. On the Ministry of Labour, see Rodney Lowe, *Adjusting to Democracy: The Role of the Ministry of Labour in British Politics, 1916–1939* (Oxford, 1986).

19. Sir Frederick Ponsonby to Hodge, June 21, 1918, PIN 15/3650, PRO. For registers of war charities, see 4, PRO. Char 4/6 for Lancastershire, for instance, registered 782 war charities, though not all were for wounded soldiers. In total, 10,000 new charitable societies were founded during the war. Frank Prochaska, *Royal Bounty: The Making of a Welfare Monarchy* (New Haven, 1995), 176.

20. J. Worsfold [MP] to C. G. L. Syers, November 15, 1939, PRO.

21. An initiative of the Ministry of Labour, the King's Roll attempted to place disabled veterans in employment. To qualify for the roll, employers had to fill at least 5 percent of their workforce with disabled ex-servicemen; in return, they were permitted to use the King's Roll Seal on their letterhead, and, after 1920, granted preferences in government contracts.

22. Short Memorandum on Work of Employment Department for Disabled Men, October 1919, Lab 2/1196/EDX 1922/1919, PRO. "King's National Roll," Hansard, vol. 324, no. 115, June 3, 1937, 1151, MSS 200/B/3/2/c243 pt. 2. Select Committee on Pensions, August 9, 1920, Lab 2/522/TDS 3947/7/1919, PRO; King's National Roll, Ministry of Labour, B.S. 23/14. In 1924, there were 28,524 firms on the roll, employing 330,000 disabled men (of a total of 680,000). More than 20,000 firms (each employing 25 or more) were not on the roll. See T. J. MacNamara, "The King's Roll," *British Legion Journal,* May 1924, 337. As of December 31, 1926, there were 27,500 employers on the King's Roll employing approximately 375,000 disabled ex-servicemen. Ministry of Labour, *Annual Report* (London, 1926), 25. In June 1929, there were 26,948 employers on the King's Roll; in June 1930, 26,454; in June 1931, 25,514; in December 1938, 24,526 employers. "King's Roll," Hansard, vol. 255, no. 154, July 16, 1931; "24,526 Employers on the King's Roll," *The Times,* December 7, 1938, MSS 200/B/3/2/c243 pt. 2, Modern Records Centre.

23. The statistics offered by the King's Roll must be treated cautiously. First, they do not differentiate between those in receipt of pensions and those who had been awarded gratuities. Second, local committees had the discretion to grant the King's Roll Seal on a lower basis if the circumstances warranted. Third, there was very little oversight to ensure that employers, once on the roll, maintained their quota of disabled

employees. "Unemployment," Hansard, vol. 310, no. 68, April 9, 1936, 2967, MSS 200/B/3/2/c243 pt. 2; E.D. Circ. 14/52 [December 14, 1921] and E.D. Circ. 14/51 [December 2, 1921], Lab 2/224, EDX 5308/1921, PRO; M. F. Hoare, "King's National Roll, Report on the Position of the Above on 3 October 1921," October 4, 1921, Lab 2/224, EDX 4880/1921, PRO.

24. James Sime Waterston, Chairman, "Notes on the Problem of the Disabled Ex-Service Man," Lab 2/224, EDX 993/1921, pt. 2, PRO. On problems with the King's Roll, Bolderson, *Social Security, Disability, and Rehabilitation: Conflicts in the Development of Social Policy, 1914–1926* (London, 1991), 41.

25. On the Weimar welfare state more generally, Christoph Sachße and Florian Tennstedt, *Geschichte der Armenfürsorge in Deutschland,* vol. 2: *Fürsorge und Wohlfahrtspflege, 1871 bis 1929* (Stuttgart, 1988), 68–87; Detlev Peukert, *Die Weimarer Republik: Krisenjahre der klassischen Moderne* (Frankfurt am Main, 1987), 46–52; David Crew, *Germans on Welfare* (Oxford, 1998), 16–31; Elizabeth Harvey, *Youth and the Welfare State in Weimar Germany* (Oxford, 1993), 152–85; Young-Sun Hong, *Welfare, Modernity, and the Weimar State, 1919–1933* (Princeton, 1998), 44–75; Ludwig Preller, *Sozialpolitik in der Weimarer Republik* (Düsseldorf, 1978), 34–85; Werner Abelshauser, "Die Weimarer Republik— ein Wohlfahrtstaat?" in *Die Weimarer Republik als Wohlfahrtstaat,* ed. Abelshauser (Stuttgart, 1987); Edward Ross Dickinson, *The Politics of Child Welfare from the Empire to the Federal Republic* (Cambridge, 1996).

26. On the corporatization of charity, see Hong, *Welfare, Modernity, and the Weimar State,* 44–75, 181–202; on state consolidation, see Cohen, *The War Come Home,* chap. 2; Index, Rep. 191, Geheimes Staatsarchiv Preußischer Kulturbesitz.

27. Heidrun Homburg, "From Unemployment Insurance to Compulsory Labour," in *The German Unemployed,* ed. Richard Evans and Dick Geary (New York, 1987), 73–107; Joan Campbell, *Joy in Work, German Work* (Princeton, 1989), 213–42; Peukert, *Die Weimarer Republik,* 135–36.

28. "Entwurf eines Gesetzes über die Beschäftigung Schwerbeschädigter," Verhandlungen der verfassunggebenden Deutschen Nationalversammlung, Bd. 340, Anlagen zu den Stenographischen Berichten, Nr. 1750, p. 1783.

29. See Dr. G. Hohmann, "Die Kriegsbeschädigten und die neue Zeit," *Münchner Neue Nachrichten,* January 11, 1919, Staatskanzlei, Auschnittsammlung, Nr. 1553, Sächsische Hauptstaatsarchiv—Dresden. Franz Schweyer, "Der Wiederaufbaugedanke," *Kriegsbeschädigtenfürsorge,* December 1919, 178.

30. Dr. Wölz, quoted in International Labour Office, *Employment of Disabled Men,* 223. Reichsbund representative Dr. Pfänder agreed. Merely to restore to the disabled the standard of living that they enjoyed before the war was not sufficient. He said that "they should be able to improve their social position by means of their work" (226).

31. Dr. H. Fr. Ziegler, *Die Leistungen kriegsverletzter Industriearbeiter und Vorschläge zur Kriegsbeschädigtenfürsorge* (Düsseldorf 1919), 48.

32. See, for example, *Der Tag*'s report on the Cologne conference, September 20, 1916, R 8034 II/2330, ff. 2–3; "Die deutsche Kriegsbeschädigtenfürsorge," *Reichspost,* December 31, 1916, R 8034 II/2330, f. 46; "Neue Wege in der Kriegsbeschädigtenfürsorge," *Das Volk,* October 12, 1917, R 8034 II/2330, ff. 113–14; "Die Verwendungsmöglichkeiten der Kriegsbeschädigten," *Mitteilungen des Kriegsausschuses der deutschen Industrie,* April 22, 1916, R 8034 II/2330, f. 125; Kriegsministerium [von Stein]

an die sämtlichen Bundesregierungen (außer Preussen, Bayern, Königreich Sachsen und Württemberg), September 6, 1918, 111–2, Senat-Kriegsakten, CII c 1 b, f. 27, Staatsarchiv Hamburg.

33. "Lazarett-Beratung und Berufs-Beratung," *Frankfurter Zeitschrift,* October 31, 1916, R 8034 II/2330, f. 21; C. Zetzsche, "Die Beschäftigung der Kriegsverletzten in den Lazaretten," *Das Land,* January 15, 1916, R 8034 II/2329, f. 46, BAP.

34. Konrad Biesalski, *Kriegskrüppelfürsorge: Ein Aufklärungswort zum Troste und zur Mahnung* (Leipzig, 1915), 4.

35. See for instance Landesrat Gerlach, "Zehn Jahre Kriegsbeschädigten- und Hinterbliebenfürsorge in der Rheinprovinz," *Sonderabdnick ans dem Werk, Die rheinische Provinzialverwaltung, ihre Entwicklung und ihr heutiger Stand* (Düsseldorf: L. Schwann, 1925); Roman Bachmeier, *Programm und Organisation einer Heilschule für Kriegsbeschädigte* (Halle, 1916); Edward Devine, *Disabled Soldiers and Sailors Pensions and Training* (New York, 1919), 294, 299; Douglas McMurtrie, *Evolution of National Systems of Vocational Reeducation for Disabled Soldiers and Sailors* (Washington, D.C., 1918): "As far as can be seen . . . the volume of work done and the efficiency of individual institutions rank extremely high" (133).

36. Gerlach, *Zehn Jahre,* 298.

37. For results of the Brandenburg questionnaire to employers, see H. Beckmann, *Die Schwerbeschädigtenfürsorge in der Provinz Brandenburg* (Berlin, 1919). See also Betty Hirsch, *15 Jahre Kriegsblindenschule Geheimrat Silex,* 1914–29, 24. Rep. 62/36, LAB-A.

38. See C. Jackson, "Infirmative Action: The Law of the Severely Disabled in Germany," *Central European History* 26, no. 4 (1993): 417–55. Included within the Law for the Severely Disabled were also victims of industrial accidents and the peacetime blinded, approximately one-ninth of the total. However, disabled veterans were accorded preference over the peacetime disabled. Beschäftigung Schwerbeschädigter bei hamburgischen Behörden, Referent Senatsrat Schultz, February 1928 [draft], 351–10 I, Sozialbehörde I, KO 41.51 Band 2, n.f., Staatsarchiv Hamburg. For P. A. Tixier, writing in the *British Legion Journal,* the German law was a model. See "Employment of Disabled," *British Legion Journal,* February 1922, 175; June 1922, 274. On modification of the law, and court decisions regarding it, see Sammlung von Gerichtsentscheidungen zum Schwerbeschädigtengesetz, May 1927, f. 85, 351–10 I, Sozialbehörde, KO 41.10 Band 2, Staatsarchiv Hamburg.

39. On the ordinary register, D. Hoare to Mr. Barltrop, May 6, 1921, Lab 2/224, EDX 993/1921, pt. 1, PRO. In 1929, the live register for disabled ex-servicemen numbered 24,000; in April 1930, 28,000; in July 1931, 41,000; in November 1933, 36,000; in April 1938, 29,512. These figures do not include those disabled ex-servicemen whose names went onto the ordinary registers. Nor, as with all unemployment statistics, do these figures include those men who no longer registered at exchanges. On the difficulties in calculating unemployment, see W. R. Garside, *Measurement of Unemployment* (Oxford, 1980), 33–37, 46–61; Alan Deacon, *In Search of the Scrounger,* Occasional Papers on Social Administration, no. 60 (London, 1976), 21–68, 88. "The King's Roll," *Yorkshire Post,* November 28, 1929, MSS 200 B/3/2/243 pt. 2, Modern Records Centre; "The King's Roll," *The Times,* April 10, 1930, MSS 200 B/3/2/243 pt. 2, Modern Records Centre; "The King's Roll," *The Times,* July 1, 1931, MSS 200 B/3/2/243 pt. 2, Modern Records Centre; "The King's Roll," *The Times,* November 23, 1933, MSS 200

B/3/2/243 pt. 2, Modern Records Centre; "Disabled Ex-Service Men," Hansard, vol. 335, no. 107, May 10, 1938, MSS 200/B/3/2/c243 pt. 2.

40. Deacon, *In Search of the Scrounger,* 88; Pilgrim Trust, *Men Without Work* (Cambridge, 1938), 63. Disabled ex-servicemen were required to make fewer contributions for standard benefit than their able-bodied counterparts. Eveline Burns, *British Unemployment Programs, 1920–1938* (Washington, D.C., 1941), 39.

41. "The King's Roll," *The Times,* March 18, 1927.

42. Captain Donald Simpson, Comrades of the Great War, Committee on the Employment of Severely Disabled Ex-Service Men, November 17, 1920, PIN 15/37, PRO.

43. In August 1920, the Roehampton Employment Bureau reported that nearly 8,717 of the hospital's patients had returned to their previous employers by previous arrangement (43.7 percent of the total). 4,383 men were either passed on for further training or found work (21.9 percent). 6,850 men refused to consider work except in the vicinity of their own homes and were passed onto their local committees (34.3 percent). See Final Report of the Employment Bureau, August 1920, Executive Committee Minutes II, Greater London Record Office.

44. William Towers, Tape 741 and 742, Peter Liddle Collection, Leeds.

45. Samuel Peers, Tape 743, August 1989, Blesma Home, Crieff, Peter Liddle Collection, Leeds.

46. George Ayling to the Ministry of Labour, received August 30, 1921, Lab 2/529/TDS4433/1921. See also W. Rankine, Ministry of Labour to Captain Haydn Parry, Training Dept., September 1, 1921, same file. T. B. Wheeler, Divisional Director of Industrial Training to Mr. Vernon Dier, Controller, MP, May 5, 1922, Lab 2/529/TDS4433/1921.

47. J. Bennett to Lord Derby, received March 3, 1922, 920 DER (17) 21/3, Liverpool Record Office.

48. E. Wight Bakke, *The Unemployed Man: A Social Study* (London, 1933), 129–30. On transportation in London, Kimball, "Ex-service Movement," 220.

49. What percentage of these men were returning to prewar jobs is not stated. Statement Relating to the Employment of Ex-Service Men in Government Offices on July 1, 1927, Cmd. 2932. For 1932, see Ex-Service Men Employed in Government Departments. London: HMSO, 1932, Cmd. 4099, MSS 200/B/3/2/c243 pt. 2, Modern Records Centre. Ex-Service Men, Hansard, vol. 344, no. 50, February 22, 1939, 382, MSS 200/B/3/2/c243 pt. 2, Modern Records Centre. On women civil servants, Meta Zimmeck, "Strategies and Stratagems for the Employment of Women in the British Civil Service, 1919–1939," *Historical Journal* 27, no. 4 (1984): 901–24 and "The 'New Woman' in the Machinery of Government: A Spanner in the Works?' in *Government and Expertise,* ed. R. Macleod (Cambridge, 1988). EDX 217/4/1920, Lab 2, Box 221. In 1923, government offices employed 4.8 percent of disabled veterans; on January 1, 1923, there were 26,500 disabled men in permanent employment in the public services and 17,000 in temporary employment. See International Labour Office, *Employment of Disabled Men,* 18. E.D. Circ. 14/52 [December 14, 1921] and E.D. Circ. 14/51 [December 2, 1921], Lab 2/224, EDX 5308/1921, PRO.

50. Jack Hogg, Tape 743, August 1989, Blesma Home, Crieff, Peter Liddle Collection, Leeds.

51. Arthur Pool to M.P., February 4, 1937, Misc. 128, Item 1992, Imperial War Museum.

52. General Bertram Boyce to Mr. Kearn [Divisional Controller, Ministry of Labour], March 18, 1932, Lab 20/17, PRO.

53. James Currie's evidence, November 11, 1919, 449.

54. Foote to Beatrice Herring, January 1933, Foote Tenancy File, Stoll Foundation.

55. Statistics from the British Limbless Ex-Servicemen's Association. See "Provisions for War Disabled Pensioners: Analysis of Pensioners and their Pensions," November 1937, PIN 15/1412, PRO; Department of M.P.s on War Pensions, November 25, 1937, PIN 15/1412, PRO.

56. See Der Reichsarbeitsminister [Dr. Brauns], Entwurf eines Gesetztes zur Aenderung des Gesetzes über die Beschäftigung Schwerbeschädigter, November 28, 1922, Rep. 142, Nr. 1824, Landesarchiv Berlin—Kalkreuthstr, LAB-K; Walther Leuner, "Praktische Erfahrungen bei der Durchführung des Schwerbeschädigtengesetzes," *Die Kriegsbeschädigten- und Kriegerhinterbliebenen- Fürsorge*, 11, no. 5 (May 1921); Niederschrift der Sitzung des ständigen Ausschusses der deutschen Hauptfürsorgestellen, April 20, 1926, 351–9 Kriegsbeschädigten- und Kriegshinterbliebenenfürsorge C 3 b, Staatsarchiv Hamburg. Although disabled veterans also lost jobs during the hyperinflation, they did not suffer as badly as the general male population. See figures from the Hauptfürsorgestelle, 1924, RAM 8914, BAP. Only 851 (4.4 percent) of Westphalia's 19,476 severely disabled were unemployed in July 1923. Ewald Frie, *Wohlfahrtsstaat und Provinz, Westfalen und Sachsen, 1880–1930* (Paderborn, 1993), 154.

57. According to the Hamburg welfare office's figures, approximately 12 percent of severely disabled veterans occupied "invalid posts." See Dr. Gustav Tonkow, *Das Schicksal der Schwerkriegsbeschädigten in Hamburg* (Rostock, 1927), 91.

58. See Jackson, "Infirmative Action," 442.

59. In the other imperial ministries, severely disabled veterans averaged 3 percent of the total staff. See Schwerbeschädigte im Bereich der Reichsbehörden, 1928, RAM 8908, BAP. In Hamburg, the quota for city offices was raised to 2.5 percent in an attempt to counter long-term unemployment. Auszug aus dem Ersten Bericht des ständigen Staatshaushaltausschusses, June 1928, Nr. 13, Sozialbehörde I, KO 41.51 Band 2, f. 104, Staatsarchiv Hamburg.

60. Sondersitzung der Vertereter der Hauptfürsorgestellen in Reutlingen, October 7, 1921, 351–10 I, Sozialbehörde I, KO 41.50 Band I, f. 60, Staatsarchiv Hamburg. For employers' complaints, see W. Mielck, Schwanapotheke an Amtliche Hauptfürsorgestelle [Abschrift], May 25, 1921, 351–10 I, Sozialbehörde I, KO 41.55, f. 7, Staatsarchiv Hamburg; Betonbau Arbeitgeber Verband für Deutschland [Eichenauer] an die Hauptfürsorgestelle der Kriegsbeschädigten- und Hinterbliebenenfürsorge, November 10, 1920, 351–10 I, Sozialbehörde I, KO 41.50 Band I, f. 10, Staatsarchiv Hamburg; Der Präsident des Landesfinanzamts Düsseldorf an den Herrn Reichsminister der Finanzen, November 16, 1926, Abschrift, RAM 8921.

61. Frie, *Wohlfahrtsstaat und Provinz,* 228–29. Die Hauptfürsorgestelle für Kriegsbeschädigte, Landeswohlfahrtsamt in Hamburg an den Landeshauptmann der Provinz Westfalen, February 8, 1928, 351–10 I, Sozialbehörde I, KO 41.31 Band I, f. 109, Staatsarchiv Hamburg. Der Präsident der Reichsarbeitsverwaltung an die mit den Aufgaben der Hauptfürsorgestellen beauftragten Dienstellen, February 9, 1926, 351–10 I, Sozialbehörde I, KO 41.23 Band 1, f. 64.

62. Niederschrift über die Tagung des ständigen Ausschusses der Hauptfür-sorgestellen am 23 und 24 April 1925, 351–9 Kriegsbeschädigten- und Kriegshin-terbliebenenfürsorge C 3 b. For praise of Rhenish employers, see also Niederschrift der Besprechung über die Unterbringung Schwerbeschädigter in der Landwirtschaft im RAM, November 8, 1921, Regierungsrat Dr. Kuessner [RAM] speaking. Sondersitzung der Vertereter der Hauptfürsorgestellen in Reutlingen, October 7, 1921, 351–10 I, Sozialbehörde I, KO 41.50 Band I, f. 51, Staatsarchiv Hamburg.

63. Abtlg. für Schwerbeschädigte, Hamburg, June 7, 1921, Bericht, 351–10 I, Sozialbehörde I, KO 41.50 Band I, f. 10. f. 27, Staatsarchiv Hamburg.

64. D. B. Schmidt, "Schwerbeschädigte und Arbeitgeber," *Zentralblatt für Kriegs-beschädigte und Kriegshinterbliebene,* April 1929, 44.

65. Otto Hager to Hirsch, February 5, 1921, Rep. 62/160, LAB-A; Kurt Neuwiller to Hirsch, May 6, 1922, Rep. 62/248, LAB-A. For the employer's perspec-tive, see Report, Gustav Heyde, Dresden, n.d. [1917?], Rep. 62/38, LAB-A.

66. Erich Heinen to Hirsch, July 3, 1919, Rep. 62/167, LAB-A; Hermann Kramer to Hirsch, January 17, 1921, Rep. 62/208, LAB-A.

67. Bruno Jung, *Der Einfluß der Wirtschaftskrise auf die Durchführung des Schwerbeschädigten-Gesetzes* (Mannheim, 1932), 7.

68. Karl Noack to Hirsch, March 31, 1920, Rep. 62/251, LAB-A; Wilhelm Wix to Hirsch, June 17, 1918, Rep. 62/354, LAB-A; J. Behrendt to Betty Hirsch, February 15, 1920, Rep. 62/87, LAB-A.

69. "Kriegsbeschädigten und Kriegerhinterbliebenen im Reichs-, Staats- und Kommunaldienst," *Reichsbund,* May 1, 1922, 109.

70. "Lebensgestaltung," *Zentralblatt für Kriegsbeschädigte und Kriegshinterbliebene,* September 16, 1920, 134. G. Nowottnick, "Der Geist Macht Lebendig," *Zentralblatt für Kriegsbeschädigte und Kriegshinterbliebene,* January 1, 1927, 2. Josef Schmidt, "Zur Berufs-wahl unserer Kriegsbeschädigten," *Zentralblatt für Kriegsbeschädigte und Kriegshinterbliebene,* February 1, 1920, 18.

71. K. Junghanns to Hirsch, January 29, 1920, Rep. 62/190, LAB-A; Willi Hemeyer to Hirsch, July 23, 1919, Rep. 62/172, LAB-A; Willi Hemeyer to Hirsch, October 30, 1919, Rep. 62/172, LAB-A; Erich Heinen to Hirsch, June 25, 1920, Rep. 62/167, LAB-A; Karl Noack to Hirsch, March 31, 1920, Rep. 62/251, LAB-A.

72. P. Röhr to Hirsch, September 5, 1919, Rep. 62/278, LAB-A.

73. Tonkow, *Das Schicksal der Schwerkriegsbeschädigten,* 77, 48–54.

74. Ibid., 83.

75. Ibid., 91; "Lebensgestaltung," *Zentralblatt für Kriegsbeschädigte und Kriegshin-terbliebene,* September 16, 1920, 134.

76. J. Briefs, *Die Soziale Fürsorge der Schwerbeschädigten in der heutigen Gesetzgebung* (Berlin, 1931), 104. See also Johannes Teitz, Leiter der Abteilung für Erwerbs-beschränkte beim Landesberufsamt, *Berufsberatung und Eingliederung erwachsenen Erwerbs-beschränkter ins Erwerbsleben* (Berlin, 1925), 30.

77. Hans Weber to Hirsch, December 13, 1921, Rep. 62/345, LAB-A; Kurt Neuwiller to Hirsch, May 6, 1922, Rep 62/248, LAB-A. For more complaints about employers, see Georg Paffhausen to Hirsch, March 23, 1926, Rep. 62/256; Fritz Koepke, Report by Betty Hirsch, December 18, 1923, Rep. 62/204, LAB-A.

78. See Christopher Sachße and Florian Tennstedt, *Geschichte der Armenfürsorge in Deutschland,* vol. 2: *Fürsorge und Wohlfahrtspflege, 1871 bis 1929* (Stuttgart, 1988), 81.

79. Hauptfürsorgestelle der Kriegsbeschädigten- und Kriegshinterbliebenen-Für-

sorge in Mecklenburg-Strelitz [Dr. Bahlike] an den Herr Reichsarbeitsminister, April 28, 1923, RAM 8920, f. 135. Der Minister des Innern an den Herrn Reichsarbeitsminister, April 16, 1923, f. 189, RAM 8920; Der Landeshauptmann der Provinz Sachsen, Landesfürsorgeverband (Bernau?), Urschriftlich dem Herrn RAM, Reichsarbeitsverwaltung, June 27, 1924, RAM 8921.

80. Tonkow, 41–42. On the preference accorded the severely disabled, Der Reichsarbeitsminister an sämtliche Hauptfürsorgestellen, February 7, 1924, 351–10 I, Sozialbehörde I, KO 41.51 Band I, f. 103; Der Reichsarbeitsminister an alle Hauptfürsorgestellen, March 7, 1924, 351–10 I, Sozialbehörde I, KO 41.51 Band I, f. 117.

81. Georg Panzer, "Die Wirtschaftliche Lage der Schwerbeschädigten," *Zentralblatt für Kriegsbeschädigte und Kriegshinterbliebene,* January 1929, 16.

82. As Jackson, "Infirmative Action," notes, 6,000 veterans lost the protection of the Law for the Severely Disabled between 1931 and 1934; according to Bruno Jung, many of those were the "lightly" disabled accorded posts after longer spells of unemployment. See Jung, *Der Einfluß der Wirtschaftskrise,* 32–33, 39.

83. See Dietmar Petzina, "Arbeitslosigkeit der Weimarer Republik," in Abelshauser, *Die Weimarer Republik als Wohlfahrtsstaat.*

84. Jung, *Der Einfluß der Wirtschaftskrise,* 23–26, 39.

85. Statistisches Jahrbuch der Stadt Berlin, 1933, 105, 229.

86. From March 31, 1930, to March 31, 1931, the number of unemployed severely disabled rose from 1,881 to 4,097. See Jung, *Der Einfluß der Wirtschaftskrise,* 23; Auszug aus der Niederschrift über die Sitzung des Ständigen Ausschusses der Deutschen Hauptfürsorgestellen, January 29, 1932, 351–10 I, Sozialbehörde I, KO 41.31 Band I, f. 163, Staatsarchiv Hamburg.

87. Jung, *Der Einfluß der Wirtschaftskrise,* 27–28. NS-Kriegsopferversorgung, Bezirk Hamburg (Bode, Bezirksobmann) Aufruf an die Arbeitgeberschaft Hamburg, May 1934, 351–10 I Sozialbehörde I, KO 41.50 Band 2, f. 33, Staatsarchiv Hamburg.

88. August Cook, Kriegsinvalide an Seine Exelens Herrn Reichspräsident v. Hindenburg, September 1, 1927, RAM 9936, BAP. See also Julius Schwanitz an dem RAM, December 7, 1921, RAM 8920, f. 65.

89. H. Näther to Hirsch, June 21, 1927, Rep. 62/645, LAB-A.

90. Herr Becker to Hirsch, July 29, 1920, Rep. 62/85, LAB-A.

91. A. G. Webb, *British Legion Journal,* August 1922, 45.

92. Verbatim Report of the Annual Conference, May 20, 1929, 20, British Legion Archives; Verbatim Report of the Annual Conference of the British Legion, May 20, 1929, 15, British Legion Archives.

93. The Social Democratic Reichsbund (founded 1917) counted 639,856 members in 1921. The Kyffhäuser Bund, a prewar veterans' organization, followed, with 225,392. The moderate Einheitsverband, founded in 1919, had 209,194 members. Another 1919 founding, the conservative Zentralverband, had 156,320 members; the Communist Internationaler Bund, founded 1919, 136,883; the Deutscher Offiziersbund, 27,435; the Bund erblindeter Krieger, founded 1916, 2,521. Throughout the Republic, membership in war victims' organizations fluctuated significantly, declining in most cases from 1922. In January 1924, for instance, the Reichsbund had only 245,410 members in 4,075 local branches. By December 1926 it had 324,580 members organized in 5,156 branches. Geschäftsbericht des Bundesvorstandes und Bundesausschusses für die Zeit vom 1.Januar 1924 bis 31 März 1927. *Reichsbund,* 1927, 5, 351–10 I, Sozialbehörde

I, KO 80.11, f. 42, Staatsarchiv Hamburg. There is a large literature on Weimar veterans. Among others, Volker Berghahn, *Der Stahlhelm: Bund der Frontsoldaten, 1918–1935* (Düsseldorf, 1966); James Diehl, *Paramilitary Politics in Weimar Germany* (Bloomington, Ind., 1977); Karl Rohe, *Das Reichsbanner Schwarz-Rot-Gold* (Düsseldorf, 1966); Kurt Schuster, *Der rote Frontkämpferbund, 1924–1929* (Düsseldorf, 1975).

94. Ewald Frie, "Vorbild oder Spiegelbild? Kriegsbeschädigtenfürsorge in Deutschland, 1914–1919," in *Der erste Weltkrieg,* ed. Wolfgang Michalka (Piper, 1993), 564.

95. Whalen, *Bitter Wounds,* 107–24; James Diehl, "Victors or Victims? Disabled Veterans in the Third Reich," *Journal of Modern History* 59 (December 1987): 718, 719; Michael Geyer, "Ein Vorbote des Wohlfahrtsstaates: Die Kriegsopferversorgung in Frankreich, Deutschland und Grobritannien nach dem ersten Weltkrieg, *Geschichte und Gesellschaft* 9 (1983): 230–77, esp. 257–58.

96. "Aufruf an das deutsche Volke!" *Zentralblatt für Kriegsbeschädigte und Kriegshinterbliebene,* February 1, 1920, 2.

97. "Zustände beim städtischen Fürsorgeamt für Kriegsbeschädigte," *Arbeiter-Zeitung,* January 11, 1923, Frankfurt City Archive, Mag. Akte V/65.

98. Resolution Mehrer Hundert Kriegsopfer, Kb und Kh aus Stadt u. Krs. Fraustadt, beauftragen heute den Vorstand der Ortsgruppe des Reichsverbandes deutscher Kriegsbeschädigten und Kriegshinterbliebenen [J. A. Franke] to the Reichsarbeitsministerium, n.d. [received March 5, 1924], RAM 9238—foliated, p. 139, BAL.

99. Ibid.

Mary Tremblay

Lieutenant John Counsell and the Development of Medical Rehabilitation and Disability Policy in Canada

War brings about an epidemic of disease and of disability, and World War II was no exception. Improvements in medical care for veterans during the war resulted in dramatically increased survival rates for veterans with serious disabilities, such as spinal cord injury. At the end of World War II, new developments in medical rehabilitation enabled more veterans with disabilities to leave veterans' hospitals and return to civilian life. In addition to improvements in medical care, a number of Western countries, such as Canada, the United States, and Australia, developed comprehensive veterans' legislation to reestablish all veterans into civilian life. Veterans with disabilities were included within these new programs and services and were often given special benefits and preferences.

One of the most significant examples of the impact of these new programs and services was in the area of spinal cord injury. Changes in medical treatment and rehabilitation for veterans with spinal cord injury reduced mortality rates from over 80 percent in World War I to about 10 percent by 1946. New programs for education and retraining, improved disability pensions, and entitlements to new services and equipment supported the return of veterans with spinal cord injury to independent life in the community, "beyond the confines of hospitals or paraplegic colonies."[1]

Canadian veterans with spinal cord injury were among the first veterans in the world with spinal cord injury to return to live and work in their communities, the first to use wheelchairs to travel about the community and to enter the workplace. Many of these innovations in rehabilitation were pioneered by Lieutenant John Counsell, a Canadian veteran who had sustained a spinal cord injury during the ill-fated Dieppe raid in 1942.

Counsell was initially treated by Dr. Harry Botterell, a young Canadian neurosurgeon, who was developing a new approach to medical treatment of spinal cord injury. In 1943, after returning to Canada, Counsell began what became his life's work, the development of programs and services for veterans and civilians with spinal cord injury.

In May 1945, Counsell founded the Canadian Paraplegic Association (CPA), the first association in the world organized and administered by individuals with spinal cord injury. Its goals were to provide mutual aid and support for both veterans and civilians with spinal cord injury and to lobby government to develop new programs and services. Central to his work was the philosophy that spinal cord injury was not the end of life, and that individuals with spinal cord injury could fully participate in all aspects of life in their communities, in the mainstream of life. Throughout his career Counsell worked closely with Dr. Harry Botterell and Dr. Al Jousse, a new medical graduate who joined them in 1945, to develop a unique Canadian approach that revolutionized the life experiences and life expectancy of veterans and civilians with spinal cord injury.[2]

This essay describes Counsell's unique philosophy of rehabilitation and adaptation to disability and the role of CPA, under Counsell's leadership, in the development of rehabilitation and disability policy in Canada.

Spinal Cord Injury Prior to World War II

Both the mechanism of spinal cord injuries and the paralysis that followed an injury to the spinal cord have been described throughout medical history. The Edwin Smith surgical papyrus (dated between 3000 and 2500 B.C.) is the first recorded document that discussed the symptoms of a lesion of the spinal cord following either dislocation or fracture of spinal vertebrae.[3] In later eras a number of physicians recorded unsuccessful attempts to prevent, reduce, or cure paralysis. However, prior to World War II, no successful method of treatment had been adopted, and most physicians agreed with the unknown author of the papyrus that spinal cord injuries were an "ailment not to be treated" because of limited life expectancy.

Harvey Cushing, the American neurosurgeon, reporting on World War I, noted that "fully 80 percent died in the first few weeks in consequence of infection from bed sores and catheterization."[4] The British experience was similar. Sir Frederick Treves, founder of the Star and Garter Home for English veterans with spinal cord injury, eloquently described their fate in 1917:

There will be no more lamentable and pathetic figure than the soldier who . . . is paralysed and left utterly helpless. . . . here is a man in the very flower of his youth, bedridden for life, unable to move hand or foot, and dependent, at every moment of the day, upon the ministrations of others. . . . the mind is as vigorous and as alert as ever; the eagerness and independence of youth are still aglow in the brain; there are still the intense longing to do, the stimulus to venture, the desire to lay hold of the joys of life; . . . this mental energy is associated with a body that cannot feel, limbs that cannot move, fingers without touch, and hands as listless as *the hands of the dead*.[5]

In Canada, veterans with spinal cord injury were not offered newly developed vocational training; instead they were housed at Euclid Hall, a Toronto mansion with "a massive pipe-organ and space for forty patients."[6]

In the interwar period, civilians with spinal cord injuries were not treated. Families were told that an individual had "a [life] expectancy of four or five years . . . and the anticipation was that he would get kidney and bladder disease or pneumonia, one or the other of those and that he would die within a short time."[7] In Canada, James Burke was injured in a car accident in 1940 that resulted in paraplegia. Burke, who lived for over five decades, recalled that "the attitude at that time was to pray and die. . . . the life expectancy was very low for paraplegics."[8]

One physician, Dr. Donald Munro of Boston, however, began in the 1930s to develop a variety of new approaches to the management of spinal cord injury that resulted in improvements in survival. By 1943, Munro called for a new philosophy in dealing with spinal cord injury.

A defeatist attitude on the part of everybody concerned must be avoided at all costs. Nothing less than an active self-supporting wheel chair life is to be considered for a moment as an end result, and ambulatory activity with the aid of splints should be the eventual goal if at all possible. Time must not be allowed to be a factor and the physician, the patient and his relatives should all constantly be striving toward that end.[9]

Later, in his text on injuries to the nervous system, Munro acknowledged the work of Botterell and Counsell and wrote: ". . . To these men should go the credit for really setting in motion the rehabilitation of the spinal cord casualties of World War II."[10]

In Canada, in the late 1930s, Dr. Harry Botterell, used some of Munro's ideas and developed a new team approach to caring for three men with spinal cord injury.[11] During World War II, Botterell became the chief neurosurgical officer at the No. 1 Canadian Neurological Hospital at Basingstoke, England, and he developed a specialized medical, surgical, nursing, and physiotherapy team to provide care for soldiers with spinal cord injury. The unit at Basingstoke successfully demonstrated that pressure sores could be prevented, and urinary and respiratory infections reduced. Botterell argued that a soldier with spinal cord injury should be expected to survive the initial injury and return "to the main stream of life rather than be set aside as a hermit."[12] He was, however, one of a small group of physicians in the world who argued that full participation in community life was possible. Most physicians continued to believe that if paralysis was permanent, survival rates would be low and there was no appropriate treatment. Individuals who survived were expected to remain as hopeless invalids to be cared for in chronic care hospitals or at home.[13]

At Basingstoke, Botterell treated John Counsell in 1942. Botterell and his team initially worked to stabilize his medical condition. Once this was accomplished, they began to teach him how to regain independence in activities of daily living such as dressing and personal hygiene. Counsell, depressed about his injury, sought to delay his return to Canada.[14] Botterell, however, urged Counsell, who was financially independent, to return to Canada and take on the leadership of other spinal-cord-injured veterans to ensure the development in Canada of new programs for spinal cord injury.

John Counsell was born in 1911, in Hamilton, Ontario, the only son of prominent and wealthy parents. His father was a lawyer and sportsman and his mother a member of an elite Canadian family. Counsell went to Ridley College, a private school for upper-class young men, for his secondary school education but never attended university. Prior to the war, he began work in Montreal as an insurance broker and married. During the war, Counsell was an officer in the Royal Hamilton Light Infantry. He received the Order of the British Empire and the Military Cross for his actions at Dieppe.[15]

Counsell returned to Canada in 1943 and received additional medical care at the Montreal Neurological Centre. He found, as Botterell had predicted, that no programs were available to help him regain independence. While in Montreal, his physician arranged for him to meet James Darou, a jockey, who had a spinal cord injury in the late 1930s. Darou had developed his own series of exercises to regain strength and mobility in his upper body and devised a number strategies and skills to adapt to his disability. With financial help from friends, he had opened an auto garage that he managed in downtown Montreal. Counsell later described their meeting to others: "seeing is believing, they gave me all kinds of books to read, but it didn't mean a thing until Jimmy Darou swung into his room in Montreal. . . . he gave me proper hell for lying there feeling sorry for myself. . . . but seeing what he could do gave [me] the courage to try."[16] Counsell and Darou became friends who shared a love of horseracing.

In 1943, Counsell and his wife moved to Toronto and lived with his sister and her husband Walter Gordon, a prominent Canadian businessman. During this period, Counsell worked alone at his sister's home to regain his physical strength. He had round-the-clock nursing care, but no rehabilitation programs were available. Initially he spent most of his time in bed and used a large wooden wheelchair to get from bedroom to a sunporch. Then, in 1943, Counsell got his first Everest and Jennings collapsible, self-propelling wheelchair, from a friend, veteran John McCarthy, the son of the Canadian ambassador to the United States.[17] Counsell taught himself to transfer independently in and out of the wheelchair and into an automobile. He quickly recognized that the combination of a folding, self-propelled wheelchair and an automobile with hand controls could provide a new means of independent transportation for disabled veterans. The first managing secretary of the Canadian Paraplegic Association described Counsell's early experiences.

> Through sheer determination he rehabilitated himself. Solved most of his own problems. Financial problems he didn't have. He and his wife lived quite independently for many years at the Park Plaza Hotel, in a suite. They moved to a house that they adapted by adding an elevator and a few minor structural changes. He was a very strong personality. At the time he was trying to sort out his own life, he became acquainted with a bridge crony of his mother's, Lew Wood. It was Lew who had established, after World War I, with Eddie Baker, the CNIB [Canadian National Institute for the Blind]. Lew's attitude was that nothing is impossible; if we need help, we'll get it. He encouraged John to try and copy what the CNIB had done for the blind twenty years before. Through John's determination and Lew's advice [they] got the paraplegic association going.[18]

Lew Wood was a wealthy Toronto financier and philanthropist and chairman of the Toronto Rehabilitation Committee of the Citizens' Committee for Troops in Training. Wood, who was not disabled, played a major role in the development of not only the CNIB and CPA but also the National Society for the Deaf and Hard of hearing and the Canadian Arthritis and Rheumatism Society. He has been described as "a very modest and retiring man, . . . never retiring in using his many influential contacts in the service of the less fortunate."[19] He joined forces with Counsell during 1943 to lobby the government for programs for veterans with paraplegia. Their first effort to convince the government to purchase the Everest and Jennings wheelchairs for Canadian veterans was unsuccessful. According to Wood, Counsell believed "the rehabilitation of paraplegic, double amputation, and other cases requiring chairs, [to be] a practical problem in need of intensive study and the application of a new point-of-view. . . . He regards *mobility as the initial road to Rehabilitation.*"[20]

The provision of these wheelchairs was significant because veterans with spinal cord injury were cared for as invalids or bed patients, often bedridden because of a limited supply of invalid chairs and the belief among hospital staff that these chairs were for patient transport and not for independent mobility. Jack Higman was a dispatch rider in England in 1943 when he became paraplegic following a motorcycle accident. After treatment at Basingstoke, he returned to the Christie Street Military Hospital, in Toronto. He remembered:

They fed us, they changed the bed, they gave us enemas. That was about our life. Outside of reading . . . listening to the little radios we had, that was our life. . . . We had the old wooden ones [wheelchairs] which you couldn't fold up. There was only one. . . . You wheeled this great big tractor down the halls. We were getting up at six o'clock in the morning, the first one up got the wheelchair [laughter]. You knew darn well you weren't going to get out of bed the rest of the day.[21]

Counsell met with physicians and veterans officials at Christie Street Military Hospital in Toronto and, as he often would do in the future, used himself as a model to demonstrate the potential of new equipment or programs. John Catto, a veterans' welfare officer, described this demonstration. "We might say that it is only since obtaining this chair that Mr. Counsell has been able to be around to any great extent. The way in which he handles himself, getting in and out of motor cars, and in and out of ordinary chairs, on to this wheel chair, is really amazing."[22] While Counsell gained the support of most of those present at the meeting, the superintendent in charge of wheelchairs in Toronto argued that "the price of $162.50 is quite high, and the intrinsic value of the chair certainly would not warrant payment of such a figure."[23] His view was to prevail, at least until February 1945, when the Privy Council of Canada passed P.C. 924 authorizing purchase of the Everest and Jennings wheelchairs, 14 months after Counsell's initial recommendation.[24]

In 1943, Counsell and Wood, along with Botterell in England, began to lobby the Canadian government to "provide a separate building, preferable within the city limits, in charge of a competent neuro-surgical doctor who is fully cognisant with the necessity of getting these men up and active . . . up and around in chairs, and in many cases, gainfully employed."[25] The government agreed and in 1944 began to convert a large mansion in central Toronto, Lyndhurst Lodge, into a treatment center.

In January 1945, Botterell returned to Toronto to become chief of neurosurgery at the Christie Street Military Hospital. He found, as he had expected, veterans confined to their beds with little hope of leaving the hospital. Once again he developed a specialized unit for early medical treatment at Christie Street and, along with Counsell and Wood, undertook the development of a new rehabilitation program at Lyndhurst Lodge. The new programs at Lyndhurst were to help the veterans, following discharge from hospital, learn new skills to live in the community. Early in January 1945, Botterell invited Donald Munro, the Boston pioneer in treatment of spinal cord injury, to visit Toronto and advise them on their programs. One of the new ideas discussed was development of a program to help some paraplegics regain the ability to walk. Following an extensive exercise program to regain upper-body strength, veterans were taught how to walk using calipers (now called braces) and crutches. Following Munro's visit this new program, called gait training, was introduced at Lyndhurst. Counsell moved into Lyndhurst to help with the early administration, to provide support to the veterans as they began to transfer from Christie Street, and to begin his own gait-training program.

Botterell and Counsell chose to call the building Lyndhurst Lodge, as opposed to Lyndhurst Hospital, because they wanted to establish it as a non-institutional setting where veterans could learn to readjust to civilian life. Many rules that usually existed in hospitals, particularly military hospitals, were relaxed or eliminated at Lyndhurst. Dr. Al Jousse, the first medical director of Lyndhurst, recalled once trying to establish a list of rules, which he showed to Counsell for his review. Counsell's only comment was: "You may have as many rules and regulations as you like, as long as you never enforce any of them."[26]

Counsell's sister later described her brother's views on the development of Lyndhurst:

He wanted Lyndhurst to be a friendly, casual place. The paraplegics had all had enough of hospitals and uniforms, so the staff wore "civvies." The therapists came to work in slacks and sweaters, not uniforms. They wanted to get people up and moving and learning how to live and be independent from a wheelchair—cooking, caring for themselves, job skills, hand controls on cars. . . . Before the war they lived in institutions or with their families but didn't look after themselves. Perhaps because there were so many *young* men paralyzed in the war, no one could see them being institutionalized for life, and they wanted more. So the thinking changed, and thus Lyndhurst . . . began as a rehabilitation center, not just physical, but mental, emotional, and readjustment to living and working from a chair.[27]

A newspaper reporter in 1945 described Lyndhurst as a "friendly cheerful environment . . . considerably more like that of a fraternity house than that of a hospital. It's something like a Y.M.C.A. gymnasium, too, particularly when the boys get to work on their parallel bars, punching bag, wall weights and mat exercises."[28]

In March 1945, Dr. Al Jousse was recruited to be the medical director of Lyndhurst, responsible for the coordination of all aspects of treatment. Jousse, a recent medical graduate from the University of Toronto, had been unable to serve in the armed forces during the war because of a physical disability that required the use of two canes for walking. Counsell, Botterell, and Jousse worked together throughout their lives as pioneers in the development of rehabilitation for spinal cord injury.

By May 1945, the success of Lyndhurst was already apparent, and Dr. Bill Warner, director general of Treatment Services in the Department of Veterans Affairs (DVA) agreed to develop three more special treatment centers across Canada, modeled after Lyndhurst. Warner, later wrote that the establishment of these four centers and the development of rehabilitation for spinal cord injury were two of the most significant aspects of his work in Treatment Services.[29]

The Canadian Paraplegic Association

During 1944 and 1945, Counsell and Wood developed plans to form an association that would provide services to veterans and civilians and lobby different levels of government for programs and services for all who had suffered spinal cord injury. The new association was modeled after the CNIB and had veterans with spinal cord injuries play central roles on both the board of directors and in the administration of the association. However, in at least one respect Counsell and Wood did not imitate CNIB, which had established a separate wing of the association, the Sir Arthur Pearson Association for the Blind, to represent blinded veterans. Instead, CPA included both the 200 World War II veterans and civilians equally in its mandate. Counsell and Wood used their contacts with prominent business, political, and military leaders to gain political and financial support for the new association. Indeed, their first constitution had the support of Prime Minister Mackenzie King, a friend of Wood and of Counsell's family.[30] The first office of the association, at Maple Leaf Gardens in Toronto, was provided at no charge by Conn Smythe, a wealthy sports promoter and World War II veteran who had also sustained a spinal cord injury.

On May 1, 1945, Counsell and seven other World War II veterans with spinal cord injury founded the Canadian Paraplegic Association.[31] It was the first organization in the world founded and administered by individuals with spinal cord injury. Counsell was elected as the organization's first president. Counsell, working with Wood, recruited a number of prominent Canadian political, medical, military, and civic leaders who were not themselves disabled, to join the board of directors. They chose board members, including Warner, who were well placed in business and government to assist with fund-raising and lobbying efforts for the association. Initial fund-raising for the association was handled by Wood and Smythe, who contacted business and financial leaders and sought donations. There were no public subscriptions or charity campaigns to raise funds. Instead this was undertaken by the members of the board through their personal contacts.[32]

In the early stages of planning, there had been a suggestion that Counsell should be employed by DVA; however, this idea was rejected by the board of directors, who felt it would limit his independence to lobby government. Instead, the association sought an annual grant from the DVA to cover its costs related to veterans' services. When the initial grant was not forthcoming, Counsell's brother-in-law was sent to call on the minister of finance. Gordon, a partner in Canada's leading accounting firm, had been a senior financial consultant to the government during the war. In 1946, the first annual grant of up to $10,000 per year was provided. CPA agreed to provide services to paraplegic and near paraplegic veterans in special counseling and vocational guidance; assistance in obtaining suitable employment; advising the DVA on all matters affecting rehabilitation; and aftercare services to ensure satisfactory adjustment to civil life. In addition they agreed to maintain the association as an organization that would contribute to the development of a spirit of independence and reliance.[33]

Beginning in 1945, Counsell began to travel across Canada to help establish the association as a national organization with regional divisions. The regional divisions were led by veterans with spinal cord injury and had close ties to the DVA special treatment centers. The structure of the new divisions followed Counsell's early principle of a board of directors composed of veterans with spinal cord injury; civilians with spinal cord injury would be added later, along with prominent civic, medical, military, and political leaders. The national office supplied some early financial support and advice, but the new divisions were set up to be self-governing and autonomous, controlling their own finances. Each division would have a representative on the national board of directors. Finally, to spread its new philosophy of rehabilitation, CPA developed a national newsletter, *Caliper*. Originally started in 1945 at the veterans hospital at Ste. Anne de Bellevue, Quebec, *Caliper* became the official newsletter of the association in 1946.

Philosophy of Rehabilitation

The central philosophy of the association was that "paraplegics could be made to lead useful, reasonably normal lives."[34] This philosophy was shared by others in the field of veteran's rehabilitation following World War II. Edward Dunlop, supervisor of casualty rehabilitation in DVA, defined rehabilitation broadly "as the restoration of the disabled to the best possible physical, mental, social, economic and vocational adjustment and usefulness of which they are capable. This is a continuous and indivisible process which begins at the time of diagnosis and is not complete until the individual is restored to a *suitable job and satisfying life*."[35] Dunlop, who had been blinded in the war, was both a friend and early supporter of Counsell and the CPA.

The goals of the association were very comprehensive for this era and designed to address the needs of all men and women disabled by paraplegia (as illustrated in figure 10) At an early meeting with DVA officials in 1945, Counsell summarized the goals of the association: "to fraternize all paraplegics, assist and foster their professional and vocational training, promote investigations of best possible treatment and equipment, operate employment and information bureaux, etc. for their benefit."[36]

GOALS OF THE CANADIAN PARAPLEGIC ASSOCIATION, MAY 10, 1945

1. To bind together in a spirit of fraternity all men and women who are disabled by paraplegia;
2. To obtain mutual aid and protection and to make provision for all paraplegics;

3. To foster and assist the vocational and professional training of all paraplegics;
4. To promote education, profitable employment and social well-being as far as possible of all paraplegics;
5. To investigate and promote the study of paraplegia and to establish or assist in the establishment of a research laboratory or laboratories with the necessary appliances for the purpose of ensuring that the best possible treatment and equipment is provided for all paraplegics;
6. To make representations to appropriate departments of Government concerning adjustment of pensions and any other claims to which any paraplegics may be entitled;
7. To establish, maintain and operate employment and information bureaus, libraries and establishments for the benefit, treatment and advancement generally of paraplegics;
8. To establish, organize and regulate provincial local branches or chapters in convenient centres throughout Canada, or to affiliate or co-operate with other bodies or associations with similar aims and objects throughout Canada;
9. To raise funds for all purposes of the Association by fees from its members, by private or public subscription, by subsidies from the Dominion and Provincial Governments and urban and rural authorities, and any other ways and means which the Association may determine.

Mutual Aid/Self-Help

Mutual aid had been used by veterans' associations following World War I, when veterans with amputations or blindness formed organizations, such as the War Amputations Association of Canada and the Sir Arthur Pearson Association, and shared their experiences with other disabled veterans. However, it gained considerably more prominence following World War II. Under the leadership of Walter Woods, deputy minister, DVA actively recruited veterans with disabilities to be casualty rehabilitation officers and work with other disabled veterans. Woods, the leading architect of Canadian veterans' policy, argued that "a man who has been seriously disabled and who has regained control, as it were, and mastered the ordinary functions of life despite his disability can, by his mental attitude and his physical mastery of handicaps, be a tremendous inspiration to others."[37]

FIG. 10. *Caliper,* the publication of the veteran-founded Canadian Paraplegic Association, encouraged its members to enjoy an active lifestyle. This
cartoon humorously suggested opportunities for recreation made possible by
lightweight, self-propelling wheelchairs. (*Caliper,* winter 1950, 20. Courtesy
of the Canadian Paraplegic Association.)

Another supporter of mutual aid was Dunlop, who had supported
DVA funding for the association because of its importance of raising morale.

> There are two ways in which morale can be raised—one is by the pro-
> vision of physical rehabilitation centres . . . the other is by the devel-
> opment of group consciousness on the part of the paraplegics. There is
> a place for the development of associations of disabled veterans within
> the scope of the Government programs, for example the War Ampu-
> tations of Canada. The active participation of paraplegics in their own
> rehabilitation will be of great assistance to Departmental officials. This
> active participation can only be achieved where they are enabled to
> organize to help themselves.[38]

Finally, the belief in the importance of mutual aid was supported by
Counsell's earlier personal experience, his first meeting with James Darou in
Montreal. Recognizing that they would be pioneers in entering the workforce and living in the community, a mutual aid approach enabled members
to share the successful strategies they developed to return to full participa-

tion in community life. In addition, the early veteran members recognized the fate of the civilian paraplegic who in the past "was taken to hospital and regarded as a good bet for the undertaker."[39] Members would later seek out civilian paraplegics and aid them in gaining access to programs and services. As veterans leave "behind our war time mode of life . . . and take up normal positions in our communities," they argued, "[we] must back and promote the association . . . so that it may offer to civilian paraplegics the benefits which we have shared."[40]

Pioneers in Independent Living

The veteran members of CPA were pioneers in independent living. They introduced new examples of independence into Canadian society using the wheelchair as a means of mobility. Members argued for full participation in all aspects of civilian life: education, employment, recreation, and family life. They rejected a philosophy of special services for the disabled and instead sought to return to the mainstream of civilian life.

For Counsell, who often used his experience as a role model, this presented an early unique dilemma. Counsell had been one of the first to argue for the use of the wheelchair as a means to independence. In 1945, however, following the visit to Toronto by Munro, the new concept of walking with calipers and crutches had been introduced. Counsell had been one of the first veterans to master the skill of crutch walking and tried to use it as an example for others. Dorothy Smith, one of the first secretaries at CPA, remembered: "When we went to see a new patient, John Counsell always went in on the calipers and crutches. He never went in a wheelchair."[41] Later, on a cross-Canada tour of veterans hospitals, he tried to avoid using the wheelchair but found it exhausting. Tony Mann, one of the founding members of the Western Division of CPA, remembered that experience:

> On his first trip to Winnipeg, he was so well rehabilitated that he came only using his crutches and braces. He didn't use the chair, and it was just an agonizing trip for him. He was totally exhausted, [but] . . . he was supposed to be a perfect example of rehabilitation. . . . Over time, we accepted that walking was not practical for spinal cord injuries. By the time you got from Point A to Point B, you'd be so exhausted that you couldn't possibly conduct any business. . . . It just wasn't a practical option.[42]

The veterans had found that the wheelchair was a vehicle to expand independence rather than to confine it. Gait training remained a central part of rehabilitation, however, for it permitted individuals the opportunity to try walking and then make their own decisions on which mode of mobility they would use to return to the community.

A major factor in the success of veterans, as pioneers in independent living, was their veteran status. Ken Langford, the first managing secretary of CPA, described the attitude of the veterans.

> We were all the same age group, had all been in the army or navy or air force. The Canadians, not being professional soldiers, their main objective in the services in wartime is to get the thing over with and get out. . . . That attitude included hospital, that was universal among all the patients. Some found it easier than others, but within a couple of years of Lyndhurst opening most of the veteran patients were out of there.[43]

Accompanying the new focus on independent life was the belief that it was possible to adapt to the community, to participate as full members. Thus, special classes for disabled veterans were rejected by CPA, and veterans were encouraged to enroll in vocational training programs and university courses offered to all veterans. The pages of *Caliper* throughout the postwar period contained stories and photographs of veterans, and later civilians, returning to university, entering the workplace, and participating in a wide range of sport and recreation activities. *Caliper* developed a series of cartoons that explored the experience of using a wheelchair in a community that had not planned for wheelchairs. A cartoon of horseracing using a wheelchair was a reference to Counsell's main recreational interest.

The employment policy for all Canadian veterans, disabled or nondisabled, was to reestablish them in significant remunerative civilian jobs, not in sheltered workshops.[44] Under Counsell's leadership, CPA rejected the use of sheltered workshops or low-skilled jobs such as elevator operators, an approach that had been used following World War I. The use of sheltered workshops was also supported by Ludwig Guttman, the founder of spinal cord rehabilitation in England, who believed that not all veterans with spinal cord injury could fully return to work in the community. Later, the Quebec division would develop links with a sheltered workshop in Montreal. However, in principle, the association, under Counsell's leadership, rejected the use of sheltered workshops.

Canadian veteran policy encouraged employers to hire disabled veterans and not penalize them for their service to their country. For some veterans this view was new. Jousse remembered the ironic response of some veterans:

That struck some of them as being amusing. They couldn't get a job during the thirties when they were able-bodied. . . . Having been in the army, having become a paraplegic, they were now expected to go to work. Nobody wanted them before. Now they were encouraged to do what they were never able to do of their own volition.[45]

Members of the association argued that "no disabled person need fear a limited life"; they recognized, however, that they had to convince employers that individuals with spinal cord injury could be successfully employed.[46] They used a combined approach that included the use of local service clubs, mutual aid, employment counseling, and public education. Stories in national magazines portrayed the impact of rehabilitation and described the successful return of veterans with spinal cord injury to employment.

The Canadian approach encouraged veterans to return to their former leisure activities rather than become involved in specialized activities for the disabled or specialized wheelchair sports, a policy favored in England. Canadian veterans developed various strategies to return to fishing, hunting, bowling, and other community sports. In addition, veterans began to venture out into travel, using trains and airlines, for both business and leisure. In 1946, when Counsell learned that the airlines might develop safety regulations to prevent individuals using wheelchairs from flying, he organized a small fishing party of CPA members. They took a newspaper reporter from a national newspaper for a flight to Algonquin Park for a fishing expedition. On the trip they were guests of a member of the provincial legislature. They used the subsequent story and pictures to demonstrate that flying could be done successfully using a wheelchair. By December 1946, they had reached an agreement with Trans Canada Airlines to ensure travel on their airlines with the presentation of a medical certificate of approval.[47]

Veterans were also pioneers in the areas of marriage, family life, and adoption. Following the war, veterans with spinal cord injury were encouraged to marry, something not usually accepted in this period. In addition, as they became established in their marriages, a number of veterans and their wives began to try to adopt children. At that time Canadian adoption policy generally prevented individual's with a disability from adopting children. Once again the veterans used their contacts through the association to lobby successfully for changes in policy across Canada. Their successful example provided an important precedent for civilians.[48]

Pensions, Benefits, and Entitlements

In the postwar period, Counsell, along with the members of the Canadian Paraplegic Association, worked to ensure that veterans with spinal cord injury were included within all aspects of the Veterans' Charter, the federal government's legislation that governed the provision of pensions, programs, and special benefits and entitlement. Pensions for disability were awarded by the Canadian Pension Commission. These pensions were free from income tax and did not decrease when the veteran was employed. Medical review for pension was carried out by physicians employed directly by the Pension Commission. The amount of pension was related to the level of disability, rated on a 100-point scale.

Initially, spinal cord injury was rated as a 100 percent disability, the maximum amount of pension. However, as veterans with spinal cord injury became independent in dressing and self-care and returned to live and work in the community, a new dilemma arose, and some pension ratings were lowered. The table of disabilities used to assess level of disability was related to the "incapacity to perform work in the general labour market."[49] Counsell and the members of the association lobbied the Pension Commission to recognize that spinal cord injury should be recognized as a permanent physical disability and consistently awarded at 100 percent level. Members of the Pension Commission met with the veterans at Lyndhurst and, following the meeting, agreed to restore the 100 percent pension level for paraplegia.[50]

Veterans with spinal cord injury were among the first veterans in Canada to receive funding for assistance with daily living activities. A new "helplessness allowance" was provided, following World War II, for veterans who were "totally disabled and helpless, and in need of attendance."[51] In 1946, Counsell met with the head of the Pension Commission to argue that the full allowance of $750.00 per annum be consistently given to all veterans with spinal cord injury. By 1947, he was able to report to the members of the association that (as a result of the "close personal interest in our problems") "Almost all of those who have been discharged . . . have received eminently fair awards."[52]

In addition to a concern about the level of allowance, Counsell and others were concerned about the use of the term *helplessness*. This was not the image of disability Counsell and the members of the association were trying to promote. Certainly veterans needed assistance with some activities, but the language of the initial legislation, the Veterans' Charter, used the negative term *helplessness*. Counsell and other veterans associations sought to change the language. However, in this early postwar era, the veteran pioneers of independent life in the community, such as Counsell, found it difficult to change existing views of disability within the Pension Commission. This term *helplessness* continued in use until 1957, when the new and more acceptable term "attendance allowance" replaced it.[53]

In 1946, Counsell and the association joined the National Council of Veterans' Associations, a coalition of five organizations representing disabled veterans: Army, Navy, and Air Force Veterans; Canadian Corps Association; Canadian Pensioners' Association of the Great Wars; Sir Arthur Pearson Association of War Blinded; and War Amputations of Canada. The council lobbied the Canadian government for improved pensions and other benefits for all disabled veterans. In 1948, Counsell and other members of the CPA played a central role in presentations before Parliament resulting in a 25 percent increase in basic disability pension rate and an increase in the "helplessness allowance" from a maximum of $750 per year to $1,400 per year.

Counsell, Jousse, and Botterell all recognized that the veterans were pioneers and that their status as veterans was important to the early successes in rehabilitation and community living. The veteran group had men from all ranks and social classes, and from its ranks arose the first group of leaders in CPA. Jousse recalled:

> The veterans were first-class people. We were able to mobilize them, get them up and going to a degree that would have been very difficult if it were not for the caliber of the individuals and the fact that they had economic security that would include provision for being in the community, for education, either at university or trade schools that were then developing. We had a lot of support from the civilian community.[54]

The examples of the success of the veteran members of CPA as pioneers provides an important insight into the relationship between the cause of disability and the development and provision of services. The Canadian government placed considerable importance in the postwar period on returning all veterans to civilian life, including disabled veterans. Underlying the Canadian Veterans' Charter was a recognition of the poor treatment that had been provided to the veterans of World War I. The deputy minister summarized the Canadian philosophy in 1953. "This time it was not a question of 'how little can we get away with?' But, 'How much do we owe?' What did the war do to the lives of these young people and how can we best repay the damage?"[55]

Impact on Civilian Rehabilitation: 1945–1960

By 1946, four Canadian special treatment programs were well developed, and veterans were successfully returning to their communities. Botterell, Counsell, and Jousse became concerned that, as the veterans completed their treatment, the specialized teams of "physiotherapists, nurses, doctors and orderlies [would] inevitably, in the course of the next six to eighteen months, disintegrate unless new patients [were] admitted."[56] In August 1946, they were successful in convincing DVA to allow the admission of a limited number of civilian paraplegics to all four DVA special treatment centers. Civilians were charged six dollars per day, and CPA assumed the responsibility for reimbursing the department. This was the first time in Canada that civilians with spinal cord injury had access to an organized medical rehabilitation program. Unlike the veterans' funding, which was provided by the DVA, funding for civilians came from a variety of sources, including private donors, workman's compensation boards, municipal and provincial government grants, and local service clubs and charities. By 1948, Counsell reported that the association had reimbursed the DVA $40,000 for treatment for civilians.[57]

Counsell and the association undertook the responsibility for lobbying various levels of government to secure funding for civilians. In 1947, they were successful in persuading George Drew, premier of Ontario, to provide the first grant of $25,000 dollars to the association to cover some of the costs of treatment for civilian paraplegics admitted to Lyndhurst Lodge.[58] Drew had been kept closely informed of the developments at Lyndhurst through his son-in-law, Edward Dunlop, Counsell's friend, and through Conn Smythe, a friend and colleague of Drew and a member of CPA board of directors. In 1950, the association purchased Lyndhurst Lodge from the DVA for one dollar, and over the next two decades CPA continued to seek special provincial grants and direct funding from local governments to cover the costs of rehabilitation for civilians. They were only relieved of this responsibility in the late 1960s, when national health insurance was introduced in Canada.

Following the discharge and successful reestablishment of veterans into civilian life, Counsell and the association were able to focus on the needs of civilians for a new Canadian approach to disability policy. An early editorial in *Caliper* argued,

> The raising of funds by public subscription is at best a loose way of providing for the crippled and helpless. A plan to finance the crippled

should properly come from the government. The re-training of these cases makes them into assets and prevents them from becoming liabilities upon government.[59]

They were, however, not successful, and securing funds for the costs of rehabilitation, retraining, and equipment for civilians continued as a major focus of the association throughout the period of Counsell's leadership.

Counsell and other CPA members across Canada tried to locate civilians with spinal cord injuries and find means to help them gain access to medical, economic, and social rehabilitation. The first groups of civilians who took part in the medical rehabilitation programs offered at the veterans centers found the same dramatic experience as the veterans. One of the first civilians Counsell visited was James Burke, who had been in a hospital since he was injured in 1940. Burke remember his impact.

> John Counsell, the head of the Canadian Paraplegic Association, brought me over a wheelchair. I didn't have a wheelchair. There were only half dozen wheelchairs in the hospital, and they had to be shared. One was often confined to bed for long periods of time. These were those old type of wicker chairs, but you couldn't go anywhere in them. This gift of a wheelchair from the Canadian Paraplegic Association (or it might have been a Department of Veterans Affairs acquisition)—that changed my life. I could get out, go around the neighborhood. I was curious to see the world after all this time. I went on my own. . . . I was never an in-patient at Lyndhurst. I came about two afternoons a week for perhaps a year. Lyndhurst brought me out of the atmosphere of putting in time till that last moment that I was living with. Lyndhurst was still a Department of Veterans Affairs institution, and I was not really supposed to be there. They were sticking their necks out and squeezing me in there.[60]

While civilians were beginning to have limited access to medical rehabilitation, they did not have access to the pensions, benefits, and entitlements provided to veterans to support their full economic and social rehabilitation. Recognizing the importance of funding for equipment such as wheelchairs, CPA undertook to supply equipment to civilians. It loaned wheelchairs to individuals, who were given long periods to pay back the cost, or it worked with local service clubs to raise funds. During the 1950s and 1960s, CPA was one of the major Canadian suppliers of equipment, as there were few government programs available to fund the cost of equipment needed for independence.

By the late 1940s, the dramatic example of the success of veterans' rehabilitation programs led to calls for new government policy to provide for rehabilitation for civilians. In 1951, the federal government established a National Advisory Committee on the Rehabilitation of Disabled Persons. This advisory committee held the first national conference on disability in Canada in 1952, and the work of the committee laid the foundation for the development of disability policy for civilians. Throughout its early deliberations of the committee, Counsell was one of three delegates of organizations representing people with disabilities.

The early planners of civilian disability policy, however, did not follow the veterans' model of comprehensive programs to cover the costs of disability with disability pensions, training allowances, funding for equipment, and attendance allowances. Instead, the disability policy for civilians used a social welfare model with pensions provided only to the unemployed, with limited funding for vocational training and education, and with funding for equipment generally remaining the responsibility of the individual or local charities or service clubs. Attendance allowances were never considered during this period and, indeed, are still very limited today.

Despite the early recognition by Counsell and CPA that the government needed to develop a firm funding policy for disability, no record has been found that either Counsell or the other veteran members of CPA called for the adoption of the veterans' model of funding for civilians. During the postwar period, when Canada had neither organized programs for medical rehabilitation nor any national disability policy, they may have recognized that the use of the veterans model would not gain acceptance. The difference in philosophy between veterans disability policy and civilian disability policy continues to this day. For example, a new program, developed in the 1970s to meet the needs of aging veterans with disabilities, was called the Veterans Independence Program. The program offers the most comprehensive range of services in Canada and is designed to enable veterans to remain in their home. Programs for aging civilians with disabilities did not begin to develop until the late 1980s and provide access to a limited range of health care services.

During the 1950s, Counsell and the members of the CPA worked with provincial governments to establish medical rehabilitation centers and provide counseling and employment programs for civilians with spinal cord injury across Canada. Regional divisions were led by veterans with spinal cord injury who were often actively involved in all aspects of the expansion of rehabilitation in their regions. By 1960, when Counsell retired as president, there were nine divisions in CPA spread across Canada. Its members worked with local committees to establish new rehabilitation centers, and its members were often leaders in developing new community programs and services for all Canadians with disabilities.

Another impact of Counsell's work through CPA was the introduction of mutual aid in civilian organizations for people with disabilities. The CNIB had used mutual aid in its civilian programs following World War I but had used a two-part model to separate veterans and civilians. CPA, with its joint veteran and civilian mandates, was one of the first organizations to adopt a mutual aid philosophy to meet the needs of civilians with physical disabilities. Most organizations meeting the needs of civilians with disabilities used a charitable model of organization with leadership provided by nondisabled members of voluntary boards and services provided by nondisabled staff. CPA's use of mutual aid and its philosophy of full participation in community life provided an early archetype for the self-help and independent-living movements that developed in the 1970s in North America. These new organizations were established by Canadians with disabilities, many of whom were led by individuals who had themselves been mentored by the early veteran leaders of CPA.

John Counsell continued as president and managing director of the Canadian Paraplegic Association until 1961, when Ken Langford replaced him as managing director. Counsell continued as president of the association until 1967. That year he received the Order of Canada. He died in Toronto in 1977 at the age of 66.

Conclusion

This essay has described the role of John Counsell and the veteran members of CPA in the development of medical rehabilitation and the introduction of disability policy in Canada following World War II. Counsell and the early veteran members were pioneers in living and working in the community using a wheelchair. They provided examples demonstrating that it was possible to return to civilian life with a spinal cord injury. They acted as trailblazers, providing role models for the civilians with spinal cord injury that followed. Counsell's early role in establishing programs for spinal cord injury was described in 1947 by William O'Connor, a veteran with spinal cord injury:

He knows the despair which accompanies each new set-back, and he realizes the tremendous physical and psychological adjustments which the paraplegic must make before he can mingle in society freely and without fear and embarrassment. . . . whole new vistas of living are opened up for those who might otherwise eke out their existence as mere fragments of human beings ignorant of the fact that life has not ended for them.[61]

The CPA, under Counsell's leadership, was the first association in the world to be organized and administered by individuals with spinal cord injury. Under his leadership, the association played a major role in opening up new vistas of living and helped lay a groundwork for the development of rehabilitation and disability policy in Canada.

NOTES

The author wishes to thank the members of the Canadian Paraplegic Association and their families who participated in the research for this essay. I am also indebted to Eric Boyd, Executive Director, Canadian Paraplegic Association, Ken Hawke, Canadian Department of Veterans Affairs, and Professor Charles Roland, McMaster University. Funding for this research was generously provided by the Hannah Institute for the History of Medicine.

        1. Quoted from E. H. Botterell, A. T. Jousse, C. Aberhart, and J. W. Cluff, "Paraplegia following War," *Canadian Medical Association Journal* 55 (September 1946): 249–59.

        2. Mary K. Tremblay, "The Canadian Revolution in the Management of Spinal Cord Injury," *Canadian Bulletin of Medical History* 12 (1995): 101–32.

        3. Charles Elsberg, "The Edwin Smith Surgical Papyrus: The Diagnosis and Treatment of Injuries to the Skull and Spine 5000 years Ago," *Annals of Medical History* 3 (1931): 271–79.

        4. Harvey Cushing, "Organization and Activities of the Neurological Service American Expeditionary Force," in *The Medical Department of the United States Army in the World War*, ed. M. W. Ireland (Washington, D.C.: Government Printing Office, 1927), 757.

        5. Sir Frederick Treves, "The Star and Garter, Richmond; A Permanent Home for Paralysed and Disabled Sailors and Soldiers," *American Journal of Care for Cripples* 5 (1917): 146, emphasis added.

        6. Desmond Morton and Glenn Wright, *Winning the Second Battle: Canadian Veterans and the Return to Civilian Life, 1915–1930* (Toronto: University of Toronto Press, 1987), 93, 97.

        7. Margo Gewurtz, interview by author, November 2, 1990, Toronto, tape recording.

8. James Burke, interview by author, December 20, 1991, West Hill, Ontario, tape recording.

9. Donald Munro, "Thoracic and Lumbosacral Cord Injuries: A Study of Forty Cases," *Journal of the American Medical Association* 122 (August 1943): 1059.

10. Donald Munro, *The Treatment of Injuries to the Nervous System* (Philadelphia: Saunders, 1952), vi.

11. E. H. Botterell and A. T. Jousse, *The Evolution of Spinal Cord Rehabilitation* (Toronto: Hannah Institute for the History of Medicine, 1988), videotape.

12. Dr. E. H. Botterell, interview by Valerie Schatzer, Kingston, Ontario, April 26, 1979, transcript at Hannah Institute for the History of Medicine, Toronto, 32–33.

13. Dr. D. Allen described his appointment as a medical officer at the Star and Garter Spinal Unit in England: "In the Spring of 1944 I was called to group headquarters for interview with the group officer, a surgeon of formidable character. 'Allen,' he said to me, 'I am sorry to have to inflict this on you, but we have been ordered to open a spinal unit . . . and I want you to take charge of it. Of course, as you know, they are hopeless cases—most of them die, but you must do your best for them.' With these words of encouragement I returned home sadly." D. Allen, "Spinal Unit at the Star and Garter Home," *Cord* 17 (1967): 14.

14. E. Harry Botterell, interview by author, August 10, 1993, Kingston, Ontario, tape recording.

15. *Dictionary of Hamilton Biography,* vol. 3 (Hamilton: W. L. Griffin, 1992), 39–40; *The Macmillan Dictionary of Canadian Biography* (Toronto: Macmillan, 1978), 294.

16. Dorothy Smith, interview by author, February 10, 1997, Hamilton, Ontario, tape recording.

17. Mary K. Tremblay, "Going Back to Civvy Street: A Historical Account of the Impact of the Everest and Jennings Wheelchair for Canadian World War II Veterans with Spinal Cord Injury," *Disability and Society* 11 (1996): 149–69.

18. Kenneth Langford, interview by author, November 4, 1991, Toronto, tape recording.

19. Marian Holleman, *The Founding of the Canadian Paraplegic Association* (Toronto: Canadian Paraplegic Association, 1992), 20.

20. L. M. Wood to Major Austin Bell, December 16, 1943, Department of Veterans' Affairs Archives, Charlottetown, Prince Edward Island (hereafter DVA), box 163, vol. 6, file 31–15, emphasis added.

21. Jack Higman, interview by author, March 3, 1992, Toronto, tape recording,

22. John Catto to Director of Rehabilitation, Department of Pensions and National Health, Re: Paraplegia, Serious Orthopaedic and Double Amputation Cases, December 20, 1943, DVA box 163, vol. 6, file 31–15.

23. R. Wilson to Major C. A. Bell, December 11, 1943, DVA, box 163, vol. 6, file 31–15.

24. Tremblay, "Back to Civvy Street," 156.

25. John Catto to Director of Rehabilitation, December 20, 1943.

26. A. T. Jousse, "Unpublished Speech to Veterans Dinner in Memory of John Counsell," 1978, photocopy.

27. Elizabeth Gordon, interview by author, January 25, 1994, Toronto, tape recording.

28. Trent Frayne, "Walking and Working, Paraplegics Zestful," *Toronto Star,* November 15, 1945, n.p.

29. Mary K. Tremblay, "The Right to the Best Medical Care: Dr. W. P. Warner and the Canadian Department of Veterans' Affairs," *Canadian Bulletin of Medical History* 15 (1999): 3–25.

30. Higman, interview.

31. The seven board members had decided on January 16, 1945, to seek incorporation as the Canadian Paraplegic Association. They were John Counsell, Arthur Hay, Joseph Wrangham, Jack Higman, Douglas Quirt, Edward Higginbottom, and Andrew Clarke. "First Annual Report," *Canadian Paraplegic Association* (Toronto, 1946), 9.

32. Kenneth Langford, interview by author, July 13, 1993, Toronto, tape recording.

33. Walter S. Woods, *Rehabilitation: A Combined Operation* (Ottawa: Edmond Cloutier, 1953), 290–92.

34. William O'Connor, "Societate Fortiores," *Caliper* 2 (March 1947): 12.

35. Edward Dunlop, "Report on the Vocational Rehabilitation of Disabled Veterans as at January 31, 1948," *Treatment Services Bulletin* 3, no. 5 (1948): 39–42, emphasis added.

36. W. P. Warner, Minutes of Conference on Paraplegia, August 15, 1945, DVA box, 66, vol. 1 & 2, file 3–26–2–1.

38. Walter S. Woods to Dr. A. W. Park, May 19, 1944, National Archives of Canada, Ottawa, RG 38, vol. 187, file 7297.

38. Edward Dunlop to Director General of Rehabilitation, October 9, 1945, DVA, box 66, vols. 1 and 2, file 3–26–2–1.

39. B. Wiggins, "John Counsell Stresses Unity," *Caliper* 1 (January 1946): 2.

40. D. George Petrie, "Our Association," *Caliper* 1 (June 1946): 2.

41. Smith, interview.

42. Tony Mann, interview by author, May 31, 1995, Winnipeg, tape recording.

43. Langford, interview, November 4, 1991.

44. Woods, *Rehabilitation,* 359–61.

45. Dr. Al Jousse, interview by author, January 17, 1991, Toronto, tape recording.

46. Charles Kelsey, "The Physically Disabled in Canadian Industry," *Caliper* 2 (March 1947): 24.

47. William O'Connor, "Babes in the Woods," *Caliper* 1 (October 1946): 1, 3, 8; D. G. Petrie, "Flying Wheelchairs," *Caliper* 2 (December 1946): 2.

48. Langford, interview, November 4, 1991; Higman, interview.

49. Woods, *Rehabilitation,* 420–24.

50. Higman, interview.

51. Woods, *Rehabilitation,* 423–24.

52. D. George Petrie, "C.P.A. Officers Confer with Pensions Commission," *Caliper* 1 (August 1946): 1.

53. F. L. Barrow, *A Post-war Era: A Study of the Veterans Legislation of Canada, 1950–1963* (Ottawa: Queen's Printer, 1964), 134.

54. Jousse, interview.

55. Woods, *Rehabilitation,* 458.

56. E. Harry Botterell to Dr. van Nostrand, December 6, 1945, DVA, box 552, vol. 2, file 5260–1.

57. J. G. Counsell, Report for the Year 1947–1948, Canadian Paraplegic Association, DVA box 66, vols. 1–2, file 3–26–2–1.

58. "Minutes of the Thirteenth Meeting of the Directors," *Canadian Paraplegic Association,* May 20, 1947, photocopy.

59. Charles Kelsey, "Finance for the Paraplegic," *Caliper* 2 (March 1947): 19–20.

60. Burke, interview.

61. William O'Connor, *Caliper* 2 (March 1947): 13.

Contributors

Deborah Cohen received her Ph.D. in History at the University of California at Berkeley in 1996 and is Assistant Professor of History at American University. She is currently at work on an extended study of disabled veterans of World War I, *The War Come Home: Disabled Veterans in Great Britain and Germany, 1914–1939*.

Ethel Dunn is Executive Secretary of the Highgate Road Social Science Research Station in Berkeley, California. In addition to publishing both poetry and translations of Russian works, she is the author, or coauthor with Stephen P. Dunn, of numerous essays in both Russian and American scholarly journals of anthropology, sociology, and Slavic studies, and is a contributing editor of the publication *Russia and Her Neighbors*.

Martha Edwards received her Ph.D. in Classics from the University of Minnesota and is Assistant Professor of Ancient History at Truman State University. She is currently working on a study of disability in the Ancient Greek world.

David A. Gerber is Professor of History at the State University of New York at Buffalo. His principal interest as a scholar has been in individual and group identities in American history, and in this connection he has published extensively on race, religion, and ethnicity as well as disability.

Robert I. Goler is Executive Administrator of the National Museum of Health and Medicine in Washington, D.C. and an Assistant Professor in the Arts Management Program at American University. In addition to organizing exhibitions, he publishes widely in the fields of history, medical history, and museum studies. Among his recent publications, he is the editor of *"What about AIDS?": Workshop Proceedings* (Washington, D.C.: National Museum of Health and Medicine, 1994).

Geoffrey L. Hudson received his D.Phil. in History at St. John's College of Oxford University in 1996 and is currently preparing his thesis, "Ex-Servicemen, War Widows, and the English County Pension Scheme, 1593–1679," for publication. He is the author of "Negotiating for Blood

Money: War Widows and the Courts in Seventeenth Century England," which appeared in *Women, Crime, and the Courts in Early Modern England*, ed. J. Kermode and G. Walker (1994).

James Marten is Associate Professor of History at Marquette University. The author of numerous articles and books on the American Civil War and on the American West, he has recently published *The Children's Civil War* and is now completing *Let Me Talk to You My Children: Selections from Children's Magazines during the Civil War*.

Martin F. Norden teaches film as Professor of Communications at the University of Massachusetts–Amherst. The author of many works on American movies, he is best known for the definitive study, *The Cinema of Isolation: A History of Physical Disability in the Movies* (1994).

Jeffrey S. Reznick is Assistant Director of Emory University's Institute for Comparative and International Studies, and a Research Fellow at the Center for the Study of Health, Culture, and Society in the Rollins School of Public Health. He is preparing *Rest, Recovery, and Rehabilitation: Healing and Identity in the First World War* for publication.

Michael G. Rhode is Chief Archivist at the Otis Historical Archives of the National Museum of Health and Medicine. The author of numerous archival guides and collections descriptions, he is currently completing a coedited work, *Faces of the Civil War Wounded*.

R. B. Rosenburg is Associate Professor of History at the University of North Alabama. He is the author of *Living Monuments: Confederate Soldiers' Homes and the New South* (1993) and is completing a study of Goldstar Mothers during World War I.

Mary Tremblay is Associate Professor in the School of Rehabilitation Science and a member of the Program in Medical History of the Faculty of Health Sciences at McMaster University in Canada. She is currently working on a book on the lives of Canadians with spinal cord injury in the mid–twentieth century and is also involved in research on disability in its connections to human rights, to aging, and to war.

Gregory Weeks received an M.A. in History at Purdue University in 1993 and is currently a doctoral candidate in Contemporary History at the Karl-Franzens-Universität in Austria.

Isser Woloch is Moore Collegiate Professor of History at Columbia University. Among his many publications in French and European history are *The French Veteran from the Revolution to the Restoration* (1979), and most recently, *Revolution and the Meanings of Freedom in the Nineteenth Century* (1996).